Michael J. Leitner, PhD
Sara F. Leitner, MA
and Associates

Leisure Enhancement
Third Edition

Pre-publication
REVIEWS,
COMMENTARIES,
EVALUATIONS . . .

"Leisure plays a significant role in personal development at all life stages and serves as the manifestation of values and meanings within a society. It is, therefore, not surprising that leisure attracts considerable attention from researchers, policymakers, community organizations, entrepreneurs, service providers, and educators. It is a difficult task to define and capture the essence of leisure for the twenty-first century, but the authors have found a way to make the complex both informative and accessible.

Students fortunate enough to be using this book when studying leisure will quickly realize that the philosophies, theories, and concepts are connected to all spheres of life. Leisure is not a phenomenon that exists in isolation. As the book progresses, the reader is carefully guided on a systematic journey that uncovers how the many notions of leisure have changed over time and have become an integral and important part of the way we define ourselves and the community in which we live. A particular strength of the book is the way it engages the reader and allows for an easy connection to everyday life experiences.

The authors cover a diverse range of topics and discuss issues, practical ideas, and constraints to and opportunities for leisure. The content is carefully woven using a blend of concepts, trends, and issues that all warrant attention at an individual and societal level. The associated instructor's manual provides a plethora of ideas for initiating discussion and numerous tasks for assessing student learning. Students who use *Leisure Enhancement* as a source of information will embrace leisure in its broadest sense, and because of this, enhance the leisure life of themselves and others."

Bevan C. Grant, PhD
Director of Sport and Leisure Studies
University of Waikato

More pre-publication
REVIEWS, COMMENTARIES, EVALUATIONS . . .

"*Leisure Enhancement, Third Edition,* maintains its preeminent position as the most easily adopted, comprehensive, and well-grounded text for introducing leisure conceptually and in personal life practices to students, and people generally, in search of life satisfaction. The authors' purpose of creating a foundation for self-understanding and social wisdom develops smoothly into approaches for lifestyle planning and rewarding choice-making. Every chapter is learning-oriented with well-conceived exercises requiring critical and reflective thinking. A marvelous advantage for faculty, however, is the accompanying instructor's manual, which demonstrates an awareness of the difficulties most teachers experience in making a shift to updated editions. In the manual, the Leitners provide a particularly valuable brief outline of changes in contents with their suggestions of where teaching time can be refocused to make better use of new information during the semester schedule.

This text is so successful at leading its readers into understanding issues and experiences with a real-life perspective, it should also be considered for use with educational programs oriented to helping people cope with self-development, lifestyle change, or achieving balance in life. In essence, *Leisure Enhancement* makes sense as a tool for creating or improving quality of life—Who would not benefit from that?"

Maureen Glancy, PhD
Professor and Chair,
Department of Recreation
and Leisure Studies,
San Jose State University

The Haworth Press®
New York • London • Oxford

Leisure Enhancement

Third Edition

HAWORTH Leisure and Recreation
Michael J. Leitner, PhD and Sara F. Leitner
Senior Co-Editors

Leisure Enhancement, Third Edition by Michael J. Leitner and Sara F. Leitner

Leisure in Later Life, Third Edition by Michael J. Leitner and Sara F. Leitner

Leisure Enhancement

Third Edition

Michael J. Leitner, PhD
Sara F. Leitner, MA
and Associates

The Haworth Press®
New York • London • Oxford

The Haworth Press, Inc., 10 Alice Street, Binghamton, NY 13904-1580.

Cover design by Brooke Stiles.

Library of Congress Cataloging-in-Publication Data

Leitner, Michael J.
  Leisure enhancement / Michael J. Leitner, Sara F. Leitner, and Associates. — 3rd ed.
    p. cm.
  Includes bibliographical references and index.
  ISBN 0-7890-1533-1 (case : alk. paper) — ISBN 0-7890-1534-X (soft : alk. paper)
  1. Leisure. 2. Leisure—Social aspects. I. Leitner, Sara F. II. Title.
GV174.L46 2004
306.4'812—dc22
                                                          2003018000

Dedicated to our two wonderful daughters,
Arielle and Jessica,
who have enhanced our leisure so much!

CONTENTS

ABOUT THE AUTHORS

Michael J. Leitner, PhD, is a professor in the Department of Recreation and Parks Management at California State University in Chico, California. **Sara F. Leitner, MA,** is an instructor in special education and adapted physical education at Butte College in Oroville, California. They are co-authors of the textbook *Leisure in Later Life: A Sourcebook for the Provision of Recreational Services for Elders, Third Edition* (Haworth) and *How to Improve Your Life Through Leisure.* They are also the authors of several articles, primarily on the topic of recreation and aging.

CONTRIBUTORS

William Bowness was director of the Ability First Disabled Sports and Recreation program at California State University, Chico, offering recreational opportunities to physically disabled individuals. He is also the current world champion and record holder for the sit water-ski slalom event.

Tracy M. Claflin, MA, is a certified recreation therapist and is the director of the Chico Montessori Elementary School.

Amy Hornick received an MA in recreation administration from California State University, Chico, and specializes in fitness and dance.

Kelli Cliff McCrea teaches for the University of Phoenix Online and has conducted workshops at various educational institutions and U.S. Armed Forces installations in the United States and Europe.

Laura J. McLachlin, PhD, is a professor in the Department of Recreation and Parks Management at California State University, Chico, and is a certified recreation therapist.

David E. Simcox, PhD, is a professor in the Department of Recreation and Parks Management at California State University, Chico.

Preface

This textbook is intended for use as an introduction to leisure for nonmajors. Many universities are offering introduction to leisure courses as part of their general education requirements. To attain and maintain general education status, introduction to leisure courses should demonstrate that they contribute to lifelong learning and have substantial rigor. *Leisure Enhancement* is a unique introductory textbook in that it presents intellectually challenging information in a format that enables its practical application to improvement of the reader's leisure and life in general.

The ultimate goal of this book is to facilitate the enhancement of leisure and life. In order to improve leisure, a person first needs to understand leisure, which is why the first part of the book focuses on gaining a basic understanding of leisure theory, concepts, and philosophy. The second part of the book builds on the material presented in Part I and examines how specific theories, concepts, data, and philosophies can be applied to attempts to enhance specific benefits of leisure such as social development, fitness, and stress reduction. The third part of the book goes beyond the scope of personal leisure in examining topics such as leisure in foreign countries and leisure in the future. The thesis of this section is that through broadened horizons, individuals can better work toward continued leisure enhancement throughout their lives.

In summary, the three parts of this book reflect its three major goals:

1. To foster a better understanding of personal and societal leisure behavior,
2. To facilitate the application of theories, concepts, and data to improve personal leisure well-being, and
3. To broaden perspectives on leisure and enable adaptation to future changes.

These three goals, if met, will lead to the attainment of the ultimate purpose of this book, which is to facilitate maximal leisure well-being.

The first edition of this book was published in 1989, and the second edition was published in 1996. We have incorporated a great deal of recent research in the third edition and have made some other changes. In particular, Chapters 2, 4, 7, 10, 11, 13, and 16 have been updated a great deal, with many new references in each of these chapters.

However, despite all of the changes in the world since 1989, so many of the principles upon which this book is based have remained the same. For example, the theories and concepts discussed in Chapters 1 and 5 still provide an excellent basis for understanding leisure. The time-management principles in Chapter 6 and the ideas regarding the development of a personal philosophy of leisure in Chapter 12 are in some respects even more relevant today than they were in 1989.

It has been a wonderful experience to use this book in teaching "Leisure and Life" courses over the past twenty-two years, as well as helping other instructors use this book in teaching introductory courses to leisure for both recreation majors and nonmajors. We hope that you enjoy the third edition of this book and that it really does help to enhance your leisure.

Acknowledgments

The authors wish to acknowledge the important contributions of numerous individuals and organizations to the successful completion of this book:

Gloria Leitner, for her assistance with the review of literature for the third edition;

Lesley Allen, for typing the original manuscript; and Aaron Kenedi for typing the second edition;

Don Penland, Dawn Balzarano, David Gamse, and the Association of Americans and Canadians in Israel/Netanya Region for computer assistance;

the Department of Recreation and Parks Management, California State University, Chico, for its help and support;

the Zinman College of Physical Education, and the Nat Holman School for Coaches and Instructors at the Wingate Institute, Netanya, Israel, for their help and support;

Amy Hornick (Chapter 7), Kelli Cliff McCrea (Chapter 9), Professor Laura J. McLachlin and Tracy Claflin (Chapter 14A), William Bowness (Chapter 14B), and Professor David E. Simcox (Chapter 15) for their excellent contributions;

Professor Edward Seagle, for the photographs in Chapter 14A;

Tina Kelly of the World Leisure and Recreation Association for assistance in identifying professional contacts in foreign countries;

Nicole Samuel (France), Olga and Bessie Plaitis (Greece), Dr. Hillel Ruskin (Israel), Dr. Hilmi Ibrahim (Egypt), Professor Tej Vir Singh and Professor B. Bhattacharya (India), Hari Pokhrel and Raj B. Gunuig (Nepal), Dr. Samarng Puangbootr (Thailand), and Dr. Dicken Yung (Hong Kong) for their helpful information for Chapter 16;

and special thanks to all of our family and close friends for their inspiration and support.

PART I:
INTRODUCTION TO RECREATION AND LEISURE

Chapter 1

Concepts of Leisure

INTRODUCTION

One of the most frequently debated topics in the professional literature of the field of recreation is the definition of leisure. Perhaps an entire book could be written on this subject, and how to define leisure could be the major focus of an entire college course. Is leisure a category of time? Is leisure a form of activity? Is leisure really not time, but rather a subjective state of being? Can leisure only be positive, or can it be negative as well?

The answers to these questions will be discussed in this chapter. More specifically, the learning objectives for this chapter are as follows:

1. Compare and contrast the terms leisure and recreation.
2. Compare and contrast different categories of time expenditure.
3. Identify the different classifications of recreational activities and several examples of activities for each classification.
4. Contrast the definition of leisure used in this book with other concepts of leisure discussed in the literature.

LEISURE AS A CATEGORY OF TIME

Leisure Defined

For the purposes of this book, leisure is defined as free or unobligated time during which one is not working or performing other life-sustaining functions. This definition is being utilized mainly for practical purposes. It is by no means the most complete or profound definition. However, it is probably the most commonly used definition.

In a study by Neulinger (Maclean, Peterson, and Martin, 1985), 77 percent of a sample population defined leisure as discretionary or unobligated time. On the first day of class, before students have read this chapter, when asked to define leisure, by far the most common response in my "Leisure and Life" class over the past twenty years has been "free time." This definition is often used in leisure research because it allows an objective identification and quantification of leisure.

Another reason why this definition is utilized in this book is that it enables the identification and discussion of "negative" leisure activities. The reality is that free time can be used for either positive or negative purposes. Since 1981, when I began teaching a "Leisure and Life" course, a major problem on college campuses in the United States has been, and still is, binge drinking, a problem related to the negative use of free time by students. This problem can and should be addressed as a leisure-related problem. It would be irresponsible to cling to the classical definition of leisure as a positive state of being (as discussed later in this chapter) and therefore not discuss this problem, claiming that it is not related to leisure.

Nevertheless, other definitions are presented later in the chapter for comparison purposes. First, however, the definition of leisure as free time will be further explained, mainly by citing examples and contrasting leisure with other key terms.

Leisure and Other Key Terms

To better understand the definition of leisure as free or unobligated time, other terms such as work, personal care, and recreation should also be discussed.

1. *Work* is obligated time. Whereas leisure is free time (no obligations), work involves constraint or commitment. The term work can be used as both a category of time expenditure and as an activity.
2. *Personal care* refers to time devoted to maintenance of an individual's well-being. Although leisure is also essential to one's well-being, personal care refers to basic necessities of life that must be met even before one can experience work or leisure.

3. *Recreation* refers to activity performed during leisure (free time), usually for the purpose of enjoyment. The terms leisure activity and recreation are used synonymously in this book.

Utilizing the Definitions

The following examples of activities are presented to further clarify the terms work, personal care, recreation, and leisure:

1. Sleep—is it personal care or a leisure activity? It can be both. Suppose a person usually sleeps six hours per night. Without that much sleep, the person feels tired all day. Those six hours are considered personal care time. However, if the same person sleeps nine hours per night on the weekend, are the extra three hours of sleep necessary to help deal with an illness or buildup of stress, or is the motivation for the extra sleep simply that it feels good? If the latter reason is given, then the additional three hours of sleep are considered leisure time. However, if the former reason is the explanation given, then all nine hours are classified as personal care time.
2. Enjoyable work (athletics, music, art, teaching). Can work time actually be considered leisure time instead, because it is so enjoyable? Even time spent in the most enjoyable job is still classified as work time.
3. Conversely, consider unenjoyable free time activities (e.g., jogging or aerobics strictly for health reasons). Is the time spent in these activities work time or leisure time? It is leisure time, because the activity is voluntary.

In attempting to distinguish between work and leisure, the key factor to consider is perceived freedom. If the activity is one of free choice, it is a leisure activity, whether it is enjoyable or not. However, obligatory activity is classified as work. Clearly, there are many different types of work and leisure activities. The paradigm of leisure presented in the following section (Neulinger, 1981) clarifies the different types of activities.

NEULINGER'S PARADIGM OF LEISURE

In Neulinger's paradigm (1981), six types of activities are identified: three that are leisure, three that are nonleisure (see Table 1.1). The leisure and nonleisure types of activities are distinguished from one another on the basis of perceived freedom (leisure) versus perceived constraint (nonleisure).

The concept of intrinsic versus extrinsic motivation is used to further divide the two major types of activities (leisure and nonleisure) into three categories each, thereby creating a total of six activity categories. Intrinsic motivation refers to internal motivation: wanting to participate in the activity for its own sake. In contrast, extrinsic motivation refers to external motivation: wanting to do an activity for the external rewards (e.g., money) associated with the activity. According to Neulinger (1981), some activities are intrinsically motivated, others are extrinsically motivated, and perhaps the largest number of activities is caused by a combination of intrinsic and extrinsic motivation.

In order to facilitate a clear understanding of this paradigm, each cell of the paradigm is explained as follows:

1. *Pure leisure* refers to those activities freely engaged in that are totally intrinsically motivated. The activity is engaged in for its own sake, with extrinsic rewards not considered. This cell represents one of the smallest categories of activities. In most leisure activities, at least some attention is paid to external rewards. An example of a pure leisure activity is hiking in the mountains if the only motivation for doing the activity is the good feelings experienced during the activity. However, if the mountain hike is also motivated by the external reward of obtaining exercise that would contribute positively to one's health, then the activity is classified in cell 2, "leisure-work."

2. *Leisure-work* refers to activities that are engaged in freely and that are motivated by a combination of both intrinsic and extrinsic rewards. A very large number of leisure activities are likely to be classified as leisure-work. For example, any sport participated in not only for the enjoyable aspects but also for the fitness benefits would be classified as leisure-work activity.

3. *Leisure-job* refers to activities freely engaged in but motivated solely by the extrinsic rewards obtained from participation. A common example of a leisure-job activity is exercise such as jogging or aerobics that is participated in only for better health, weight reduction, or other positive consequences and is not motivated at all by enjoyment of the activity itself.

4. In contrast, *pure work* refers to activities engaged in under constraint but which provide only intrinsic rewards. Similar to the first cell, this category probably represents only a select group of activities. One example of pure work is a professional basketball player obligated to play because of a binding legal contract but who plays totally for the enjoyment of playing basketball and does not think about the financial rewards of playing. There probably are some professional athletes whose work could be classified in this cell, but it is more common for a professional athlete's work to be classified in the next cell, "work-job."

5. *Work-job* refers to activities engaged in under constraint and motivated by both intrinsic and extrinsic rewards. An example of a work-job activity is a professional baseball player who is contractually obligated to play and who is motivated to play both because of the financial rewards and the enjoyment of playing baseball. Similarly, a college professor who is contractually obligated to teach a course but does so both for financial gain and the joys of teaching is performing a work-job activity.

6. Last, and perhaps least appealing, are *pure job* activities. Pure job refers to activities engaged in under constraint that have no intrinsic rewards; participation is motivated exclusively by extrinsic rewards. An example of a pure job activity is a menial job such as custodial work that is motivated solely by an extrinsic reward (money).

Exercise 1.1 provides an opportunity to examine how your work and leisure activities fit into Neulinger's paradigm. List those work and leisure activities that fit into each of the various cells of the paradigm. Reviewing Exercise 1.1, in which cell of Neulinger's paradigm do most of your leisure and work activities fit? Are any of the cells blank? How much of your leisure is "pure leisure"?

Therefore, beyond the simple distinction of work being characterized by perceived constraint and leisure being characterized by per-

TABLE 1.1. Neulinger's Paradigm of Leisure

Perceived freedom = leisure			Perceived constraint = nonleisure		
1	2	3	4	5	6
Pure Leisure	Leisure-Work	Leisure-Job	Pure Work	Work-Job	Pure Job
(intrinsic motivation)	(both intrinsic and extrinsic motivation)	(extrinsic motivation)	(intrinsic motivation)	(both intrinsic and extrinsic motivation)	(extrinsic motivation)

Source: Adapted from Neulinger, 1981.

8

EXERCISE 1.1. Categorizing Activities According to Neulinger's Paradigm

1	2	3	4	5	6
Pure Leisure	Leisure-Work	Leisure-Job	Pure Work	Work-Job	Pure Job

Source: Adapted from Neulinger, 1981.

ceived freedom, many categories of work and leisure can be identified. In addition to the definition of leisure presented previously in this chapter and the categories of leisure and work in Neulinger's paradigm, many other definitions or concepts of leisure are described and contrasted in the next section of this chapter.

CONTRASTING VIEWS OF LEISURE

The definition of leisure being used for the purposes of this book is known as the *discretionary time* or *unobligated time* concept (Maclean, Peterson, and Martin, 1985). However, there is considerable debate over whether leisure can or should be viewed as a category of time expenditure.

Classical or Traditional View of Leisure

One contrasting view is the classical or traditional view (Kraus, 1984), which describes leisure as a highly desired state of mind or state of being that is realized through participation in intrinsically motivated activities. Implicit in this subjective view of leisure is the idea that leisure is highly valued and must involve a positive state of being to be considered leisure. Therefore, if this definition is utilized, free time and leisure are not considered synonymous. For example, suppose a mediocre movie is viewed during one's free or unobligated time. According to the traditional or classical view of leisure, the time spent watching the movie is not leisure time, whereas according to the discretionary time concept, this time is leisure time, but it is a negative or poor utilization of leisure time. This example illustrates some of the strengths and weaknesses of these two concepts of leisure. In a research study on the proportion of leisure time spent watching movies, using the traditional definition of leisure would create serious problems. Meanwhile, utilizing the unobligated time definition would not allow discrimination between positive and negative movie-viewing experiences, although this information could certainly be ascertained through an interview or questionnaire.

To further illustrate the difficulty of utilizing the classical definition, try to define your leisure time using this definition. Can it be done? Try comparing your leisure time estimates using the classical and discretionary time definitions of leisure.

Antiutilitarian View of Leisure

Similar to the traditional view, the antiutilitarian view envisions leisure as a state of mind (Neulinger, 1981). The antiutilitarian view further states that leisure need not serve any useful purpose and needs no justification. A positive aspect of this definition is that it suggests a more relaxed orientation to leisure than exists in the fast-paced, high-stress lifestyle of modern society.

However, the antiutilitarian view, like the classical view, is difficult to utilize in objectively quantifying leisure for research purposes. Yet another possible drawback to the antiutilitarian concept of leisure is that it can be used to justify leisure activities that are detrimental to healthy self-development (e.g., excessive television viewing, use of recreational drugs, or heavy recreational drinking). Applying the antiutilitarian definition, a chronic television watcher can argue that watching television for eight hours per day is fine as long as it is enjoyable and does not cause any physical harm, because leisure need not serve any purpose or useful function.

Social Instrument View of Leisure

In opposition to the antiutilitarian view of leisure is the social instrument view (Neulinger, 1981), in which leisure is seen as a means of promoting self-growth and helping others. According to this view, leisure should serve a useful purpose.

A drawback to this concept is that it can lead to a stressful attitude toward leisure, in which achievement during leisure activity is overemphasized. Leisure can become worklike in nature, approached with an emphasis on end results rather than on the experience itself. In defense of the social instrument view, it helps prevent uses of free time that detract from healthy self-development. Another desirable and likely outgrowth of having the social instrument orientation to leisure is a greater degree of volunteerism and community involvement emanating from the desire to utilize leisure to help others.

Leisure As a Symbol of Social Class

The view of leisure as a symbol of social class is quite different from the social instrument view. According to Veblen (Kraus, 1984), leisure can be viewed as a symbol of social class in that one of the most noticeable signs of wealth is the possession and use of free time. In support of this concept of leisure, one can argue that in modern society some of the most visible indices of high socioeconomic status are owning boats and fancy swimming pools, engaging in exotic world travel, attending exciting parties, and eating at the finest restaurants. All of those indices are leisure related, supporting Veblen's assertion that leisure is utilized as a symbol of social class.

Fortunately, this negative view of leisure is not as relevant to modern society as it was in the past. In many cases, people of lower socioeconomic status have more leisure than people of higher socioeconomic status. In contrast, during several periods in history the lower classes worked long hours and had very little free time, while the nobility was free to engage in a wide variety of leisure pursuits. In addition, in modern society, the recreation behavior patterns of people of different socioeconomic strata are much more similar than they were in past societies. Today both rich and poor might participate in the same activities (e.g., swimming), the major difference being the type of facilities or equipment used (e.g., private pool versus public pool). Therefore, the concept of leisure as a symbol of social class does not seem to be as relevant today, but even so, the leisure-related rewards associated with wealth are still perhaps the primary motive for aspiring to higher socioeconomic status.

Leisure As Activity

Leisure has also been defined as nonwork activity (Weiskopf, 1982). In contrast, for the purposes of this book, leisure has been defined as free time, recreation as the activity engaged in during free time. Thus, the leisure-as-activity concept equates the term leisure with the term recreation (as it is used in this book). If the leisure-as-activity concept is utilized, then the terms leisure and recreation are synonymous, but the terms leisure and free time are not synonymous. It seems that using the leisure-as-activity definition creates confusion because of the terminology changes it necessitates. Are not recreation and leisure commonly conceived of as two different concepts?

Casual Leisure and Serious Leisure

Stebbins (2000) makes a distinction between two types of leisure: casual leisure and serious leisure. In his view, casual leisure involves activities that are immediately intrinsically rewarding, have short-lived benefits, and require little or no special training. In contrast, serious leisure activities require significant personal effort and even an occasional need to "persevere." Serious leisure activities have durable, lasting benefits. Participants identify strongly with the activity and may even find a career in it, meaning that they experience different stages of achievement/involvement in the activity during their lifetime.

Exercise 1.2 asks you to attempt to categorize your leisure activities as either "casual" or "serious," utilizing Stebbins's descriptions of these terms in the previous paragraph. You can utilize the same activities you listed in Exercise 1.1.

Based on your categorization of your leisure activities in Exercise 1.2, answer the following questions:

1. Which activities that are currently casual could become serious if you dedicated more effort to them or took a different attitude toward them?
2. Which activities that are currently serious could become casual if you approached them differently?
3. Next to each activity listed, briefly explain your rationale for categorizing it as you did.
4. Which activities are more enjoyable, the casual or the serious ones? Why?
5. What are some serious leisure pursuits that you would like to develop?
6. According to your own personal feelings about leisure, how do you feel about the concept of "serious leisure"? Can an activity be serious and still be leisure?
7. Which categorization of activities is more helpful to you in understanding different types of leisure, Neulinger's paradigm, or Stebbins's definitions of casual versus serious leisure?

Holistic View of Leisure

The holistic view of leisure sees leisure and work as being so closely interrelated that the two cannot be separated (Edginton et al., 2002). According to the holistic view, elements of leisure can be found in work, education, and other social spheres. Because leisure is

EXERCISE 1.2.
Categorizing Activities As Casual or Serious Leisure

Casual leisure activities   **Serious leisure activities**

_____   _____

_____   _____

_____   _____

_____   _____

_____   _____

_____   _____

_____   _____

_____   _____

_____   _____

_____   _____

_____   _____

_____   _____

_____   _____

_____   _____

_____   _____

_____   _____

_____   _____

_____   _____

_____   _____

so interrelated with work and other aspects of life, a holistic explanation or definition of leisure also includes an analysis of the concepts of work and time.

A study by Shaw (1986) lends support to the contention of the holistic view that elements of leisure can be found in many different aspects of life. In Shaw's study, 120 adults reported their subjective leisure time, daily free time, and time devoted to recreational activities via a 48-hour diary and interviews. The results indicated that leisure can be experienced in work and other obligatory activities and that not all recreation time or free time is necessarily considered to be leisure. Specifically, average daily subjective leisure time was 7.26 hours, compared with daily averages of 5.26 hours of free time and 3.22 hours of recreation time, meaning that two hours per day of leisure occurs during nonfree time, and over four hours per day of leisure occurs during time other than recreation time. In addition, approximately 8 percent of recreation time and 15 percent of free time was reported as being nonleisure. Therefore, this study provides evidence that the holistic view is accurate in its assertion that work, education, leisure, and other spheres are intertwined at least to some extent.

It is worthwhile to consider the following questions in relation to the holistic view of leisure:

1. Will the holistic view of leisure be the most widely accepted view in future society?
2. Will greater acceptance of the holistic view lead to a more humanistic approach to life, in which concern for humans supersedes concern for material goods?
3. Currently, how widely accepted is the holistic view of leisure?

Summary of Leisure Concepts

This section presented most of the major concepts of leisure, although several more concepts of leisure are discussed in the literature that are not discussed in this chapter. The key point is that for the purposes of this book, leisure is defined as free or unobligated time, time during which individuals might choose to participate in positive, beneficial activities or negative, detrimental ones.

Now that some concepts of leisure have been examined, what is recreation?

RECREATION

Characteristics of Recreation

The term recreation was defined previously as activity conducted during leisure time. However, to really understand what recreation is, a number of characteristics of recreation should be explained. According to Weiskopf (1982), the following are basic characteristics of recreation:

1. Participation is voluntary, not obligatory.
2. Some of the major purposes of participation are enjoyment, fun, personal satisfaction, and revitalization.
3. Recreation usually involves activity as opposed to total idleness or rest.
4. Participation is usually motivated by internal goals or rewards.
5. Perhaps the most important factor in determining whether an activity is a recreational experience is the participant's attitude toward the activity, not the activity itself. Although it was previously stated that recreation participation is voluntary and is motivated by internal rewards such as personal satisfaction, many activities might also have some element of obligation and external rewards. However, it is the degree to which the participant psychologically focuses on the voluntary versus obligatory and the internal versus external reward aspects of the activity that determines whether the activity is a recreational experience.

    Example: A friend calls, asking you to play racquetball tomorrow. Analyzing this activity, you might find that your motivation for participation is comprised of a mixture of internal and external factors. On the one hand, you feel that playing would be fun (internal rewards). On the other hand, you feel that you should agree to play just to please your friend and to burn some calories (external rewards). Participation is voluntary in that the decision to play is totally in your hands, yet you feel a sense of obligation because your friend asked you to play. If you focus upon the external rewards of playing and the obligatory aspect of participation, this activity will not be a recreational experience. Have you ever observed someone who seemed to have a negative attitude while playing a sport and appeared to have a miserable time throughout the activity instead of having a recreational experience? Conversely, if you focus on the internal rewards and voluntary aspects of participation, then the activity is a recreational experience. Attitude is the key!

6. Recreation usually benefits a person physically, mentally, and/or socially, in addition to being an enjoyable experience. (The various benefits/needs/satisfactions derived from recreation are expounded in Chapter 5.)

7. Recreation services provided as part of a community service program should meet appropriate ethical standards and provide a healthy and constructive experience.

8. Recreation is a very broad concept. It involves an extremely diverse range of activities. The different categories of recreational activities are discussed in the next section of this chapter.

Classification of Recreational Activities

Refer to the Appendix for a listing of specific recreational activities associated with each of the categories of recreational activity identified as follows.

1. *Simple entertainment:* This category includes spectator sports, movies, television, and any other type of activity that provides pleasure without placing much physical, mental, or social demand on the participant.

2. *Mental activity/contemplation and self-awareness:* An excellent example of a recreational activity in this category is meditation. Other common activities under this heading are reading and writing (for pleasure).

3. *Sports and exercise:* This category includes a very wide range of activities, such as basketball, aerobics, windsurfing, and weight lifting.

4. *Music:* The category of music encompasses a broad span of listening and participation activities, including composing.

5. *Art:* Art covers a diverse spectrum of media, such as oil painting, sculpture, and stained glass, as well as art appreciation activities.

6. *Dance:* The category of dance includes both spectator and participant activities. The categories of music, art, and dance together form a cluster commonly referred to as cultural/aesthetic activities.
7. *Hobbies:* The hobbies category is also very broad. It includes collecting activities such as stamp collecting and handicrafts such as model building.
8. *Play/games:* Included are numerous childhood games and board games as well as noncompetitive games and spontaneous play activity.
9. *Relaxation:* Hot tubbing and massage are prime examples of activities in the relaxation category.
10. *Social activity:* Family gatherings, parties, and involvement in clubs are only three of many types of social recreation activity.
11. *Humanitarian services:* Service activities encompass many types of volunteer work and involvement in organizations providing humanitarian services.
12. *Nature activities/outdoor recreation:* This category covers those activities in which the outdoors or a natural resource is the focal point, such as hiking and fishing.
13. *Travel and tourism:* This category covers perhaps the largest segment of the leisure services industry and spending on recreational activities. In a sense, it encompasses the other twelve categories in that while traveling or on a tour, participation in any or all of the other twelve categories can be attempted.

These thirteen categories are intended to provide a classification that covers the broad spectrum of recreational activities. However, the categories are not intended to be mutually exclusive. Many activities could fit into two or more categories. For example, volunteering to help with a camping trip for a group of children with physical disabilities could be considered humanitarian service as well as outdoor recreation or social activity. Listening to music is another activity that could fit into several categories. Depending upon the type of music and one's attitude toward the activity, it might be considered primarily a social activity, relaxation, or mental activity/contemplation and self-awareness, as well as a music activity.

The purpose of the classification of recreational activities is to illustrate the broad spectrum of activities included under the term recreation, not necessarily to place every single recreational activity into its appropriate category. The lists of activities in the Appendix are provided to further emphasize the enormous variety of recreational pursuits that exist.

SUMMARY

If such varied recreational pursuits are available, then why would anybody complain of boredom, lack of motivation, or "being in a rut"? Clearly, the problem is not a lack of opportunities, but rather a lack of knowledge or awareness of these opportunities. As discussed in the next chapter, there is a growing need for leisure education in society today to help make people more aware of their leisure possibilities.

REFERENCES

Edginton, C.R., Jordan, D.J., DeGraaf, D.G., and Edginton, S.R. (2002). *Leisure and life satisfaction: Foundational perspectives* (Third edition). New York: McGraw-Hill.

Kraus, R.G. (1984). *Recreation and leisure in modern society* (Third edition). Glenview, IL: Scott, Foresman.

Maclean, J.R., Peterson, J.A., and Martin, W.D. (1985). *Recreation and leisure: The changing scene.* New York: Wiley.

Neulinger, J. (1981). *To leisure: An introduction.* Boston: Allyn and Bacon.

Shaw, S.S. (1986). Leisure, recreation, or free time? Measuring time usage. *Journal of Leisure Research,* 18(3), 177-189.

Stebbins, R.A. (2000). Leisure education, serious leisure and community development. In A. Sivan and H. Ruskin (Eds.), *Leisure education, community development, and populations with special needs* (pp. 21-30). New York: CABI Publishing.

Weiskopf, D. (1982). *Recreation and leisure: Improving the quality of life.* Boston: Allyn and Bacon.

Chapter 2

Leisure Education:
Vital to the Well-Being of Society

INTRODUCTION

The purpose of this chapter is to illuminate the accuracy of its title. Leisure education is indeed vital to the well-being of society. More specifically, the learning objectives of this chapter are as follows:

1. Define leisure education.
2. Identify the goals of leisure education.
3. Describe the connection of leisure to education.
4. Identify factors that have led to a growth in free time and made leisure education a more critical concern in modern society.
5. Contrast the importance of leisure education with other types of education, in light of data on time expenditure in a typical life span.
6. Cite references to research on the importance of leisure well-being in determining physical and mental well-being, in support of the importance of leisure education.
7. Compare the economic costs to society of leisure misuse with projected costs of expanding leisure education programs.
8. Identify factors that affect the quantity and quality of leisure, in support of the assertion that leisure education should be a life-long process.

WHAT IS LEISURE EDUCATION?

Definition and Goals of Leisure Education

Leisure education is a process designed to facilitate maximal leisure well-being. Leisure education courses are offered at colleges and universities, at elementary and secondary schools, and even in corporations as part of a comprehensive wellness program. This textbook is written for university-level leisure education courses. The authors advocate that the goals of a university-level leisure education course should include the following:

1. Gaining a basic understanding of leisure and recreation
2. Understanding theories and concepts of leisure and how they apply to one's life
3. Gaining an understanding of time-management and leisure-planning principles and how they can be applied to improving one's leisure
4. Applying qualitative and quantitative methods to solving leisure-related problems
5. Understanding how leisure behavior can affect physical and mental health
6. Understanding how stress can be either reduced or increased by leisure activities
7. Understanding the role of recreation in socialization
8. Understanding the leisure-related aspirations and constraints to leisure of ethnic minorities and women
9. Understanding global issues affecting leisure in the United States and in other nations
10. Exploring future leisure possibilities

These goals and areas of responsibility for leisure education coincide with the aims of this textbook, as this book is designed for use in university-level leisure education courses. Even though the goals of leisure education certainly seem very worthwhile, the appropriateness of leisure education as a part of school and university curricula is still questioned by some people. Perhaps if you are a student at a university enrolled in a leisure education course to fulfill a general education requirement, or if you are a recreation major enrolled in a foundations of leisure course, you have had a parent or friend make fun of the idea that you are receiving three units of credit for a course on the topic of leisure. Maybe a parent even tried to persuade you to take a different, more "worthwhile" course. The next section of this chapter explains the importance of incorporating leisure education into school and university curricula.

Leisure and Education

According to Ruskin and Leitner (2002), the idea that leisure education should be incorporated into schools and universities has its roots in the early twentieth century (e.g., the 1918 Commission on the Reorganization of Secondary Schools identified "the worthy use of leisure" as one of the seven cardinal principles of education) and is still advocated in the twenty-first century by organizations such as the United Nations (UN), which recognizes the right of children to have rest and leisure and to engage in play and recreational activities. In a convention on the rights of children, the UN also urged governments to encourage the provision of equal opportunities for cultural, artistic, recreational, and leisure activity. A world conference on ministers responsible for youth stated that leisure activities should be integrated into the regular school curriculum. In summary, many prominent organizations and individuals advocate the idea that leisure education should be integrated into school and university curricula. It is vital that schools integrate leisure education into their curricula starting at an early age, given the great influence that schools have on almost all aspects of the lives and development of youth.

According to Ruskin and Leitner (2002), there are a number of different ways to implement leisure education in schools. These include teaching special courses in areas related to leisure, incorporating leisure education in existing subject areas such as social sciences, literature and languages, arts and crafts, and music, and creating social activities for students.

The benefits of leisure education to the educational process in general and for society as a whole include the following:

1. Leisure experiences can provide valuable exercises in utilizing and reinforcing skills (both physical and mental) taught in school (Brightbill, 1960).
2. Leisure activities incorporated into the leisure education curriculum can provide an outlet for surplus energy, enabling students to concentrate better in class (Kelly, 1982).
3. Leisure activity can provide intrinsic motivation for developing physical skills, reading skills, and even mathematical skills. Many leisure activities require a certain level of proficiency in these and other skills taught in the curriculum (Kelly, 1982).

Thus, the intrinsic motivation for participation in certain leisure activities can contribute to motivating students to develop academic skills. Leisure activity can also provide positive experiences that give students confidence in these skills.

4. Leisure education can contribute to an understanding and appreciation of other cultures and societies (Brightbill, 1960). Exposure to the literature, art, music, and games of other ethnic groups and countries can foster better cross-cultural relations.

5. Leisure education exposes students to leisure experiences that contribute to reaching a deeper level of understanding of the world and life in general (Brightbill, 1960). Is that not the ultimate aim of education?

6. Adequate preparation for leisure can help ensure the strength of present and future society. For example, leisure-related problems such as recreational drug use pose a threat to the well-being of society. Leisure education can play a significant role in attempting to alleviate problems such as these. Leisure education can also help individuals make the most of the great leisure opportunities available to many people in later life, after retirement.

Ruskin and Sivan (2002) present the World Leisure and Recreation Association's international charter for leisure education, including its principles and strategies for implementing leisure education in schools. They are outlined in the following list.

1. Leisure education is an essential part of every stage of formal and informal education.

2. The potential leisure content in every subject in the curriculum should be identified.

3. Every subject should be infused with leisure content.

4. The topic of leisure should be integrated into all educational, cultural, school, and extracurricular activities.

5. Out-of-school involvement should be enhanced by curriculum flexibility and freedom of choice in the selection of educational activities.

6. Schools should implement the sharing of leisure cultural experiences in the learning process.

7. Educators should promote enjoyment without fear of failure by incorporating principles of trial and error.
8. A variety of personnel should help implement these leisure education principles and strategies, including school and class leisure coordinators, teachers, counselors, and leisure out-of-school specialists.

Clearly, leisure and education have a strong connection. As discussed in the next section, leisure education is more important than ever before as a result of the greater prominence of leisure in modern society.

PROMINENCE OF LEISURE IN SOCIETY

Leisure As the #1 Block of Time in a Lifetime

In Chapter 2 of the first two editions of this book, a study from Weiskopf's (1982) book was cited, which calculated that during a seventy-year life span, an "average" person would spend 27 years in leisure, 24 in sleep, 7.33 in work, 4.33 in formal education, 2.33 eating, and 5 years in "miscellaneous." According to Pawlowski (2000), ten of the twenty-seven years of leisure are spent watching television, with children age two to five averaging twenty-five to thirty-two hours per week in front of the television.

Students sometimes question the accuracy of these figures, so for this edition of the book, new calculations are presented, with a slightly different twist. Table 2.1 lists figures for the remaining sixty years of a seventy-eight-year life span of an eighteen-year-old college freshman.

The key point of Table 2.1 is that leisure is the largest category of time in the remaining life span of a college freshman. More than twice as much time will be devoted to leisure than to work. It would be foolish to not include leisure education in the university curriculum and to instead focus entirely on career preparation, as much more time will be spent at leisure than at work. The figures shown in the table are conservative estimates. In fact, if sleep time is less than seven hours per night, if the life span increases, if the retirement age lowers, if the workweek is reduced, or if vacation time increases, the figure

TABLE 2.1. Years Spent in Life Activities, Ages Eighteen to Seventy-Eight

Number of years	Life activities
18.08	Leisure, including retirement
17.80	Sleep (seven hours per night)
8.33	Work (forty years, thirty-six hours per week)
1.00	Formal education
7.12	Personal care (includes some eating)
5.34	Family and other obligations
1.53	Commuting
0.80	Miscellaneous
60.00	Total

for leisure would rise significantly. For example, if a person were to sleep six hours per night instead of the seven hours per night assumed in the calculations in Table 2.1, the time for leisure would increase to 20.5 years! College students should note that during four years of college, you are projected to have 1.34 years of leisure to enjoy. That figure assumes that a student enrolled in sixteen units of courses does thirty-two hours of homework per week in addition to attending class sixteen hours per week and working ten hours per week.

At this point, some people might argue that although leisure is the number one block of time in a lifetime, leisure education is not necessary, because people should know what to do in their leisure, as it is not complicated or technical in the way that many careers are. Two sections later in this chapter show how false and even dangerous this argument is. The section on leisure-related problems (as well as Chapter 11, which addresses this topic in more detail) explains how many people are misusing leisure in ways that cause harm to themselves, others, and society in general. The section on the relationship between leisure and psychological well-being (as well as Chapter 7 on the topic of fitness) discusses the enormous but unfortunately underutilized potential of leisure to enhance physical and mental health. Furthermore, the statistics on recreational activity participation patterns of Americans cited in Chapter 4 indicate that extensive leisure education efforts are needed to facilitate more positive leisure behavior patterns.

However, will the free time of Americans continue to grow? This issue is examined in the next section.

LEISURE: CONTINUED GROWTH, DECLINE, OR STABILIZATION?

The Nineteenth- to Twentieth-Century Leisure "Explosion"

The free time of Americans has grown tremendously since the mid-nineteenth century. Some factors that have contributed to this growth include the following:

1. The workweek has declined from seventy hours in 1850 to approximately thirty-five to forty hours by the 1980s (Weiskopf, 1982).
2. According to Leitner and Leitner (2004), the proportion of retirement-age (age sixty-five and over) persons in America has tripled since 1900. This has led to the rise of a new, large "leisure class." Never before has industrialized society had so many nonworking adults. Therefore, the growth in the older population has contributed significantly to an overall increase in the free time of Americans.
3. Technological advances such as microwave ovens and clothes dryers have contributed to reducing time needed for household obligations, thereby allowing more free time (Godbey, 1981).
4. The decline of the work ethic and rise of the "leisure ethic" has caused people to accept and seek greater free time (Godbey, 1981).
5. The decline in family size due to a lower birthrate (Kelly, 1982) has resulted in less time devoted to household and family obligations and more free time.

Undoubtedly, from 1850 to 1980, a tremendous growth in leisure occurred. However, a subject of debate is whether free time in the United States has stabilized, continued to grow, or experienced some decline since the 1980s. Another question is whether leisure will grow, decline, or stabilize in the next fifty years. Numerous articles have been written on this subject, some claiming that leisure has declined, others explaining that free time is still increasing and will continue to increase. Although statistics cited in some articles seem to support the idea that leisure has been in decline, an analysis of the research indicates that overall, leisure has been increasing since the 1980s and will continue to increase. First, an overview of some of the literature that discusses the decline of leisure in recent years is presented. This is followed by facts and concepts contradicting the idea that free time has been declining, instead supporting the notion that leisure has in fact been increasing in recent years and will continue to increase.

The Apparent Decline of Leisure

Some compelling statistics would seem to indicate that there has been a decline in leisure since the 1980s:

1. According to the Bureau of Labor Statistics, an average married couple works 26 percent more each year than similar working couples did twenty to thirty years ago (O'Sullivan, 2000).
2. According to research cited by Slatalla (2000), the free time of children ages three to thirteen decreased 16 percent, from sixty-three hours per week in 1981 to fifty-one hours per week in 1997.
3. Statistics cited by Lardner (1999) claim that those working fifty or more hours per week rose from 24 percent to 37 percent, and that the average workweek of those working at least twenty hours per week rose from forty-three to forty-seven hours per week during the 1990s.

Schor (2002) argues that leisure in America has been declining in recent years. She correctly points out that compared to other industrialized nations, Americans are far behind in terms of vacation time (one or two weeks per year, compared to five or six weeks per year in many European countries) and national holidays and celebrations. Also in support of Schor's assertion of declining leisure in America are the results of a 1987 Harris Poll, indicating that from 1973 to 1987 the median number of leisure hours per week declined from 26.2 to 16.6 (Kilborn, 1990). Schor's (1991) book on the decline of leisure in the United States received a great deal of publicity and acceptance.

The widespread belief that leisure has declined can in part be explained by sociological research which has found that increasing wealth and education brings about a sense of tension about time (Lewis, 2000). As explained in the next section, the idea that we have too little free time or that leisure has been declining is a myth. Some of the statistics cited in this section are refuted in the next section.

More Real Leisure, Less Perceived Leisure

Scott (1999) explains that even though it is true that some Americans are working more than they used to, others are working less, and overall Americans have more free time even if a significant portion of society is working longer hours. It is true that some of the highest-paid professionals are working longer hours, but on the other hand, many people are retiring early and many young adults are postponing child rearing or are having fewer children. Also, it might actually be true that overall, work hours have decreased rather than increased in recent years. A survey of businesses by the Bureau of Labor Statistics (Scott, 1999) indicates that the average workweek declined from 38.8 hours in the mid-1960s to 36.1 hours in the mid-1970s, 34.9 in the mid-1980s, and 34.6 in 1998.

The statistics cited regarding the decline of free time among children might also be misleading. True, children seem to have less *unstructured* leisure today than they used to have, but is playing on a soccer team or taking dance classes not leisure? Yes, children's free time is more structured than it used to be, but it does not necessarily mean that children have less free time. In fact, it could be argued that because of the increased structure, children's leisure today is of a higher quality (more enriched) than it used to be.

In examining whether to believe the statistics pointing to decreased leisure versus those indicating continued growth in leisure, it is important to consider the research methods employed in the different research studies. One problem with the statistics on declining leisure is that the data are obtained from a *single question* in which survey respondents *estimate* how much free time they have in a week (Robinson and Nicosia, 1991). Robinson (1990) also points out that most surveys have only a 10 percent response rate.

Meanwhile, Robinson (1990) cites statistics from his own research which indicate that since 1965, leisure hours per week increased from approximately thirty-four to forty. Robinson and Nicosia (1991) point out that although many Americans might psychologically perceive a decline in their leisure time, millions of Americans actually have more free time than they did twenty years ago. Robinson's most recent research indicates that free time has continued to increase, mainly because of a decrease in the amount of time spent on eating and grooming (Scott, 1999).

Robinson's research employed a time diary method. Unlike the surveys, which asked respondents to estimate their leisure for an entire week, the time diary method requires respondents to recall their activities for a specific period, usually only a day. Robinson and Nicosia (1991) explain that an advantage to this method is that it lessens the reporting burden for respondents, thereby making the data obtained more accurate. In contrast, people tend to exaggerate their work hours when asked to recall them from memory in the survey research.

Therefore, it appears Americans perceive that they have less free time when in fact they have more. In fact, it seems that Americans have *more than twice the amount* of free time than they think they have. What could cause such a disparity between actual and perceived leisure?

Perhaps the main cause is the passive nature of most people's leisure activities. Cutler (1990) states that the number of hours spent watching television has increased since 1985, and Robinson and Nicosia (1991) explain that almost the entire increase in free time in America since 1965 has been taken up by an increase in television viewing time. Also, adults age forty-five and over now spend an average of over seventy minutes per day at their computers and have increased time spent talking on the phone from 36.5 minutes per day in 1980 to fifty-two minutes per day in 2000 (Lewis, 2000). Another area of leisure that has seen an increase in time expenditure is shopping for, watching, and returning videos and DVDs. Meanwhile, participation in many active sports has been declining (Robinson, Godbey, and Walker, 1993). The increasingly passive nature of leisure in America is one likely cause for the discrepancy between actual and perceived leisure. Passive leisure is less memorable than active leisure.

Davidson (1994) discusses other factors that may also be contributing to the feeling that leisure has decreased and stress has increased, such as population density, the information explosion, keeping records, and having to make choices from many options. Perhaps the tendency for people to spend their free time in activities that are easy to do rather than doing what they enjoy most (Spring, 1993) might also cause leisure to be less memorable and lead to the perception that free time is scarcer than it actually is.

In conclusion, leisure time has increased dramatically during the twentieth century, and despite survey research indicating a decline in leisure, it appears that leisure time has continued to increase during the past twenty to thirty years. Research indicates that Americans actually have more than twice the amount of free time than they perceive to have (forty hours per week of actual leisure versus 16.6 hours of perceived leisure).

Factors Affecting Future Trends in Free Time

Numerous factors will influence whether leisure continues to increase or whether it will decrease or stabilize. Some of the factors that may cause free time to stabilize or possibly decline are the following:

1. The *attitude of "limitless materialism"* in modern society could cause leisure to decline (Godbey, 1981). The desire for more material goods can lead people to seek more work and less leisure. According to Vacek (1994), if Americans had been satisfied with living at 1950s standards, they would now be working only six months a year. Instead, they have chosen to double the amount they own and consume. For example, the average starter home has more than doubled in size, from 900 square feet in 1950 to 1,850 square feet in 1990 (Keyes, 1991). What were once considered luxuries (e.g., video equipment, personal computers) are now deemed to be necessities. Bryce (2001) describes how much more packed homes today are with material goods such as televisions, computers, and other electronic equipment.

   The philosophy of limitless materialism seems to be the greatest force opposing continued growth in leisure in America. As stated by Prasch (2000), "The longer you work, the more you spend. The more you spend, the longer you have to work. And the longer you work, the less time you have for family, community, and leisure activities" (p. 679).

O'Sullivan (2000) cites some statistics indicating that the attitude of limitless materialism is as strong as ever: 30 percent of Americans say that they would like to increase their income by working more hours; 53 percent would not trade money in order to have more time; and only 9 percent of American workers would accept a pay cut in order to work fewer hours. Exercise 2.1 gives you an opportunity to examine if you are caught up in the attitude of "limitless materialism." This exercise asks you to project a few years into the future, after you have graduated from college and are working and perhaps married or living on your own. In the left column, list the material items you feel you would want or need in order to live a "good life." Try to estimate the cost of these items and compute how much annual salary you would need to earn in order to afford this lifestyle. In the right column, try to "downshift" and list "minimized" material needs that would enable you to make ends meet with a smaller salary, fewer work hours, and therefore more leisure.

After completing Exercise 2.1, answer the following questions:

- How many hours per week would you have to work in order to make enough money to afford the possessions listed in the left column?
- How many hours per week would you have to work in order to make enough money to afford the possessions listed in the right column?
- Which lifestyle do you feel would make you happier? Why?
- To what extent are you influenced by the philosophy of limitless materialism?

2. The changing roles of men and women in society are related to *an increased presence of women in the workforce* (Kelly, 1982). Should this trend continue, the free time of women might decrease, possibly contributing to an overall decline in the free time of society.

3. Although manual labor might decline, the *demands of service occupations* might grow. According to Godbey (1981), statistics indicate an increase in overtime work and in dual job holding. Godbey (1981) states that although the workweek declined

drastically since the turn of the twentieth century, it has been fairly stable since World War II.
4. Godbey (1981) makes another argument against increasing leisure by considering *the increasing level of complexity* and change in society. Much of what could be considered free time is absorbed by the increasing demands of keeping up with new information and changes.

On the other hand, there are factors that could cause a continued increase in free time in society:

1. Technology might eliminate a larger number of manual jobs, causing massive unemployment (Kraus, 1984). How would society be able to cope with this "enforced" leisure if this prediction comes true? Alternatively, the decreased amount of work available could be distributed evenly among people, creating less unemployment but decreasing the workweek for most people.
2. Projections cited by Leitner and Leitner (2004) indicate that there will continue to be rapid growth in the proportion of elders in future society, thereby increasing the number of nonworking adults in society. If medical technology continues to progress and people continue to live longer, the possibilities for growth in the population of retirees are mind-boggling.
3. Improved technology will continue to help reduce time devoted to household obligations, thereby enabling more free time.
4. Educational levels are increasing. As educational levels increase, birthrates tend to decline. Smaller family size usually means less household and child-rearing obligations and more free time.

Although future trends are not totally clear, the sure growth in the population of retirees and the technological advances which will reduce certain types of work should lead to an overall increase in leisure in society. Leisure education is of great importance in facilitating adjustment to an increasingly leisure-centered society. As discussed in the next section, the leisure well-being of society is a critical concern, given the ample data that point to the strong relationship between psychological well-being and leisure.

EXERCISE 2.1.
Limitless Materialism versus Limited Materialism

Ideal material possessions
and their cost

Minimized material needs

_____ _____

_____ _____

_____ _____

_____ _____

_____ _____

_____ _____

_____ _____

_____ _____

_____ _____

_____ _____

_____ _____

_____ _____

_____ _____

_____ _____

_____ _____

_____ _____

_____ _____

THE RELATIONSHIP BETWEEN LEISURE
AND MENTAL HEALTH

The main focus of this section is the relationship between leisure and mental health. Leisure is also a very important factor influencing physical fitness and health, but this topic is explored in detail in Chapter 7. Siegenthaler (1997) presents an overview of research that shows the many ways leisure can positively affect mental health:

1. Certain leisure activities *promote psychological well-being.* In one study, participation in hobbies/crafts, visiting with friends, and swimming were leisure activities that had a positive impact on psychological well-being. However, watching television was a leisure activity that was negatively related to psychological well-being.

2. High levels of participation in a variety of leisure pursuits help to *balance life's demands and increase perceived physical, mental, and social health.* Research with college students indicated that those who were more active in social activities and competitive sports perceived better mental health. Those who were more active in social, adventure, entertainment, nature, and competitive sports perceived better social health.

3. Students who experience *less boredom in their free time report better mental and physical health.* Participation in a variety of recreational activities helps to prevent boredom and promotes healthier behavior.

4. *Leisure can provide a morale boost during times of major life crises.* Social leisure activities can be especially helpful in boosting morale in times of grief. Leisure enables people to face negative events in life and still be happy. This idea is supported by a research study conducted in Brazil with 552 women that found participation in leisure activities was negatively correlated with depression and anxiety, and helped to maintain mental health under adverse life conditions (Ponde and Santana, 2000). Because people face many crises and challenges throughout the life span, Kleiber (2001) advocates that leisure education must be a lifelong process, not just an intervention directed at children in schools.

5. *Meaningful and fulfilling leisure activities promote higher perceived wellness.* The meaning and quality of leisure experiences can be more important in promoting wellness than is the actual participation in the activity.

6. *Leisure congruence,* meaning that individuals participate in leisure activities that match their personality type, seems to be a key factor in promoting a sense of well-being.

7. *Perceived freedom in leisure helps people resist stress-induced illness.* In particular, participation in leisure activities helps to prevent illness when stress is high. Other ways in which leisure can help in dealing with stress are discussed in more detail in Chapters 8 and 9.

Many previous studies support the assertion that leisure participation and satisfaction are positively related to psychological well-being and life satisfaction: Brooks and Elliott (1971); Campbell, Converse, and Rogers (1976); DeCarlo (1974); Flanagan (1978); Graney (1975); Haavio-Mannila (1971); Keller (1983); Kelly, Steinkamp, and Kelly (1986); Kleiber (1972); Larson (1978); London, Crandall, and Seals (1977); Mancini and Orthner (1980); Palmore (1979); Peppers (1976); Ragheb and Griffith (1982); Riddick and Daniel (1984); Sneegas (1986); and Yankelovich (1978). Furthermore, some of these studies indicate that leisure behavior is the most important or one of the most important determinants of life satisfaction and psychological well-being (Campbell, Converse, and Rogers, 1976; Flanagan, 1978; London, Crandall, and Seals, 1977; Yankelovich, 1978).

According to Iso-Ahola (1980), research indicates that active recreation contributes more strongly to positive mental health than does passive recreation. Iso-Ahola (1980) offers the explanation that active recreation is more optimally arousing than passive recreation and that optimally arousing activity is conducive to psychological well-being. The arousal theory is discussed in detail in Chapter 5. Albrechtsen (2001) discusses the need for leisure education to encourage greater participation in active forms of leisure, in order to counteract the increasingly sedentary lifestyles induced by technology.

Research (Iso-Ahola, 1980) indicates that leisure activity is an even more important source of life satisfaction for unmarried adults than it is for married adults. According to Kraus (2000), the proportion of adults who are single rose from 28 percent in 1970 to 39 percent in 1991. If the proportion of single persons in the adult population continues to increase, leisure education will become even more critical to the well-being of society.

Two concrete ways in which leisure education can contribute to enhanced leisure well-being are by improving knowledge of leisure resources and leisure values. A study by Riddick (1986) of 221 adults aged eighteen to sixty-five indicates that knowledge of leisure resources and leisure values has a significant effect on leisure satisfaction. A four-year study by Leitner (1987) of 193 college students enrolled in a leisure education course and a control group of seventy-five students not enrolled in the course indicates that being enrolled in the leisure education course has a statistically significant effect on knowledge of leisure resources.

Obviously, leisure participation and satisfaction are important determinants of psychological and physical well-being, but can most people attain a high level of leisure satisfaction without leisure education? Apparently not, as evidenced by the prevalence of leisure-related problems in society.

LEISURE-RELATED PROBLEMS

The widespread existence of a variety of leisure-related problems in society reflects the need for leisure education. For example, the following behavioral problems can be viewed as being leisure related: alcohol abuse, drug abuse, compulsive gambling, and stress. Each of these problems has a tremendous negative impact on society, in terms of both human and economic costs. The theoretical connection of these problems to leisure and specific data on their prevalence in society are discussed in later chapters.

It seems wise to devote more resources to leisure education, given the costs to society of the aforementioned problems versus the costs of increasing leisure education efforts, assuming that leisure education can contribute to alleviating the problems. Table 2.2 provides a comparison of the costs of increasing leisure education versus the costs of some leisure-related behavioral problems.

As illustrated by Table 2.2, the costs of leisure-related problems are enormous, while the costs of the different methods of enhancing leisure education are much lower. In addition, Brightbill (1960) dis-

TABLE 2.2. Costs of Leisure Education versus Costs of Leisure-Related Problems

Methods of expanding leisure education and their costs	Leisure-related problems and their costs
1. University-level leisure education courses could be incorporated into the required general education curriculum. Cost: None. Students would simply be enrolling in a leisure education course instead of a course in another discipline. 2. Leisure education courses could be incorporated into elementary and secondary school curricula. Currently employed teachers could be trained to teach the courses, so the main costs of this approach would be teacher training programs and curriculum materials. Estimated costs would be fairly low for each school, probably only several hundred dollars or a few thousand dollars for a very large school. 3. Leisure education workshops could be offered to employees as part of an employee enrichment program. Costs would be minimal: Curriculum materials would be needed and leisure educators would need to be hired to lead the workshops. An example of a successful program is reported by Holser (1992). A leisure education program was conducted on a combat support ship, and the crew of a second ship was studied as a control group. The leisure education recipients significantly reduced their alcohol consumption and had significantly fewer alcohol-related disciplinary actions. 4. Leisure counseling services could be provided at schools, universities, and big corporations. Costs for leisure counseling personnel could be as high as several million dollars. If currently employed guidance and counseling personnel received training in leisure counseling and leisure education, costs would be lower.	1. *Substance abuse:* The economic cost of alcohol abuse alone is estimated as $166 billion annually (Arnold, 1999). Alcohol abuse is also a major factor in violent crime and family problems. As discussed by Weissinger (1994), leisure boredom is often associated with negative behaviors such as substance abuse, and leisure education can work directly at alleviating leisure boredom, thereby helping to reduce the problem of substance abuse. 2. *Stress:* The costs to society of work-related stress alone are over $200 billion annually, and 75 to 90 percent of all physician visits are estimated to be for stress-related complaints and illnesses (Verespej, 2000). 3. *Gambling:* Americans spend more than $500 billion a year on gambling, a 100 percent increase in spending since 1990 (Brody, 1999). 4. *Juvenile delinquency:* The number of juveniles arrested for violent crimes rose sharply in the United States in the late 1990s (Kraus, 2000). As documented by Robertson (2001), juvenile delinquency can in some cases be prevented or alleviated through leisure education programs. 5. *Family unrest:* The economic costs of family unrest are more difficult to estimate, but the human costs are apparent: The number of single-parent families increased 12 percent from 1990 to 1995 (Kraus, 2000).

5. Continuing education courses could be offered through community colleges, universities, and municipal parks and recreation departments at a very low cost to individuals or families. For example, Michaelis and O'Connell (1987) report the success of a family leisure education program, designed to help families learn how to recreate successfully together. Leisure education programs can also be offered in correctional institutions. In one study (Robertson, 2001), incarcerated youth indicated that increased leisure education could lessen or eliminate their participation in unacceptable social behaviors.

cusses many other leisure-related problems prevalent in society that are more difficult to quantify. These problems seem to be just as relevant in the twenty-first century as they were in 1960.

1. *Spectatorship:* Brightbill expresses concern over the tendency to observe rather than to participate. In particular, the spectatorship tendency with regard to sports must surely contribute to the poor level of fitness of Americans.
2. *Boredom:* According to Brightbill, of all leisure-related problems, boredom is potentially the most devastating because it "dampens the human spirit." In addition, many cases of alcohol and drug abuse, compulsive gambling, eating disorders, and juvenile delinquency can probably be linked to boredom.
3. *Nonliving:* This term is used by Brightbill to depict the emphasis on materialism and consumerism, the idea that to be happy, one needs to buy more and do more of nothing. As Iso-Ahola (1980) emphasizes, research clearly shows that "money can't buy happiness." Many studies indicate that leisure activity is more important than economic and materialistic considerations in determining life satisfaction.

In summary, leisure-related problems are widespread and costly, indicating that leisure education efforts should be expanded. One means of expanding leisure education mentioned in Table 2.2 is to expand leisure counseling services. Leisure counseling is quite different from leisure education, as discussed in the next section.

LEISURE COUNSELING

Leisure Education and Leisure Counseling Contrasted

Although leisure counseling can be viewed as an aspect of leisure education (Epperson, Witt, and Hitzhusen, 1977), the two terms describe very different processes. Leisure counseling is defined as a helping process in which a counselor works with an individual client or in small groups to enhance the leisure well-being of the clients, whereas leisure education refers to a self-help process involving a leisure education facilitator and a large group. Although the ultimate purpose of both leisure counseling and leisure education is to promote maximal leisure well-being, the process (education versus counseling) of each one is different. There are several types of leisure counseling.

Types of Leisure Counseling

Developmental-educational leisure counseling is similar to leisure education in that values clarification and self-awareness exercises are utilized to identify desired ideal leisure lifestyles. This type of leisure counseling is designed for people who wish to pursue an in-depth counseling process directed toward expanding leisure horizons. Developmental-educational clients are motivated to enter the counseling process by a desire to bring their real leisure lifestyle closer to an idyllic state. These clients do not necessarily exhibit symptoms of leisure-related problems. In fact, developmental-educational clients might be satisfied with their leisure *before* commencing counseling, but may simply wish to improve their leisure.

In contrast, *therapeutic-remedial* leisure counseling is designed for people who do exhibit specific behavioral leisure-related problems, such as alcohol and drug abuse, boredom, depression, and eating disorders. Therapeutic-remedial leisure counseling often takes place within institutional settings as part of a therapeutic recreation program. Counselors work intensively with clients to try to alleviate their problems by facilitating positive changes in leisure attitudes and activities.

A less intensive type of leisure counseling is *leisure resource guidance* counseling. In this approach, clients are motivated to enter the process to obtain information on leisure resources available to them that meet their leisure needs and interests. These clients do not necessarily exhibit leisure-related behavioral problems, nor do they necessarily desire to be involved in an intensive process designed to expand their leisure horizons. They are aware of what they would like to do but need information on resources to enable them to pursue their leisure interests. Some municipal parks and recreation departments offer this type of leisure counseling service.

Current Status of Leisure Counseling

Leisure counseling is a growing field within the broader leisure services profession. Research studies such as McDowell's (1976) indicate that leisure counseling can have a positive effect on leisure attitudes and leisure self-concept, thereby positively affecting psychological well-being and mental health. Additional information on leisure counseling can be obtained from books by Dowd (1984), Epperson, Witt, and Hitzhusen (1977), Loersch and Wheeler (1982), and McDowell (1976).

SUMMARY

Leisure education can make significant contributions to the well-being of society, because, as discussed in this chapter, research points to a strong connection between leisure well-being and psychological well-being. Leisure education should be a continuous, lifelong process, because leisure well-being and psychological well-being are constantly being challenged by changes in social norms, family structure, technology, the environment, personal health, employment status, and other areas. Leisure education is needed to help individuals adapt their leisure to these and other changes likely to be faced in the future. The historical overview presented in the next chapter should provide insight into how some of the leisure-related problems experienced in past societies evolved as a result of being unable to deal effectively with changes.

REFERENCES

Albrechtsen, S.J. (2001). Technology and lifestyles: Challenges for leisure education in the new millennium. *World Leisure,* 43(1), 11-19.

Arnold, L. (1999). Survey finds gambling woes could affect 20 million in U.S. *The Boston Globe,* March 19, p. A3.

Brightbill, C.K. (1960). *The challenge of leisure.* Englewood Cliffs, NJ: Prentice-Hall.

Brody, J.E. (1999). Compulsive gambling: Overlooked addiction. *The New York Times,* May 4, p. D7.

Brooks, J.B. and Elliot, D.M. (1971). Prediction of psychological adjustment at age thirty from leisure time activities and satisfactions. *Human Development,* 14, 51-61.

Bryce, J. (2001). The technological transformation of leisure. *Social Science Computer Review,* 19(1), 7-16.

Campbell, A., Converse, P., and Rogers, W. (1976). *The quality of American life: Perceptions, evaluations, and satisfactions.* New York: Russell Sage Foundation.

Cutler, B. (1990). Where does the free time go? *American Demographics,* 12(11), 36.

Davidson, J. (1994). Overworked Americans or overwhelmed Americans? Learning to relax and choose which decisions to make and inputs to respond to is the key to getting rid of that overwhelmed feeling. *Business Horizons,* 37(1), 62.

DeCarlo, T.J. (1974). Recreation participation patterns and successful aging. *Journal of Gerontology,* 29, 416-422.

Dowd, E.T. (Ed.). (1984). *Leisure counseling: Concepts and applications.* Springfield, IL: Charles C Thomas.

Epperson, A., Witt, P.A., and Hitzhusen, B. (1977). *Leisure counseling: An aspect of leisure education.* Springfield, IL: Charles C Thomas.

Flanagan, J.C. (1978). A research approach to improving our quality of life. *American Psychologist,* 33, 138-147.

Godbey, G. (1981). *Leisure in your life: An exploration.* Philadelphia: Saunders.

Graney, M.J. (1975). Happiness and social participation in aging. *Journal of Gerontology,* 30, 701-706.

Haavio-Mannila, E. (1971). Satisfaction with family, work, leisure, and life among men and women. *Human Relations,* 24, 585-601.

Holser, M.A. (1992). Naval recreation: A low-alcohol mixed drink. *Parks and Recreation,* 27(10), 40-44.

Iso-Ahola, S.E. (1980). *The social psychology of leisure and recreation.* Dubuque, IA: Wm C. Brown.

Keller, J.M. (1983). The relationship between leisure and life satisfaction among older women. Paper presented at the NRPA Research Symposium, National Recreation and Park Association, October, Kansas City, KS.

Kelly, J.R. (1982). *Leisure.* Englewood Cliffs, NJ: Prentice-Hall.

Kelly, J.R., Steinkamp, M.W., and Kelly, J.R. (1986). Later life leisure: How they play in Peoria. *Gerontologist,* 26, 531-537.

Keyes, R. (1991). *Timelock: How life got so hectic and what we can do about it.* New York: HarperCollins Publishers.

Kilborn, P.T. (1990). Tales from the digital treadmill. *The New York Times,* June 3, section 4, pp. 1, 3.

Kleiber, D.A. (1972). Free time and sense of competence in college students. Unpublished doctoral dissertation, University of Texas at Austin.

Kleiber, D.A. (2001). Developmental intervention and leisure education: A life span perspective. *World Leisure,* 43(1), 4-10.

Kraus, R.G. (1984). *Recreation and leisure in modern society* (Third edition). Glenview, IL: Scott, Foresman.

Kraus, R.G. (2000). *Leisure in a changing America* (Second edition). Needham Heights, MA: Allyn and Bacon.

Lardner, J. (1999). World class workaholics. *U.S. News and World Report,* December 20, pp. 42-53.

Larson, R. (1978). Thirty years of research on the subjective well-being of older Americans. *Journal of Gerontology, 33,* 109-125.

Leitner, M.J. (1987). The effects of a leisure education course on college students' leisure awareness and attitudes. Unpublished manuscript, California State University, Chico.

Leitner, M.J. and Leitner, S.F. (2004). *Leisure in later life* (Third edition). Binghamton, NY: The Haworth Press.

Lewis, D.E. (2000). Time out! Speed isn't all that we need. *The Boston Sunday Globe,* March 26, p. F3.

Loersch, L.C. and Wheeler, P.T. (1982). *Principles of leisure counseling.* Minneapolis, MN: Educational Media.

London, M., Crandall, R., and Seals, G. (1977). The contribution of job and leisure satisfaction to quality of life. *Journal of Applied Psychology, 62,* 328-334.

Mancini, J. and Orthner, D. (1980). Situational influences on leisure satisfaction and morale in old age. *Journal of the American Geriatrics Society, 28,* 446-471.

McDowell, C.F. (1976). *Leisure counseling: Selected lifestyle processes.* Eugene, OR: University of Oregon, Center of Leisure Studies.

Michaelis, B. and O'Connell, J. (1987). Family leisure education: A model, some strategies and program development case studies. *California Parks and Recreation,* 43(1) (January), 20-24.

O'Sullivan, E. (2000). Play for life. *Parks and Recreation,* 35(10), 98-106.

Palmore, E.B. (1979). Predictors of successful aging. *Gerontologist, 19,* 427-431.

Pawlowski, C. (2000). *Glued to the tube: The threat of television addiction to today's family.* Naperville, IL: Sourcebooks, Inc.

Peppers, L. (1976). Patterns of leisure and adjustment to retirement. *Gerontologist, 16,* 441-446.

Ponde, M.P. and Santana, V.S. (2000). Participation in leisure activity: Is it a protective factor for women's mental health? *Journal of Leisure Research,* 32(4), 457-472.

Prasch, R.E. (2000). Reassessing the labor supply curve. *Journal of Economic Issues,* 34(3), 679-693.

Ragheb, M.G. and Griffith, C.A. (1982). The contribution of leisure participation and satisfaction to life satisfaction of older persons. *Journal of Leisure Research, 14,* 295-306.

Riddick, C.C. (1986). Leisure satisfaction precursors. *Journal of Leisure Research,* 18, 259-265.

Riddick, C.C. and Daniel, S.N. (1984). The relative contributions of activities and other factors to the mental health of older women. *Journal of Leisure Research,* 16, 136-148.

Robertson, B.J. (2001). The leisure education of incarcerated youth. *World Leisure,* 43(1), 20-29.

Robinson, J.P. (1990). The leisure pie. *American Demographics,* 12(11), 38.

Robinson, J.P. (1992). Assessing free time through time diary research. Invited lecture at California State University, Chico, February 20.

Robinson, J.P., Godbey, G., and Walker, C. (1993). Has fitness peaked? *American Demographics,* 15(9), 36-41.

Robinson, J.P. and Nicosia, F.M. (1991). Of time, activity and consumer behavior: An essay on findings, interpretations, and needed research. *Journal of Business Research,* 22(2), 171-186.

Ruskin, H. and Leitner, M.J. (2002). Leisure education perspectives worldwide: World Leisure Association Commission on Education (EDCOM). Paper presented at the First Pacific Rim Conference on Leisure Education, January 11-14. Honolulu, HI, Hawaii Tokai International College.

Ruskin, H. and Sivan, A. (2002). *Leisure education in school systems.* Jerusalem, Israel: Cosell Center for Physical Education, Leisure, and Health Promotion, The Hebrew University of Jerusalem.

Schor, J. (1991). *The overworked American: The unexpected decline of leisure.* New York: Basic Books.

Schor, J. (2002). Why Americans should rest. *The New York Times,* September 2, p. A17.

Scott, J. (1999). Working hard, more or less. *The New York Times,* July 10, pp. A15, A17.

Siegenthaler, K.L. (1997). Health benefits of leisure. *Parks and Recreation,* 32(1), 24, 26, 28, 30-31.

Slatalla, M. (2000). Overscheduled. *Time,* 156(7), 79-80.

Sneegas, J.J. (1986). Components of life satisfaction in middle and later life adults: Perceived social competence, leisure participation, and life satisfaction. *Journal of Leisure Research,* 18, 248-258.

Spring, J. (1993). Exercising the brain. *American Demographics,* 15(3), 56-60.

Vacek, E. (1994). Never on Sundays: Whatever happened to leisure? *Commonweal,* 121(3), 13-16.

Verespej, M.A. (2000). Stressed out. *Industry Week,* February 21, pp. 30-34.

Weiskopf, D. (1982). *Recreation and leisure: Improving the quality of life.* Boston: Allyn and Bacon.

Weissinger, E. (1994). Recent studies about boredom during free time. *Parks and Recreation,* 29(3), 30-34.

Yankelovich, D. (1978). The new psychological contracts at work. *Psychology Today,* 12(May), 46-50.

Chapter 3

Historical Influences on Leisure Today

INTRODUCTION

The purpose of this chapter is to foster a better understanding of historical influences on leisure today. This chapter is not intended to be a complete overview but rather a brief synopsis of interesting aspects of leisure throughout history and their relevance to leisure in modern society. More specifically, the learning objectives for this chapter include the following:

1. Identify the purposes and benefits of studying the history of leisure.
2. Contrast various aspects of leisure in different societies throughout history with leisure in present American society.
3. Identify similarities of leisure in primitive societies and ancient civilizations to leisure in modern society.
4. Identify recent historical influences on the development of the recreation movement in America.
5. Appropriately utilize knowledge of leisure history in making leisure-related decisions.

This chapter is divided into several sections, one for each of the major historical periods: primitive and early civilizations; the Middle Ages, the Renaissance, and the Protestant Reformation; the Industrial Revolution; and twentieth-century influences on the recreation movement in America. However, before proceeding with this historical overview, it is important to understand the purposes and benefits of studying leisure history.

PURPOSES AND BENEFITS
OF STUDYING LEISURE HISTORY

The purposes and benefits of studying leisure history are numerous:

1. A knowledge and understanding of leisure history can promote a better understanding of leisure-related problems in society today (e.g., excessive consumption of alcohol) and thereby facilitate the alleviation of these problems. Without a firm understanding of history, society is more likely to repeat past mistakes. As stated by philosopher George Santayana (Kraus, 1984): "Those who do not understand the past are condemned to relive it."

2. Understanding leisure history can help provide explanations for leisure behavior in society—not just the leisure-related problems in society, but leisure activity participation patterns in general. The better that leisure behavior can be understood, the easier it is to determine how to work to improve society's leisure services and well-being.

3. A knowledge of leisure history provides a basis for comparison and evaluation of leisure services in today's society. Are leisure opportunities better or worse than they were in recent history and early history? Specifically, in what areas has progress been made? In what areas has the situation declined or remained as it was?

4. Society can learn to more effectively deal with leisure-related social and technological changes in the future by better understanding how such changes affected the leisure behavior of past societies. Society should not repeat its mistakes (e.g., the invention of television leading to an overly passive pattern of leisure behavior), but should certainly repeat its successes (e.g., greater wealth leading to more varied leisure opportunities for all people, including lower socioeconomic groups).

5. Examining leisure history facilitates a clearer understanding of the multitude of factors that affect leisure in society. Some of these factors are religion, technology, influential people, wars, and economics.

6. If there is greater consciousness of history, then perhaps individuals will view present leisure behavior patterns with a broader,

more philosophical historical perspective. Clearly, present society views many forms of recreation of early civilizations as immoral. If today's society is more conscious of how future societies might view leisure behavior in society today, then perhaps society will be moved toward a higher level of morality in leisure and life in general.

Examining the history of leisure can be beneficial. Even the leisure behavior of primitive and early civilizations has great relevance to leisure today.

PRIMITIVE AND EARLY CIVILIZATIONS

Primitive Societies

Some interesting similarities and differences are apparent in comparing leisure in modern society with that in primitive cultures. Curtis (1979) states that in primitive societies no clear distinction was made between work and leisure, sharply contrasting today's society in which there seems to be a segmentation of time as being either work or leisure. Is it more desirable to have a pronounced separation of work and leisure as opposed to a fusion of work and leisure? In other words, is it healthier to have definite time periods set aside for work and definite time periods for leisure, or to have elements of leisure mixed in with work and elements of work mixed in with leisure?

Apparently modern society is aspiring toward the ambiguous work/leisure relationship of primitive societies. Murphy (1975) discusses the holistic concept of leisure, which views work and leisure as overlapping spheres. The holistic concept is often discussed as a potentially positive philosophical force that will steer society away from a materialistic orientation to a more humanistic orientation.

Furthermore, people in today's society who are in fact "ambiguous free timers" (Neulinger, 1981) seem to be held in high esteem. According to Neulinger, an ambiguous free timer is one whose leisure and work are intertwined. Examples are professional artists, musicians, and athletes. It is difficult for such individuals to distinguish between their work and their leisure, partly because these individuals enjoy their work and establish their own work hours. Aren't these people held in high esteem by society? Therefore, in a sense, isn't society aspiring toward primitive society's orientation toward work and leisure? Even though people today have greater control over their environment than people did in primitive societies, are people today desiring greater self-determination over their time, in a sense similar to the greater spontaneity that primitive people seemed to have?

An interesting characteristic of primitive societies discussed by Kraus (1984) is that work was varied and creative, in contrast to the greater specialization of work in modern society. One leisure-related implication of the change in the nature of work is that there is perhaps a greater need in modern society for meaningful leisure experiences as an antidote to work. A positive recreational experience is often more meaningful after performing specialized work (e.g., assembly line work) as opposed to having just completed a more varied and creative work activity (e.g., photography).

Another interesting characteristic of leisure in primitive societies is that play and games seemed to evolve from religious rituals and vestiges of warfare (Kraus, 1984). Modern society is similar to primitive society in this respect. For example, the most highly celebrated holiday in America is religious—Christmas. Many other holidays are also based on religious rituals. Perhaps the most popular sport in America, football, can be viewed as related to warfare (the idea of trying to cross territorial boundaries despite physical resistance from an opposing group), so present society may be viewed as being similar to primitive society in this respect.

An additional similarity between leisure today and leisure in primitive societies is the notion of children's play preparing children for adult life. According to Kraus (1984), in primitive societies, young boys' play was intended to prepare them to be good warriors. Today, do games and other war-related toys also prepare boys to be good warriors? Do the dolls that young girls play with help prepare them for a caring, nurturing role in adult life? There is certainly strong debate whether these are the roles that children should be taught through their childhood play experiences. Nevertheless, it does seem that childhood play today, just as in primitive societies, helps to prepare children for adult life.

Ancient Civilizations: Greece, Rome, Egypt, Israel

An examination of leisure in early civilizations also provides some interesting comparisons with leisure in modern society. For example, Kraus (1984) states that in ancient Egypt, recreational opportunities for the upper classes were very rich and diverse (e.g., art, music, drama, and athletics), whereas the opportunities for the lower classes were much more limited (virtually no opportunities for participation in art, music, and drama). Today, are the recreational opportunities for people of lower socioeconomic status also much more limited than those of the rich? Some might say yes, because the rich can engage in glamorous activities such as yachting, which are not as available to lower socioeconomic status groups. However, leisure opportunities of the rich and the poor differ much less today than they did in ancient Egypt. In modern society, music, art, dance, sports, and games are available to people of any status. Therefore, in terms of leisure opportunities for the lower classes, modern society seems to be far ahead of ancient Egypt.

Kraus (1984) also discusses the prevalence of "immoral" forms of recreation in early civilizations, such as drunkenness and prostitution. In contrast, these forms of recreation were condemned by the ancient Israelites. In modern society, conflicting views of the morality of various recreational activities still exist.

The religion of the ancient Israelites also made a very significant philosophical contribution to leisure. Judaism's major leisure "innovation" was the Sabbath, a day of rest from work. All work is forbidden on the Sabbath, thus it is in a sense a day of leisure. Isn't the idea of a day of total rest from work especially appealing in today's high-paced society? Could adopting this idea help counteract executive burnout and stress caused by workaholism?

Leisure in ancient Greece and Rome also has important ramifications for modern society. These societies were characterized by a rich variety of leisure pursuits, such as music, theater, dance, art, gymnastics, and athletics. According to Kraus (1984), mass participation in sports and games in Greece was later weakened by athletic specialization and commercialism, whereas in Rome, the decline of society was linked to an inability to deal with mass leisure. Some writers compare ancient Rome to the United States in this regard. Bertrand Russell wrote that the ability to use leisure wisely is the final test of civilization, but it is questionable whether American leisure is wise or merely efficient (Anonymous, 1997). According to Bucher, Shivers, and Bucher (1984), sport and entertainment in ancient Rome became corrupted with wild and cruel celebrations, such as the Circus Maximus, a spectacle with approximately 385,000 spectators viewing bloody battles between animals and humans. Tax money was collected and spent by the government to provide this seemingly cruel entertainment.

The Circus Maximus of the Romans is viewed by most people in modern society as being grotesque. The idea of government sponsorship of such an event is revolting. However, is modern society very different? How will future societies view the popularity of violent sports such as boxing, wrestling, and even football and ice hockey in late twentieth-century America? Furthermore, cannot the existence of tax write-offs for corporations that buy tickets to these sporting events be likened to the Roman government's support of the Circus Maximus? Is American society, similar to ancient Rome, being weakened by corruption in sports and entertainment?

THE MIDDLE AGES, THE RENAISSANCE, AND THE PROTESTANT REFORMATION

The Middle Ages

The influence of religion on leisure is clearly apparent in the Middle Ages. The Catholic Church held a powerful influence on society from approximately A.D. 400 to 1350 and sought to eliminate many of the immoral forms of recreation indulged in by the Romans. What are the similarities between the rise of religious influence in this time period and the religious revival in the United States in the 1970s and 1980s?

It is interesting to note that during the period of restricted leisure opportunities of the Middle Ages, the peasants often resorted to drinking and crude brawling during their free time (Kraus, 1984). Ironically, in modern society, teenagers involved in substance abuse or vandalism often state that their reason for participation in these negative activities is boredom, because "there's nothing better to do." In recent history, the provision of leisure services for youth has been supported by the argument that it will help prevent them from engaging in negative or destructive activities. It seems that this argument has historical support. However, as Yukic (1970) cautions, recreation by itself does not have magical powers to overcome delinquency. Recreation is only one of many factors (family, education, etc.) that must be considered in assessing and preventing delinquency.

The Renaissance and the Protestant Reformation

The Renaissance, which began in approximately A.D. 1350, brought about a rebirth of the arts, music, theater, dance, and athletics (Maclean, Peterson, and Martin, 1985). Religious influence declined temporarily, allowing people to participate in a much wider variety of leisure pursuits than was possible during the Middle Ages. However, the Protestant Reformation, a religious movement which began in the 1500s, reestablished a strong religious influence in many countries, and many forms of recreation (sports, arts, and amusements) were once again restricted (Dulles, 1965).

Thus throughout history religious influence has fluctuated, causing a corresponding flourishing or restriction in certain leisure opportunities. An excellent modern example of this phenomenon is the Iranian Revolution. Over a period of many years religious influence in the country lessened, and a wide variety of leisure pursuits became widespread. The revolution in the late 1970s established a much firmer religious influence in Iran and increased restrictions on many forms of recreation. Chapter 16 will further illuminate the varying degrees of religious influence and the variety of leisure pursuits among different countries in the world today.

Curiously, despite the curtailment of many leisure activities during times of greater religious influence, hunting was one of the few sports held in esteem. Hunting has been viewed as a morally defensible activity throughout history. Based on the criteria identified in Chapter 12 for judging the morality of leisure activity, the morality of hunting as a recreational activity is questionable.

Although religion obviously had a negative effect on recreational opportunities at certain points in history, religion has also exerted a very positive effect on recreational opportunities. In recent times, organized religion has facilitated the expansion of sports and camping programs for youth and leisure services for elders. In fact, religious organizations are one of the largest nonprofit providers of leisure services. Therefore, the historical overview of religion's influence on leisure opportunities should not be misinterpreted as a negative factor in the provision of leisure services. In fact, in many ways, just the opposite seems to be true in modern American society.

THE INDUSTRIAL REVOLUTION

The Industrial Revolution, which began in the 1800s, stimulated a rapid growth in many forms of recreation. Some of the leisure pursuits that experienced growth were professional sports; popular amusements such as music and theater; hobbies such as photography, hiking, camping, and swimming; and participant sports such as golf, tennis, bowling, bicycling, archery, football, baseball, basketball, and skating (Kraus, 1984). Commercial recreation, such as amusement parks and dance halls, also flourished. Despite the growth in sports and other "wholesome" leisure pursuits, "immoral" recreation such as drinking, gambling, and prostitution also became increasingly popular (Dulles, 1965). It was the growth of these "immoral" activities, along with several other factors, that stimulated the development of the recreation movement beginning in the late 1800s.

THE RECREATION MOVEMENT
IN TWENTIETH-CENTURY AMERICA

Bucher, Shivers, and Bucher (1984), Knapp (1972), Kraus (1984), Weiskopf (1982), and Yukic (1970) discuss many factors that have influenced the development of the recreation movement. Comprehension of these factors will promote a better understanding of the recreation profession as it exists today. These factors include the following:

1. *Technological advances* have led to a shorter workweek and increased free time. In part, the recreation profession's growth was stimulated by a concern for how society would deal with increased free time. An examination of leisure-related problems in today's society (e.g., drinking, compulsive gambling, use of recreational drugs) indicates that the recreation profession still has a great deal of work to do in combating leisure-related social ills. Furthermore, with technology continuing to

progress, additional increases in free time are possible. How well will society deal with future increases in free time? Can potential leisure-related problems related to the growth in free time be prevented if free time increases further?

2. *Urbanization* (the migration of people to the cities) also influenced the development of the recreation movement. The crowded, dirty conditions of early twentieth-century cities posed a special challenge in attempting to provide a quality life for the masses. Recreation was viewed as a means of combating the social and environmental threats to maintaining a decent quality of life in the cities.

3. Another factor that spurred the development of the recreation movement was the *increased specialization of work* caused by the Industrial Revolution. Working conditions in the factories in early twentieth-century America were abysmal. Work for many people was boring and tedious. Recreation was viewed as a means of satisfying the need for an outlet or release from work. Furthermore, if human needs such as socialization were not being met at work, then it was essential that leisure activities provide an opportunity for meeting these needs.

4. The increasing popularity of certain *philosophical concepts* also contributed to the growth of the recreation movement. These concepts included the idea of play having an important role in education (Dewey, 1921) and the use of play as a positive outlet for negative emotions (catharsis theory).

5. *Improved transportation* had a tremendous impact on the recreation movement. Recreational opportunities such as outings in natural resource or outdoor recreation settings and sightseeing greatly expanded as a result of society's enhanced mobility. One particular aspect of the broad field of recreation that was perhaps most affected by improved transportation was tourism.

6. The *growth in physical education* and play programs in the schools also contributed positively to the recreation movement. The result of more people acquiring sports skills through the educational system was an increased demand for physical recreation opportunities.

7. The expansion of *"immoral" forms of commercial recreation* such as drinking establishments and burlesque shows contrib-

uted to the development of the recreation movement. The movement sought to ensure that recreation opportunities which contributed positively to the well-being of society would be provided to counteract the immoral commercial recreation opportunities being offered by private enterprises.

8. The increasing *pollution* of outdoor recreation resources caused by increasing industrialization created a need for an organized movement to work for conservation of these resources. The recreation movement was instrumental in the creation of national, state, and municipal parks.

9. *Wars* have greatly affected the recreation movement, especially in the area of therapeutic recreation. The large number of disabled veterans of World War II and the Vietnam War stimulated the development of therapeutic recreation services as a separate field of specialization within the broader profession of recreation.

10. Related to the increased number of individuals with disabilities was the passage of *legislation ensuring the rights of people with disabilities*. Legislation such as Public Law 94-192, the Education for All Handicapped Children Act (Kraus, 1983), had a profound impact on the expansion of therapeutic recreation services.

11. The *women's liberation movement* had a significant impact on leisure behavior patterns of women, such as greater opportunities in athletics, as well as on family life. The recreation movement is still exploring new ways to deal effectively with these changes. One change already evident is the provision of more sports programs for females.

12. The private enterprise recreation aspect of the recreation profession received a big boost from the *fitness enthusiasm* of the 1970s and 1980s, as discussed in Chapter 7.

13. *Tax-reform legislation* (e.g., Proposition 13 in California) created a greater consciousness of the need for accountability in publicly provided leisure services. The documentation of program benefits became increasingly important.

14. The *post–World War II baby boom* created a need for the recreation movement to more carefully address the recreational needs and desires of youth during the 1950s, 1960s, and early 1970s.

15. The *aging of American society* has mind-boggling implications for the recreation movement. A tremendous expansion in leisure services for elders has already been necessitated by the recent growth in the older population. However, if the over-sixty population grows to 40 percent to 50 percent of American society by the year 2035 as hypothesized by Leitner and Leitner (2004), will the recreation movement be able to provide adequate leisure services for this enormous older population? This is perhaps the greatest challenge presently facing the recreation movement.

THE RECREATION MOVEMENT IN THE TWENTY-FIRST CENTURY

Recreation in the twenty-first century will be discussed in greater detail in Chapter 17, under the topic of leisure in the future. However, the twenty-first century not only represents the future but also is the present and is already part of our history. The following is a list of some of the factors that have already affected and will continue to affect the recreation movement in the twenty-first century:

1. *Increasing globalization* is affecting the recreation movement all over the world. As discussed in Chapter 16, people in some countries complain about the "Americanization" of their culture and leisure. In the United States, other countries are increasingly influencing leisure activities. For example, tai chi, from China, has gained much popularity in recent years, especially among elders.
2. Related to globalization is the problem of *worldwide terrorism.* More specifically, the horrific events of September 11, 2001, can be viewed as a historical event that might have tremendous influence on the recreation movement in the twenty-first century. The long-term effects of 9/11/01 are unclear, but it is possible for the recreation movement to actually turn the events into a positive opportunity for leisure services provision by addressing the following:
   • Improve security for all recreational programs, not just for air travel. The truth is, before 9/11/01, dangers existed. The dangers to the safety of participants and spectators of recre-

ational programs and events are numerous and are not just related to terrorism. By improving security, safety risks (terrorism included) can be minimized.

• Immediately after 9/11/01, leisure-related domestic and international travel dropped sharply, and people sought leisure activities that were close to home. Again, this is an opportunity for local recreation departments to increase the provision of leisure services that can be participated in within one's community. It is also an opportunity for private enterprise recreation to fulfill a need for activities that are both close to home and that are viewed as safe. As discussed in Chapter 16, the participation of Israelis in classes and activities at health clubs seems to have increased as a result of the rash of terrorist bombings in their country since September 2000. The health clubs are close to home for most Israelis, and the presence of security guards at the entrances enhances their feelings of safety.

• The tragic events of 9/11/01 have helped some people to realize the wisdom and importance of appreciating the simple things in life. In turn, the recreation movement can seize the opportunity to provide programs that fulfill basic needs through simple leisure activities.

• Greater feelings of unity seem to prevail in the United States since 9/11/01. These positive feelings can be a positive force in bringing communities together for a variety of recreational activities.

3. *Technology,* especially computers, is a major factor affecting the recreation movement in the twenty-first century. In some ways, technology, including computers, can enhance leisure services provision. However, in other ways, technology, especially computers, is competing with more active, beneficial recreational programs. Keeping people active in the face of the proliferation of passive forms of leisure created by computers and other technological advances is a major challenge facing the recreation movement.

Exercise 3.1 is an opportunity to examine the relevance to personal leisure of the factors influencing the recreation movement in twentieth- and twenty-first-century America. In the left column, list your ten favorite leisure activities. In the right column, identify at least one factor from the list of factors on the previous pages that has influ-

EXERCISE 3.1.
Impact of Factors Influencing the Recreation Movement
on Personal Leisure

Ten favorite leisure activities	Factors that affect this activity and explanation
1. *Example:* Playing on the women's rugby team.	The women's liberation movement—sports for females at universities expanded due to this movement, and aggressive sports such as rugby became more socially acceptable.
2._____	_____
3._____	_____
4._____	_____
5._____	_____
6._____	_____
7._____	_____
8._____	_____
9._____	_____
10._____	_____

enced or affected the activities, and explain how the factors have affected these activities.

SUMMARY

This chapter highlighted only some of the major aspects of leisure throughout history and their implications for leisure today. Refer to books by Dulles (1965) and Kraus (1984) for more complete information on the history of leisure. Hopefully, by understanding the past, the positive aspects of leisure will be more fully realized in the future.

REFERENCES

Anonymous (1997). The American way of leisure. *The Economist,* March 1, p. 36.

Bucher, C.A., Shivers, J.S., and Bucher, R.D. (1984). *Recreation for today's society* (Second edition). Englewood Cliffs, NJ: Prentice-Hall.

Curtis, J.E. (1979). *Recreation theory and practice.* St. Louis: C.V. Mosby.

Dewey, J. (1921). *Democracy and education.* New York: Macmillan, Inc.

Dulles, F.R. (1965). *A history of recreation: America learns to play* (Second edition). New York: Appleton-Century-Crofts.

Knapp, R.F. (1972). Play for America: The National Recreation Association, 1906-1950. *Parks and Recreation Magazine,* 7(10) (October), 21-23.

Kraus, R.G. (1983). *Therapeutic recreation service: Principles and practice.* Philadelphia: Saunders.

Kraus, R.G. (1984). *Recreation and leisure in modern society* (Third edition). Glenview, IL: Scott, Foresman.

Leitner, M.J. and Leitner, S.F. (2004). *Leisure in later life* (Third edition). Binghamton, NY: The Haworth Press.

Maclean, J.R., Peterson, J.A., and Martin, W.D. (1985). *Recreation and leisure: The changing scene.* New York: Wiley.

Murphy, J.F. (1975). *Recreation and leisure service.* Dubuque, IA: Wm C. Brown.

Neulinger, J. (1981). *To leisure: An introduction.* Boston: Allyn and Bacon.

Weiskopf, D. (1982). *Recreation and leisure: Improving the quality of life.* Boston: Allyn and Bacon.

Yukic, T.S. (1970). *Fundamentals of recreation* (Second edition). New York: Harper and Row.

Chapter 4

Leisure and Recreation in the United States Today

INTRODUCTION

The purpose of this chapter is to provide an overview of the status of recreation and leisure in the United States today. Included is statistical information on the amount of free time Americans have and their recreation participation and recreational spending patterns in the United States. In addition, the current status and future outlook for the recreation profession are addressed briefly. The learning objectives for this chapter follow.

1. Compare the number of hours of leisure per week by defining leisure as time left over versus defining leisure as "memorable" free time.
2. Identify recreational activities in which Americans most frequently participate.
3. Identify the most popular forms of *active* recreation of Americans.
4. Cite statistics on the prominence of leisure in the U.S. economy.
5. Identify the largest categories of leisure expenditures in the United States.
6. Identify and describe the major categories of employment within the leisure services field.
7. Identify similarities and differences in leisure activity participation patterns of racial and ethnic minorities and women as compared to general societal patterns.

FREE TIME IN THE UNITED STATES

Statistics cited in Chapter 2 indicate that leisure is the largest category of time in a life span and that the free time of Americans increased greatly since the early 1900s, mainly as a result of a shortened workweek, technological advances, and a greater life expectancy. However, it seems that many Americans desire more free time. According to Collins (1991), 70 percent of Americans would like more free time, and according to Robinson (1991), 50 percent of over 1,000 American workers interviewed in a national survey said that they would be willing to sacrifice a day's pay for an extra day off. However, survey findings cited by O'Sullivan (2000) indicate that only 9 percent of workers would work fewer hours if it included a cut in pay, 53 percent would not make the choice of having more free time instead of more money, and 30 percent said that they would like to work more hours in order to increase their income. Did attitudes toward work and leisure change that much during the 1990s, or is it a matter of obtaining different results from research using different methods? Perhaps the reality is that views are mixed on this subject.

One reason why Americans' views on the desire for more leisure might be mixed is that there are significant differences in the amount of free time enjoyed by different segments of the population. Retired persons tend to have the most amount of free time, while single parents and dual-career couples with children living at home have the least amount of free time. Their leisure hours per week might be as little as half of that of retired persons. Teenagers, college students, and young adults also tend to have more leisure hours per week than other segments of the population, though it is difficult to generalize. I have taught many students who have calculated their free time to average around seventy hours per week, while other students (enrolled in school full-time and also working full-time) estimate their free time to be less than ten hours per week.

Research conducted by Robinson (Anonymous, 1996) indicates that the average amount of free time for both men and women is approximately forty hours per week. How much free time do you have in an average week?

Exercises 4.1a and 4.1b are presented as a means of comparing individual leisure hours per week when utilizing two different methods of calculating leisure. Complete this exercise twice. The first time, calculate your leisure hours using the "leisure as memorable time" method (Exercise 4.1a). First, write in the number of leisure hours per day, then, fill in the numbers for the other categories. The second time, calculate leisure hours using the "leisure as time left over" method (Exercise 4.1b). Begin by filling in the hours for all of the other categories, leaving the spaces for leisure blank. Then, for each day, total the numbers of hours spent in these other categories, and subtract this figure from twenty-four. The resulting figures are the number of leisure hours for each day.

After completing Exercises 4.1a and 4.1b, answer the following questions:

1. Did the daily hours add up to twenty-four the first time you completed the chart? Did the daily hours tend to total more than twenty-four or less than twenty-four?
2. What was the total number of leisure hours on the first chart? How did this figure compare to the national average of forty hours per week?
3. How did the total number of leisure hours for the two charts compare? Was the total number of leisure hours greater on the second chart? If so, how can this finding be explained?

An interesting answer to the last question is that free time often comes in relatively small (thirty- to sixty-minute) blocks of time (Anonymous, 1981). These short periods of free time are often not recognized or utilized as opportunities for meaningful leisure experiences and instead are spent by individuals doing unrewarding activities that later cannot be vividly recalled. Does this explanation seem to be true for you? To test the relevance of this concept to your life, keep a leisure time log for the next few days, carefully noting the short segments of free time and what you did during those time periods. Perhaps being more attuned to the phenomenon of leisure time coming in short segments will help you make better use of it.

EXERCISE 4.1a. Inventory of Leisure (As Memorable Time) Hours per Week

Category of time expenditure	Sun.	Mon.	Tues.	Wed.	Thu.	Fri.	Sat.	Total
Leisure								
Sleep								
Work								
School								
Personal care								
Household chores								
Commuting								
Personal/family obligations								
Total								

EXERCISE 4.1b. Inventory of Leisure (As Time Left Over) Hours per Week

Category of time expenditure	Sun.	Mon.	Tues.	Wed.	Thu.	Fri.	Sat.	Total
Sleep								
Work								
School								
Personal care								
Household chores								
Commuting								
Personal/family obligations								
Leisure								
Total								

RECREATIONAL PARTICIPATION PATTERNS

Although statistics indicate that Americans have ample leisure time, their participation rate in active forms of recreation is still low. In the first two editions of this book, research was cited which indicated that Americans were sedentary in their leisure. In recent years, leisure in the United States has perhaps become even more sedentary. O'Sullivan (2000) states that the average American adult spent 22 percent more time in 1999 using consumer media (television, videos, etc.) than he or she did in 1998. According to Pawlowski (2000), Americans spent an average of fifteen hours per week, or 38 percent of their free time, watching television, but when "secondary" viewing is counted (time spent doing other activities while the television is on), watching television consumes more than half of all free time. According to Lewis (2000), other sedentary activities that have increased in recent years include usage of home computers (seventy minutes per day) and talking on the telephone (fifty-two minutes per day, up from 36.5 minutes in 1980). Meanwhile, participation is low in physically active forms of leisure. Only 15 percent of Americans achieve recommended levels of leisure-time physical activity. Furthermore, approximately 25 percent of adults do not participate in any physically active leisure pursuits (O'Sullivan, 2000).

In the second edition of this book, statistics on participation in active forms of recreation were cited from a survey conducted from 1985 to 1990. This survey indicated that walking for exercise was the most popular in 1990 (45 percent participation rate), followed by gardening (26 percent), calisthenics and general exercise (18 percent), and bicycling (11 percent); all other activities had a participation rate of less than 10 percent (Robinson, Godbey, and Walker, 1993). More recent statistics, based on U.S. Census Bureau data, indicate that the most popular active forms of recreation of Americans in 1997 were as follows (Leonard, 1998):

1. Exercise walking (73.3 million people)
2. Swimming (60.2 million people)
3. Bicycling (53.3 million people)
4. Exercising with equipment (47.8 million people)
5. Camping (44.7 million people)

The apparent widespread participation in fitness walking might be misleading, because it is difficult to assess how many people really engage in walking that is truly strenuous enough to be considered fitness walking, from among those who claim to walk for exercise. Similarly, among those who claim to swim or ride a bicycle for exercise, many might not in fact be participating in the activity in a strenuous way (e.g., many people might say they went swimming when in reality they were simply wading or floating in a pool). Also, camping is unfortunately often a recreational activity that involves consuming calories rather than burning them.

Watching television continues to be the most prevalent use of free time in the United States. Other common leisure activities include the following (Leonard, 1998):

1. Going to the movies (66 percent)
2. Attending religious services (60 percent)
3. Going to amusement parks (57 percent)
4. Volunteering (49 percent)
5. Attending sports events (41 percent)

However, it is important to consider that whereas watching television or surfing the Internet are *daily* activities for many people, most of the activities in the previous list are at best *weekly* activities, and in the example of amusement parks, might be participated in only a few days out of the entire year.

A more interesting and humorous way of summarizing the leisure pursuits of Americans was developed by Parker (1985). He compiled annual figures and divided by 365 to determine what Americans do (collectively) on a typical day. As you look through this list, try to *visualize* the statistics and estimate what the figures would be today (e.g., how many football fields would Americans now be filling with pizza on a typical day?). According to Parker (1985), on an average day Americans

- Spend $700 million on recreation ($8,000/second);
- Drink enough bottles and cans of beer and ale to fill a baseball stadium 30 feet deep;
- Eat the equivalent of 2,250 cattle at McDonald's;
- Snort a bathtub full of cocaine (325 pounds);

- Spend $40 million on prostitutes;
- Place 70 million quarters in arcade game machines;
- Eat 3 million gallons of ice cream and 5,000 tons of candy;
- Smoke a bale of marijuana the size of a small house (85,000 pounds);
- Eat 75 acres worth of pizza, enough to fill sixty football fields;
- Drink 1.2 million gallons of hard liquor, enough to get 26 million people drunk;
- Buy 5 million books;
- Buy 38,000 Ken and Barbie dolls and 55,000 pieces of Barbie clothes;
- Snap 21 million photographs; and
- Jump out of airplanes at the rate of approximately 5,000 people/day.

Seldom mentioned in the discussion of Americans' recreational habits is sexual activity, largely because it is a potentially sensitive issue. Although some might view sex as one of the most important leisure activities, others might be horrified by a casual discussion of sex as a form of leisure activity. Therefore, because of the sensitivity of the topic, sex as a leisure activity is scarcely addressed in this book, even though it can be viewed as a most enjoyable and beneficial (physiologically and psychologically) form of recreational activity. Its role in stress reduction is discussed briefly in Chapter 8. Many excellent books on human sexuality provide a comprehensive overview of this topic. In terms of the prominence of sex as a leisure activity, 60 percent of all unmarried women had intercourse in the past twelve months (Leonard, 1998), but the average amount of time per day devoted to sex by all Americans was only four minutes, even though it is identified as their favorite activity (Lewis, 2000)!

What are the recreational participation patterns of *college students?* How do they compare with the facts and statistics cited thus far in this chapter? Based on unscientific research (open-ended discussion with and informal observations of hundreds of college students), the most common uses of free time by college students are the following (not necessarily in rank order):

1. Using the computer to play games, surf the Internet, etc.
2. Watching television and movies at home

3. Listening to music
4. Drinking alcohol and using other drugs for "recreational" purposes
5. Socializing (often in combination with #3 and #4)
6. Recreational reading (newspapers and magazines)

How accurate is this list? Compare this list with your most time-consuming recreational activities of the past week by completing Exercise 4.2.

What were your most time-consuming leisure activities of the past week? How do you feel you could have used your leisure more wisely? How satisfied are you with your use of free time?

Research indicates that many people are not satisfied with how they spend their leisure. A survey of working-age Americans indicated that on Sunday night, 64 percent usually ask themselves "Where did the weekend go?" Only 60 percent of working-age adults say they are satisfied with their leisure, reflecting a 15 percent decrease since 1963. Even though television viewing consumes the largest share of the average American's leisure, watching television is only ninth on the list of people's favorite activities. Other indications of dissatisfaction with usage of free time are that only 19 percent of Americans say they like doing chores around the house, but 44 percent spend a great deal of time doing them, and only 10 percent enjoy running errands, yet 26 percent say that a major portion of the weekend is spent doing them (Anonymous, 2000).

Another troubling trend in leisure behavior in the United States is the decline in certain types of social activity. Since the mid-1970s, attending club meetings has declined 58 percent, family dinners are down 33 percent, and having friends over is down by 45 percent (O'Sullivan, 2000). According to Hunnicutt (2000), not only have people become spectators at sports events, but they have also become passive in the building and maintenance of their own culture. This statement should be contemplated. Picture people watching a sporting event on television. They react to what is occurring, but they are not in control of the action. Similarly, according to Hunnicut, people have become so passive that instead of helping to define their own culture through active participation in art, music, and even social activity, they are for the most part passively following along with trends set by the media and influential people. The millions of people

EXERCISE 4.2. Leisure Activities of the Past Week

Instructions

1. Think about the past week and all of the recreational activities you participated in during that time period.
2. Begin by identifying the activity that you feel was the most time-consuming during this past week.
3. Then, continue listing leisure activities, in descending order of perceived time spent in each one during the past week.
4. Next to each activity, estimate how much time was spent in each one during the past week.

Activities	Time spent in the activity during the past week
1. _____	_____
2. _____	_____
3. _____	_____
4. _____	_____
5. _____	_____
6. _____	_____
7. _____	_____
8. _____	_____
9. _____	_____
10. _____	_____

watching a football game on television do not decide whether the quarterback should call a running or passing play, it is the quarterback and/or the coaches who do. Similarly, instead of making individual decisions on what music we listen to, what clothes we wear, and other aspects of popular culture, many people passively go along with trends that are set by a small number of individuals.

The statistics cited in this section represent an aggregate of data for all segments of the population. However, it is interesting to examine characteristics of the leisure activity participation patterns of racial and ethnic minorities and women, to better understand the recreational needs and desires of various segments of the population.

RECREATION PARTICIPATION PATTERNS OF RACIAL AND ETHNIC MINORITIES

It is difficult to make generalizations about recreation participation patterns of racial and ethnic minorities. First, there are many different groups to consider, and each one has unique characteristics. Second, within each group are vast differences to consider.

For example, Gomez (2002) studied differences within the Puerto Rican population in central Massachusetts in their use of public parks and perception of benefits derived from recreation. Highly assimilated and less-assimilated Puerto Ricans were compared, assimilation being defined as the extent of acquisition of cultural characteristics of the majority group (e.g., English language skills). Contrary to findings from previous studies, the less-assimilated Puerto Ricans in this study used parks significantly more than the highly assimilated Puerto Ricans. Also, the more highly assimilated Puerto Ricans perceived less benefits derived from recreation.

In contrast, a study of Hispanic Americans conducted by Shaull and Gramann (1998) found that more assimilated Hispanics placed greater value on participation in outdoor recreation than did the less-assimilated Hispanics. However, the importance of family seemed to be unaffected by assimilation. Bicultural families seemed to more highly value family-related recreation benefits than did the least-assimilated Hispanics or Caucasians.

Similarly, Shinew and colleagues (1996) found some differences in leisure activity preferences among different groups of African Americans. For example, females with higher levels of education preferred fine arts and games, whereas females with lower levels of education preferred association/sociability activities. In this study, males of different education levels did not differ much in terms of activity preferences. High- and low-income females differed more in their activity preferences than did the males. High-income females preferred games and art, while low-income females preferred team sports. Both groups of males preferred sedentary activities, team sports, hunting, fishing, and exercise activities.

Earlier research also provides some insight into the topic, even though it is difficult to draw conclusions or make sweeping generalizations. For example, Stamps and Stamps (1985), based on their examination of black/white differences in leisure activities, concluded that race seemed to be more important than social class in influencing leisure participation. Meanwhile, Hutchinson (1987) felt that the differences among blacks, whites, and Hispanics in leisure activities found in his study in Chicago's public parks were more strongly related to social class than to race or ethnicity. Similarly, Woodward (1988) found social class to affect the leisure activities of urban black Americans. Hutchinson (1987) cites past research indicating that black/white differences seem to disappear among blacks living in predominantly white areas. Hutchinson (1988) concluded that black/white differences in leisure activities are caused by a combination of racial and social class factors.

Statistics cited by Parks (1990) support Hutchinson's statement. Parks states that the average income for blacks is 35 percent below that of whites. However, blacks spend 85 percent as much as whites spend on television and cable, but less than 25 percent of what whites spend on sports, recreation, and exercise equipment. These figures on leisure-related expenditures are not totally indicative of leisure participation trends. For example, Stamps and Stamps (1985) found sports participation to be the third highest-ranked leisure activity for blacks and only the fourth highest one for whites. Television and radio were ranked second by both blacks and whites.

One of the more striking differences in leisure participation between blacks and whites is in the category of outdoor recreation (camping, hiking, etc.). Stamps and Stamps (1985) found it to be the third highest-ranked activity of whites, but only eighth for blacks. Dwyer and Gobster (1992) also found blacks to have a lower rate of participation in outdoor recreation, higher participation in ball playing and picnicking, and a tendency to participate more in recreational activities close to home. Similarly, in Detroit, West (1989) found that blacks tended to use city parks more than whites, but whites used surrounding regional parks more. West cited restricted access to automobiles for blacks and interracial relations as being causes of this trend. Woodward (1988) also found activities close to home or home-based as being central to black American life.

Meanwhile, budget cutbacks in publicly provided leisure services have disproportionately hurt people of color in urban areas (Washington, 1990). In particular, Hispanics tend to rely on neighborhood parks as an integral part of their leisure (Hutchinson, 1987), and it would appear that more public funding for the maintenance of the parks is needed. Hutchinson reports that predominant activities of Hispanics in these parks are the use of playgrounds, picnicking, lounging in the grass, and watching sporting events, but that many differences among Hispanic subgroups exist.

Similarly, there are many differences in the leisure activities of various white ethnic groups and Asian subgroups. Some of these differences are more obvious, such as different customs and traditions with regard to holiday celebrations. Sensitivity to these differences is very important in the increasingly diverse population of the United States.

Kraus (1994) documents some of the special contributions various racial and ethnic groups have made in leisure-related fields such as sports, music, and popular media, yet there are still areas of concern. For example, in a study of interracial couples' experience of leisure, it was reported that the couples had a low level of comfort in leisure participation in public spaces, caused by feelings of social isolation stemming from perceived racism (Hibbler and Shinew, 2002). Clearly, although great strides have been made in enabling racial and ethnic groups to participate in leisure activities and to express their affinity to their cultural background, much more needs to be done. As is the case with leisure and women, although there are signs of progress, there are still areas of concern.

LEISURE PARTICIPATION PATTERNS OF WOMEN

One of the key aspects of leisure is perceived freedom. Unfortunately, several factors restrict the freedom of women with respect to leisure. These factors include the following:

1. *Lack of free time:* According to Levine (2001), women have less leisure than men because they work two to three hours per day more than men, when work both inside and outside the home is considered. In countries where birthrates are higher and social norms require even less of men in terms of housework, women have correspondingly less free time. Horna (1991) reports that in a study of dual-career households, 90 percent of the women often cook and do housework, while only 25 percent of the men perform these chores often. Yet, surprisingly, in this study, only 21 percent of the women said they were dissatisfied with the division of labor in their household. Horna's explanation is that society dictates the wife's subordination into the marriage script. Horna (1993) states that contrary to the popular belief that the division of labor in households has become more equitable, traditional sex roles persist.

2. *Fear of violence:* According to James and Embrey (2001), 70 percent of Australian women fear attack after dark, and this fear constrains their nighttime recreational choices. In the United States, where violent crime rates are higher than in most other developed nations, the fear of violence is a major factor limiting women's recreation choices, both at night and during the day. The following questions are presented to create an awareness of how much the fear of violence actually constrains women's recreational choices. If you are a female, please answer the questions on a personal level. If you are a male, answer the questions in terms of whether you would feel comfortable if your wife, sister, mother, or a close female friend wanted to engage in these activities. Please answer yes or no as to whether you would feel comfortable about the following:
   - Going alone for a walk or run in the park at night
   - Going alone for a walk or run in the park during the day
   - Going alone for a run or walk on the beach at night
   - Going alone for a bike ride at night
   - Going into town alone at night, dressed up nicely

- Going into town with a girlfriend at night, dressed up nicely
- Going alone at night to a local health club or gym, if it involved taking a bus or train and walking a block or two

After answering these questions, males should answer these questions again, this time on a personal level. Compare these answers to the first set of answers you had. How do the answers compare? How much more freedom do men have than women?

3. *Stigmas inhibiting participation in physical activities:* Even in the twenty-first century, large national surveys indicate that women are less likely to be physically active than men (Brownson et al., 2000). Kane (1990) discusses the barriers women face in terms of leisure participation in general and involvement in physical recreation in particular. Women's sense of commitment and responsibility to others seems to lead them to feel guilty about taking care of their own needs, which in turn can result in a self-imposed lack of leisure. Kane also states that many dual-career women simply have no time or energy for leisure after their homemaking responsibilities and work are completed. Interestingly, women with more masculine and androgynous personalities are less constrained by psychological barriers to leisure (Kane, 1990). As discussed by Little (2002), some women do have the ability to take control of their own leisure and overcome the common constraints to leisure activity participation, as shown in a study of women participating in adventure recreation.

   Yet it is the hurtful masculine stigma regarding female involvement in sports that Cahn (1994) believes poses a dilemma for women wishing to compete in sports. Although women have made great strides in sports, Cahn feels that sporting resources and institutions are still dominated by men and that a great effort is needed in order for women to attain unrestricted access to sports and the ability to experience meaningful leisure.

Clearly, some efforts have been made and have produced tangible results. According to Simon (1991), in 1970-1971, 3.7 million boys and only 300,000 girls participated in interscholastic sports. By 1978-1979, 4.2 million boys and 2 million girls (an almost 700 percent increase) were participating in interscholastic sports.

However, more recent research reported by Kolata (2002) indicates that girls become so sluggish in their teenage years that many barely do any physical activity at all! By age sixteen or seventeen, 56 percent of black girls and 31 percent of white girls reported no physical activity at all.

Hargreaves (1993) has an interesting view of how to create more equality for women in sports. Rather than trying to break down the barriers to female involvement in aggressive, competitive male-dominated sports, she sees the key to greater equality as a societal shift toward a more participating, cooperative model of sports. According to this view, instead of trying to get more females involved in aggressive sports such as football, a more healthy approach would be to encourage greater male and female involvement in activities such as hiking and bicycling, which are less aggressive in nature and more heavily emphasize the recreational, health, and social benefits of participation.

As Kane (1990) so strongly states, meaningful leisure experiences are important to women because they can empower and help women to feel the freedom and authority that they may have been socialized into not feeling. The benefits of physical recreation and other positive leisure pursuits have a significant spillover effect to other aspects of women's lives. It is important to society as a whole that progress continues in this area.

LEISURE IN THE U.S. ECONOMY

Another way of viewing the recreational habits of Americans is through statistics on leisure spending. If a fairly broad definition of recreation is used, recreation could probably be considered the largest industry in the United States, ahead of even the defense industry and agriculture. Annual spending on recreation is estimated to be between $500 billion and $1 trillion (Kraus, 2002). According to the Department of Commerce (Bryce, 2001), recreation spending includes the following:

1. Home electronics
2. Radio and television
3. Music
4. Entertainment
5. Sporting goods
6. Amusements

7. Home gardening
8. Toys
9. Books and magazines
10. Recreation equipment such as boats, motor homes, and bicycles

The following statistics illustrate how important recreation is to the U.S. economy:

1. Consumers spend three times more on recreational goods and services than they do on new cars (Bryce, 2001).
2. Americans spent approximately $22 billion on renting or buying movies in 1996 (Bufkin, 2000).
3. Approximately $81 million was spent in 1998 on online games (Bryce, 2001).

To further clarify the importance of leisure in the economy, complete Exercise 4.3 on personal spending. Under each category, estimate (in round numbers) how much money you spent last month. The most difficult aspect of this exercise will probably be making a distinction between necessity and recreation in the categories of food and clothing. Defining what is necessity and what is recreational is entirely subjective. Another consideration in completing Exercise 4.3 is to average out recurring expenses that are paid in lump sums (e.g., $360 tuition paid twice per year averages out to $60 per month).

What percentage of your total monthly spending is devoted to recreation? Is it more or less than you would have guessed? Which is your largest expenditure category under recreation?

Given the prominence of leisure in the nation's economy and in your personal budget, it should be apparent that leisure services is a broad field with many career opportunities.

THE LEISURE SERVICES FIELD

Careers in leisure services exist in commercial and private enterprise recreation, community recreation, military recreation, industrial recreation, outdoor recreation, and recreation for special popula-

EXERCISE 4.3. Personal Spending (One Month)

Necessities   **Recreation**

Food: _____   Sports equipment and supplies: _____

Rent: _____   Admissions: _____

Maintenance: _____   Electronic media: _____

Clothes: _____   Recreational eating and drinking: _____

Utilities: _____   Alcohol and other drugs: _____

Education: _____   Recreational reading material: _____

Commuting: _____   Recreational shopping: _____

                                          Membership in clubs: _____

                                          Vacations: _____

                                          Miscellaneous: _____

TOTAL: _____   TOTAL: _____

                     Total Spending: _____

tions/therapeutic recreation. Each of these areas within the field of leisure services is discussed in this section to elucidate the breadth and scope of the leisure services field.

Commercial and Private Enterprise Recreation

Kraus (1984) identifies five categories within the area of commercial recreation:

1. *Travel and tourism:* This category encompasses approximately 1 million different businesses ranging from small resorts, tour companies, and commercial campgrounds, to amusement and theme parks, hotels, and motels.
2. *Facilities and areas for self-directed activity:* This category includes golf courses, bowling alleys, bars, swimming pools, and other recreational facilities and areas where people can recreate without supervision.
3. *Enterprises providing entertainment:* This category includes nightclubs and sports stadiums.
4. *Enterprises providing instructional services:* This category encompasses music, dance, physical fitness, and other activities in which instruction is given.
5. *Manufacturers and suppliers of recreational equipment:* This category is extremely broad, including toys, games, musical equipment, books, magazines, radios, televisions, gardening equipment, and sports apparel.

Clearly, commercial and private enterprise recreation encompasses diverse aspects of leisure. Likewise, community recreation is an umbrella for a wide variety of leisure services.

Community Recreation

Careers in community recreation include community center directors, youth leaders, activity specialists, recreation workers in voluntary and religious organizations, and municipal recreation administrators.

Military Recreation

The armed forces was one of the most promising areas of employment within the leisure services field during the 1970s and 1980s. Defense spending cuts and the closing of military bases during the 1990s has changed the employment picture in this field somewhat. Nevertheless, some excellent jobs are still available in the United States and overseas in leisure services provision for military personnel and their families. Leisure services include concerts, movies, sports and fitness activities, tours, and teen activities.

Industrial Recreation

Industrial recreation is another area of employment within the field of recreation. According to Mendell (1984), companies provide recreation for their employees because it enhances productivity, improves employee morale, and is cost effective (i.e., the health benefits of recreation and savings in health care costs more than compensate for the cost of providing facilities and programs). Fitness programs are a major part of many employee recreation programs.

Outdoor Recreation

Jobs in the area of outdoor recreation often sound quite appealing. The images conjured up by the terms park ranger, naturalist, and nature center manager are those of natural beauty, fresh air, and wildlife. Employment opportunities in outdoor recreation have improved since the late 1970s, partly due to agencies recognizing the economic values of recreation, the need to deal with population/user growth problems, and the desirability of hiring personnel with a recreation background as opposed to the common practice in the 1960s and 1970s of hiring biologists, geologists, and other specialists for outdoor recreation positions (D. Simcox, personal communication).

Recreation for Special Populations/Therapeutic Recreation

Employment in the special populations/therapeutic recreation area involves the provision of meaningful leisure opportunities for the physically disabled, developmentally disabled, substance abusers, inmates of correctional facilities, emotionally disturbed, elders, and other special populations. Programs are conducted in hospitals, residential facilities, and community facilities. Chapter 14 explains the diversity of recreational programs provided for special populations.

An especially dire need exists for recreational personnel trained to work with elders. In light of statistics projecting a vast increase in the older population in the future (Leitner and Leitner, 2004), there will be a tremendous need for an expansion in leisure services for elders and personnel qualified to provide those services.

SUMMARY

In summary, recreation is an extremely important aspect of American society. Both directly and indirectly, recreation has a profound impact on the physical, psychological, and economic well-being of all Americans.

REFERENCES

Anonymous (1981). Our endless pursuit of happiness. *U.S. News and World Report,* August 10, pp. 58-67.

Anonymous (1996). You have plenty of time to read this story. *San Francisco Chronicle,* December 19, p. A13.

Anonymous (2000). Where did the weekend go? *USA Today,* 129(2667), pp. 12-14.

Brownson, R., Eyler, A., King, A., Brown, D., Shyu, Y., and Sallis, L. (2000). Patterns and correlates of physical activity among U.S. women 40 years and older. *American Journal of Public Health,* 90(2), 264-303.

Bryce, J. (2001). The technological transformation of leisure. *Social Science Computer Review,* 19(1), 7-16.

Bufkin, J. (2000). Images of sex and rape. *Violence Against Women,* 6(12), 1317-1345.

Cahn, S.K. (1994). *Coming on strong: Gender and sexuality in twentieth century women's sport.* New York: The Free Press.

Collins, G. (1991). Why no one wants to work anymore. *Working Woman,* 16(11), 160.

Dwyer, J.F. and Gobster, P.H. (1992). Recreation opportunity and cultural diversity. *Parks and Recreation,* 27(9), 22-31.

Gomez, E. (2002). Puerto Ricans and recreation participation: Methodological, cultural, and perceptual considerations. *World Leisure,* 44(2), 46-62.

Hargreaves, J.A. (1993). Gender on the sports agenda. In A.G. Ingham and J.W. Coy (Eds.), *Sport in social development: Traditions, transitions, and transformations* (pp. 167-185). Champaign, IL: Human Kinetics Publications.

Hibbler, D.K. and Shinew, K.J. (2002). Interracial couples' experience of leisure: A social network approach. *Journal of Leisure Research,* 34(2), 135-156.

Horna, J.L.A. (1991). The family and leisure domains: Women's involvement and perceptions. *World Leisure and Recreation,* 33(3), 11-14.

Horna, J.L.A. (1993). Married life and leisure: A multidimensional study of couples. *World Leisure and Recreation,* 35(3), 17-21.

Hunnicutt, B. (2000). Our reform heritage: Recovering the vision of community leisure service. *Journal of Leisure Research,* 32(1), 58-62.

Hutchinson, R. (1987). Ethnicity and urban recreation: Whites, blacks, and Hispanics in Chicago's public parks. *Journal of Leisure Research,* 19(3), 205-222.

Hutchinson, R. (1988). A critique of race, ethnicity, and social class in recent leisure-recreation research. *Journal of Leisure Research,* 20(1), 10-30.

James, K. and Embrey, L. (2001). "Anyone could be lurking around!": Constraints on adolescent girls' recreational activities after dark. *World Leisure,* 43(4), 44-52.

Kane, M.J. (1990). Female involvement in physical recreation-gender roles as a constraint. *Journal of Physical Education and Recreation,* 6(1), 52-56.

Kolata, G. (2002). 5 Decades of warnings fail to get Americans moving. *The New York Times,* September 10, pp. D5, D8.

Kraus, R.G. (1984). *Recreation and leisure in modern society* (Third edition). Glenview, IL: Scott, Foresman.

Kraus, R. (1994). *Leisure in a changing America: Multicultural perspectives.* New York: Macmillan College Publishing Company.

Kraus, R.G. (2002). Careers in recreation: Expanding horizons. *Journal of Physical Education, Recreation, and Dance,* 73(5), 46-49, 54.

Leitner, M.J. and Leitner, S.F. (2004). *Leisure in later life* (Third edition). Binghamton, NY: The Haworth Press.

Leonard, M. (1998). A snapshot of a prosperous America. *The Boston Globe,* December 4, p. A3.

Levine, J.A. (2001). Work burden of women. *Science,* 10, 812.

Lewis, D.E. (2000). Time out! Speed isn't all that we need. *The Boston Sunday Globe,* March 26, p. F3.

Little, D.E. (2002). Women and adventure recreation: Reconstructing leisure constraints and adventure experiences to negotiate continuing participation. *Journal of Leisure Research,* 34(2), 157-177.

Mendell, R. (Ed.). (1984). *Leisure today: Selected readings, volume III.* Reston, VA: American Alliance for Health, Physical Education, Recreation, and Dance.

O'Sullivan, E. (2000). Play for life. *Parks and Recreation,* 35(10), 98-106.

Parker, T. (1985). *In one day.* Boston: Houghton Mifflin.

Parks, F.C. (1990). Is the recreation industry color blind? *Parks and Recreation,* 25(12), 42-44.

Pawlowski, C. (2000). *Glued to the tube.* Naperville, IL: Sourcebooks, Inc.

Robinson, J.P. (1991). Your money or your time. *American Demographics,* 13(11), 22-26.

Robinson, J.P., Godbey, G., and Walker, C. (1993). Has fitness peaked? *American Demographics,* 15(9), 36-41.

Shaull, S.L. and Gramann, J.H. (1998). The effect of cultural assimilation on the importance of family-related and nature-related recreation among Hispanic Americans. *Journal of Leisure Research,* 30(1), 47-63.

Shinew, K.J., Floyd, M.F., McGuire, F.A., and Noe, F.P. (1996). Class polarization and leisure activity preferences of African Americans: Intra group comparisons. *Journal of Leisure Research,* 28(4), 219-232.

Simon, R.L. (1991). *Fairplay: Sports, values, and society.* Boulder, CO: Westview Press.

Stamps, S.M. and Stamps, M.B. (1985). Race, class, and leisure activities of urban residents. *Journal of Leisure Research,* 17(1), 40-56.

Washington, S.J. (1990). Provision of leisure services to people of color. *Journal of Leisure Research,* 6(8), 37-39.

West, P.C. (1989). Urban regional parks and black minorities: Subculture, marginality, and interracial relations in park use in the Detroit metropolitan area. *Leisure Sciences,* 11, 11-28.

Woodward, M.D. (1988). Class, regionality, and leisure among urban black Americans: The past civil rights era. *Journal of Leisure Research,* 20(2), 87-105.

Chapter 5

Why People Recreate:
Theoretical Explanations

INTRODUCTION

This chapter is extremely important because it provides a theoretical foundation for developing a personal leisure philosophy as well as a theoretical context for understanding other chapters appearing later in the book. The concept presented in this book that is probably most critical to attaining maximal leisure well-being is the development of a strong personal philosophy of leisure. A strong personal leisure philosophy is emphasized in later chapters as the central challenge in improving leisure-time management, in dealing most effectively with stress, and in being able to positively adapt to future personal changes and societal changes.

A strong personal leisure philosophy must have a solid theoretical foundation. Theories facilitate reaching a level of understanding to be able to explain past events and predict future events (Ellis, 1973). If a personal leisure philosophy cannot be justified or supported by theoretical concepts, then its validity is in question.

The purpose of this chapter is to provide information on theoretical explanations of the needs, benefits, and satisfactions derived from leisure and to help the reader understand how to utilize this information to justify leisure activity choices and to develop a sound personal philosophy of leisure. More specifically, the learning objectives of this chapter are to

1. Describe the following needs/benefits/satisfactions theories: surplus energy, recreation, relaxation, compensation, generalization, instinct-practice, learning, catharsis, self-expression,

arousal, flow, competence-effectance, and the psychological explanations of Erikson and Menninger.
2. Identify personal applications of and drawbacks to the aforementioned theories.
3. Utilize Nash's pyramid of leisure to categorize and analyze various leisure activities.
4. Utilize Maslow's hierarchy of needs to justify or explain needs/benefits/satisfactions derived from various leisure activities.
5. Utilize Iso-Ahola's model of causality of leisure behavior to examine motivation for personal leisure behavior.
6. Utilize the theoretical explanations presented in this chapter to justify leisure choices and to develop a sound personal philosophy of leisure.

EARLY PLAY THEORIES

Defining Play

The terms play and recreation are frequently used interchangeably in the literature, and the early play theories can be utilized to explain needs, benefits, and satisfactions derived from a wide variety of recreational activities. According to Kraus (1984), play is a form of recreation commonly defined as enjoyable, consisting of spontaneous activities participated in for their own sake. Holmes (1999) conducted a study that compared kindergarten children's and college students' views of play. Both groups agreed that play must be fun. The kindergarten children said that play meant playing with a friend or a toy. Male college students remained more object oriented, citing sports and activities involving physical movement as play, whereas female college students listed social interactions and events as play. As discussed in Chapter 1, recreation is a broad concept, encompassing a wider spectrum of activities than just play. Nevertheless, the play theories presented in this section will be analyzed in terms of their relevance to a broad realm of recreational activities, not just play.

The Surplus Energy Theory

According to the surplus energy theory (Ellis, 1973), the primary motivation for play is the need to expend surplus energy. One example of this theory in action is the play of children during a recess period on a school day. It seems logical to allow children a period during the school day to play in order to release the enormous energy that accumulates after sitting in a classroom all morning.

Does the surplus energy theory have relevance to adult play as well as children's play? It would certainly appear to be relevant in explaining the leisure behavior patterns of college students on weekends (e.g., when students "let loose" on Friday night after a hard week of school). Another example is jogging or participating in a physically exerting sport after a long period of sedentary work. Is there a feeling of frustration or fidgetiness when there is not an outlet for the surplus energy built up over a period of time of sedentary work? Isn't it often easier to concentrate on work or studies after having the opportunity to release this surplus energy?

There are also some criticisms or drawbacks to the surplus energy theory. According to Ellis, research on children's play supports some of these criticisms. For example, if the need to release surplus energy is the primary motivation for play, then how can it be explained that people often play or continue to play when they have no surplus energy or feel tired? For example, many children will continue to play for hours after expending their surplus energy. Also, after long hours of sedentary work, one might feel tired and need a leisure activity to restore energy, rather than to use excess energy. Therefore, the surplus energy theory can explain *some* forms of recreation, but certainly not all forms.

The Recreation Theory

Contrary to the surplus energy theory, the recreation theory (Weiskopf, 1982) views the primary motivation for play as being the need to restore or re-create energy. For example, after several hours of attending boring lecture classes, one's energy level might be very low; therefore, to go home and study immediately after classes would be futile because of the low energy level that has set in. An invigorating leisure activity such as bicycling or roller-skating could have the effect of restoring or re-creating energy and help provide the impetus for working or studying effectively.

The recreation theory can be a useful motivational tool for encouraging participation in physically active recreation. After long hours of sedentary work or studying, fatigue is a very common feeling. People in a tired state will often choose a sedentary recreational activity, such as napping or watching television. Unfortunately, these sedentary leisure activities often induce an even lower energy level and lower productivity. Even though it might seem overwhelming to initiate a physically demanding recreational activity when feeling run-down, the physical activity might very well have the effect of producing renewed energy and motivation.

However, one glaring weakness of this play theory is that after some forms of play, the participants feel even more tired than before the activity. For example, after a two-hour study break of vigorous racquetball and swimming, one might feel more inclined to go to sleep than to resume studying. Therefore, the recreation theory, like the surplus energy theory, can explain the motivation for some forms of play, but not all forms.

The Relaxation Theory

According to the relaxation theory of play (Kraus, 1984), the primary motivation for play is relaxation. This theory has great relevance in modern society. As discussed in Chapter 8 on stress reduction through recreation, stress is a major problem in modern society. Recreation can be a deterrent to a buildup of negative stress by providing an opportunity for relaxation. For example, an executive able to take a midday break for calisthenics, a swim, or a walk could significantly reduce the personal tension accumulated during the high-stress workday.

The relaxation theory provides an excellent justification for many forms of recreational activity besides play, games, sports, and exercise (e.g., massage or hot tub). However, the relaxation theory does not apply to many recreational activities. Does not recreation sometimes produce greater stress instead of relaxation? For example, a person in a high-stress job (such as a heart surgeon) who plays tennis as a break from the high-stress workday might often find his or her personal stress level increased, not decreased, by tennis because of the frustration of missed shots, bad line calls, distractions from other courts, the wind, and so on. Clearly, some forms of recreation are supported by the relaxation theory while others are not.

The Compensation Theory

According to the compensation theory (Weiskopf, 1982), leisure behavior is influenced by the desire to meet needs not met through work or other activities. For example, a worker in a somewhat undemanding, uncompetitive job (such as clerical work) may be more likely to seek competitive leisure activities such as sports. Conversely, a person in a highly competitive job (such as sales) may select more relaxing leisure activities, such as listening to music, to compensate for the competitiveness of work.

The compensation theory is certainly applicable in many situations, but it is not relevant in others. As discussed previously, people in high-stress jobs often choose to participate in competitive, stressful activities. Why people choose this seemingly self-defeating pattern of leisure behavior is partially explained by the generalization theory.

The Generalization Theory

According to the generalization theory (Ellis, 1973), play is caused by the transference to leisure of behaviors rewarded at work or another setting. This theory can help explain why someone in a stressful, demanding job might choose stressful, demanding recreational activities (such as competitive sports). According to the generalization theory, surgeons may acquire skills in dealing well with stressful situations through their work and therefore seek to use these skills in recreational activities.

Apparently, the generalization theory is relevant in some cases, the compensation theory is relevant in other situations, and neither theory is relevant in explaining children's play (children cannot generalize or compensate for work if they do not work).

The Instinct-Practice Theory

Quite different from the previously discussed theories, the instinct-practice theory (Kraus, 1984) views the motivation of play as stemming from the need to practice inherited traits needed for survival. For example, the doll playing of young girls can be viewed as practicing innate nurturing traits needed for survival in later life (caring for a family). Meanwhile, the war games played by young boys can be viewed as practicing innate combative skills needed for survival in later life (fighting wars).

Although this theory can explain some forms of play, there are certainly many problems with applying this theory to a variety of play situations. Even in the doll playing and war games examples, it is questionable whether the skills being practiced (particularly the combat skills) are really necessary for survival. Even if these skills are really needed for survival, are they instinctual or learned?

The Learning Theory

The learning theory of play (Millar, 1968) presents a view quite contrary to the instinct-practice theory. The learning theory assumes that most skills are learned, whereas the instinct-practice theory assumes that most skills are inherited. Similar to the instinct-practice theory, the learning theory is also perhaps most applicable to children's play. According to the learning theory, children are motivated to play by the desire to learn. Play is viewed as an outlet or opportunity for learning to take place. For example, by playing team sports, children can learn social skills, while word games can help teach important verbal skills.

Furthermore, play in earliest childhood can be viewed as experimentation leading to a growth in intelligence. Millar (1968) discusses Piaget's concepts of assimilation and accommodation in relation to the learning process that occurs during children's play. During play experiences, children assimilate or "digest" new information (adapt the information so that it can be incorporated into their life). Accommodation also occurs in that adjustments must be made by the children in order to incorporate the information into their life. Thus, childhood play can be viewed as a process of assimilation and accommodation resulting in learning.

The learning theory can also be utilized as an explanation or justification for a wide variety of adult recreational activities. In fact, two of the most frequently participated in leisure pursuits of Americans, watching television and reading newspapers, are often justified on the basis of their information transmittal/learning potentials. In addition, adult recreational activities ranging from a nature walk (to learn about the natural environment) to foreign travel (to learn about other cultures) can be very rich learning experiences. Thus the learning theory serves as a reminder that formal education and work are not the only opportunities for learning; recreational activity can provide some of the most enriching learning experiences.

Not all forms of play contribute to learning (e.g., a game played repetitively for simple amusement, such as some card games). Furthermore, play can sometimes contribute negatively to learning (e.g., children can acquire aggressive and destructive skills by playing war games). Gorney (1976) states that children learn aggressive behavior through play and sports and that to foster a more cooperative and harmonious society, people need to learn more cooperative, less competitive behaviors through play and sports. Therefore, the learning theory can be applied to explaining or justifying a variety of recreational activities, but certainly not all activities.

The Catharsis Theory

The catharsis theory (Ellis, 1973) views play as a positive, safe outlet for the release of pent-up emotions (including negative emotions). According to this theory, negative emotions such as aggression, if not given a safe outlet, will be built up and let out in a harmful way, such as fighting. However, playing football or even hitting tennis balls can have the cathartic effect of purging one's aggressive emotions. The catharsis theory can be extended to justify the provision of extensive recreational opportunities for teens to prevent juvenile delinquency.

The catharsis theory has widespread application in modern society. Many people experience the purging of negative emotions through participation in a variety of physically active sports and even through audience participation at concerts or sporting events. According to Smolev (1976), a research study involving 593 college students found that physical activity participation significantly decreased aggression, especially for females.

However, a criticism of the catharsis theory is that play sometimes increases negative emotions instead of releasing them. For example, at a sporting event, do spectators sometimes become increasingly hostile if their team is losing? Similarly, can athletes also become increasingly aggressive, frustrated, and angry if they are losing? As discussed by Ellis (1973), frustration leads to an increase in aggressive feelings; losing in a competitive sport can be quite frustrating. Furthermore, media coverage of professional sports that involve violence and aggression might be contributing to a widespread increase in the expression of these negative emotions because of the societal acceptance implied by media coverage and the tendency to imitate what is portrayed in the media.

Gelfand and Hartmann (1976) cite experimental research indicating that children's involvement in competitive sports and observation of aggressive adults cause increased aggression. Sipes's (1976) comparison of ten warlike and ten peaceful societies found that nine of the ten warlike societies had combative sports, whereas only two of the ten peaceful societies had combative sports. These results also seem to dispute the catharsis theory. Therefore, the catharsis theory is applicable in some cases but also has some serious weaknesses.

Each of the play theories discussed so far can be utilized to explain a great variety of leisure activities, but each also has shortcomings in explaining various forms of recreational activity. The self-expression theory is an attempt to provide a more comprehensive explanation of what motivates people to play.

The Self-Expression Theory

According to the self-expression theory (Weiskopf, 1982), play is motivated by the need or desire for self-expression. Self-expression is manifested through play in very diverse ways for different people and even in diverse ways for one person at different points in time. The self-expression theory explains these differences as being caused by a variety of factors.

1. *Physiological structure* or anatomical structure is a more permanent characteristic of an individual influencing leisure behavior. For example, a tall, muscular male might be more likely to seek self-expression through football than would a short, thin man. Conversely, the slightly built man might be more likely to seek self-expression through gymnastics than would the large man. Because height and weight are fairly stable for most people, the physiological structure of an individual tends to have a more permanent influence on leisure behavior.
2. Conversely, *physiological state* has a more temporary effect on leisure behavior. Physiological state refers to one's physical sta-

tus (e.g., sick, tired, injured, sleepy, hungry, energetic) at the moment. Because one's physiological state frequently changes, an individual chooses different leisure activities at different times. For example, dining out is an appropriate recreational activity when feeling hungry, whereas basketball is a likely choice when feeling energetic.

3. *Psychological state* is another constantly changing factor that strongly affects leisure behavior. Moods can range from happy to melancholy within a short period of time, causing drastic changes in leisure behavior. In a happy state, one might choose social interaction activities, whereas solitary activities would more likely be selected when feeling melancholy. Ironically, it is likely that the social interaction activities that might be shunned when one is feeling down are the activities that can help bring a person up from a depressed mood.

4. The *physical environment* also greatly influences leisure behavior. Physical environment refers to weather conditions, availability of natural resources (e.g., mountains, lakes, oceans), congestion, pollution, and so on. The effects of the physical environment are obvious. For example, more people surf in Hawaii than Maine, while skiing is probably more popular in Maine than in Hawaii. In addition, the physical environment affects moods and attitudes, which in turn affect leisure behavior. For example, gloomy, overcast weather adversely affects some people and causes them to stay indoors and participate in sedentary forms of recreation.

5. The *social environment* is perhaps just as strong an influence on leisure behavior as the physical environment. Social environment refers to social norms and attitudes as well as characteristics and desires of friends, roommates, and family. Other people can have a great influence on leisure behavior. An interesting question to ask is whether one's leisure behavior is more self-determined or more a function of others' desires.

6. *Learned habits* are also very influential in shaping leisure behavior. Habits learned in childhood are often continued through adulthood. For example, if reading the Sunday paper is done habitually for many years, it may be difficult to eliminate reading the newspaper from the Sunday itinerary.

7. *Personal wishes and desires* also influence leisure behavior significantly. The tremendous individual differences in need for achievement and recognition can help account for the great variation in participation in competitive sports. Variation in desire for adventure and excitement can account for individual differences in high-risk recreation participation and travel. Thus, wishes and desires, whatever they may be, strongly affect recreational activity participation patterns.

In summary, the self-expression theory recognizes that many factors influence leisure behavior. However, there are still other theoretical explanations of why and how people recreate.

OTHER THEORIES OF PLAY AND RECREATION

Optimal Arousal

Another theory explains leisure behavior as a quest to attain an optimal level of arousal (Iso-Ahola, 1980). Because people have different optimal arousal levels, they pursue different recreational activities; because an individual also has different optimal arousal levels at different times, different activities are selected.

Arousal refers to both physiological and psychological stimulation. The same stimuli can cause a high level of arousal for one person and a low level of arousal for another person, depending on the individual's perception of the stimuli. For example, an intermediate skier may find the stimuli of skiing down an intermediate slope to be arousing to a moderately high degree and therefore enjoy this activity greatly and desire to repeat it. Meanwhile, this same slope might be very boring to an advanced skier because skiing down this slope elicits a much lower level of arousal than this person seeks when skiing. On the other hand, a person afraid of speed and heights who has never skied previously could find the arousal level induced by skiing down the slope to be so high that he or she chooses not to try the activity again.

The skiing example illustrates how individuals seek an optimal level of arousal from recreational activities. When the arousal level is too high or too low, the activity is not an enjoyable experience. However, a recreational activity can be adapted in order to bring the level of arousal produced by the activity closer to the optimal level of arousal. For example, an expert skier can attempt trick moves on the intermediate slope in order to raise the arousal level of the activity, and the frightened novice can seek the assistance of an advanced skier in order to lower the arousal level of the activity.

It is hypothesized that biological differences exist among people in terms of their need for arousal. These biological differences can help account for the seemingly high level of risk-taking behavior of some people, contrasted with the passive, isolationist, low-arousal-seeking leisure behavior of others.

Loy and Donnelly (1976) discuss several different theories that attempt to explain the causes of individual differences in need for stimulation:

1. Zuckerman's theory relates differences in optimal levels of stimulation to variability in physiological differences in the central and autonomic nervous systems, age, learning experiences, task demands, and diurnal cycles.
2. Sales believes that the optimum level of arousal is similar for most individuals but that exposure to the same stimulus affects people differently because some individuals' nervous systems "dampen" stimuli, whereas others' nervous systems "augment" stimuli.
3. According to Gray, level of arousal is largely a function of the reticular activating system (RAS). Confronted with the same stimulus, person A's RAS bombardment of the cerebral cortex might be high, whereas person B's level of bombardment might be low. Person A would require less stimulation to reach an optimal level of arousal than would person B.
4. Eysenck's theory of cortical inhibition is closely related to Gray's RAS theory. According to Eysenck, when confronted with a stimulus, an organism produces an inhibiting response. Some individuals produce stronger inhibiting responses than others. The higher the level of inhibition, the lower the level of cortical bombardment. Thus, the level of inhibiting responses helps to determine optimal level of stimulation.

A concept related to stimulation and arousal is incongruity. Incongruity refers to the difference between all previously stored information and new information being presented in a situation (Iso-Ahola, 1980). Just as individuals seek an optimal level of arousal, they also seek an optimal level of incongruity. When the difference between stored information and new information is too great, the situation is perceived as overwhelming and perhaps frightening (e.g., ice-skating for the first time). Conversely, an activity seems boring if there is little or no difference between already-stored information and information presented by the activity (e.g., watching reruns on television). The level of incongruity of a stimulus or activity is a prime determinant of the level of arousal it causes. According to Ellis (1973), the meaningfulness and intensity of the stimulus or activity also determines its impact on arousal level.

"Flow"

The "flow" concept is related to the optimal arousal theory. Jackson (2000) defines flow as an optimal psychological state, experienced during an activity when things are going well, where participation is almost automatic and effortless, yet characterized by a highly focused state of consciousness. Nine dimensions of flow are identified:

1. There is a balance between perceived challenges and skills.
2. There is a merging of action and awareness.
3. Clear goals are apparent.
4. Unambiguous feedback is received.
5. There is total concentration on task.
6. There is a sense of control over what one is doing.
7. The participant is *not* self-conscious.
8. The participant loses track of time because he or she is so absorbed in the activity.
9. High levels of intrinsic satisfaction are experienced in the activity.

In which of your leisure activities do you experience this optimal psychological state called flow? Complete Exercise 5.1 to identify the leisure activities that produce the feeling of flow and to understand why these activities make you feel this way.

EXERCISE 5.1. Comparing Two "Flow" Activities

Instructions

1. Identify two diverse leisure activities that produce flow.
2. Write the title of one activity in the middle column and the title of the other one in the last column.
3. Explain how each of the nine dimensions of flow applies to each activity.

Dimension	Leisure activity #1	Leisure activity #2
1. Balance		
2. Merging		
3. Goals		
4. Feedback		
5. Concentration		
6. Control		
7. *Not* self-conscious		
8. Absorbed		
9. Intrinsic satisfaction		

The Competence-Effectance Theory

The competence-effectance theory (Kraus, 1984), similar to the arousal theory, also examines the effects of situational and environmental stimuli on motivation to engage in recreational activities. According to the competence-effectance theory, the primary motivation for play is the desire to manipulate the environment and produce a desired effect. For example, the sight of a basketball swishing through a basketball net is the desired effect of shooting a basketball. If this desired effect is produced with at least a small rate of success, then the individual is motivated to repeat this activity.

The awareness of the outcome of one's behavior is crucial in this theory. Therefore, a blind person playing basketball would need a feedback mechanism such as a basketball goal with a buzzer in order to be aware of the outcome of shooting the ball. Without this feedback, the individual would not be interested in playing.

The competence-effectance theory is applicable to most sports, art (immediate visual discovery of what is being produced), and music (immediate auditory discovery of what sounds are being produced). However, the competence-effectance theory has limited applicability to leisure activities such as passive entertainment, nature activities, and mental activity in which the environment is not manipulated by the participant.

Play As an Escape from Social Reality

A very different psychological explanation of motivation to play is Erikson's (Kraus, 1984) description of play as a means of escaping from social reality. Clearly, the importance of "escaping" is emphasized in marketing many diverse forms of recreation, ranging from movies to resorts and vacation packages. Although Erikson's theory was developed through his work with disturbed children, the concept of using recreation as an escape from social reality is very relevant for most adults.

For example, what are the various aspects of social reality for a typical first-year college student? In terms of time, there might be a great deal of constraint, given the commitments to classes, homework, and part-time employment. The economic aspects of life may be just as difficult (living on a limited budget). In terms of social status, many freshmen feel inferior or on the bottom of the totem pole. Thus, the social reality for a freshman can seem very bleak at times.

However, play can help any student to temporarily escape this somewhat difficult social reality. During a simple, fun recreation activity such as "orange pass under the chin," doesn't everyone in the group have equal social status? Are not economic and time constraints totally irrelevant during the activity? Therefore, is not play a very effective way for an adult to escape social reality? Don't college students justify the use of recreational drugs or getting drunk often as a way to escape? Couldn't play be as effective or more effective as an escape (without any harmful side effects)?

Recreation As a Religious Experience

Rather than escape from reality, a recreational experience can facilitate a deeper understanding of reality and in a sense be likened to a religious experience (Godbey, 1981). A true recreational experience can be thought of as a spiritual celebration, a totally joyous experience, akin to the positive feelings experienced through a religious celebration. According to Pieper (Godbey, 1981), celebration is the highest form of religious expression, thus a true recreational experience can be analogous to a religious experience.

Another similarity between religion and recreation is belief. The "belief" in jogging among avid joggers is perhaps comparable to faith or belief in religion. Godbey cites one survey of joggers in which over half the respondents reported feeling a spiritual high while running.

An interesting explanation of the stages of participation one goes through in order to reach the level of spiritual celebration and belief in a recreational activity is offered by Bryan (Godbey, 1981):

1. In the initial stage of participation, a newcomer to an activity is merely interested in obtaining some results.
2. In the second stage, the participant seeks to display greater competence in the activity by increasing the level of challenge in the activity and increasing the number of successes obtained.
3. In the third stage, the participant becomes more specialized in the activity (e.g., a baseball player who now only plays one position).

4. In the final stage, the participant engages in the activity for its own sake, the quality of the experience being paramount. It is in this stage that the activity can assume spiritual qualities and participants "believe" in its value.

Certainly, these four stages of participation do not apply to passive activities such as watching television. The idea of recreation being a form of religious experience would apply primarily to activities more likely to be viewed as "peak" experiences. Similar to religion, peak recreational experiences can provide spiritual uplift and meaning to life.

Many theoretical explanations of the needs, benefits, and satisfactions derived from leisure activity have been discussed in this chapter so far, but most of these theories seem to apply to only certain types of recreational activities.

Summary of Play Theories

- Surplus energy (play to *release* excess energy)
- Recreation theory (play to *restore* energy)
- Relaxation theory (primary motive is *relaxation*)
- Compensation theory (recreate to meet needs *not* met at work)
- Generalization theory (transferring work-related skills to leisure)
- Instinct-practice (primary motive is practicing inherited traits)
- Learning theory (play, recreate in order to *learn*)
- Catharsis (play as a positive, safe release for pent-up emotions)
- Self-expression (seven factors that help explain differences in how people seek self-expression through leisure)
- Optimal arousal (primary motive is quest for perfect level of arousal)
- Flow (an optimal psychological state)
- Competence-effectance (play to produce a desired effect on the environment)
- Play as an escape from social reality (primary motive is to escape from social reality)
- Recreation as a religious experience (recreation can be a spiritual celebration, leading to a deeper understanding of reality)

The following models and categorizations of leisure needs, benefits, and satisfactions provide a better overview of the different needs that are met by different activities.

CATEGORIZATION/MODELS OF LEISURE NEEDS/BENEFITS/SATISFACTIONS

Menninger's Categorization of Hobbies and Interests

Dr. Karl Menninger explored the use of recreation in treating mental illness (Weiskopf, 1982). According to Menninger, a balanced leisure life is critical in attempting to maintain a high level of emotional health. Menninger (Kraus, 1984) viewed play as providing the opportunity for "miniature victories" that could counteract the "miniature defeats" (e.g., minor problems at work, school, or in relationships) encountered in everyday life. Table 5.1 is a categorization of psychological needs and leisure activities, based on Menninger's work.

TABLE 5.1. Psychological Categorization of Leisure Activities

Psychological needs	Appropriate leisure activities
1. Tension release	Creative activities such as crafts, music, sculpting, writing, etc.
2. Creating feelings of security	Collective activities such as antiques, stamps, coins, etc.
3. Mental stimulation	Knowledge and skill acquisition activities such as reading, travel, sports, etc.
4. Release of aggressive impulses	Competitive games and sports such as football, tennis, etc.
5. Eliminating feelings of inferiority or superiority	Noncompetitive sports and games such as dancing, hiking, skiing, etc.
6. Emotional involvement	Spectator activities such as athletic contests, movies, etc.
7. Social involvement	Group participation activities such as volunteer work, participation in clubs and organizations, etc.

The categorization presented in Table 5.1 is a fairly comprehensive overview of needs, benefits, and satisfactions derived from various leisure activities. It is interesting to note the similarities in Menninger's categorization to Maslow's hierarchy of needs.

Maslow's Hierarchy of Needs

According to Maslow (1971), humans have a hierarchy of needs as follows:

1. *Physiological:* Hunger, thirst, exercise, etc.
2. *Safety:* Protection from danger, the need to exist under a system of rules and boundaries.
3. *Love and belongingness:* Socialization and intimacy.
4. *Self-esteem:* Recognition and achievement.
5. *Self-actualization:* Realizing one's full potential.

Maslow states that higher-level needs (love and belongingness, self-esteem, and self-actualization) can only be met once the lower-level needs (physiological and safety) are met. However, Ruskin (1988) suggests that the higher-level needs can be met even if the lower-level ones are not. He cites as an example concentration camp prisoners whose physiological and safety needs were not met but who were nevertheless engaged in cultural activities such as poetry, an activity that meets self-esteem and possibly self-actualization needs as well.

Maslow's hierarchy can be a useful basis for self-examination of one's leisure lifestyle. Some appropriate self-exploration questions to ask are the following:

1. Are all of the needs on Maslow's hierarchy being met through the recreational activities currently being participated in?
2. Are some needs being met more completely than others?
3. What activities can be engaged in that would contribute to self-actualization? What is self-actualization?

In answer to the last question, self-actualization is a somewhat intangible concept, not as easy to define as the first four levels of needs. Self-actualization is described as "realizing one's full potential," but can people ever really reach their full potential? How would anyone know if his or her full potential was reached?

Although the term *self-actualization* is a bit vague, it is quite possible to identify recreational activities that contribute to self-actualization. Such activities would place a great demand on the participant to improve a variety of skills. Recreational activities that contribute to self-actualization could also involve the aspect of challenge or reaching for a long-range goal. The goal would have to be set high enough that the individual constantly has something to strive for, but not so high that the person becomes frustrated.

The following are examples of recreational activities that could contribute to meeting each of the needs in Maslow's hierarchy:

1. *Physiological:* Running (exercise), dining out (hunger, thirst), bicycling (exercise)
2. *Safety:* Tennis, volleyball, soccer (All are activities with rules and boundaries, thereby contributing to the need for existing under a set of rules and boundaries.)
3. *Love and belongingness:* Volunteer work, membership in an organization or club, socializing (All of these activities usually involve a great deal of social interaction.)
4. *Self-esteem:* Art work (receiving praise for completed projects raises self-esteem), tennis (beating a worthy opponent feels great), dancing (Receiving compliments would enhance the positive effects of the activity on self-esteem, although just participating in the activity may have a significant positive effect on self-esteem.)
5. *Self-actualization:* Drama, badminton, performing music (In each of these activities, there is almost limitless potential for improvement, and striving for excellence in each activity would help develop a variety of skills and abilities.)

The examples of activities cited for each of the levels of needs are merely illustrative. Recreational activities cannot and should not be categorized permanently into one level or another. In fact, many recreational activities can meet all five of the needs on the hierarchy, depending on one's attitude toward the activity. For example, basketball is such an activity.

1. The *physiological* need for exercise can be met through basketball, and it can be the only need met in the activity if the participant is simply playing informally to unleash some surplus energy.
2. *Safety* needs can be met in that while playing basketball, the players exist under a very specific set of rules and boundaries. The rules are designed to protect the participants from physical harm, although it does not always work that way.
3. *Love and belongingness* needs can be met extensively, especially if the coach of the team emphasizes and facilitates team unity. Basketball or any team sport can provide the opportunity to develop many close friendships.
4. *Self-esteem* is certainly enhanced if the team wins or if recognition is given for significant contributions to the team's effort.
5. *Self-actualization* is facilitated through basketball if the participant exerts maximal effort to realize his or her full potential. At the highest level of play, players can use their physical and mental abilities to their fullest and perhaps push themselves beyond previous levels of skill, concentration, and endurance. However, at lower levels of play, basketball meets only physiological needs or physiological and safety needs. In fact, at the lowest levels of play (a simple informal game played at half-speed, simply to kill time and involving little or no social interaction), basketball might be entertaining but not meet any needs (not even the physiological need for exercise). Therefore, the key is how the participants approach the activity.

Exercises 5.2 and 5.3 are presented to foster the application of Maslow's hierarchy to personal leisure behavior. Exercise 5.3 focuses on the concept that one particular leisure activity, depending on the attitude toward the activity, can contribute to meeting all five needs on Maslow's hierarchy.

In summary, Maslow's hierarchy can be a useful tool in evaluating the worthiness of various leisure involvements. Nash's pyramid of leisure is another useful tool for self-evaluation and understanding the different benefits of various recreational activities.

EXERCISE 5.2.
How Personal Leisure Activities Fit into Maslow's Hierarchy

Instructions

1. In each need column, list all recreational activities you participate in that you feel contribute significantly to meeting that need. Begin listing activities from the bottom of the table, working up.
2. In the bottom row, enter the number of activities listed in each column. Enter the total number of activities in the space at the bottom far right.
3. Answer the following questions: How well-balanced are your activities in terms of need fulfillment? Which areas are lacking? Which needs are met most completely? (Consider the frequency of participation of each activity, not just the number of different activities in each column.)

Physiological	Safety	Love and belongingness	Self-esteem	Self-actualization
Total number of activities				
			TOTAL	

EXERCISE 5.3. Applying Maslow's Hierarchy to Leisure

Instructions

1. Select any activity for analysis, but preferably one that you engage in often.
2. For each need, explain how the activity could contribute to meeting that need.
3. Answer the following questions: What are some other recreational activities that could also potentially meet all five needs? What activities do you regularly engage in that you feel could not meet all five needs?

Activity _____

Need	Explanation of how the activity could contribute to meeting that need
Self-actualization	_____ _____ _____
Self-esteem	_____ _____ _____
Love and belongingness	_____ _____ _____
Safety	_____ _____ _____
Physiological	_____ _____ _____

Nash's Pyramid of Leisure

In Nash's pyramid (1960) (Figure 5.1), the higher levels of the model represent more highly valued categories of recreational activities; the lower levels represent less valued and even undesirable categories of recreational activities.

The following is an explanation of how various recreational activities would be categorized according to Nash's pyramid:

4. *Creativity:* Activities such as creating art work, composing music, inventing new games, or even inventing new strategies in a particular sport classify as creative pursuits.

3. *Active participation:* Playing music, engaging in participant sports, volunteer work, or any form of recreation involving physical and mental effort fit in this category.

2. *Emotional participation:* Listening to music, engaging in spectator sports, and attending a theatrical or dance performance all usually classify as emotional, not active, participation activities.

1. *Simple amusement and entertainment:* Activities such as watching movies and television or even engaging in spectator sports and listening to music can be placed in this category if the participant is entertained but not moved to a significant level of emotional involvement.

0. *Retardation of self-development:* Almost any leisure activity done in excess fits into this category. Prime examples are gambling, drinking, the use of recreational drugs, and chronic television watching. Even a usually healthy activity, such as basketball, can become a "retardation of self-development" activity if it is participated in so much that it becomes mentally and physically unstimulating. However, a much lower level of alcohol use is considered excessive; only in more extreme cases are activities such as basketball considered to be retarding self-development.

–0. *Acts performed against society:* Juvenile delinquency and vandalism are prime examples of activities in this category.

Nash's pyramid provides a conceptual model for evaluating the worthiness of various recreational activities. Nash (1960) empha-

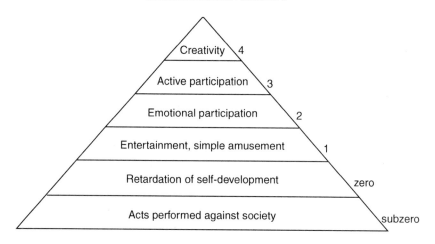

FIGURE 5.1. Nash's Pyramid of Leisure (Adapted from Nash, 1960, p. 89)

sizes a concern that society has become more passive in its leisure. He views simple amusement and entertainment activities such as television and spectator sports as less worthy pursuits than music, art, dance, and other creative and active pursuits.

Nash (1960, p. 132) quotes Albert Schweitzer: "The great sickness of man is that he is constantly seeking entertainment and more entertainment, sometimes of the stupidest and more cruel type, instead of finding stimulation from within." How would Schweitzer view the popularity of spectator events such as professional wrestling, boxing, and violent movies in today's society? Schweitzer's quote unfortunately seems to be highly relevant to leisure pursuits of Americans in the twenty-first century. As documented in Chapter 4, the leisure behavior patterns of Americans tend to be heavily focused on entertainment, much of it involving violence in various simulated forms.

Exercise 5.4 utilizes Nash's pyramid in self-evaluation of leisure activities. This exercise can hopefully be a motivational tool for trying new leisure activities that contribute to healthy self-development and self-actualization and for attempting to eliminate harmful leisure activities. The next model examines the various factors that influence or motivate leisure behavior.

EXERCISE 5.4. Self-Evaluation of Leisure Using Nash's Pyramid

Instructions

1. List all of your recreational activities.
2. Categorize your leisure activities into the levels of the pyramid in the illustration. In some cases, an activity might fit equally into two levels, but when possible, choose only one level per activity.
3. After completing this exercise, examine the distribution of activities among the different levels. Are there too many activities in the bottom three levels? Are there not enough activities in the top three levels? Which levels of the pyramid seem to be most representative of your leisure? Based on this exercise, what changes would you make in your leisure behavior?

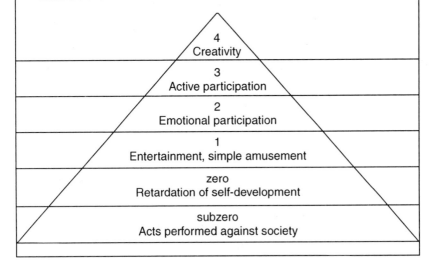

Iso-Ahola's Model of Causality of Leisure Behavior

Iso-Ahola's model (1980) is presented toward the end of this chapter because it integrates many of the theories and concepts discussed previously. The theories and models presented in this chapter offered explanations of the needs, benefits, and satisfactions derived from recreational activities. The model in Figure 5.2 presents an even broader view of motivation for participation in recreational activities.

According to Iso-Ahola, the factors above the dotted line represent "open" causes of leisure behavior that are easier to assess than the

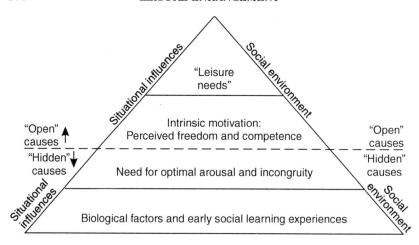

FIGURE 5.2. Iso-Ahola's Model of Causality of Leisure Behavior (*Source:* Adapted from Iso-Ahola, 1980.)

"hidden" causes below the dotted line. For example, in a research study on why people go bowling, subjects would likely be able to identify "open" causes, such as "It makes me feel good; I'm good at it" (intrinsic motivation) or "It helps fulfill my socialization needs" ("leisure needs"), but would not likely state "hidden" causes, such as "I bowl because of inherited biological traits and early social learning experiences." Thus, the causes below the dotted line are termed "hidden" and those above the line are termed "open."

Another interesting aspect of the Iso-Ahola model is that situational influences and social environment affect both the "hidden" and "open" causes of leisure behavior. Situational influences refer to the specific situation in which the leisure behavior is occurring. Social environment refers to more general ideas about societal norms that affect leisure behavior in a broader sense.

In order to illustrate this point, examination of causal factors for an activity such as playing guitar would point out that there are both hidden and open causes for the activity, with each type of causal factor affected by both situational influences and the social environment. Specifically, "leisure needs" such as relaxation and self-expression would be likely "open" causes of the activity. Situational influences (e.g., if the individual feels tense after working a long day) would create the need to relax through guitar playing at a particular moment. The social environment (e.g., knowing that many people choose to play guitar as a means of self-expression) would elicit the desire to incorporate guitar playing into a regular schedule of activities as an outlet for self-expression.

In this example, the social environment and situational influences would also likely affect "hidden" causes of the activity. Growing up in a time when playing the guitar was very popular (e.g., the 1960s) would be an example of the social environment affecting early social learning experiences. Receiving positive reinforcement as a child from parents for guitar playing would be an example of a situational influence (specific to the individual) affecting early social learning experiences.

The four levels of causal factors presented in the Iso-Ahola model integrate many of the theories and concepts presented in the chapter, making this model a very comprehensive view of why people recreate. The bottom level, biological factors and early social learning experiences, is addressed in the self-expression theory. The self-expression theory also considers social environment to be an important influence on leisure behavior. The next level, the need for optimal arousal and incongruity, was a theory discussed in the section of this chapter on other theories of play and recreation. The third level, perceived freedom and competence, was considered in detail in the discussion of Neulinger's paradigm in Chapter 1. Finally, the top level, "leisure needs," encompasses the wide variety of needs identified by the early play theories and other theories of play and recreation discussed in the chapter, as well as those identified in Maslow's hierarchy of needs and Nash's pyramid. In order to ensure a clear understanding of the Iso-Ahola model, another example is presented in Table 5.2.

Example: John, age twenty-six, over six feet tall, with a muscular build, is an avid weekend football player. Table 5.2 presents a hypothetical analysis of the causes of John's avid football playing.

Exercise 5.5 is designed to give the reader the opportunity to use Iso-Ahola's model to examine causes of personal leisure behavior. Select two activities for analysis, and for each one complete a table of causal factors as illustrated in Table 5.2.

TABLE 5.2. Hypothetical Analysis Using Iso-Ahola's Model of Causality

Level of causality	Causes affected by situational influences	Causes affected by social environment influences
"Leisure needs"	After a buildup of frustrations caused by events at school during the week, John plays football on Saturday as a catharsis for his negative emotions.	John plays football to enhance his self-esteem, knowing that friends will be impressed if he plays well. John knows that in general, society holds good athletes in high esteem.
Perceived freedom and competence (intrinsic motivation)	John looks forward to playing on Saturday because the field is muddy and he knows that he plays exceptionally well on a muddy field.	John's intrinsic motivation is heightened by the fact that all of his good friends also feel that playing football will be the most enjoyable activity to do on Saturday.
Need for optimal arousal and incongruity	John's arousal level will be optimal, because his team is very evenly matched with the opposing team.	John is seeking a high arousal activity and knows that football will be just that, especially with all of his friends and teammates creating an air of excitement in anticipation of the game.
Biological factors and early social learning experiences	John's size and strength make him feel confident and competent in football.	John has been somewhat influenced to play football by the societal stereotype that big strong guys should play football or other "macho" sports.

After completing Exercise 5.5, answer the following questions:

1. How do the causal factors of the two activities compare?
2. Is it more difficult to identify "hidden" causes than "open" causes?
3. Was it difficult to do a personal analysis of the causal factors of a recreational activity? If so, attempt an analysis for the leisure behavior of a friend or relative, then reattempt a personal analysis.
4. What did you learn about causal factors for your leisure behavior?
5. Does the Iso-Ahola model seem to be a comprehensive model for explaining causes of your leisure behavior? Were you able to incorporate theories and concepts previously discussed in this chapter in Exercise 5.5? Which ones?

EXERCISE 5.5. Applying Iso-Ahola's Model of Causality

Activity

Level of causality	Causes affected by situational influences	Causes affected by social environment influences
"Leisure needs"		
Perceived freedom and competence (intrinsic motivation)		
Need for optimal arousal and incongruity		
Biological factors and early social learning experiences		

SUMMARY

This chapter presented many theories, concepts, and models that attempt to explain leisure needs, benefits, and satisfactions. Being aware of the various needs that can be fulfilled through leisure activities can have some important behavioral ramifications. According to Weissinger (1994), awareness of the potential for leisure to meet psychological needs is a significant factor influencing the extent to which people become bored during their leisure. Leisure boredom is associated with negative behaviors such as substance abuse and smoking.

College students who are more bored during their leisure tend to rate themselves as being less physically and mentally healthy (Weissinger, 1994). Thus, awareness of the needs that can be fulfilled through leisure (the main topic of this chapter) can help prevent a variety of negative behaviors and help people feel healthier and not bored.

There are even more theories on the needs fulfilled through leisure than were covered in this chapter, such as psychoanalytic theories; refer to Millar's (1968) and Ellis's (1973) books for explanations of these theories. As a minimum, theories, concepts, and models that were presented in this chapter should be considered in developing a comprehensive personal philosophy of leisure. If greater awareness is developed of the variety of needs, benefits, and satisfactions that can be derived from leisure, there is a greater probability of being able to develop a personal philosophy of leisure that will facilitate maximal fulfillment of needs, benefits, and satisfactions through leisure.

REFERENCES

Ellis, M.J. (1973). *Why people play.* Englewood Cliffs, NJ: Prentice-Hall.

Gelfand, D.M. and Hartmann, D.P. (1976). Some detrimental effects of competitive sports on children's behavior. In T.T. Craig (Ed.), *The humanistic and mental health aspects of sports, exercise and recreation* (pp. 46-49). Chicago: American Medical Association.

Godbey, G. (1981). *Leisure in your life: An exploration.* Philadelphia: Saunders.

Gorney, R. (1976). Human aggression. In T.T. Craig (Ed.), *The humanistic and mental health aspects of sports, exercise, and recreation* (pp. 37-42). Chicago: American Medical Association.

Holmes, R.M. (1999). Kindergarten and college students' views of play and work at home and at school. In S. Reifel (Ed.), *Play and culture studies,* Volume 2 (pp. 59-72). Stamford, CT: Ablex Publishing Company.

Iso-Ahola, S.E. (1980). *The social psychology of leisure and recreation.* Dubuque, IA: Wm C. Brown.

Jackson, S.A. (2000). Joy, fun, and flow state in sport. In Y.L. Hanin (Ed.), *Emotions in sport* (pp. 135-155). Champaign, IL: Human Kinetics.

Kraus, R.G. (1984). *Recreation and leisure in modern society* (Third edition). Glenview, IL: Scott, Foresman.

Loy, J.W. and Donnelly, P. (1976). Need for stimulation as a factor in sport involvement. In T.T. Craig (Ed.), *The humanistic and mental health aspects of sports, exercise, and recreation* (pp. 80-89). Chicago: American Medical Association.

Maslow, A. (1971). *Toward a psychology of being.* New York: Van Nostrand Rheinhold.

Millar, S. (1968). *The psychology of play.* Baltimore, MD: Penguin Books.

Nash, J.B. (1960). *Philosophy of recreation and leisure.* Dubuque, IA: Wm C. Brown.

Ruskin, H. (1988). Perspectives on international recreation. Paper presented at the California State University, Chico Anthropology Forum, April 21, Chico, California.

Sipes, R.G. (1976). Sports as a control for aggression. In T.T. Craig (Ed.), *The humanistic and mental health aspects of sports, exercise, and recreation* (pp. 46-49). Chicago: American Medical Association.

Smolev, B.A. (1976). The relationship between sports and aggression. In T.T. Craig (Ed.), *The humanistic and mental health aspects of sports, exercise, and recreation* (pp. 49-54). Chicago: American Medical Association.

Weiskopf, D. (1982). *Recreation and leisure: Improving the quality of life.* Boston: Allyn and Bacon.

Weissinger, E. (1994). Recent studies about boredom during free time. *Parks and Recreation,* 29(3), 30-34.

PART II:
APPLICATION OF THEORY
TO ENHANCE LEISURE WELL-BEING

Chapter 6

Leisure Planning and Time Management

INTRODUCTION

This chapter presents guidelines for effectively managing leisure time. As discussed in Chapters 2 and 4, many Americans are not utilizing their free time to its full potential, as evidenced by the large number of people who feel that much of their leisure is spent in activities that they really do not want to do or that are not memorable. The purpose of leisure planning and time management is to enable people to make the best possible use of their free time, meaning that people obtain maximal enjoyment and other benefits from their leisure. In contrast, the purpose of time management at work is to increase efficiency (making more money in less time).

Principles of effectively managing work time are discussed in books by Davidson (1978), Fanning and Fanning (1979), and Lakein (1973). However, can principles of time management be applied to leisure time? Is leisure time used more effectively when it is planned, or is the concept of leisure totally destroyed when an attempt is made to manage or plan leisure time? Certainly spontaneity can be one of the more desirable characteristics of a leisure experience, but there is a danger in using the argument for spontaneity as an excuse for not making any attempt to plan or manage leisure time.

The application of time-management principles to leisure is described in detail in this chapter. Following the section on benefits of leisure planning is a detailed explanation of guidelines for setting leisure goals and writing personal daily time schedules. Criticisms of this approach to leisure time management are then discussed and refuted. Other leisure time-management techniques are discussed in the chapter, including a separate section on using sleep reduction to increase leisure time.

117

The intent of this chapter is to present a time-management approach to leisure that might be helpful to people who are attempting to improve their leisure and the quality of their life in general. Many of the techniques discussed in this chapter can at least be experimented with and evaluated. The ideas presented should not be rejected just because they seem different or unusual. On the other hand, the suggestions made in this chapter should not be viewed as a prescription for leisure wellness for everyone, even though the potential benefits of leisure planning (as discussed in the next section) are quite impressive. The learning objectives for this chapter include the following:

1. Identify potential benefits of leisure planning and goal setting.
2. Identify different types of leisure goals and describe their relationship to one another.
3. Identify guidelines for setting leisure goals.
4. Effectively utilize the guidelines for leisure goal setting in writing personal leisure goals.
5. Identify guidelines for devising daily time schedules.
6. Construct a time schedule for a weekend or a week that effectively incorporates the guidelines for devising daily time schedules.
7. Identify suggestions for improving leisure time management.
8. Identify suggestions for overcoming common time wasters.
9. Describe the theoretical basis for sleep reduction as an effective means of increasing leisure time.
10. Identify guidelines for attempting a gradual sleep-reduction program.

BENEFITS OF LEISURE PLANNING AND GOAL SETTING

Effective leisure planning and time management involves setting short-term and long-term leisure goals and managing time to ensure meeting these goals. There are several potential benefits of this approach:

1. Setting goals helps to establish priorities and gain a perspective on what is most important in life.

2. Leisure planning and goal setting can serve as a positive motivational force. Leisure goals can provide a sense of direction and purpose. Lack of commitment and motivation are serious problems and can be overwhelming obstacles that prevent participation in leisure activities. Setting leisure goals that are clearly connected to potential benefits can act as a strong motivational force.

3. Related to the concept of motivation is the idea that planning leisure can offer a desirable sense of structure. Some people are highly motivated and work more effectively in structured situations; the same can be true in leisure. Large blocks of unstructured time can be threatening and difficult to approach. The idea of planning leisure time can make leisure a less threatening concept. It might not seem nearly as difficult to simply follow a structured plan of activities as being faced with constant decisions on how to utilize free time.

4. Planning leisure time can be an enjoyable activity in its own right. The process of planning leisure can evoke memories of pleasant experiences and fill the mind with positive thoughts. Knowing that an especially enjoyable leisure activity is upcoming can help make it easier to deal with less pleasant circumstances in the present. During the planning process, the anticipation of future leisure activities can perhaps elicit positive emotions as strong as actually participating in the activities.

5. Leisure planning and goal setting require taking greater control and responsibility for personal leisure well-being and overall life satisfaction. One is no longer a victim of circumstances and future changes, but rather has established control over how time is spent and what happens in life. This feeling of control can result in a more positive attitude in general.

6. Similarly, leisure planning and goal setting can facilitate more effective responses to future changes. Without a plan, leisure behavior patterns can be diverted drastically by future changes without ever realizing that leisure behavior has been directed away from a more positive time-utilization pattern to a more negative one. This concept can be understood by examining

recent changes in society and how leisure has been affected by these changes.

An example is the invention of the television and its effects on leisure behavior patterns. Society's response to television was a vast increase in the percentage of leisure time devoted to passive entertainment and a corresponding decrease in other types of leisure activities, such as social activities. With a sound leisure philosophy, clearly defined leisure goals, and a conscious effort to effectively manage leisure time, society probably would not have immersed itself in watching television quite so much and would have maintained a healthier balance of leisure activities.

The idea of leisure planning enabling more positive responses to future changes also relates to smaller changes within a shorter time frame. A prime example is change in weather (e.g., from sunshine to rain). A sudden change in weather can ruin a weekend if no thought was given to alternative rainy-weather plans. However, an effective short-range leisure plan that identifies satisfying rainy-weather alternative activities will help prevent becoming overly distraught by a sudden change in the weather. Leisure planning facilitates effective coping with short-range and long-range, minor and major changes.

7. Yet another benefit of leisure planning and goal setting is that it can help prevent negative uses of free time. Leisure goals should be established on the basis of affecting the individual positively. Structuring free time to enable meeting leisure goals should leave little or no room for negative uses of free time (activities that have negative effects on health, such as use of alcohol and other recreational drugs, or activities that can retard personal growth, such as excessive television watching or excessive sleeping). Furthermore, leisure planning can provide greater control over utilization of free time and reduce susceptibility to being persuaded by others to participate in negative free-time activities. Negative activities often appear very attractive and are difficult to resist. However, leisure planning and goal setting can help provide a deeper understanding of the possible consequences of various free-time

utilization patterns, thereby enabling more discriminating leisure activity selection.

8. Leisure planning and time management can facilitate greater leisure "achievement." In some cases, the only desired end product of leisure is enjoyment. In other cases, the enjoyment of leisure is related to the production of achievements, such as finishing a painting, learning to play a song on the piano, or winning a tournament in a particular sport. Whatever the desired end product, establishing leisure goals related to these desired achievements and then planning and managing leisure with these goals in mind will help to ensure that leisure is more productive.

9. Related to the concept of achievement is the idea of being able to evaluate the desirability of free-time utilization patterns. The identification of leisure goals establishes a set of criteria for determining the desirability of free-time utilization patterns. The achievement of or failure to meet the leisure goals can provide objective evidence of whether free time was utilized effectively.

10. Furthermore, setting leisure goals can enhance self-esteem. Self-esteem is enhanced by the ability to objectively evaluate the attainment of leisure goals and see that progress in goal attainment has been achieved.

11. Leisure planning and time management can help reduce feelings of guilt. An often-cited barrier to leisure fulfillment is guilt (Mundy, 1984), usually related to the philosophical conflict created by the work ethic. However, a comprehensive leisure plan enables visualization (on paper) that adequate time has been set aside for work as well as leisure, thereby eliminating feelings of worry and guilt that might stem from the thought that work might not be completed.

12. Another potential benefit of leisure planning and time management is that it can encourage spontaneity. Perhaps the most frequently mentioned argument against planning leisure is that doing so robs leisure of spontaneity. However, effective leisure planning and time management can have the opposite effect.

Some of the key principles of writing leisure plans (discussed later in this chapter) are to set aside ample time for essential commitments, leave at least one hour of time uncommitted every day, and identify alternative leisure activities (to allow for changes in mood, weather, etc.). A leisure time utilization plan that incorporates these principles therefore helps encourage greater spontaneity. Without a plan, an opportunity for a spontaneous leisure experience might be rejected if one is unsure if participation in the activity will prevent meeting already-established commitments. Effective planning can permit greater spontaneity by enabling the visualization of how essential commitments can be met even if the spontaneous leisure opportunity is seized. Also, a leisure plan can encourage greater spontaneity by ensuring that time is set aside for spontaneous or unplanned activity. Furthermore, spontaneous activities can often help meet already-established leisure goals; the awareness of the connection of spontaneous activities to goal attainment can increase motivation to take advantage of such opportunities. As Porat (1980, p. 36) states, "greater control of time provides greater freedom."

13. Leisure planning and goal setting is in some cases necessary to ensure that a person has any leisure time. Especially for dual-career parents (the segment of the population with the least leisure hours per week), finding time for leisure can be quite a challenge. Specific time-management tips for parents of young children can be found in Chapter 13.

14. Last, but not least, leisure planning and goal setting can enhance the enjoyment of leisure time. Careful planning can yield more time for participation in those activities that are most enjoyable and less time in semienjoyable activities. Many special, highly valued leisure activities (e.g., a ski trip) are not possible without a good deal of planning. There is truth in the statement "*not* planning is planning to fail."

In the next section of this chapter, time-management principles and their applications to planning and managing leisure time more effectively are discussed.

TIME-MANAGEMENT PRINCIPLES

List Goals, Set Priorities

As identified by Lakein (1973), the principle of listing goals and setting priorities is one of the keys to effective time management. This principle is also applicable to improving leisure satisfaction. Setting leisure goals provides a guiding philosophy for leisure. Prioritizing these goals helps ensure that leisure time is spent in the best possible activities. It is useful to set three types of leisure goals: ultimate, long-term, and short-term.

Ultimate Goals

Ultimate goals provide an overall guiding philosophy for leisure. These goals should facilitate the viewing of leisure and life in a broad perspective and help determine the ultimate purpose(s) of leisure. Whereas long-term and short-term goals should be specific, ultimate goals should be general.

Examples. Students in an "Introduction to Recreation" class identified the following examples of ultimate leisure goals:

1. To help others.
2. To enjoy life as much as possible.
3. To travel all around Europe.
4. To bowl a 300 game.

Critique. Goals 1 and 2 might seem a bit vague but are good examples of ultimate goals because they help establish an overall guiding philosophy for leisure. Although goals 3 and 4 do identify difficult-to-attain ultimate activities, they do *not* establish a guiding philosophy for leisure and are *not* good examples of ultimate leisure goals. Ultimate goals should provide a foundation or basis for setting long-term and short-term goals.

Ultimate goals can be more specific than goals 1 and 2. For example:

1. To stay as fit as possible through my later years.
2. To make many true friends and socialize as much as possible.

These goals are more specific than those such as "helping others," but they still provide a framework for clustering a good number of more specific short-term and long-term goals. A greater number of these more specific ultimate goals should be identified to adequately understand one's guiding philosophy of leisure. Complete Exercise 6.1 to begin establishing your own ultimate leisure goals.

Long-Term and Short-Term Goals

Once a guiding philosophy for leisure has been established through setting ultimate goals, long-term and short-term goals that clearly contribute to meeting the ultimate goals should be identified. The relationship of short-term, long-term, and ultimate goals can be viewed in the following way:

Short-term goals (contribute to meeting long-term goals)
↓
Long-term goals (contribute to meeting ultimate goals)
↓
Ultimate goals

Avoid having short-term goals that interfere with meeting long-term goals or long-term goals that interfere with meeting ultimate goals. For example:

Ultimate goal: To stay as fit as possible through my later years.
Long-term goal: To make as many new friends as possible by increasing my visits to bars to at least twice a week (as opposed to once a week now) for the next five years.
Short-term goal: To reduce recreational alcohol consumption from five drinks a week to one a week.

In this example, the short-term and long-term goals clash and the long-term goal interferes with meeting the ultimate goal. By identifying a set of goals, better leisure choices can be made because the relationship of short-term activities to long-term and ultimate goals can be visualized. Frequently a decision must be made whether to indulge in an activity that will definitely bring short-term satisfaction but might inhibit the attainment of a particular long-term or ultimate goal

---

EXERCISE 6.1. Establishing Ultimate Leisure Goals

1. In the space below, list a minimum of five leisure goals that you consider to be *ultimate* leisure goals.

a. _____
   _____

b. _____
   _____

c. _____
   _____

d. _____
   _____

e. _____
   _____

2. Analyze the goals listed above and try to determine if there is a common theme to the goals. In the space below, write one or two ultimate leisure goals that you feel would accurately summarize the leisure philosophy reflected by the goals identified in task one.

3. Contemplate the goals identified and determine which one would be the best to utilize as the basis for setting long-term and short-term leisure goals.

(e.g., alcohol consumption might be enjoyable at the moment but interferes with meeting a long-term fitness goal).

*Guidelines for Setting Long-Term and Short-Term
Leisure Goals*

1. Determine if the goal contributes to or inhibits the attainment of ultimate goals.
2. Link goals to specific theories and concepts on needs/benefits/satisfactions of leisure (refer to Chapter 5 on theories and concepts).
3. Do not confuse leisure goals with work goals. For example, getting a high-paying job will provide more money for leisure activities, but it is not a valid leisure goal.
4. Remember that goals are not set in concrete. Goals should be reviewed and revised at least once per month (Lakein, 1973).
5. State goals in measurable, observable terms.
6. Clearly state the direction of change (increase or decrease).
7. Identify the time frame for short-term (one month? six months? one year? two years? five years?) and long-term (five years? ten years? fifty years?) goals.
8. Try to make each goal specific enough so that the means by which to approach the goal are recognizable.
9. Goals should identify something to strive for—not unrealistic and out of reach, but not easily attainable either. As Dr. Hans Selye states, "Fight always for the highest attainable aim, but never put up resistance in vain" (Selye, 1956, p. 300). This philosophy is appropriate in setting leisure goals.

It should be noted that in leisure services and in other fields, goals are used as more broad statements of purpose, and objectives are used as the measurable statements of purpose that clarify goals. However, throughout this chapter, the authors refer to goals as being specific and measurable statements, akin to what other writers might refer to as objectives. If you are already familiar with the concept of setting goals and objectives, then for the purposes of this chapter, simply think of the terms *goals* and *objectives* as being synonymous.

The following are short-term and long-term leisure goals identified by students in an "Introduction to Recreation" class. A critique in terms of following the aforementioned guidelines appears after each goal.

> *Goal:* To relax more.
> *Critique:* This goal is too vague and unspecific, is not stated in measurable, observable terms, and has no time frame.

> *Goal:* To continue swimming forty laps three days per week for the next fifty years.
> *Critique:* This goal is stated in measurable and observable terms, has a time frame, and is specific. However, this goal does not allow the individual to strive or reach for greater achievements. Even though being able to swim forty laps at age seventy may seem like quite an accomplishment, goals that merely involve continuation of a current activity are not as motivating as goals that involve striving for higher levels of achievement.

> *Goal:* To buy a ski boat within the next ten years.
> *Critique:* This goal is really a "consumer" goal, not a leisure goal. How often will the individual go water skiing after the boat is purchased? Perhaps the goal would be better stated as a water skiing goal. How many people acquire a wealth of leisure goods but do not have adequate free time to use them? Beware of "purchase" goals. Larsen (1994) states that busy people often purchase products advertised by showing models in relaxed poses with the unconscious belief that the leisure displayed in the picture will be transferred to them.

> *Goal:* To decrease getting drunk on Friday and Saturday nights from twice a month to only twice a year in the next two years.
> *Critique:* This goal is a good example of a specific leisure-related goal stated in measurable, observable terms with a clearly stated direction of change and a clearly defined time frame. Leisure goals can involve decreasing a negative activity, increasing a positive one, or initiating a new activity. Caution: State goals that you really want to achieve. Do not write goals merely intended to please someone else (teacher, parent, friend, etc.).

Goal: To increase recreational reading from one-half hour per week to two hours per week within the next ten years.
Critique: Excellent!

Exercise 6.2 provides an opportunity to apply the guidelines for leisure goal setting.

Once a satisfactory list of goals has been identified, the next step is to prioritize these goals.

Prioritizing Goals

The A, B, C rating system suggested by Lakein (1973) can be utilized for prioritizing leisure goals. Although all goals should contribute to the attainment of ultimate goals and should also incorporate a theoretical basis (i.e., the activity's benefits should be explained by a particular theory or concept), some goals will be rated higher than others for several reasons. For example, which activities have several benefits, not just one or two? Which activities yield more benefits in less time? Which activities not only provide specific benefits but also are the most enjoyable or appealing in which to participate? Which activities will drain one's resources (financial and personal) the least? These considerations are all important, but probably the most important factor to keep in mind is the extent of long-term benefits that are derived by meeting the goal.

Using the prioritization system advocated by Lakein (1973), the highest-priority goals should receive an "A" rating, medium-priority goals are rated "B," and low-priority goals are rated "C." The medium-priority goals should be reexamined to see if some are not actually As and some are not really Cs. The goals can then be further prioritized as A1, A2, A3, etc., to more specifically establish priorities. Again, it is important to remember that the goals and their prioritization are not permanent; they should be reviewed regularly and revised as necessary.

One of Lakein's key points is "do As, not Cs!" The prioritization of goals is critical to overcoming the tendency to spend more time in lower-priority, easier to do activities instead of the higher-priority activities. Apparently the principle of "doing As, not Cs" is just as important for leisure as it is for work.

The "do As, not Cs" principle can be modified somewhat to allow participation in moderately beneficial and enjoyable "B" and "C" ac-

EXERCISE 6.2. Setting Long-Term and Short-Term Leisure Goals

Instructions

   List a minimum of five short-term and five long-term leisure goals. Be sure to follow the aforementioned guidelines for setting leisure goals. Do this exercise with a partner; after listing personal goals, exchange lists with your partner and critique each other's goals in terms of their conformity with the guidelines for setting leisure goals.

Short-term goals	Critique

Long-term goals	Critique

tivities. The principle could be restated as "do As first, and spend more time doing As than Bs or Cs." This principle can be put to practical use in making daily "to do" lists, which is another key to Lakein's time-management approach.

Making Daily "To Do" Lists/Daily Schedules

According to Lakein, a common characteristic of many highly successful people is that they utilize daily "to do" lists. The approach advocated in this chapter is to write daily time-management schedules, going one step beyond the concept of the daily "to do" list. Suggested guidelines for writing daily schedules are listed in the following section.

Guidelines for Devising Daily Time Schedules

1. Try to plan one week in advance. Use a pocket calendar to write down appointments that are scheduled more than a week ahead.
2. Schedule a time once per week for a personal time-management planning session, preferably at the end of the week.
3. Begin by making a separate blank time schedule for each day of the upcoming week.
4. Next, mentally review the past week and list of goals and determine what activities seem to be most important in the upcoming week, based on the goal-attainment successes and failures of the past week.
5. Block out time in the daily schedules for the already-existing commitments listed in the pocket calendar.
6. Block out time in the daily schedules for definite, ongoing, essential commitments and activities, such as classes, work, and personal care.
7. At this point, a better perspective of unobligated time in the upcoming week (how much there is and when it occurs) should have been obtained.
8. The first step in allocating time for leisure activities should be to consult one's list of goals. First, reevaluate the goals and make changes, additions, and deletions, or reprioritize as appropriate. Make sure the goals and their prioritization have a clear, logical theoretical basis. Next, begin allocating time for

high-priority ("A") leisure goals/activities. Before allocating time for "B" and "C" activities/goals, decide if even more time should be allocated for the high-priority goals and activities to create a more beneficial use of time.

9. Allocate adequate *transition* time between activities. The next activity usually cannot begin immediately after the preceding one ends. Allocating inadequate transition time in a daily schedule would lead the follower of such a plan through a frantic, frustrating day.

10. Identify appropriate alternative activities for any activity that can be affected by the weather.

11. Leave a minimum of one hour each day uncommitted. According to Lakein, it is important to leave an hour uncommitted to prevent the problem of running behind schedule all day if one activity happens to take longer than anticipated. This uncommitted hour (or more) can create a more relaxed attitude about following a time schedule (wouldn't it be terrible to feel rushed all day?). The uncommitted time can also promote an enhanced sense of freedom and control over time, perhaps leaving room for spontaneous activities.

12. Consider moods and the concept of "internal and external prime time" when allocating time for various activities. Lakein believes internal prime time is that time in which one tends to work best alone. In many cases, internal prime time occurs in the morning. If so, then activities such as reading and studying should be planned for the morning hours. On the other hand, external prime time is that time during which one works best with others (Lakein, 1973). Many people find that their external prime time usually occurs in the evenings. If so, then evenings would be the best time to plan social recreation activities. It would be counterproductive to plan solitary activities during external prime time and social activities during internal prime time. For example, the student who plans to do homework on a Saturday night (if the student knows it is a definite external prime-time period) is doomed to fail. However, internal and external prime-time are not always easy to predict. To compensate for unpredictable moods, daily schedules should be written to allow the flexibility to switch activities. For ex-

ample, a plan can allow the option of playing tennis in the morning and studying in the evening or vice versa.

13. Do not plan to procrastinate. How many students plan to do all their weekend homework Sunday night and then do not feel in the mood to do it when Sunday night comes around?

14. Recognize the necessity of "idiot work," but do not let it dominate. According to Fanning and Fanning (1979), idiot work refers to activities that are necessary but require limited ability or skill. Some examples of idiot work are mowing the lawn, vacuuming the rug, doing laundry, and washing dishes. These activities are essential but require little demand on mental and physical abilities. According to Fanning and Fanning (1979), some of the problems with idiot work are that it often expands to take up more time than initially anticipated (thereby reducing time available for leisure activities), and it can be physically draining, reducing the physical energy level and psychological motivation to participate in more highly valued activities. In daily time schedules, planning to accomplish meaningful leisure activities before doing idiot work can prevent this potential problem. Idiot work can be left for late at night, after more satisfying activities have been completed.

Another suggestion made by Fanning and Fanning is to allocate only a specific amount of time for idiot work. A timer can be set to go off when the idiot work time period is over, and the individual will thus be forced to complete idiot work within the specified time period, not allowing it to interfere with leisure time.

One final comment on idiot work: Idiot work can be a leisure experience, with the right frame of mind. Listening to music or working with friends can greatly enhance the leisure potential of idiot work.

15. Do not allocate time in daily schedules for activities that do not qualify as essential activities (related to work, school, or personal care) or as priority leisure activities. For example, if watching television or reading the newspaper are not identified as being essential or priority leisure activities, then a plan should not include time for them. However, if these activities have not been listed as priority activities yet there is a compelling desire to engage in them, question the accuracy of the pri-

oritization of leisure activities and goals. Perhaps there was a lack of honesty or thoughtfulness in writing the prioritization, and these activities *do* belong in the priority list as "A" or "B" leisure activities.

16. If you are not the "planning type," Lakein (1973) suggests that you say to yourself, "I can't plan, but if I could plan, this is what the plan would be." Doesn't that sound like an effective way of tricking yourself into writing a time schedule?

17. Review the plan once it is completed and compare it with the list of goals. Be sure that there is a strong relationship between planned time expenditure and ultimate, long-term, and short-term goals. If adequate time is not being devoted to goal attainment, then revise the daily plans. Lakein (1973) emphasizes that at least some time should be devoted to long-term goals each and every day.

Key Elements of Daily Time Schedules

- Allocate time for "A" leisure goals first.
- Identify rainy-weather alternatives.
- Allow adequate transition time.
- Leave one hour or more *uncommitted.*
- Consider internal and external prime time.
- Do not procrastinate.
- Do "A" activities *before* "idiot work."
- Maximize time spent doing "As."

Criticisms of Writing Daily Time Schedules

Students who experiment with devising and following daily time schedules sometimes find the experience frustrating and express doubt that such a time-management practice can work well in their lives. However, the causes of their frustration usually stem from poor planning on their part, not the concept of planning time expenditure.

For example, one common negative comment is "I felt rushed all weekend, trying to follow my plan, going from one activity to the next, nonstop." However, if adequate transition time is set aside between activities and uncommitted time is allocated in the daily plan, this problem can be avoided.

Another common criticism heard is "Planning takes away all my spontaneity. I couldn't do spur-of-the-moment activities I would have loved to do with my friends because I felt I had to follow my time-expenditure plan." This problem can also be prevented. First, one can list special spontaneous activities that might become available under the list of high-priority ("A") activity possibilities and then incorporate a contingency plan into the daily schedules should these spontaneous opportunities become available. Using this technique could even help to increase spontaneity.

Students experimenting with leisure planning for the first time sometimes say that because of their plan, they cannot participate in leisure activities that they would enjoy even more than the leisure activities in the plan. The question to be asked of these individuals is "Why were those 'great' leisure activities not listed in your plan as high-priority activities?" Imagination is a key element in the success of a daily time-expenditure schedule. A plan that lacks imagination will exclude a person from participating in some of the most enjoyable and beneficial leisure activity possibilities. However, by being thoughtful and imaginative in listing and prioritizing leisure activities and goals, it is possible to have more leisure activity opportunities than ever before. In this way, planning can help prevent a person from falling into a leisure rut.

In summary, there are many possible reasons for the failure of a leisure time-expenditure plan. If the first experiment with this approach is unsuccessful, make some adjustments and try it again. Before rejecting this concept, make sure that the reason for the failure of this approach is an individual reaction to the concept, *not* mistakes or inadequacies in a particular plan. In order to facilitate the identification of time-expenditure planning problems, two examples of weekend plans written by students are presented in the following section. The first plan is a poor one, and the problems with the plan are discussed. The second plan is a good one.

Sample Plan A: Example of an Inadequate Plan

School/Work/Personal Care

> Sleep: 8 hours per day
> Homework: CHEM (4 hours)
> RECR (2 hours)
> ENGL (3 hours)

Personal care: 1 hour per day
Eat: 1 hour per day

Leisure Activity Possibilities

A1 Go dancing
A2 Ski
A3 Tennis
A4 Play softball with friends

B1 Partying
B2 Listen to music
B3 Write letters
B4 Long-distance calls to parents, friends

C1 Watch TV
C2 Play Scrabble with friends
C3 Go to arts and crafts fair
C4 Play table tennis

Time Schedule

	Friday
3:00 p.m.	Last class ends
3:00-5:00 p.m.	Relax, listen to music
5:00-6:00 p.m.	Read newspaper
6:00-8:00 p.m.	Watch TV, eat dinner
8:00-midnight	Party with friends

	Saturday
8:00-9:00 a.m.	Personal care
9:00-10:00 a.m.	Eat breakfast
10:00-11:00 a.m.	Long-distance phone calls
11:00-noon	Write letters
12:00-2:00 p.m.	RECR homework
2:00-4:00 p.m.	Softball game
4:00-6:00 p.m.	Shower, eat, listen to music
6:00-9:00 p.m.	Invite friends over for Scrabble, table tennis
9:00-10:00 p.m.	Watch TV
10:00-midnight	Dancing

	Sunday
8:00-9:00 a.m.	Personal care
9:00-11:00 a.m.	Eat breakfast, read Sunday newspaper
11:00-1:00 p.m.	Watch basketball games on TV
1:00-5:00 p.m.	Skiing at Lassen Park
5:00-6:00 p.m.	Eat dinner, watch TV
6:00-10:00 p.m.	CHEM homework, watch *60 Minutes*
10:00-midnight	ENGL homework

Critique

This plan is poor. Some glaring errors and omissions are the following:

1. No allowance is made for transition time between activities.
2. There is no uncommitted time in the daily schedules.
3. Reading the newspaper is not listed as a priority activity, yet it is included in the schedule.
4. Watching television is a "C," yet it is scheduled for Friday, ahead of many "A" activities. This violates the principle of doing As before Cs.
5. The plan lacks flexibility; there is no room for spontaneous, alternate activities or mood changes.
6. No rainy-weather alternative activities are identified.
7. Procrastination is preplanned, with homework slated for Sunday night.
8. Tennis is an "A," but it never appears in the schedule.

Sample Plan B: Example of a Good Plan

School/Work/Personal Care

Sleep: 8 hours per day
Homework: HEM (4 hours)
               RECR (2 hours)
               ENGL (3 hours)
Personal care: 1 hour per day
Eat: 1 hour per day

Leisure Activity Possibilities

Good-Weather Leisure Activity Possibilities		Rainy-Day Leisure Activity Possibilities	
A1	Go dancing	A1	Same as fair-weather activity
A2	Bike ride	A2	Ride stationary bicycle at health club
A3	Hike in mountains	A3	Walk in park with rain gear
A4	Volunteer work at retirement home	A4	Same
A5	Volleyball	A5	Same
A6	Watch sunset	A6	Listen to relaxation music
B1	Write letters	B1	Same
B2	Go out for Chinese food	B2	Same
B3	Write letters	B3	Same
B4	Long-distance calls to relatives	B4	Same
B5	Shopping	B5	Same
B6	Board games	B6	Same
B7	VCR with friends	B7	Same
C1	Magazine collage	C1	Same
C2	Bake cookies	C2	Same
C3	Coffee drinks	C3	Same
C4	Soccer	C4	Indoor soccer
C5	Record tapes and records	C5	Same
C6	Skiing	C6	Indoor roller-skating
C7	Listen to music	C7	Same
C8	Sleep	C8	Same
C9	Visit grandparents	C9	Same
C10	Board games	C10	Same

Justification for "A" Activities and Rainy-Weather Alternatives

A1. After a stressful week of school, relaxing and visiting with friends is an optimal arousal-level experience (i.e., low level of arousal). It also fulfills the love and belongingness level of needs on Maslow's hierarchy. Furthermore, it meets my need to relax (relaxation theory). Because this activity can occur indoors or outdoors, no alternate activity is needed.

A2. The bicycle ride meets the physiological need for exercise on Maslow's hierarchy. It is a highly active participation activity on Nash's pyramid, and being in the outdoors provides an escape from social reality. If raining, riding a stationary bicycle indoors will meet similar needs. By listening to good music with headphones while riding, the escape from social reality need can be met.

A3. Hiking in the mountains not only helps release surplus energy but also is a rejuvenating, energizing activity (recreation theory). It also is an activity that is simple, allowing the opportunity to utilize basic, *instinctual skills*. Because it is the outdoors and very active, hiking helps to *compensate* for being indoor and sedentary much of the school week. The rainy-weather alternative is also outdoors and active, and therefore it is also a good release for *surplus energy,* can be rejuvenating, enables the practicing of instinctual skills (what can be more basic than walking?), and also is in opposition to the indoor, sedentary nature of the school week.

A4. Volunteering is a great love and belongingness and self-esteem activity because of the warmth and gratitude expressed by the retirement home residents (Maslow's hierarchy). It is also a creative activity (top level of Nash's pyramid) in that devising new activity ideas to implement at the home requires a great deal of innovation. It also provides an opportunity to apply material learned in recreation and gerontology classes (generalization theory).

A5. Whether it is played indoors or outdoors, *volleyball* is a good outlet for pent-up emotions (*catharsis* theory); it is so therapeutic to hit some good spikes! The *competence-effectance* theory also applies because hitting balls hard and seeing them land on the opponent's court (the desired effect) elicits feelings of competence and raised self-esteem.

A6. Watching a sunset is both a *relaxation* and *escape from social reality* activity. If it is raining, listening to relaxation music can, to a somewhat lesser degree, meet both of these needs.

Time Schedule

	Friday
noon-3:00 p.m.	Work on and complete lifestyle packet, eat a quick lunch

3:30-5:30 p.m.	Volleyball
6:00-8:00 p.m.	Eat quick dinner, complete R80 home-work, start on CDES 97 assignment
8:00-9:00 p.m.	Free time
9:00-11:30 p.m.	Relax, visit with friends, perhaps play board games or cards

Saturday

7:00-8:00 a.m.	Personal care, breakfast
8:00-9:00 a.m.	CDES 97 assignment
9:30-1:30 p.m.	Hike in mountains or walk in the rain
1:00-3:00 p.m.	Free time
3:00-5:00 p.m.	Volunteering
5:30-7:30 p.m.	Picnic dinner, watch sunset or dinner, listen to relaxation music
8:00-8:30 p.m.	Write letters or read magazines
9:00-11:30 p.m.	Relax, socialize, visit with friends

Sunday

7:00-8:00 a.m.	Personal care, breakfast
8:00-10:00 a.m.	Finish CDES 97 assignment
10:30-12:30 p.m.	Bicycle ride or stationary bicycle
12:30-1:30 p.m.	Free time
1:30-3:30 p.m.	More volleyball or Rollerblade/roller-skate or soccer or other activity
4:00-5:30 p.m.	More volunteering
6:00-6:30 p.m.	Call grandparents or write letters
9:30-11:30 p.m.	Collage or bake cookies or coffee drinks or record tapes, and record or listen to music or VCR with friends.

Critique: This plan is obviously much better than sample A. The guidelines for writing daily time schedules were effectively incorporated in this plan.

Potpourri of Time-Management Tips

In this section, a variety of suggestions for improving leisure time management are presented. These suggestions include philosophical approaches to time, methods for eliminating or reducing common leisure time robbers, and other techniques and ideas for improving leisure time management.

Make Use of Transition Time

Lakein defines transition time as the time between activities, such as waiting in lines, commuting, and the like. According to Lakein, many people waste transition time and could make better use of this time if they carried with them a list of activities that are possible to engage in during transition time.

In a related vein, as stated in Chapter 4, most leisure time occurs in relatively short (thirty- to sixty-minute) blocks of time. These short blocks of leisure time are often wasted because people either are not aware that they have this free time or simply do not know what to do with it. For example, a common time waster is watching television while waiting the half-hour it will take for dinner to be ready. Another example is the time college students have between classes. Occasionally, I will see students sitting in the hallway, and when one student asks the other one what he or she is doing, the response is often "I'm just *killing time* until my next class." Instead of "killing time," try having with you the following list of activities for short blocks of time:

1. Doing artwork, such as drawing or painting
2. Creative writing
3. Letter writing
4. Playing a musical instrument
5. Listening to music
6. Meditation and other relaxation techniques
7. Exercise, such as running, walking, bicycling, roller-skating, skateboarding, or basketball
8. Reading
9. Laughter and humor
10. Games
11. Hobbies
12. Leisure planning

In addition to having this list of activities with you at all times, it is possible to *be prepared* for transition time by taking with you the items you might need in order to participate in these transition time recreational activities. For example, if you are going to the doctor and you think that you might have to wait for a half-hour or more, take a good book with you or paper to work on artwork or creative writing. If you have time between classes and there are nice outdoor areas on campus, consider bringing sneakers with you so that you can go for a walk or a beach towel so that you can lie on the grass to meditate, do yoga, or simply sit and enjoy nature. Some of the activities on the list, such as hobbies, are intended more for transition time that occurs at home; instead of carrying hobby or craft materials with you to campus, the idea is to have the materials at home and easily accessible to enable work on a hobby or craft when short blocks of leisure time occur.

Making maximal use of transition time and short blocks of free time can enable participation in a much wider variety of activities than previously thought possible. As discussed in the next section, transition time and short blocks of free time can also be utilized to make progress in attaining high-priority leisure goals that seem to be overwhelming.

Apply Lakein's "Swiss Cheese" Approach

Lakein discusses how to make an overwhelmingly big, important work-related goal easier to deal with by "poking holes in it" and accomplishing small tasks related to achieving that goal in very short blocks of time. This concept can easily be applied to leisure goals.

For example, suppose an "A1" short-term leisure goal is to increase foreign travel from none at all to taking a one-month tour of Europe within the next year. The following is a list of some of the tasks that could be accomplished in short blocks of time that would contribute to meeting this goal:

- Call travel agents or read travel ads to get information on ticket prices.
- Read travel brochures or books to learn about sightseeing, travel, and accommodations in the European countries.
- Call a friend who has been to Europe to obtain ideas and information on European countries.
- Write letters to various consulates requesting travel information.

In this way, transition time and short blocks of free time can be utilized effectively to contribute toward the attainment of a high-priority leisure goal. Implementing this technique will also help prevent using the common excuse for procrastinating: "I don't have enough time to do it." People avoid working on high-priority activities by employing a variety of escapes, as discussed in the next section.

Understand Procrastination/"A"-Avoidance Behavior

Lakein suggests identifying common escapes from working on high-priority goals and then asking friends for help in cutting off these escape routes. Some of the more commonly used escapes are the following:

- Indulgence (e.g., sleeping late, eating an especially long meal)
- Socializing (e.g., semisatisfying chitchat in the library when studying for an exam usually is not as enjoyable as true recreational socializing, and it prevents progress being made in studying)
- Reading (e.g., reading a newspaper thoroughly, cover to cover)
- Doing it yourself (e.g., copying something by hand instead of photocopying it or cooking dinner instead of simply buying something)
- Overdoing it (e.g., cleaning one's room before studying and being incredibly neat in order to avoid studying)
- Running away (finding excuses for physically leaving the situation where the work or activity should take place)
- Daydreaming
- Creating distractions or irrelevant stimuli (e.g., turning on the TV or radio while studying)
- Putting it off ("I'll do it later; I work best under pressure!")

It is important to cut off these escape routes and to overcome the problem of procrastination. A research study on procrastination among college students (Hackett, 2002) found that procrastination was associated with the use of alcohol and other drugs, smoking, higher levels of stress, and higher rates of digestive ailments, insomnia, and cold and flu symptoms. Procrastination can be hazardous to your health!

Walk Faster

This simple suggestion, offered by Levinson (1990), has several benefits. It will not only shorten the time needed to do errands but will also enhance the potential fitness benefits of performing errands on foot. Furthermore, it just might help make simple errands seem more meaningful, in harmony with the "on time" concept.

Limit Purchases

As explained by Keyes (1991), learning to make do with less can create more free time. Keyes points to a paradoxical connection between people having too much income but too little time. He feels that if people could live a simpler lifestyle, they would be able to slow down and spend their time more wisely.

Related to the idea of limiting purchases is the suggestion to be wary of memberships at "warehouse/discount" stores, especially if they are not conveniently located near your house. The lure of these mammoth stores is the wide selection of items available and the expectation that prices are lower. Sometimes the savings are real and worthwhile, but in many cases, buying in bulk does not really save as much money as people might think. The key is to evaluate your use of time. For example, on a Saturday morning, suppose you have the opportunity of doing your shopping at the supermarket five minutes from your house, getting the shopping done quickly, and then going out to play tennis for an hour or two. Suppose that your other option was to drive a half-hour each way to the warehouse store, do your shopping there and save about five or ten dollars, but not be able to have time to play tennis. Which option would you choose? Judging by the full parking lots at the warehouse stores on Saturdays, it seems that most people would choose the more time-consuming shopping option, but is that really the best choice? The other problem about the big shopping trip to the warehouse store is buying more than you really need, which goes back to the original suggestion of *limiting purchases* as a way to create more leisure time.

Beware of Time-Saving Devices

Keyes (1991, p. 79) quotes Duncan Caldwell: "Americans have more time saving devices and less time than any other group of people in the world." Keyes offers several reasons why time-saving devices often do not save time and might even detract from leisure: (1) they create new tasks (e.g., video shopping); (2) they raise standards (e.g., letters to family and friends now have to be perfectly typed on a computer instead of handwritten); and (3) the devices require time to learn how to use and master, maintain, and repair. Be aware of how supposed time-saving devices are utilized, cut back usage on ones that are overused and waste time, and perhaps eliminate those that are totally time wasters.

Decelerate

Keyes (1991) cites the example of walking instead of driving as a way to go slower and to gain more satisfaction from one's time. Approaching some tasks with a more relaxed attitude (as opposed to rushing) can help bring out the leisurely characteristics of many of life's activities that people typically do not view as leisure.

Count All Time As "On Time"

How common is the attitude that a given situation is a waste of time, that it is not worth trying to enjoy or learn from the situation? Certainly if one takes that attitude toward a situation, it is unlikely that any satisfaction can be gained from the time spent in that situation. Lakein's tip, "Count all time as on time," can be helpful in preventing such an attitude from prevailing.

This simple statement can have a very positive impact on leisure satisfaction. For example, one might be playing in a tennis match in which the score is lopsided and there is no chance of winning. If the last few games of the match are considered "off time," the remaining few games will most likely be very unsatisfying and could be considered a waste of time. However, if the remaining games are considered to be "on time," satisfaction could be derived by simply being outdoors, from the exhilaration of physical exertion, from enhanced self-esteem from hitting some good shots, and by learning some new strategies and techniques.

Another good leisure-related example in which the "on time" approach would be useful is a social recreational activity involving people you do not like (e.g., your partner makes a commitment to go out to dinner with a couple of friends you find to be annoying). If the entire evening is "written off" even before it takes place, the dinner date will surely be a miserable experience. However, if a conscious effort is made to consider the dinner as "on time" and satisfaction is sought from the situation, then perhaps enjoyment can be derived from the food, the atmosphere, and perhaps even the conversation.

Cut Off Nonproductive Activities As Quickly As Possible

The idea of counting all time as "on time" must be balanced with the concept of cutting off nonproductive activities as quickly as possible (Lakein, 1973). What is a nonproductive leisure activity? Essentially, it is one that is not enjoyable and does not provide physical, psychological, or social benefits. A good example is a terrible party (awful music, congestion, and people relating superficially). Even though the "on time" philosophy is being tried, it is not working. Do you stay all night because you feel obligated to stay, or do you leave quickly and pursue another activity? Leave the party as soon as possible!

Apply the "80/20 Rule" to Leisure

In terms of business, Lakein's 80/20 rule suggests that in many cases, 80 percent of one's profits are derived from a mere 20 percent of one's customers. Is it possible that in leisure 80 percent of the benefits and satisfactions are derived from a mere 20 percent of your activities? Carefully examine how your free time is utilized; if the 80/20 rule holds true for your leisure, then it would make sense to attempt to spend more time in the highly satisfying activities and less time in the less satisfying activities.

Identifying Leisure Goals Through "Life Patterning"

As described by Fanning and Fanning (1979), "life patterning" can be a useful tool in determining leisure goals. Figure 6.1 is a sample life pattern. The lines connected to the center circle represent major leisure roles of the person (e.g., athlete, musician, etc.). The branches connected to these lines represent specific activities related to each major leisure role (e.g., connected to the main branch for "athlete" are branches for tennis, soccer, etc.). The solid lines represent activities that are ongoing or have been completed. The broken lines repre-

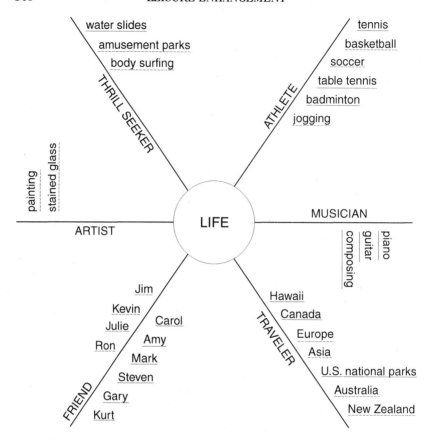

FIGURE 6.1. Sample Life Pattern

sent unfinished or unstarted activities (e.g., the person who wrote this sample life pattern had not yet traveled to Australia and New Zealand).

A truly complete life pattern is more detailed than the sample illustration. The life patterning technique can facilitate leisure goal setting by presenting a broad, visual perspective of leisure. The broken lines in the pattern are the activities for which to set goals. Exercise 6.3 presents an opportunity to utilize the life patterning technique as an aid in goal setting.

EXERCISE 6.3. Personal Life Pattern

Instructions

Follow the previously discussed guidelines for drawing a "life pattern" and construct one for yourself. Then, based on the life pattern, examine the need to revise, add, or delete goals from Exercise 6.2.

LIFE

Once sound leisure goals have been established, the next challenge is to dedicate adequate time to attaining these goals. The next section focuses on ways to overcome common time wasters that might prevent devoting adequate time to goal attainment.

Overcoming Common Time Wasters

Watching Television

If you love watching television, please do not be offended by reduced television viewing as the first topic discussed under overcoming common time wasters. Watching television can, at times, be an extremely satisfying leisure experience. Favorite television shows can be entertaining, laughter inducing, educational, and perhaps intellectually stimulating. You need not reduce time spent viewing your favorite shows (unless you have dozens of favorite shows). What would be desirable to reduce is the type of television viewing engaged in just to alleviate boredom. For example, with only thirty minutes to kill before going out, if you flick the channels to find something to watch, is this type of television viewing usually very satisfying, or is it merely a time filler?

It appears that most television viewing time could be replaced with other, more beneficial and enjoyable leisure activities. Kubey and Csikszentmihalyi (1990) report that according to research, watching television rates significantly lower than other leisure activities in terms of concentration, challenge, skill, and eliciting feelings of cheerfulness, happiness, strength, alertness, and friendliness. Yet, as discussed previously in this book, watching television usurps more leisure time than any other activity.

Another example of television viewing that wastes time is habitual viewing. This involves having regular, set hours to watch television (e.g., every evening after dinner), regardless of whether there is a program on you really like.

Why is it important to reduce wasted television viewing time? A common excuse for not being able to attain leisure goals is lack of time. The short and large blocks of wasted television viewing time can be utilized to contribute to the attainment of high-priority leisure goals.

How does one deduce if time is being wasted watching television? Ask these questions: Is all of your television viewing time satisfying?

Are there activities you do not participate in that would be more satisfying than some of your television viewing time? If you can definitely answer "yes" to the first question and "no" to the second one, do not read on. However, if your answer is "no" to the first question and "yes" to the second one, then you will probably benefit from the following suggestions for reducing television viewing, based on ideas from Lakein's (1973) and Fanning and Fanning's (1979) books, and from students at California State University, Chico.

Ideas for Reducing Television Time (Choose the Ones That Work Best for You)

1. Do not own a television. When a special event is broadcast, arrangements can be made to view it at a friend's house or a public setting with a television. Likewise, if there are a few shows you really enjoy watching regularly, arrangements can be made to watch these shows with friends. A benefit of this approach is that it enhances the potential of television viewing as a social activity.
2. Do something else while watching television, such as stretching exercises or riding a stationary bicycle. If the activity is one that does not require much concentration, then watching television simultaneously might be a good idea. However, if it is an activity that requires a great deal of concentration (e.g., writing, reading, or studying), then watching television simultaneously is obviously a distracting time waster.
3. Limit hours of television viewing by establishing a schedule for television time, with viewing not allowed at any time other than the preplanned times.
4. Place a big sign on the television that says "Don't turn on!" as a deterrent to idle channel flipping to kill time.
5. Perhaps more effective than a "Don't turn on!" sign might be to make a list of more enjoyable, easy-to-do leisure activities that can be accomplished in thirty- to sixty-minute time periods and taping this list either on the remote control or the television itself. Activity ideas for short blocks of leisure time are discussed in this chapter.
6. Keep the television in the closet. If the television is out of sight, you will not be as likely to think of turning it on (out of

sight, out of mind). Furthermore, if watching television is made a little more difficult, it is more likely that effort will be made to go through the trouble of setting up the television only if a special program is broadcast.

7. Lakein discusses a progressive method for reducing television viewing. First, turn off the sound when commercials are shown. The next step is to delay turning the sound back on for a few seconds after the commercials are over. Gradually increase time delay in turning on the sound, the idea being that you will eventually lose interest in television and drastically reduce or totally eliminate television viewing.

8. Do not subscribe to cable television or get any other enhanced television reception service such as digital television or a satellite dish. The more channels you have, the more appealing channel surfing becomes, which is the form of television viewing that is the biggest waste of time. Watching a favorite television show can be an enjoyable experience, but using the remote control to search through a hundred or more stations, hoping to find an entertaining program is really an empty time killer.

9. A related suggestion is to hide the remote control. You will still be able to watch your favorite shows, but it will be more difficult to waste time in the activity of channel surfing.

10. Keep the television unplugged. Having to go to the trouble of plugging in the television every time you want to watch it will make you think twice before turning it on. Similarly, keeping the television covered can be just the little reminder you need that you should think twice before turning it on.

11. Learn how to record your favorite television shows so that you do not have to be home at the time they are on. It is problematic if the urge to watch a television show causes you to turn down an invitation for a potentially more enjoyable leisure experience. Recording shows not only creates more flexibility in your schedule but also saves time in that you can fast-forward through the commercials when you watch the recorded show.

12. The first suggestion was *not* to own a television; a compromise can be not to own a *fancy* television. The nicer the set, the more appealing it is to turn on. Also, try to get by with only one television in the house. Avoid having a television in the

bedroom, as the convenience of a set in the bedroom makes it that much easier to waste time watching television.

Reading Newspapers

Similarly, the extent of satisfaction derived from reading newspapers should be questioned. Watching television and reading newspapers are probably the two most frequently participated in leisure activities of Americans, but how satisfying are these activities? Could more satisfying leisure activities be substituted in their place? Honestly, is reading the Sunday paper the ultimate way to spend Sunday mornings? In a ten-minute break between classes, is the best use of time reading a newspaper, or could a small hole be poked in an important leisure goal?

Lakein suggests not reading the entire newspaper, just the headlines in order to keep pace with the news. If a story is really interesting, a newspaper or news magazine can be bought or borrowed to learn more about the particular story or issue.

The suggestion to not read newspapers might seem a bit odd and contrary to the ethic that it is important to be aware of world events. However, how much information is redundant? Beyond the headlines, how much of what one reads in the paper is really important?

Over the years, in discussing this idea with university classes, I have found a number of my students to misinterpret the suggestion to not read newspapers to imply that it is not important to be well informed. False! The fact is, there may be better ways to be well informed that save time as compared to reading a newspaper. Some excellent Web sites can provide in-depth information and analysis on news topics, far beyond the depth that a newspaper can offer. Another option is a weekly or monthly news magazine. Although not all of them are necessarily of a high quality, some of them do go more in depth into stories than do newspapers, and because of their smaller page size, they are less cumbersome to read than newspapers while riding an exercise bicycle. Similarly, it is fairly easy to watch a news show on television while working out on a variety of exercise equipment. Some excellent, in-depth news shows can be found on the radio, and these can be listened to on headphones while going for a walk or a jog. Therefore, it is possible to stay well informed and keep fit in the process.

Watching television and reading newspapers are very strongly established habits for many people. Reducing or eliminating time spent in these activities might be difficult, and the very idea of attempting to reduce or eliminate time spent in these activities may be offensive because it is contrary to well-established beliefs. Nevertheless, if the time saved by reducing or eliminating these activities can be devoted instead to top-priority leisure goals, it is probably worth trying. After all, old television-viewing and newspaper-reading habits can be resumed if changing these habits causes displeasure.

Recreational Uses of Computers

Many uses of home computers can be viewed as recreational, such as the following:

1. Sending and receiving e-mail messages
2. Chat rooms
3. Games
4. Surfing the Internet

The recreational uses of computers need not be eliminated, but they should be limited. Similar to television, the computer screen can be mesmerizing, and a great deal more time can be spent at the computer than was originally intended. Some of the problems related to recreational computer use include the following:

1. It seems to be cutting into exercise and fitness activities. Many people claim to not have enough time to exercise, yet they spend an hour or more per day at their computer. This problem also exists for children, as they are spending more time behind the computer and less time in active play, with the result that fitness levels are declining.
2. It is not a social activity, and it can even alienate members of a household. There is an emerging problem of "e-mail junkies," men or women who stay up late at night communicating via e-mail, long after their partner has gone to bed. This situation cannot be good for long-term relationships!
3. E-mail communication can actually cause communication problems. E-mail, when used wisely, is a valuable, time-saving communication tool. However, when it is used in place of personal

contact or telephone communication, it can lead to miscommunications and bad feelings. It can also prevent the formation of friendships or good working relationships. For example, a student who visits a professor during office hours will most likely develop a good relationship with that professor much more quickly than a student who has a dozen e-mail exchanges with that professor.

The following suggestions are offered for limiting recreational computer use:

1. Try some of the suggestions offered for reducing television time (e.g., cover your computer) to eliminate uses of the computer that are merely time killers. Keeping a list of alternative activities to do in short blocks of time by the computer as well as by the television can help to reduce the time-wasting uses of the computer.
2. Whenever possible, call or visit a person rather than sending an e-mail message. A phone call is more direct and can save time, as opposed to an endless loop of messages going back and forth. A phone call or a personal visit is also more recreational in nature than sitting in front of a computer screen, isn't it?
3. Do not send e-mail to people that are not worth a phone call. A good use of e-mail is to send an informational message to many people at the same time. It is easy to use and enables you to communicate with more people in less time. However, when e-mail is used for the purpose of engaging in personal communication with people that are not important in your life (you do it just because it is easy to do), then it becomes a time waster. Two minutes here, five minutes there can really add up.
4. Avoid chat rooms. This activity can usurp much more time than you intend. Some people would argue that it is a form of social interaction, but actually it is an activity that prevents you from engaging in more satisfying social interaction. Instead of being at the computer, your time could be spent actually conversing with friends or family.
5. Do not surf the Internet. Is it really as much fun as other leisure activities that you could be enjoying? Similarly, try to use books instead of the Internet when seeking certain kinds of informa-

tion. Contrary to what many people believe, it can often be quicker to find needed facts in books rather than on the Internet.

6. Limit the use of computer games. When there is an opportunity to play interactive games with others, put the computer games away. The addictive nature of computer games is particularly evident with children and adolescents. For example, in some schools, students now use laptop computers in their classes. During recess, instead of playing and talking with one another, some children will opt to play games on their computer.

In summary, it is important to distinguish between the sensible, beneficial uses of home computers and the time-wasting, minimally enjoyable ones. If you can succeed in limiting the time spent in the less beneficial recreational uses of the home computer, a great deal of time will be made available for more enjoyable leisure activities.

Cellular Phones

Similar to recreational uses of home computers, the use of cellular phones, when used wisely, is good. However, there are problems related to the tremendous increase in the use of cellular phones in recent years. These include the following:

1. Talking on the phone while driving a car. It causes accidents.
2. Talking on a cellular phone when you are with someone else. How would you feel if you went out with your boyfriend or girlfriend and during the evening your "companion" was talking on the phone half of the time instead of talking to you?
3. Talking on a cellular phone when you are in the park, at the beach, in a museum, or other recreational place. Do you really want to be spending your time talking on the phone, or did you go to the beach or the park to relax and enjoy nature? Imagine being at the beach, lying in a comfortable beach chair and taking a nap, and being woken by an unimportant phone call. Or imagine being woken from a nap by someone else's cellular phone call.
4. Interrupting meals or other quality time with friends or family in order to answer a phone call.

Obviously, the easiest way to limit the use of cellular phones is not to own one. However, it is possible to own one, use it wisely, and avoid the problems cited. The following suggestions are offered for limiting/improving cellular phone usage:

1. Use the cellular phone only to make calls, not to receive calls. Do not give your cellular phone number to people. Keep the phone off when you are not using it to make calls. By doing so, the phone will not interrupt you in the middle of a leisure activity. People can leave voice-mail messages and you can return the calls at your convenience.
2. Do not use the phone while you are driving. It is too dangerous.
3. Focus on the people you are with, not those who call. Screen incoming calls on both the cellular phone and the home phone.
4. Use an earpiece and microphone rather than holding the phone. Being "hands free" while talking on the phone can enable you to do a variety of mindless tasks (e.g., ironing) as you talk or even go for a walk.

In summary, when used wisely, cellular phones can actually enhance leisure rather than detract from it. Unfortunately, many people currently overuse or misuse their phones, to the detriment of their leisure.

Thinking Negative Thoughts

Lakein advocates not wasting time regretting failures and feeling guilty about incomplete tasks. Whether the guilt is major or minor and the failures being regretted are trivial or important makes no difference. Regret and guilt are a waste of time. They do not contribute to improving the situation. Dwelling on guilt or regret takes away from time that could be spent working to improve matters and is also emotionally draining, making it more difficult to devote full energy to improving the situation.

How can regretting failures or feeling guilty about what was not done be controlled? The first step is to realize the benefits of making an effort to eliminate these negative thoughts. Next, simply determine that you have the power to shove these thoughts aside when they do surface.

Not Concentrating on One Thing at a Time

Have you ever tried to do two things at once when both required total concentration? What happened? Clearly, work performance is more efficient when concentrating on one task instead of two or more tasks.

This philosophy also has important ramifications for leisure satisfaction. Have you ever been on a vacation with someone who continuously was thinking about and planning for the next part of the trip and never totally focusing on the present? Can such a person really be fully enjoying the present if his or her mind is somewhere else? This idea also relates to the use of cellular phones—is it really possible to be fully enjoying or appreciating an outdoor activity or a social activity if you are talking on the phone? The concept of concentrating on one thing at a time relates to leisure as well as to work.

Failing to Relax and Do Nothing Rather Frequently

Is it surprising to see the suggestion to do nothing in a chapter on time management? It seems appropriate to end this section of the chapter with this statement. After reading all the previously discussed time-management suggestions, it might seem that one should be frantically trying to accomplish as much as possible all of the time. Such an attitude would be mentally and physically destructive. Relaxing and doing nothing can be an enjoyable activity in itself. It can surely help prevent burnout, although if taken to the extreme it also prevents the accomplishment of very much. The key is moderation.

Relaxing and doing nothing rather frequently can be put into action in several different ways. One technique is the "two-minute vacation," which involves lying down or reclining, eyes closed, for two minutes while fantasizing about being in a far-away, ideal vacationland. Another technique is to set aside larger blocks of time (several hours long) a few days a week for passive relaxation such as sunbathing, listening to music, or meditation. This type of passive relaxation can have a rejuvenating effect.

However, the "do-nothing" aspect of this time-management tip is perhaps more important than the suggestion to relax frequently. Unfortunately, many people will set out to relax and then turn on a television show or music that prevents relaxation. Rock and roll music can be very energizing, but is it usually relaxing? Is watching a television drama laden with violence a relaxing activity? Yet many people will say that they just want to relax and then watch television or listen to music that creates tension.

The key is to truly do nothing, to not create any stimuli or distress that will divert one's attention away from their own free-flowing thoughts. Ironically, although this suggestion is purely a leisure-related one, it is very likely that during these quiet moments of doing nothing, one's best ideas and solutions to problems will be realized without even trying.

The last section of this chapter focuses on perhaps the most effective technique for increasing the quantity of free time: sleep reduction.

SLEEP REDUCTION

Sleep reduction can be a very effective method for improving the quantity and quality of free time. As discussed previously, sleep is the second-largest category of time expenditure in most people's lives. Reducing sleep by two hours per night would give a person an extra fourteen hours awake every week. Think of the leisure activities that could now be possible with this newly acquired free time. In addition, sleep reduction can be good for your health and perhaps even increase your life span. A research study involving 1.1 million people over a six-year period found that compared to people who slept seven hours per night, those who slept eight hours per night were 13 percent more likely to die, and those who slept nine hours were 23 percent more likely to die (Reucroft and Swain, 2002).

Cautions

Sleep reduction is not for everyone. There is no universal minimum amount of sleep required for all individuals. Through experimentation you should be able to discover what your optimum amount of sleep is. If a sleep-reduction program is attempted, give it a good, honest try, but remember to approach sleep reduction gradually, push hard but not too hard, and make allowances for times of stress and illness.

Also consider personal feelings about sleep as a recreational activity. Is lying in bed an extra two hours every morning one of your favorite leisure experiences? Would you be happier if you spent that time in other leisure pursuits? If sleep is truly one of your favorite leisure activities, then do not try sleep reduction. However, if the idea of having more free time for other leisure pursuits is intriguing, then it is important to understand the theory of sleep reduction before following the guidelines for attempting a sleep-reduction program.

Theory of Sleep Reduction

According to Dr. German Nino-Murcia, director of the Stanford Sleep Disorders Clinic, there is no scientific evidence that a moderate amount of sleep deprivation (three or four hours reduction from a typical eight hours per night sleep time) detracts from physical performance (Green, 1986). According to Mattlin (1979), experiments indicate that people can succeed in gradually reducing their sleep time without experiencing any mental or physical harm. Although Angier (1990) reports that there are more than 40,000 sleep-related accidents per year, these accidents are mainly due to sleep disorders, not systematic sleep reduction.

Mattlin explains how natural sleep cycles are conducive to sleep reduction. Stage 1, 2, 3, 4, and REM (rapid eye movement) sleep are experienced within a complete sleep cycle. Stage 1 and 2 sleep is lighter and less restful. In REM sleep, the brain is very active and dreams occur. According to Mattlin, in eight hours of sleep, most of the stage 3 and 4 (deep sleep) occurs during the first four hours of sleep time, and the last four hours of sleep time are spent mainly in the less restful REM and stage 2 sleep. Therefore, in a reduction in sleep from eight hours per night to five or six hours per night, very little of the most restful stage 3 and 4 is lost. Thus, a gradual reduction in sleep time to five or six hours per night should not cause physical or mental harm.

What about REM sleep? Would a person's functioning be impaired if deprived of REM sleep? First, the gradual sleep-reduction program described in this chapter would not totally eliminate REM sleep, although REM sleep would be reduced. Furthermore, Mattlin states that although early, highly publicized experiments on REM deprivation indicated that people experienced great psychological problems when deprived of REM, later research found that subjects did not suffer significant psychological problems when deprived of REM.

It is also possible that reducing REM sleep can help to alleviate psychological problems that are made worse by dreams. Aren't bad dreams physically and psychologically draining? Waking up earlier (before the onset of bad dreams) can have the effect of contributing to a more refreshed, energized state of being in the morning and all day long.

Guidelines for a Sleep-Reduction Program

The following guidelines are primarily based on Mattlin's work:

1. One must be well rested before commencing the program. To attempt a sleep-reduction program during a period of stress or illness is self-defeating.
2. Define exactly what will be accomplished with the extra time gained from sleeping less. Why reduce sleep time if you have not decided what you will do with the extra time?
3. Use the extra time awake for recreation. Thus a reward system is set up for reducing sleep time, which will increase motivation to continue the sleep-reduction program.
4. The sleep-reduction program should be tied to a total lifestyle reevaluation. Previously in this chapter, leisure goal setting was discussed in detail. After setting leisure goals, it should be clear what leisure activities will be increased if sleep time is decreased. Thus sleep reduction will be utilized as a tool to facilitate the attainment of leisure goals.
5. At the beginning of the sleep-reduction program, a two-week daily log of sleep habits should be recorded without any attempt to reduce the amount of sleep time. Each day note what time you went to sleep at night, what time you awoke in the morning, nap time during the day, total number of hours slept, quality of sleep, and mood and energy level in the morning and all day. After you have kept the log for two weeks, a clearer picture will appear of the average rise and retire times, the average amount of sleep, and how the quantity and quality of sleep affects mood and energy level.
6. Based on the two-week log, set appropriate goals for a sleep-reduction program. In general, a one-hour reduction should be fairly easy; a two-hour reduction should be feasible, though

more difficult. Thus, if one sleeps an average of eight hours per night before attempting sleep reduction, an appropriate goal would be to reduce to only six hours per night. However, a person who already sleeps only six hours per night might not want to reduce sleep time as much; perhaps if a half-hour reduction goes well, more can be attempted.

7. Attempt to reduce sleep time very gradually, at a rate of only one-half hour every three weeks. For example:
   • The two-week log indicates that your average sleep time is eight hours.
   • During the next three weeks, try adjusting to only seven and one-half hours of sleep per night.
   • During the following three weeks (weeks six to eight of the program), attempt to reduce to only seven hours of sleep per night.
   • If the reduction program has been successful so far, continue reducing sleep gradually, to six and one-half hours during weeks nine to eleven and finally to only six hours per night by week twelve.

8. Continue maintaining a log of your sleep habits throughout the entire program.

9. Recognize that at the beginning of each step of the reduction program some discomfort will be experienced. Accept this discomfort as normal; it should gradually disappear during the three-week adjustment period.

10. Do not push too hard. Listen to your body.

11. In a related vein, take advantage of naps and stress reducers such as meditation in order to compensate for times of stress. Naptime should be counted into the total amount of sleep in a daily log.

12. Do not cheat! Sleeping late on the weekends will throw off sleep patterns and make it nearly impossible to succeed in the sleep-reduction program. At most, one-half hour cheating on the weekends might be acceptable.

13. Similarly, try to be as regular as possible in your sleep habits. Rise and retire at approximately the same time every day.

14. Do *not* try to make up for lost sleep. For example, if you go to sleep unusually late, it would be better to wake up at the usual time than to sleep later in order to obtain the usual amount of sleep. Also, if you sleep very little one night, do not attempt to

sleep extra hours the next night to compensate for the loss of sleep.

15. If the sleep-reduction program is focused on waking up earlier, have an exciting or fun activity scheduled for early in the morning that will help motivate you to get out of bed. Similarly, if the reduction is being accomplished by retiring later, have fun and exciting activities scheduled for the evening, although too much excitement late at night can interfere with the ability to fall asleep.

16. Another way to facilitate early rising is to set a light and a heater (in the winter) on a timer.

17. After succeeding in the original sleep-reduction goals, examine the possibility of setting new goals. Monitor all sleep habits for several months to make sure old sleep patterns are not resumed.

SUMMARY

In addition to sleep reduction, many other suggestions for improving leisure time management were made in this chapter. Perhaps the most important concept discussed in this chapter is goal setting. Without well-defined goals, the other leisure-planning and time-management principles are relatively meaningless.

REFERENCES

Angier, N. (1990). Cheating on sleep: Modern life turns America into the land of the drowsy. *The New York Times,* May 15, pp. C1, C8.

Davidson, J. (1978). *Effective time management.* New York: Human Sciences Press.

Fanning, T. and Fanning, R. (1979). *Get it all done and still be human.* New York: Ballantine Books.

Green, L. (1986). A spoonful of sleep: It may be all you really need. *Outside,* February, pp. 23-24.

Hackett, L. (2002). Tomorrow, tomorrow. *Ka Leo O Hawai'I,* September 26, pp. 1-2.

Keyes, R. (1991). *Timelock: How life got so hectic and what you can do about it.* New York: HarperCollins Publishers.

Kubey, R. and Csikszentmihalyi, M. (1990). *Television and the quality of life: How viewing shapes everyday experience.* Hillsdale, NJ: Lawrence Erlbaum Associates, Publishers.

Lakein, A. (1973). *How to get control of your time and your life.* New York: Signet Books.

Larsen, E. (1994). Buying time. *Utne Reader,* 61, 59.

Levinson, J.C. (1990). *The ninety-minute hour: Technological and psychological breakthroughs take you beyond time management.* New York: E.P. Dutton.

Mattlin, E. (1979). *Sleep less, live more.* New York: Ballantine Books.

Mundy, J. (1984). What prevents people from enjoying leisure? *Parks and Recreation Magazine,* 19(9) (September), 24-26, 94.

Porat, F. (1980). *Creative procrastination.* New York: Harper and Row.

Reucroft, S. and Swain, J. (2002). You snooze, you lose. *The Boston Globe,* April 9, p. C4.

Selye, H. (1956). *The stress of life.* New York: McGraw-Hill.

Chapter 7

Fitness and Leisure

Amy Hornick
Michael Leitner

INTRODUCTION

Exercise and sports are major categories of leisure activities. Several forms of leisure activity can enhance fitness (e.g., exercise and sports), but some types of leisure activity can adversely affect fitness (e.g., recreational drinking and eating). Care for the body through healthy recreational eating and exercise habits can help create more enjoyable and active leisure and life in general.

The purpose of this chapter is to provide an understanding of the relationship between fitness and leisure. This chapter will not attempt to cover all the aspects of fitness and nutrition—many good books have already been written for that purpose. What this chapter will do is provide the reader with useful information to improve the quality of leisure through recreational exercise and healthy recreational eating. More specifically, the learning objectives for this chapter are to

1. Describe how improved fitness can increase leisure enjoyment and how leisure can enhance fitness.
2. Identify the physiological and psychological benefits of a recreational exercise or fitness program.
3. Identify and define the components of health-related physical fitness.
4. Describe the current level of fitness of Americans.
5. Compare and contrast aerobic and anaerobic energy systems.
6. Identify recreational activities with low, moderate, and high potential for aerobic fitness.

7. Identify possible changes that can be made to low and moderate aerobic potential sports to increase their aerobic potential.
8. Identify ways to make aerobic exercise activities more fun.
9. Identify guidelines for beginning a recreational exercise program.
10. Recognize the importance of a warm-up and cooldown as part of an aerobic workout.
11. Identify common excuses for avoiding exercise.
12. Identify methods of self-motivation to exercise.
13. Identify common sports injuries and ways to prevent them.
14. Determine intensity of an aerobic fitness activity through a variety of methods.
15. Describe recreational eating.
16. Identify common recreational foods and healthier alternatives.
17. Identify safe, effective ways to control weight.

THE FITNESS–LEISURE CONNECTION

Fitness can be significantly affected by leisure activity. Consider the following:

1. Life in general has become more sedentary, making the importance of physical activity during leisure that much greater. According to Winslow (2000, p. R4), "We may be the first broad-scale society in human history to routinely consume more calories in our daily diets than we spend." Brody (1999) cites some interesting statistics related to the increasingly sedentary nature of life.
   • In Britain, average energy expenditures have dropped by 800 calories per day over the past twenty-five years.
   • If you used 100 fewer calories per day and ate the same amount, you would gain ten pounds per year.
   • If you spent two minutes an hour of each workday sending e-mail messages to colleagues rather than walking to their offices to talk with them, you would accumulate the caloric equivalent of eleven pounds of body fat in a decade.

2. Some leisure activities such as alcohol consumption, other recreational drug use, excessive television viewing, and junk food eating binges can have an adverse effect on fitness.
3. Effective leisure planning and time management can enable more time to be devoted to fitness-related activities.
4. Diverse leisure interests and creativity may encourage greater participation in fitness-enhancing activities. Variety is a key to maintaining motivation in an exercise program.
5. Understanding the needs fulfilled by different leisure activities will lead to greater participation in fitness-promoting activities.
6. The psychological state (positive or negative) elicited by leisure activities in turn affects physical well-being.

Not only can leisure affect fitness, but fitness can also have an impact on leisure.

1. Recreational exercise can have a positive psychological effect, which may increase confidence and motivation to participate in other leisure activities.
2. The energizing effects of exercise may help a person work more efficiently, thereby creating more leisure time.
3. A high level of fitness can raise the performance and stamina levels of certain leisure activities, making them more personally satisfying.
4. The enhanced self-esteem derived from improved fitness may increase both the enjoyment and number of social leisure activities.
5. Enhanced fitness may add years to life and leisure. A healthy lifestyle is the surest way to live a long life. As evidenced by the significant drop in travel and tourism after 9/11/01, many people are concerned about their safety and have and will alter their leisure behavior in such a way as to minimize perceived danger. However, according to statistics from sources such as the Centers for Disease Control and the National Safety Council (Anonymous, 2002), the most dangerous leisure behavior is a sedentary lifestyle combined with unhealthy eating habits. This combination leads to heart disease, which is still by far the biggest danger to Americans. The odds of dying from heart disease are 1 in 388; in contrast, the odds of dying in an airplane crash

are 1 in 659,779; the odds of dying in a domestic hijacking are 1 in 16,817,784; and the odds of dying from anthrax are 1 in 55,052,999. Becoming more fit can take twenty years off of a person's chronological age (Brody, 1999).

DEFINITION OF FITNESS

There are a variety of definitions for fitness. For the purpose of this book, the term *health-related physical fitness* is being used interchangeably with the term fitness. It is defined as the ability to participate, without undue stress, in normal daily tasks and recreational activities, having a healthy body, and not being at risk for disease because of physical inactivity (Mood, Musker, and Rink, 2003).

THE FITNESS ILLUSION

Statistics cited in the second edition of this book indicated that in the 1980s and 1990s, even though the amount of money being spent on fitness was increasing, the number of people exercising was decreasing. More than 50 percent of Americans do not exercise at all during their leisure (Anonymous, 2000), and only 27.7 percent of American adults exercise moderately (Macera and Pratt, 2000). Only 20 percent of high school students participate in moderate physical activity at least five times per week (Brody, 2000). Larsen (1994) discusses how people purchase products showing models in leisurely poses, with the unconscious belief that the leisure in the picture will transfer to them. Perhaps the same is true for fitness: People purchase fitness-related merchandise and services with the belief that merely owning these goods and services (not necessarily using them) will make their bodies more fit.

Despite the low rate of participation in physical activity, Americans continue to spend a great deal of money on fitness. Almost 30 million Americans belong to some form of health club, contributing to the annual industry revenue of $10.6 billion and payroll of $4.5 billion (Kulish, 2000). Further evidence of the continued boom in the *business* of fitness is the 54 percent increase in sales of sports equipment, apparel, and footwear since 1990, estimated at $46.5 billion in

1999 (Kulish, 2000). However, 50 percent of new fitness club members quit within six months of joining (Hsu, 1999).

The contradiction between spending a great deal of money on fitness but not actually exercising much is humorous when described by comedians, but the reality of the poor fitness levels of Americans is no laughing matter. Obesity, defined as a person who is thirty pounds or more overweight, increased 49 percent between 1991 and 1998. Doctors refer to the increase in obesity as an epidemic of a chronic disease; it accounts for about $50 billion in annual medical costs (Winslow, 2000). Approximately 35 percent of American adults are overweight, and 26 percent are obese (Nash, 2002). Each year, approximately 300,000 Americans die from diseases related to inactivity (McClam, 2002).

Obesity is a worldwide problem. In Great Britain and Australia, obesity rates have tripled to approximately 21 percent since 1980. Similarly, the percentage of people overweight or obese has increased in most countries since 1980 (e.g., 60 percent of adults ages eighteen to forty-nine in Mexico are overweight or obese). However, in Japan the obesity rate has increased only slightly, to just 2.9 percent (Winslow and Landers, 2002). The Japanese diet is lower in fat than the American diet, and similar to the Chinese (whose rate of obesity is also very low), they walk and ride bicycles more than Americans do (McCord and Godbey, 1995).

The fitness of children is as worrisome as that of adults. Kolata (2002) cites research from the *New England Journal of Medicine* which indicates that many teenage girls become so sluggish in their teenage years that they barely move at all.

Clearly, as Brody (1993) writes, physical education programs in schools and colleges are more important than ever to counteract the poor state of fitness among American youth and adults. However, instead of expanding physical education in schools, programs have been cut. The percentage of high school students having daily physical education declined from 42 percent in 1991 to only 29 percent in 1999 (Rothstein, 2000). In addition to the decline in physical education in schools, children are spending more time in front of computers and television at home; walking and bicycling by children ages five to fifteen dropped 40 percent from 1977 to 1995 (Rothstein, 2000).

A problem related to watching television is that when children watch television, their metabolic rate falls even lower than it would be if they just sat still, doing nothing (Brody, 1992). The reason for the low metabolic rate is the trancelike state that watching television induces. Therefore, while watching television, children are burning up fewer calories per minute than even when doing nothing (and certainly much less than if they were playing). Clearly, although the business of fitness has been growing, the fitness of American adults and children has not been improving, due to a combination of inactivity and poor diet. However, as described in the next section, by exercising more, impressive physiological benefits can be reaped and fitness can be improved dramatically.

PHYSIOLOGICAL BENEFITS OF EXERCISE

The physiological benefits of exercise are impressive (Langreth, 2000):

1. *Cardiovascular:* Regular aerobic exercise strengthens the heart muscle, keeps blood pressure and cholesterol down, and lowers the risk of death from heart disease. In one study of 25,000 men over a twenty-year period, it was found that the least fit 5,000 men in the study had a 70 percent higher risk of death from cardiovascular disease. A study involving 73,743 women ages fifty to seventy-nine (Kolata, 2002) found that those who exercised even a moderate amount had significantly less heart disease than those who were inactive. In this study, women who walked briskly at least thirty minutes per day, five days per week had 30 percent less heart disease than women who were less active.
2. *Diabetes:* Sedentary lifestyles are a major cause of this disease. Physical activity can help prevent diabetes by lowering body-fat levels. Researchers also believe that because the skeletal muscles are used during exercise and most glucose is metabolized in these muscles, exercise increases the body's sensitivity to insulin and improves the body's ability to transport blood sugar into muscle cells.
3. *Cancer:* Exercise helps to prevent colon cancer and may also prevent breast cancer and prostate cancer.
4. *Bones and strength:* Exercise reduces the likelihood of osteoporosis and helps to prevent frailty by helping to build better bones and stronger muscles.

5. *Immune system:* Exercise strengthens the immune system. Physically fit people are less likely to suffer from common illnesses such as colds and flu.
6. *Increased life span:* On the average, for every hour spent exercising, you increase your life span by two hours.

Another way to look at the physiological benefits of exercise is to examine the diseases related to physical inactivity (Mood, Musker, and Rink, 2003). These include the following:

1. Stroke
2. Osteoporosis
3. Obesity
4. Hypertension (high blood pressure)
5. Heart disease
6. Diabetes
7. Cancer

Related to the physiological benefits of exercise are the savings in health care costs associated with physical fitness. As explained by the following, corporations are finding that it pays to provide fitness centers for their employees (Chase, 2000).

1. Medical payments for fitness center participants are 20 percent lower.
2. The rate of hospital admissions is 70 percent lower for participants.
3. There is less absenteeism among physically active workers; less absenteeism means more productivity.

PSYCHOLOGICAL BENEFITS OF EXERCISE

The psychological benefits of exercise are documented in numerous studies. For example, a study by Hansen, Stevens, and Coast (2001) found that after just ten minutes of exercise, improvements in vigor, fatigue, and total mood occurred. After twenty minutes of exercise, reduced levels of confusion were found. This study suggests that psychological benefits can be gained through a total of thirty minutes of moderate exercise daily, accumulated in short segments throughout the day.

Another study, conducted with 3,403 people in Finland (Hassmen, Koivula, and Uutela, 2000), found that those who exercised at least two to three times per week experienced significantly less depression, anger, cynical distrust, and stress than those exercising less frequently or not at all. Those who exercised also reported higher levels of coherence and stronger feelings of social integration.

Other research related to the effects of exercise on depression indicates that exercise works at least as well as a popular prescription drug in treating clinical depression and keeping the condition from reappearing (Associated Press, 2000a). In this study, patients diagnosed with clinical depression who participated in an exercise program had vastly improved symptoms and were far less likely to see their depression return after ten months, compared with people taking an antidepressant drug. In yet another study on the effects of exercise on depression (O'Neil, 2001), patients suffering from moderate or severe depression who began walking on treadmills for thirty minutes per day reported that symptoms of depression dropped by over 30 percent after ten days of exercise.

It appears that exercise can have special psychological benefits for people involved in weight-loss programs. A study by Kiernan and colleagues (2001) found that adding exercise to a comprehensive weight-loss program reduced psychological distress associated with weight-loss attempts and also provided psychological benefits. Men in this study who participated in an exercise program in addition to a diet program showed greater restraint and decreased hunger.

The psychological benefits of exercise also apply to children. In a study by Williamson, Dewey, and Steinberg (2001), one group of nine- and ten-year-old children participated in aerobic exercise for fifteen minutes, while another group watched a fifteen-minute video. The children who exercised experienced decreases in negative mood and increases in positive mood after exercise. The children who watched the video experienced positive mood decreases and negative mood increases.

Also related to the psychological benefits of exercise for youth are the results of a survey of more than 14,000 teenagers (Associated Press, 2000b) which found that those who participate in team sports are less likely to use drugs, smoke, have sex, carry weapons, or have unhealthy eating habits.

College students can also benefit from exercise. According to Toskovic (2001), participation in tae kwon do caused significant reductions in tension, depression, anger, fatigue, and confusion levels, and increased vigor. Another study on the psychological effects of exercise for young adults was conducted by Ray and colleagues (2001). This study found that participation in a program of yogic exercises led to a reduction in anxiety and better mental functioning.

Exercise 7.1 is presented to summarize the psychological benefits of exercise and to examine how to maximize these psychological benefits through participation in recreational physical activity.

In summary, the psychological benefits of exercise are impressive.

BEGINNING AND MAINTAINING A RECREATIONAL EXERCISE PROGRAM

Common Excuses for Not Exercising

The most intimidating element of an exercise program may stem from preconceived ideas of exercise. Exercise is often seen as torturous work, unenjoyable, and even painful, but recreational exercise can be incorporated into daily living to improve physical fitness.

People give many reasons to explain why they do not exercise. However, most of these reasons are merely excuses. The real reason why most people do not exercise is lack of motivation or laziness. To verify the accuracy of this statement, complete Exercise 7.2.

Looking at the responses obtained in Exercise 7.2, how common were the following statements?

1. I don't have enough time.
2. I am afraid of injuring myself.
3. I am not healthy enough to exercise.
4. I am usually too tired to exercise.
5. The weather is a problem—either too hot, too cold, or too rainy.
6. I lack facilities or partners—no one to do it with, nowhere to do it.
7. I am lazy, unmotivated to exercise.
8. I lack the skills or abilities to participate in recreational physical activities.

EXERCISE 7.1. Psychological Benefits of Exercise

Instructions

1. Look at the list of psychological benefits of exercise in the first column.
2. In the second column, list the recreational exercise activities you currently do that most effectively provide you with these benefits. In the third column, list recreational exercise activities you would like to incorporate into your life that you feel would provide you with many of the psychological benefits listed in the first column.

Psychological benefits of exercise	Current recreational exercise activities	New recreational exercise activities
Elevated mood		
Relieve depression		
Reduce stress		
Think clearer		
Less anger		
Enhanced self-esteem		
Enhanced body image		
Better-perceived health		
Greater social integration		
Greater confidence		
Less fatigue, more vigor		

EXERCISE 7.2. Excuses Given for *Not* Exercising

Instructions

1. Interview a few friends or family members who do not exercise regularly. Ask them why they do not exercise regularly.
2. In the first column, record their responses.
3. In the second column, write why you think their responses are either genuine reasons or merely excuses given to mask their laziness.

Responses   **Excuse or valid reason?**

How many of the responses seem to be valid reasons and how many seem merely to be excuses? How can you motivate your friends to exercise regularly? Probably the most effective way would be to offer to exercise with them.

Lack of time has been cited in numerous surveys over the past thirty years as the main excuse Americans give for not exercising regularly. However, as discussed in previous chapters, most Americans actually have ample time to exercise. In fact, health clubs are making it even more convenient for busy people to fit in quick workouts by setting up workout centers in areas where people would go anyway, such as Laundromats, truck stops, and airports (Villarosa, 2000). In reality, the main challenges are to be adequately motivated and to plan and organize leisure time more effectively to create more time available for recreational physical activity. In addition, some people find that *beginning* an exercise program is especially challenging. Suggestions for beginning an exercise program are offered in the next section.

How to Begin

Morehouse and Gross (1976) offer three simple steps that may help change the way exercise is perceived and get more people involved in an exercise program.

1. *Accept the importance of exercise.* Several benefits of exercise have been discussed. Once you really accept and believe these facts you are on your way.
2. *Schedule the activity in spite of all else you must do.* By scheduling exercise into your daily plan, it becomes a high priority for your life. You will find the time to exercise. There is always time for the things we really want to do in life.
3. *Work on your attitude toward exercise.* The power of positive thinking can change your attitude about exercise. With a more positive outlook, you will be able to enjoy it more and stick with your program.

Some other valuable suggestions for how to initiate involvement in an exercise program are the following:

1. *Recognize the value of nonstrenuous exercise such as walking, gardening, dancing, and other common activities.* According to Dr. Steven Blair (Leary, 1993, p. A1), "the accumulation of short bouts (of exercise) produces significant and important changes in physiologic function and health benefit." Do not be discouraged if you are out of shape and incapable of engaging in strenuous activities such as running, bicycling, or aerobics. Resolve to take at least small steps in the direction of increased activity.
2. *Dive right in!* Do not delay the start of an exercise program; begin as soon as possible. A few small steps in the right direction will create the momentum needed to perpetuate a lasting pattern of increased activity.

However, once an exercise program is started, some help may be needed to adhere to the program. Ardell and Tager (1982) offer some principles to help build commitment to a fitness program. These principles include the following:

1. *Choose exercises that are enjoyable.* The craze may be walking or snowboarding, but if you do not like to walk or snowboard then choose other activities. Try dancing or swimming—or anything else that you enjoy. As Brothers (1992, p. 4) states, "If you don't enjoy it, don't do it." The idea of exercise being unenjoyable or worklike (many people say they are going to "work out" when they are going to exercise) probably causes many people to drop out of their exercise programs after a while. Having fun is the key to lasting involvement in an activity.
2. *Involve other people, especially those who are important to you.* These people can be encouraging and make exercising more fun. Kilpatrick, Hebert, and Jacobsen (2002) suggest promoting the development of social relationships through exercise as a strategy for motivation to exercise.
3. *Establish physical fitness goals.* Share your goals with others and ask them to encourage you. Writing down goals and making a contract between you and your body can be very beneficial. Have some friends witness the contract so you will be more inclined to meet your goals (see Chapter 6 for goal-setting guidelines). A study of 221 adults ages twenty-five to fifty-five found

that signing a contract to exercise regularly significantly increased the probability of following through with exercise plans (Schafer, 1991). Also related to the idea of setting goals as a motivational tool are the suggestions to promote "process" goals (improvement, rather than specific achievements) and to set goals that are moderately difficult (Kilpatrick, Hebert, and Jacobson, 2002).

4. *Know when enough is enough.* Everyone gets sick, hurt, or feels run-down. It is necessary to rest. These periods are good for healing the body and mind—just do not quit entirely.

5. *Choose a variety of activities.* A variety of activities will help prevent burnout and give you a more well-rounded workout as well. Have primary and secondary activities. It is important to choose alternate activities (secondary) that can be done when you are not able to do your favorite activities (primary).

Katch and McArdle (1983) add two more suggestions to help maximize exercise success: (1) progress slowly—if you have not exercised in a long time, do not try to accomplish everything in the first week; and (2) wear clothes that are appropriate for the exercise you are doing. Take into consideration the weather conditions and dress accordingly. Also, be sure to have a pair of good shoes.

It is important to be aware of the risks inherent in certain physical activities and to minimize the risk of injury through preventative measures, *not* by avoiding the activities entirely. Exercise 7.3 presents an opportunity to think about ways to minimize the risks of some of the most common sports injuries.

Some of the other common sports injuries among baby boomers in the United States are wrist fractures from in-line skating, ankle strains/sprains from swimming, and ankle strains/sprains from volleyball. Identify ways to minimize the risks of injuries from your favorite physical activities that were not listed in Exercise 7.3. Doing so will enable you to enjoy *all* of your recreational activities to their fullest potential. Also, take action to help your friends and family members minimize their risks of injuries in their favorite recreational activities. Collins and Gubernick (2001) identify which sports are actually the riskiest in terms of rate of incidence of severe injuries per 1,000 participants:

1. Basketball—8.8
2. Soccer—8.6 (soccer-related head injuries are the most under-recognized risk in sports)
3. Softball—8.0
4. Bicycling—4.1 (mountain bikers tend to take too many chances)
5. In-line skating—3.4 (reducing skating speed may reduce the rate of injury)
6. Tennis—2.6 (better equipment seems to be reducing the incidence of tennis elbow)
7. Golf—1.2
8. Swimming—0.7 (one of the safest sports)
9. Exercise and running—0.5 (this category includes jogging, walking, and indoor machines)

Also related to the topic of enhancing involvement in physical activities, Middendorf (1994) offers the following suggestions for how families can incorporate fitness into their lives:

1. Choose active toys for children, such as balls, bicycles, trampolines, jump ropes, etc.
2. Walk instead of drive, or use the steps instead of the elevator.
3. Dance together as a family, even if only for a few minutes at a time.
4. Plan active family outings, such as biking, hiking, or taking a walk in the park.
5. Let children set their own goals and post a chart to keep track of their progress.
6. Reduce television viewing time, but if children are watching any television, encourage them to jump rope, dance, or do some other fun, exerting activity during commercial breaks.

Another important consideration in maximizing the success of an exercise program is to be knowledgeable about the types of exercise that are most beneficial to health fitness. The following section addresses this topic.

EXERCISE 7.3. Preventing Sports Injuries

Instructions

1. In the first column is a list of the most common sports injuries in the United States, based on statistics from the Consumer Product Safety Commission and the American Academy of Orthopaedic Surgeons (Rundle, 2000). In parentheses next to each injury are the numbers of medically treated injuries in 1998 among baby boomers (people born 1946 to 1964).
2. In the second column, identify strategies for minimizing the risks of these injuries. As an example, some ideas for minimizing the risks of shoulder dislocations while bicycling are listed. (*Note:* Wearing a helmet when bicycling is advisable, but it will not help to prevent a shoulder dislocation.)

Most common sports injuries	Strategies for preventing these injuries
Bicycling: Shoulder dislocations (201,140)	1. Ride slower. 2. Avoid riding in traffic. 3. Avoid mountain-biking trails with steep declines and severe obstacles. 4. Make sure your brakes work well. 5. Lower the seat a little and perhaps use a woman's-style bicycle to prevent falling off the bicycle due to sudden stops (because there is no bar in the way you can put your feet down more easily).
Basketball: Ankle strains/sprains (116,144)	_____ _____ _____ _____ _____ _____
Skiing: Knee strains/sprains (105,220) (Shoulder sprains/strains from snowboarding totaled 10,020)	_____ _____ _____ _____ _____

Softball: Facial lacerations (76,330);
Baseball: Facial lacerations (51,570)

_____
_____
_____
_____
_____

Weight lifting: Lower trunk
sprains/strains (46,720)

_____
_____
_____
_____
_____

Football: Finger fractures (40,820)

_____
_____
_____
_____
_____

Golf: Lower trunk strains/sprains
(40,460)

_____
_____
_____
_____
_____

Soccer: Knee strains/sprains (36,820)

_____
_____
_____
_____

THE COMPONENTS OF HEALTH-RELATED PHYSICAL FITNESS

Health-related physical fitness has three primary components (Mood, Musker, and Rink, 2003):

1. Aerobic (cardiorespiratory) capacity/fitness;
2. Body composition; and
3. Musculoskeletal development (muscular strength, endurance, and flexibility).

Aerobic Capacity

Aerobic capacity is probably the most important component of physical fitness because of the extensive research linking aerobic capacity with various health factors. For example, research studies indicate that improving aerobic fitness can lower the risk of heart disease. In addition, people who are aerobically fit are less likely to have a stroke, be overweight, develop diabetes, have high blood pressure, or develop certain cancers (Mood, Musker, and Rink, 2003). Aerobic fitness is related to the frequency, intensity, duration, and type of physical activity engaged in. Therefore, aerobic capacity can be increased or improved by increasing the frequency, intensity, and/or duration of aerobic exercise (Mood, Musker, and Rink, 2003).

Body Composition

Body composition has two components: body-fat weight and lean body weight (or fat-free weight). Body-fat weight is the total of the body's fat (both essential and nonessential adipose tissue); lean body weight is the muscle, bone, skin, water, and organs of the body. According to Mood, Musker, and Rink (2003), increased weight is associated with diseases such as high blood pressure, diabetes, heart disease, stroke, gallbladder disease, osteoarthritis, and sleep apnea. However, overweight persons who are physically fit are at a lower risk for developing these diseases. Also, if a person has a high weight but the weight is mostly lean tissue, then the health risks are not as great as if the weight were from a higher percentage of fat. In addition, those whose weight is stored at the waist have a greater risk of disease than those whose body fat is stored in the hips or throughout the body.

Musculoskeletal Development/Fitness

Musculoskeletal development/fitness is actually composed of three factors: muscular strength, muscular endurance, and flexibility. Many tasks, whether work or leisure, require muscular strength (e.g., moving, lifting, or holding weight). "Muscular strength is the ability or capacity of a muscle or muscle group for exerting force against resistance" (Bucher and Prentice, 1985, p. 10).

In the same way that cardiovascular endurance exercises condition the heart muscle, muscular endurance exercises benefit local skeletal muscles. "Muscular endurance is the ability of muscles to repeat or sustain a muscle contraction" (Bucher and Prentice, 1985, p. 11).

Flexibility permits the body to move freely. Flexibility improves and maintains range of motion in a joint or group of joints (American College of Sports Medicine [ACSM], 1986).

All of these components of musculoskeletal development are important for obtaining the benefits of physical fitness activities. However, it is difficult to be highly skilled in all of these areas. A person may be muscularly strong but not very flexible, or someone may have muscular endurance but not much muscular strength. One way to include most of the components of musculoskeletal fitness in an exercise regimen is through incorporating aerobic activities into the regimen. Guidelines for aerobic fitness are discussed in detail in the next section.

THE TOTAL WORKOUT
FOR AEROBIC FITNESS

As previously discussed, the aerobic workout is one of the most efficient methods of obtaining many of the benefits of physical fitness. Every workout should consist of three parts: the warm-up, the aerobic phase, and the cooldown.

Warm-Up

The warm-up should consist of ten to fifteen minutes of flexibility and general calisthenics exercises (Mood, Musker, and Rink, 2003).

Exercises that stretch and warm the muscles (flexibility exercises) can be done during this phase of the workout. It is important to gradually increase the heart rate and prepare the body for the aerobic phase. Doing the aerobic activity at a lower intensity is often helpful in the warm-up phase. For example, if the aerobic activity is running, then it would be helpful to do some light jogging during the warm-up to prepare the body for running.

The Aerobic Phase

The guidelines for activities for developing and maintaining aerobic fitness are listed as follows (Mood, Musker, and Rink, 2003):

1. *Frequency:* Three to five days per week.
2. *Intensity:* 60 percent to 90 percent of approximate maximum heart rate or 45 percent to 85 percent of maximal oxygen consumption (VO_2 max). Measuring the intensity of exercise is discussed later in the chapter.
3. *Duration:* Twenty to sixty minutes of continuous aerobic activity. The amount of time depends upon the intensity of the activity. Lower-intensity exercise requires a longer duration of participation to attain a health benefit; the greater the intensity of the exercise, the shorter the duration can be to achieve a health benefit.
4. *Type of activity:* Any activity that uses large muscle groups (arms, legs, trunk), is aerobic in nature, and can be maintained continuously.

The Cooldown

The cooldown phase helps the body cool and return to its resting state. It can be viewed as the reverse of the warm-up. The cooldown should consist of ten to fifteen minutes of flexibility activities (Mood, Musker, and Rink, 2003). It is essential that the body be able to cool down. Try to avoid stopping exercise suddenly. A severe and dangerous drop in blood pressure may result. The drop in heart rate should take place gradually.

Exercise 7.4 is presented for you to take an inventory of your current aerobic exercise habits.

EXERCISE 7.4. Inventory of Current Aerobic Exercise Habits

Instructions

1. List the recreational aerobic fitness activities you do regularly in the first column.
2. In the second column, identify how *frequently* you participate in each activity.
3. In the third column, estimate the *intensity* (percentage of maximum heart rate) of each activity. The best way to estimate the intensity is to measure your heart rate during the activity by checking your pulse for six seconds, multiplying the figure by ten, and recording the result in this column. Alternatively, you can estimate the intensity of the activity as being high (e.g., running fast), medium, or low (e.g., walking at a moderate speed); use additional descriptors as appropriate (e.g., very high, moderately high, etc.).
4. In the fourth column, estimate the *duration* of the activity in terms of the length of time of continuous aerobic exertion during the activity.
5. In the last column, identify desired changes in each activity (e.g., increase the frequency, decrease the intensity, decrease the duration, etc.)

Current activities	Frequency	Intensity	Duration	Desired changes

MEASURING INTENSITY OF EXERCISE

When beginning an exercise program, it is important to know how hard you are exercising so you can safely and gradually progress with your program. There are three ways to measure the intensity of exercise: perceived exertion, maximal oxygen consumption (VO_2 max), and heart rate.

Without being actively aware of it, many people may use the first method, perceived exertion. These people stop exercising when they feel tired and may do well without taking heart rate or other measurements.

The second method, maximal oxygen consumption, or VO_2 max, is the amount of oxygen utilized by the body during maximum exercise. Unfortunately, the equipment used to measure VO_2 max is expensive and not readily available to the general population.

The third method measures heart rate. While exercising, the heart must pump oxygenated blood to the working muscles. As the workload increases, so does heart rate. Heart rate is related to VO_2 max, since the maximums of both are achieved at about the same time. Therefore, heart rate can be used as a relative indicator of exercise intensity. One of the key elements of using heart rate as an indicator of exercise intensity is *maximum heart rate*. As discussed in this section, the commonly used formula for maximum heart rate, used by many fitness specialists and cited in many textbooks, is somewhat inaccurate. Even the newer, more complicated formula for maximum heart rate is probably not totally accurate. Yet it is useful to utilize the concept of maximum heart rate in determining exercise intensity while recognizing its flaws. The basic concept remains the same. The goal in aerobic fitness activities is to significantly elevate the heart rate for a continuous period of time, while being careful not to raise the heart rate too much (beyond a theoretical maximum point).

Follow these steps in utilizing heart rate as an indicator of exercise intensity:

1. *Calculate your maximum heart rate:* The most widely used formula is

    Maximum heart rate = 220 minus your age.

Therefore, if you are twenty years old, your maximum heart rate would be 200 (220 − 20 = 200). If you are eighty years old, your maximum heart rate would be 140 (220 − 80 = 140). However, this formula is being challenged. According to Kolata (2001), this formula was devised in 1970 and was based on data that had limitations. In reality, maximum heart rates could deviate a great deal from the formula. Nevertheless, the formula became widely accepted.

According to an alternative formula for calculating maximum heart rate,

Maximum heart rate = 208 minus 0.7 times age.

Using this formula, if you are twenty years old, your maximum heart rate would be 194 (compared to 200 in the commonly used formula). If you are eighty years old, your maximum heart rate would be 152 (versus 140 in the other formula). In the alternative formula, maximum heart rates for people under forty are lower than they are in the widely used formula; after age forty, the maximum heart rates in the alternative formula become increasingly greater than those obtained in the widely used formula.

The alternative formula, although it is a bit more complicated, seems to make more sense. For example, according to the widely accepted formula, the maximum heart rate for an unfit twenty-year-old would be 200, and for a very fit sixty-year-old, it would be 160. Meanwhile, if the alternative formula is used, the maximum heart rate for the unfit twenty-year-old would be 194, and for the very fit sixty-year-old, it would be 166. Still, it might not be accurate to predict that the maximum heart rate of an unfit twenty-year-old would be so much greater than that of a very fit sixty-year-old, but at least the gap is smaller when using the alternative formula.

Therefore, according to some cardiologists (Kolata, 2001), it is not maximum heart rates that should be the primary concern, but rather how quickly the heart rate falls when exercise is stopped. As a guideline, an average healthy person's heart rate drops twenty beats in a minute, while those of athletes can drop by as much as fifty beats in a minute. Meanwhile, in three research studies, people whose heart rates fell less than twelve beats within a minute after vigorous exercise was stopped had a fourfold increased risk of dying within six years as compared to those whose heart rates fell by thirteen or more beats.

In conclusion, heart rates should be considered in determining intensity of exercise, but it is *not* advisable to simply use the 220 minus your age formula for maximum heart rate as the guideline. Using this formula can cause some people to dangerously push themselves beyond a safe level of intensity, while it can cause other people (especially older adults who are fit) to hold back too much and not engage in enough exercise to either maintain or improve their fitness levels. Use the alternative formula (208 minus 0.7 times age) instead, but even this one should not be used as the only means of determining intensity of exercise based on heart rate. The rate of decrease in heart rate after exercise is stopped should also be considered. Most important, perceived exertion should be considered. Slow down even if you are well below your theoretical maximum heart rate but perceived exertion is high. Conversely, it might be okay to exercise beyond the theoretical 90 percent of maximum heart rate if your perceived exertion is very low and other factors, such as the rate of decrease in heart rate after stopping exercise, indicate that your level of cardiorespiratory fitness is high.

2. *Find your resting heart rate:* Find your pulse and count how many beats there are for six seconds, then multiply this number by ten. An average resting heart rate is sixty to eighty beats per minute. An athletic person in excellent condition might have a resting heart rate as low as forty beats per minute. A slower resting heart rate means there is less wear and tear on the heart because it does not need to work as hard. It also means that the heart is likely to last longer.

3. *Calculate your heart rate during the activity:* Calculate your heart rate during the activity just as you calculated your resting heart rate. Compare this heart rate to your resting heart rate to see how effective the activity is in elevating your heart rate. Also compare this heart rate to your maximum heart rate and see to what percentage of maximum heart rate this activity brings you. For example, if your heart rate during the activity was 152 and

your approximate maximum heart rate is 190, then you exercised at 80 percent of your (theoretical) maximum heart rate.

4. *Try to exercise at an appropriate level of intensity (heart rate):* The appropriate level of intensity for exercise depends on your fitness level and your fitness goals. At the minimum, activity for aerobic fitness should elevate your heart rate to 60 percent of its (theoretical) maximum heart rate. The following guidelines for percentage of maximum heart rate at which to exercise are widely accepted:

60 percent—If you are unfit and are just beginning an exercise program, set your target heart rate for aerobic exercise to this level.

70 percent—If you have been exercising for a while and have improved a bit beyond the unfit category, exercising at this level should help you to improve to the next level of fitness.

80 percent—If you are relatively fit and wish to maintain and/or improve your fitness level, exercising at this level of intensity would be appropriate.

90 percent—If you are very fit and wish to continue to improve your fitness, then exercise at this level of intensity.

Monitor your heart rate periodically during an activity. Check your pulse after just a few minutes of the activity. If you are below your target heart rate, try to work harder; if you are above your target heart rate, slow down. However, regardless of heart rate, discontinue exercise if you feel sick, tired, short of breath, dizzy, overheated, or exhausted.

Even at the lowest levels of intensity, aerobic fitness activities raise the heart rate significantly. For example, at the 60 percent level of intensity, a person with an approximate maximum heart rate of 190 should be maintaining a heart rate of 114 during the aerobic activity. If the resting heart rate were 64, that would be an increase of 50 beats per minute. Individuals vary greatly. Some would have to work very hard to get up to a heart rate of 114, while others will elevate their heart rates significantly through less-intense exercise. It is important to monitor heart rates and perceived exertion to be sure not to overdo it and hurt yourself.

EXAMINING THE AEROBIC POTENTIAL
OF RECREATIONAL ACTIVITIES

Previously in the chapter, the following characteristics of aerobic activities were identified:

1. They should raise your heart rate to approximately 60 percent to 90 percent of your approximate maximum heart rate.
2. The activity should be continuous in nature. For example, riding an exercise bicycle at a steady pace so that your heart rate is elevated to 70 percent of maximum heart rate throughout the session would be an aerobic activity. However, riding a bicycle in traffic, raising your heart rate to 80 percent of maximum heart rate for no more than one or two minutes at a time and making frequent stops would *not* be an aerobic activity.
3. The duration of the activity should be twenty to sixty minutes (at a lower intensity, a longer duration is required to attain an aerobic benefit).

Using these criteria, the following activities can be classified as having high potential for promoting aerobic fitness:

• Treadmill/stair climber
• Swimming (lap swimming)
• Jogging/running
• Exercise bicycle
• Power (fast) walking
• Aerobic dancing
• Jumping rope
• Rowing
• Ultimate Frisbee (with minor rule changes)
• Roller-skating and in-line skating
• Cross-country skiing

The problem with most (but not all) highly aerobic activities is that many people find them to be boring because they are repetitive. On the other hand, most sports and recreational activities people enjoy would probably be categorized as having only moderate potential for aerobic fitness because of the stop-and-go nature of the activities. For example, the following sports would be in this category:

- Basketball
- Calisthenics
- Downhill skiing
- Field hockey
- Racquetball
- Soccer
- Lacrosse
- Tennis

Many benefits can still be achieved through stop-and-go activities, although it may require some skill and take more time. If a person playing tennis has ample tennis skills and can rally the ball for long periods, then two hours of tennis may be as beneficial or more beneficial than jogging for twenty minutes. The key is how the game is played. Certainly, singles is much more of a workout than doubles. Drills involving cross-court and up-and-back running, as well as utilizing a bucket of balls to eliminate having to stop to gather balls, could result in much more of an aerobic workout than playing a match. In fact, the drills might more appropriately be categorized in the "high aerobic potential" group. Similarly, modifications can be made in any of the activities on the "moderate aerobic potential" list to transform them into "high aerobic potential" activities.

Other sports and recreational activities are more appropriately categorized as having low potential for aerobic fitness. Examples of sports in this category are the following:

- Baseball
- Bowling
- Football
- Golf
- Softball
- Volleyball

Some students dispute the categorization of activities as having high, moderate, or low potential for aerobic fitness that is presented in this chapter. For example, many football players claim that football is a very exerting game and has either moderate or high potential for aerobic fitness. However, a game such as football tends to elevate the heart rate only for short periods at a time, with long rest periods between these short periods of intense activity.

Another indicator of the intensity of an activity is the rate of calorie expenditure per hour. As shown in Table 7.1, the activities in the high aerobic potential category are also the ones that expend the most calories per hour. Aerobic fitness and body composition are interrelated. The balance between calories expended and calories consumed affects body composition. Obviously, calories are expended at a faster rate in the activities that are more aerobic. It is not surprising that running at 10 mph burns calories at more than three times the rate of tennis. However, two hours of tennis singles will burn more calories than a half-hour run. In leisure, enjoyment is more important than efficiency. An enjoyable two-hour tennis match is preferable to a half-hour run that you find to be tedious. Hopefully those who choose run-

TABLE 7.1. Rate of Calorie Expenditure per Hour of Various Activities

Activity	Calories expended per hour
Running at 10 mph	1,280
Jogging at 7 mph	920
Jumping rope	750
Jogging at 5.54 mph	740
Cross-country skiing	700
Running in place	650
Swimming at 50 yard/minute	500
Walking at 4.5 mph	440
Bicycling at 12 mph	410
Tennis (singles)	400
Walking at 3 mph	320
Bicycling at 6 mph	240
Walking at 2 mph	240

Source: Based on data from the National Health, Lung, and Blood Institute (Mood, Musker, and Rink, 2003).

ning over tennis are doing so because they enjoy it more, not simply because it is a more efficient workout.

In summary, many of the most popular, enjoyable sports, because of the stop-and-go nature of the activity, have only low or moderate potential for aerobic fitness and also expend calories at a much slower rate than high aerobic potential activities such as running.

Being mindful that a key to adhering to an exercise program is having fun, it is important to find aerobic activities that are enjoyable. You might consider ways to adapt fun but not necessarily aerobic activities to be more aerobic, as well as to adapt aerobic but less inherently fun activities to be more enjoyable. A related consideration is to try to find exercise activities that have the right level of challenge in order to produce "flowlike" experiences. Some research studies (Stedman, 1999) indicate that the experience of flow (discussed in detail in Chapter 5) is a key factor in motivating people to adhere to their exercise regimens. New activities that combine fun, flow, and aerobic exercise are gaining popularity, such as circus acrobatics classes (Hendrie, 2000). The next section of the chapter presents some ideas for engaging in exercise that maximizes fun and enjoyment as well as the potential for aerobic fitness.

CREATING FUN, HIGHLY AEROBIC RECREATIONAL ACTIVITIES

Ultimate Frisbee

Ultimate Frisbee was listed in the category of activities with high potential for aerobic fitness, with the qualifier "with minor rule changes." Ultimate Frisbee is a fast-paced game in which two teams of seven players each are trying to score points by catching the Frisbee in their "end zone." Players cannot run with the Frisbee and must throw it within ten seconds after catching it. The following rule changes would enhance the aerobic potential of this game:

1. After a team scores, the other team immediately takes the Frisbee from the scoring team's end zone and starts advancing the Frisbee toward their own goal line. In the official rules, after a score, the two teams line up and the team that just scored "throws off" the Frisbee to the other team, similar to the kickoff

after a touchdown in football. Eliminating the throwoff makes the action more continuous.

2. Playing on a bigger field can create more opportunity for continuous running.

3. Playing with fewer players (four, five, or six per team) can cause each player to be more actively involved, have more fun, and get a better aerobic workout.

4. If enough players are not available to play Ultimate Frisbee, a fun, aerobic alternative is "Box Frisbee." This game can be played with as few as two players per team. Points are scored by catching the Frisbee in a "box" that is marked off in the middle of the playing area. The size of the box depends on the number of players involved and their skill levels. The idea is to make it challenging, but not too challenging, to score points. The rest of the rules of this game are similar to those of Ultimate Frisbee.

Ultimate Basketball

Basketball was listed as an activity with moderate potential for aerobic fitness. "Ultimate Basketball" is a version of basketball that involves more continuous action and actually requires less skill to play. It is played similarly to full-court basketball, with the following differences:

1. There is no dribbling in this game.

2. There are no boundaries.

3. Like Ultimate Frisbee, you cannot run with the ball and must pass it to a teammate within ten seconds.

4. If the ball touches the ground, possession goes to the other team.

5. The game can be played with a regular basketball or with softer, lighter balls.

6. The game can be played with five players per team like regular basketball, but depending on the size of the playing area, the number of players can be increased or decreased.

7. Points are scored the same way as in regular basketball. However, to encourage the involvement of all players in the game, the offensive team can be awarded an extra point for a basket scored during a possession in which all members of their team passed the ball. To discourage fouls and rough play, the basket made after a foul can be awarded an extra point.

Hand Tennis

Hand tennis requires less skill than regular tennis. It is also more aerobic, can be more fun for beginning tennis players, and help to develop skills important in tennis. The game is played on a regulation tennis court with a large, bouncy playground ball. Throwing the ball so that it lands inside the boundaries and your opponent cannot catch the ball before it bounces twice scores points. Some suggested rules include the following:

1. The ball must be thrown underhand.
2. Players must throw the ball immediately from the spot where it was caught.
3. It is permissible to catch the ball on a fly.
4. There is no serving in this game. There are no breaks between points. Play is continuous until one player wins by reaching twenty-one points (or a different point total) first. Alternatively, the player with the most points at the end of a specified time period (e.g., twenty minutes) can be declared the winner.

Aerobic Softball

Many students find this game strange at first but actually more enjoyable than regular softball. Try playing the game with soft, mushy balls to minimize the risk of injury. Weak hitters should be allowed to hit "enhanced flight" balls to make it easier for them to reach base safely. This game is an excellent alternative to boring team practice sessions in which one player hits balls and the fielders wait around for their turn to catch and throw the ball. The game works best with twelve players, the typical size of a recreational softball team that has a few extra reserve players on their roster. It can also be played with as many as eighteen players on a wider field with an extra base, or with as few as six players on half a field with just two bases. The suggested rules for the game are as follows:

1. There are always two teams on the field, with one team at bat.
2. The object of the game is to score as many runs as possible within a given time period. The team that scores the most runs wins.

3. The batting team supplies the pitcher, who tries to throw easy pitches to hit. Alternatively, a batting tee can be used. If after three pitches the batter is unable to put the ball into play, the next batter comes to the plate. If a person is due up to bat but he or she is still on base, a teammate should "pinch run" for that player so he or she can bat.

4. Play is continuous. As soon as one play is over, the pitcher and next batter should be ready to put the ball into play. It is advisable to have extra balls available to enable a continuous flow of play, especially when an errant foul ball is being retrieved.

5. Begin with a warm-up round in which each team has five minutes at bat. In the next round, have each team bat for at least twenty minutes, so that the batting team can have an opportunity to raise their heart rates enough to obtain an aerobic workout.

When this game is played well, it is both fun and aerobic. Members of the batting team are constantly moving, either batting, running the bases, pitching to teammates, or going from one role to another. The fielders also move around more than they would in an ordinary game, because play is continuous.

Game Summary

All of the games described in this section are designed to be both aerobic and fun. The following principles are involved in devising all of these games:

1. Modify the rules to minimize breaks in the action and make play as continuous as possible.
2. Modify the boundaries and number of players involved to maximize the opportunity to run freely without risk of injury.
3. Competition is involved to motivate players to try their best, thereby maximizing the aerobic potential of the activity and its enjoyment.
4. Equipment can be modified to maximize success and reduce the risk of injury.

Exercise 7.5 presents an opportunity to apply these principles to devise a game that would be both aerobic and fun for you. In addition to modifying sports and games to be more aerobic, it is also possible

EXERCISE 7.5. Devising a Fun, Aerobic Game

Instructions

1. Select any two activities (except softball, tennis, or basketball) from the lists of low and moderate aerobic potential activities.
2. Explain how you would modify each one to make it a fun, highly aerobic activity.
3. Try to devise a third, original game that would be both fun and highly aerobic.

Activity	Explanation of rules, modifications, variations
1. _____	_____
	_____
	_____
	_____
	_____
	_____
	_____
2. _____	_____
	_____
	_____
	_____
	_____
	_____
	_____
3. _____	_____
	_____
	_____
	_____
	_____
	_____
	_____

to try to make highly aerobic activities more enjoyable. Exercise 7.6 presents an opportunity to explore this concept further.

In summary, it is important to have fun during all leisure activities. Highly aerobic activities are the most important leisure activities in terms of promoting maximal health-related fitness. The typical highly aerobic activities tend not to be fun for many people, and the more enjoyable, fun sports tend not to be highly aerobic. However, this section of the chapter presented ideas for participating in recreational activities that are both fun and highly aerobic.

It should also be noted that anaerobic exercises, such as sprinting, are also beneficial because they enable the body to do short bursts of exercise. However, aerobic exercise is necessary for cardiorespiratory fitness, since anaerobic exercise cannot satisfy this need.

NUTRITION AND FITNESS

This section of the chapter could not possibly include all the information available about proper nutrition for a healthy lifestyle, but it does offer information regarding the interrelationships of recreational eating, weight control, health-related fitness, and leisure.

Recreational Eating

It appears that many Americans are not eating healthfully, and there are several reasons. One is that people are not eating for purely nutritional purposes but for recreation as well. Eating can be a leisure activity and is an ingrained element of daily living. Consider the following examples:

- Eating popcorn and candy at the movies
- Cooking hotdogs over a fire at the beach
- Munching on chips and dip and drinking alcoholic beverages at a party
- Stopping off at a fast food restaurant for a hamburger, fries, and milkshake
- Drinking soda and eating chips while watching television
- Indulging in cake and ice cream at a birthday party
- Devouring beer and pretzels during a football game
- Going out for pizza after a dance or softball game
- Going out for dinner on a date

EXERCISE 7.6. Making Aerobic Activities More Fun

Instructions

1. Select any two activities from the list of high aerobic potential activities.
2. For each one, list ideas for making the activity fun.
3. First, try to add more ideas to the list of suggestions below for making running more fun and enjoyable.

Activity	Ideas for making the activity more fun and enjoyable
1. Running	a. Join a running club and run with a group of people.
	b. Run in competitive races and charity events.
	c. Get a part-time job as a "dog runner." Earning money while running will make it more enjoyable.
	d. Try to run in the park or other pretty areas.
	e. Get a really good pair of running shoes so I'll feel better while running as well as after the run.

2. _____

3. _____

These are just a few examples of the kinds of eating that can be recreational. Eating is done in leisure environments (e.g., camping), as part of a leisure experience (e.g., snacks at a party), or as a whole leisure experience in itself (e.g., going out to dinner).

Eating has become more than just satisfying a need for survival. During humankind's early existence, most of the day and night were spent searching for food. Eating was a means of survival. Today, motivation for eating is not that clear-cut. One of the influences on recreational eating choices is advertising. The $1.5 billion spent by the five leading fast-food chains on promoting their products in 2001 (Vranica, 2002) surely had at least some impact on eating patterns of Americans. Studies show that approximately 40 percent of a family's food budget goes toward meals eaten outside the home, often at fast-food restaurants such as McDonald's (Winslow, 2000). In addition to the advertising of fast-food chains enticing people to consume excess calories, the 12,000 new foods introduced each year, many of them snack foods, also create more options that lead to excessive consumption (Winslow, 2000).

As a result, on the average, men consume 216 more calories per day and women consume 112 more calories per day than they did in the late 1970s. The implications of the increased calorie consumption are troubling. A man weighing 175 pounds who consumes an extra 216 calories per day and does not increase his exercise would gain about 22 pounds in one year (Winslow, 2000).

Going to the grocery store or to a restaurant can provide food needed for survival, but how much of it is needed for survival and how much is simply recreational? Imagine eating as a continuum (see Figure 7.1), with eating for survival on one end and recreational eating on the other. As illustrated in Figure 7.1, some eating is done solely for necessity/survival and some is purely recreational, but a wide range of eating is a combination of the two. The midpoint on the

FIGURE 7.1. Eating Continuum

continuum represents eating that is an equal mixture of the two (e.g., you have not eaten all day and go out with friends for a good meal).

A problem arises because many of the recreational foods are not high in nutritional value. Sugar, salt, and fat are some of the major ingredients in common recreational foods. For example, consider the health implications of the routine purchase of popcorn at the movies. According to Hannon and colleagues (1994), seven out of ten theaters pop their corn in coconut oil, the kind that raises cholesterol and is high in saturated fat. A medium bucket of popcorn has 901 calories and 43 grams of fat.

According to Professor Cindy Wolff, Coordinator of the Nutrition and Food Sciences Program at Chico State, and Director of OPT for Fit Kids (C. Wolff, personal communication),

> Fast foods tend to be high in fat, particularly saturated and trans fatty acids, the most health damaging types of fatty acids. "Portion distortion" is the norm in that portion sizes have steadily increased since the 1970s such that the average soda served at a fast food restaurant now is 24 ounces versus the 12 ounce serving size common 25 years ago. As a result, calorie content has zoomed. The average "value plus" fast food meal provides a whopping 1200 calories, more than half the calories the average consumer needs for one day.

Related to "portion distortion" are statistics on the steadily increasing calories of a serving of McDonald's french fries (Kakutani, 2003): 200 calories in 1960; 320 in the late 1970s; 450 calories in the mid-1990s; 540 calories in the late 1990s; and 610 calories in 2003. According to published nutritional information on popular fast foods (C. Wolff, personal communication), a typical burger and fries meal has 55 to 65 grams of fat and about 1200 calories. Topping off that meal with a 3.7-ounce Snickers bar adds 24 grams of fat and 510 calories. An eight-ounce ice cream at Baskin-Robbins would add 34 grams of fat and 540 calories, whereas seven ounces of 96 percent fat-free frozen yogurt would have only six grams of fat and 265 calories (fat-free yogurt would be even better).

A Note on Cholesterol

Cholesterol levels are important because of the implications for heart disease. High-density lipoprotein (HDL) is known as the "good" cholesterol, while low-density lipoprotein (LDL) is considered to be the "bad" cholesterol, the one associated with heart disease and arteriosclerosis. The ratio of HDL can be raised through regular participation in an exercise program, and LDL can be lowered through changes in diet. Clearly, exercise and eating habits are interrelated in attempting to prevent heart disease.

Breaking Old Eating Habits

Of course, not all recreational eating consists of junk food, and many Americans are becoming more health conscious. However, unhealthy eating can become habitual and can take place unconsciously—grabbing a soda or beer from the refrigerator and eating popcorn whenever sitting in front of the television, and so on.

Katch and McArdle (1983) offer an approach to breaking old eating habits. They believe that old behavior patterns can be replaced with new, healthier ones.

Established Eating Behavior	*Replacement Behavior*
Eat candy while driving	Sing while driving
Eat junk food daily at 3:00 p.m.	Exercise daily at 3:00 p.m.

To help modify your recreational eating, answer the following questions (adapted from Katch and McArdle, 1983):

- Where do you do most of your recreational eating?
- What kind of mood are you in? What kinds of feelings do you have?
- What kinds of activities are you doing when you are eating recreationally?

The answers to these questions and to Exercise 7.7 might help you replace your current recreational eating habits with healthier alternatives.

EXERCISE 7.7. Healthy Alternatives to Recreational Eating

Instructions

1. List some of your current recreational eating patterns.
2. Identify some alternative things to do or alternative foods to eat and list those in the healthier alternatives column. Try to make these healthier alternatives realistic, attractive, and related to the situation in which the recreational eating occurs.

Current recreational eating   **Healthier alternative**

_____   _____

_____   _____

_____   _____

_____   _____

_____   _____

_____   _____

_____   _____

_____   _____

_____   _____

_____   _____

_____   _____

_____   _____

_____   _____

_____   _____

_____   _____

_____   _____

_____   _____

_____   _____

_____   _____

_____   _____

_____   _____

The following is a list of a few tips for avoiding unhealthy recreational eating:

1. *Keep a gallon of cold water in your refrigerator.* The cold, clean water will always be available and will be the first thing you see when you open the door. Nationwide, consumption of soda has been increasing greatly, especially among youth. According to McAllister (2002), teens are consuming three times as much and children aged six to eleven twice as much soda as they did in 1979. It is important to reduce consumption of soda because of its negative effects on health-related fitness. McAllister (2002) cites studies indicating that overconsumption of sodas, especially colas, can cause osteoporosis in teens, leading to more broken bones and fractures; increase in cavities; and obesity, because soda drinkers consume an average of 200 calories more each day. It seems that even those who drink diet sodas are prone to gaining weight because of the wishful thinking that you can eat anything you want if you are drinking a diet drink. Some evidence also suggests that the artificial sweeteners in diet sodas stimulate hunger, making people more likely to snack.

2. *Eat before going to a party.* Doing so will help you avoid some of the tempting foods there.

3. *Ask for water or fruit juice instead of alcohol or soda at the next party you go to.* More people are also becoming aware of the dangers of drinking and driving and will gladly provide you with nonalcoholic drinks.

4. *Bring fruit or vegetables when you go to a potluck dinner.* Try skewering them as a kabob. Also, keep ready-to-eat fruits and vegetables in your house as a readily available snack, and take them along with you to school or work so that you have a readily available healthy snack that will keep you away from junk food.

5. *Watch less television.* Women who watch television more than four hours per day were found to snack more, exercise less, and be twice as likely to be obese as those watching less than an hour per day (Anonymous, 1991). Other studies have found similar results among men and children.

6. *Use salsa as a dip, instead of the usual fattening dips.* Most salsas are fat-free, low in calories, and tasty. Although fat-free versions of most fattening dips are available, people often com-

plain about their taste. Try to also substitute vegetables for chips, or have a combination of chips and vegetables instead of just chips.

7. *Try air-popped popcorn and pretzels as your salty snack of choice.* Although you still have to be careful not to consume excessive sodium, these snacks have little or no fat, compared to high-fat salty snacks such as chips or nuts.

8. *Carefully choose low-fat or nonfat versions of favorite snacks.* Some of these supposedly healthier versions of favorite snacks actually have almost as many calories as the regular version. Others should be avoided because of harmful ingredients added or poor taste. Is it really worth eating something that might cause you to have diarrhea? On the other hand, if you like the taste of low-fat or nonfat ice cream, substituting it for regular ice cream can be a great way to significantly reduce consumption of fat, cholesterol, and calories.

9. *Avoid alcohol.* As explained in the next section, it is unhealthy for a variety of reasons.

Recreational Alcohol Consumption

Although it is widely recognized that heavy drinking is harmful, it is widely believed that light or moderate consumption of alcohol is healthy. However, consumption of alcohol has *not* been proven to be healthy. Research indicating that light and moderate drinkers have a lower death rate from heart disease is *correlational,* not experimental, in nature. Contrary to numerous articles in the popular media on this subject, the consumption of alcoholic beverages is not healthy.

Much publicity has been given to studies which indicate that the French, despite consuming a great deal of fat, have less than half the death rate from heart disease of Americans, apparently because of their consumption of wine, red wine in particular (Brownlee and Barnett, 1994). These studies should *not* be interpreted to mean that a good way to reduce heart disease is to drink wine for several reasons.

1. Many extraneous variables could be the cause of the lower rate of cardiovascular disease among the French, not the consumption of wine. For example, perhaps the French lead less stressful lives, do not rush their meals as much as Americans do, and take

more time for leisure. In fact, while Americans work forty hours per week and receive twelve days of paid vacation, French workers by law work thirty-nine hours per week and receive 25.5 days of annual vacation (Kinsley, 1990). Therefore, it is possible that it is *not* the alcohol that causes the French to have less heart disease but rather their orientation to leisure that is the cause.

2. Other studies have shown that even among Americans, light and moderate drinkers have a lower rate of heart disease than either heavy drinkers or abstainers. Obviously, heavy drinking is harmful. However, why would light and moderate drinkers have a lower rate of heart disease than abstainers, if the alcohol itself was not healthy? Perhaps light and moderate drinkers are more relaxed individuals (on the average). Or perhaps it is the variable of self-discipline that is the key factor. Light and moderate drinkers obviously have good self-control if they are able to avoid the trap of excessive consumption. Such strong self-control might typify a more healthy personality.

3. Research on Mormons contradicts the findings that show light to moderate consumption of alcohol to be related to lower rates of heart disease. Mormons totally abstain from alcohol, yet research indicates that Mormon men have only 14 percent of the death rate from cardiovascular disease as American males in general, and a twenty-two-year-old Mormon male can expect to live eleven years longer than the typical American male (Schafer, 1990). How could such findings be possible if alcohol consumption was really as healthy as correlational studies imply?

4. Regular exercise and good eating habits are better ways to reduce the risk of heart disease than is drinking wine. The research on the physiological benefits of exercise is much more extensive and convincing than is the research on the effects of drinking wine on heart disease. A serious problem is that some people will not exercise, thinking that they are doing enough to prevent heart disease by drinking wine.

5. Being overweight increases the risk of heart disease, and drinking alcoholic beverages is related to undesirable weight gain. Leary (1995) cites research indicating that alcoholic beverages add calories to a meal, lead people to consume more food and

more calories, and temporarily cause the body to burn fat more slowly than usual.

In conclusion, do not be misled into believing that moderate consumption of alcohol is a good way to prevent heart disease. The health problems related to excessive consumption of alcohol are too great to risk, and the pull toward excessive use is too strong to warrant taking the chance of using alcohol moderately as a means of preventing heart disease. Besides, the supposed health benefits related to drinking wine and other alcoholic beverages can be obtained by drinking purple grape juice (Haney, 1997) or consuming foods such as onions, garlic, grapes, and persimmons, none of which have the danger of addiction that alcohol has. As stated by the American Heart Association (Siegel, 2001):

> If you want to reduce your risk of heart disease, talk to your doctor about lowering your cholesterol and blood pressure, controlling your weight, getting enough exercise, and following a healthful diet. There is no scientific proof that drinking wine or any other alcoholic beverage can replace these effective conventional measures. (p. 1)

Weight Loss

It may seem strange to have a section on weight loss in a recreation book, but dieting, although tortuous for some, is a recreational pursuit for others. Recreational exercise and proper recreational eating are integral parts of body-weight control, which can have serious effects on health-related fitness. Body weight will remain the same when caloric intake equals caloric expenditure. In other words, the amount of energy that enters the body (food) must equal the amount of energy that leaves the body (exercise and metabolic rate-heat).

There are three safe ways to lose weight if done properly:

1. Decrease caloric intake (alter diet),
2. Increase caloric expenditure (exercise), or
3. Combine both diet and exercise.

Many suggestions were offered in this chapter on ways to increase caloric expenditure by increasing recreational exercise. Ideas for ways to decrease caloric intake were presented in the section on recreational eating. Other ideas for weight control and weight reduction include the following:

1. *Eat high-water-content foods, such as fruits and vegetables,* because these foods help cleanse the body (Diamond and Diamond, 1985).
2. *Eat meals on small plates and with small utensils* in order to slow you down and cause you to eat less (Pearson and Shaw, 1982).
3. *Drink one or two glasses of cold water right before your meal.* The water itself is good for you, and it will also help you to feel full more quickly, causing you to eat less.
4. *Do not feel compelled to clean your plate.* If you feel satisfied, stop eating. Pack up leftover food to eat another time when you will enjoy it more.
5. *Daily, before dinner, look at yourself in the nude in a full-length mirror.* Pearson and Shaw (1982) recommend this technique as a form of biofeedback that can help motivate people to avoid overeating.
6. *Develop the philosophy of eating a minimum.* Try to take the attitude that less is better. Try to avoid taking seconds. Try to eat the minimum that will satisfy you. For example, if you crave chocolate, go ahead and eat some. A little bit will not kill you. Sometimes total deprivation is harmful, because it leads to binging later on. However, if you feel satisfied after eating one piece of chocolate, stop there. Do not go back for more.
7. *Keep a wide variety of healthy foods in your house.* A wide variety is important because it will keep you from getting bored with healthy foods and straying back to unhealthy foods. A simple rule of thumb is that you tend to eat what is most readily available. Have healthy foods in your house, and that is what you will eat; stock up on junk food, and that is what you will eat.

Related to the issue of weight control and weight reduction are the dietary goals and guidelines listed in the next section.

Dietary Goals and Guidelines

The U.S. Senate Select Committee on Nutrition and Human Needs (1977) established the following dietary goals for Americans:

1. Caloric energy consumption should equal caloric energy expenditure to avoid becoming overweight.
2. Increase consumption of complex carbohydrates (fruits, vegetables, and whole grains) and "naturally occurring" sugars that are a natural ingredient in food (fruits, vegetables, and milk products).
3. Reduce consumption of refined and processed (simple) sugars that are added to foods (cane sugar, molasses, and honey).
4. Reduce overall fat consumption.
5. Reduce specific fat consumption—saturated, monounsaturated, and polyunsaturated. Saturated fats come from animal products and can elevate cholesterol levels. Monounsaturated fats usually come from plants but can be made by animals and have little or no effect on cholesterol. Polyunsaturated fats can be made only by plants and tend to lower cholesterol levels.
6. Reduce cholesterol consumption.
7. Reduce salt consumption.

As discussed by Brody (2000), these goals have not been met. They are still worthy goals for the twenty-first century.

SUMMARY

It is important to recognize that keeping the body fit and healthy does not have to be a painful, undesirable experience. Recreational exercise and better recreational eating habits can be easily integrated into anyone's lifestyle. New insights into the importance of physical fitness and good nutrition are constantly being uncovered, so further reading is encouraged. Remember, by enhancing fitness through leisure, you will enhance your leisure as well.

REFERENCES

American College of Sports Medicine (1986). *Guidelines for exercise testing and prescription* (Third edition). Philadelphia: Lea and Febiger.

Anonymous (1991). Fascinating facts. *University of California at Berkeley Wellness Letter,* December, p. 1.

Anonymous (2000). Prevalence of leisure-time and occupational physical activity among employed adults. *Journal of the American Medical Association,* 283, 3064.

Anonymous (2002). Your odds of dying from. *Wired,* March, p. 147.

Ardell, D.B. and Tager, M. (1982). *Planning for wellness* (Second edition). Dubuque, IA: Kendall Hunt.

Associated Press (2000a). Exercise found effective against depression. *The New York Times,* October 1, p. D12.

Associated Press (2000b). Study links team sports and healthful behavior. *The New York Times,* September 15, p. A21.

Brody, J. (1992). Literally entranced by television, children metabolize more slowly. *The New York Times,* April 1, p. B7.

Brody, J. (1993). The trend toward inactivity continues with the unkindest cut of all; children's fitness. *The New York Times,* February 3, p. B6.

Brody, J. (1999). Persuading potatoes to get off the couches. *The New York Times,* February 2, p. D6.

Brody, J. (2000). On health report card, the "F" stands for fat. *The New York Times,* February 1, p. D8.

Brothers, J. (1992). Do you have enough fun? *Parade Magazine,* February 2, pp. 4-5.

Brownlee, S. and Barnett, R. (1994). A loaf of bread, a glass of wine. *U.S. News and World Report,* July 4, pp. 62-63.

Bucher, C.A. and Prentice, W.E. (1985). *Fitness for college and life.* St. Louis: Times Mirror/Mosby College.

Chase, M. (2000). Health assets. *The Wall Street Journal,* May 1, pp. R9, R15.

Collins, S. and Gubernick, L. (2001). The riskiest sports. *The Wall Street Journal,* July 6, pp. W1, W4.

Diamond, H. and Diamond, M. (1985). *Fit for life.* New York: Warner Books, Inc.

Haney, D.Q. (1997). A daily glass of grape juice may be good medicine for the heart. *Chico Enterprise-Record,* March 19, p. 5A.

Hannon, K., Smith, A.K., Brink, S., and Mannix, M. (1994). News you can use— A pox on popcorn. *U.S. News and World Report,* May 9, p. 71.

Hansen, C.J., Stevens, L.C., and Coast, J.R. (2001). Exercise duration and mood state: How much is enough to feel better? *Health Psychologist,* 20(4), 267-275.

Hassmen, P., Koivula, N., and Uutela, A. (2000). Physical exercise and psychological well-being: A population study in Finland. *Preventive Medicine,* 30(1), 17-25.

Hendrie, A. (2000). Daring to be a daredevil, in circus class. *The New York Times,* March 7, p. D8.

Hsu, K. (1999). As U.S. obesity rises, scientists see health crisis. *The Boston Globe,* October 27, p. A32.

Kakutani, M. (2003). Land of the free, home of the fat. *The New York Times,* January 7, p. B12.

Katch, F.I. and McArdle, W.D. (1983). *Nutrition, weight control, and exercise* (Second edition). Philadelphia: Lea and Febiger.

Kiernan, M., King, A.C., Stefanick, M.L., and Killen, J.D. (2001). Men gain additional psychological benefits by adding exercise to a weight-loss program. *Obesity Research,* 9(12), 770-7.

Kilpatrick, M., Hebert, E., and Jacobsen, D. (2002). Physical activity motivation: A practitioner's guide to self-determination theory. *Journal of Physical Education, Recreation, and Dance,* 73(4), 36-41.

Kinsley, M. (1990). You must be very busy. *Time,* August 20, p. 82.

Kolata, G. (2001). Maximum heart rate theory is challenged. *The New York Times,* April 24, pp. D1, D8.

Kolata, G. (2002). 5 decades of warnings fail to get Americans moving. *The New York Times,* September 10, p. D5.

Kulish, N. (2000). Putting a price on health. *The Wall Street Journal,* May 1, p. R16.

Langreth, R. (2000). Every little bit helps. *The Wall Street Journal,* May 1, p. R5.

Larsen, E. (1994). Buying time. *Utne Reader,* 61(3), 59.

Leary, W.E. (1993). If you can't run for health, a walk will do. *The New York Times,* July 30, pp. A1, A11.

Leary, W.E. (1995). Recipe for weight gain: Alcohol and fatty foods. *The New York Times,* September 6, p. B6.

Macera, C.A. and Pratt, M. (2000). Public health surveillance of physical activity. *Research Quarterly for Exercise and Sports,* 71, 97-104.

McAllister, R. (2002). Addicted to colas, teens drink 64 gallons a year. *Island Weekly,* October 31-November 6, p. 16.

McClam, E. (2002). U.S. urges adults take step toward regular exercise. *Boston Sunday Globe,* April 7, p. A32.

McCord, R.D. and Godbey, S. (1995). How in the world to stay slim. *Prevention,* September, pp. 81-96.

Middendorf, P. (1994). Family fitness: Establishing healthy lifestyles. *Shasta Parent,* February 6, pp. 6-7.

Mood, D.P., Musker, F.F., and Rink, J.E. (2003). *Sports and recreational activities* (Thirteenth edition). New York: McGraw-Hill.

Morehouse, L.E. and Gross, L. (1976). *Total fitness in 30 minutes a week.* New York: Pocket Books.

Nash, J.M. (2002). Cracking the fat riddle. *Time,* September 2, pp. 46-55.

O'Neil, J. (2001). Fight depression, on your treadmill. *The New York Times,* April 3, p. D8.

Pearson, D. and Shaw, S. (1982). *Life extension: A practical scientific approach.* New York: Warner Books.

Ray, U.S., Mukhopadhyaya, S., Purkayastha, S.S., Asnani, V., Tomer, O.S., and Prashad, R. (2001). Effect of yogic exercises on physical and mental health of young fellowship course trainees. *Indian Journal of Physiological Psychiatry,* 45(1), 37-53.

Rothstein, R. (2000). Do new standards in the three R's crowd out P.E.? *The New York Times,* November 29, p. A29.

Rundle, R.L. (2000). Cutting edge. *The Wall Street Journal,* May 1, p. R17.

Schafer, W. (1990). Mormon lifestyle. *Stress and Health Report,* pp. 1, 2. Chico, CA: Enloe Hospital Stress and Health Center.

Schafer, W. (1991). Health briefs. *Stress and Health Report* (Enloe Hospital Stress and Health Center) September/October, p. 1.

Siegel, J. (2001). Red wine may help your heart—But doctors say exercise is better. *Jerusalem Post,* Internet edition (www.jpost.com/Editions/2001/01/24/News/News.20153.html).

Stedman, N. (1999). A "flow" to fuel the reluctant athlete. *The New York Times,* April 13, p. D7.

Toskovic, N.N. (2001). Alterations in selected measures of mood with a single bout of dynamic taekwondo exercise in college-age students. *Perceptual Motor Skills,* 92(3, part 2), 1031-1038.

United States Senate Select Committee on Nutrition and Human Needs (1977). *Dietary goals for the United States* (Second edition). Washington, DC: U.S. Government Printing Office.

Villarosa, L. (2000). Crunched for time? Workout on aisle 3. *The New York Times,* July 18, p. D8.

Vranica, S. (2002). CDC ads ask children to be active. *The Wall Street Journal,* July 18, p. B4.

Williamson, D., Dewey, A., and Steinberg, H. (2001). Mood change through physical exercise in nine to ten-year-old children. *Perceptual Motor Skills,* 93(1), 311-316.

Winslow, R. (2000). Why fitness matters. *The Wall Street Journal,* May 1, p. R4.

Winslow, R. and Landers, P. (2002). Obesity: A world-wide woe. *The Wall Street Journal,* July 1, p. B1.

Chapter 8

The Role of Leisure
in Stress Reduction

INTRODUCTION

Stress is one of the most significant problems in society today. According to the American Institute of Stress (2000) and the Health Resource Network (2000):

1. Approximately 75 percent of the general population has some symptom of stress every two weeks.
2. Approximately 75 to 90 percent of visits to primary care physicians are due to stress.
3. Stress complaints cause an average of one million workers to be absent from work each working day.
4. Stress contributes to heart disease, high blood pressure, strokes, development of alcoholism, obesity, suicide, drug addiction, and other harmful behaviors.
5. Stress adversely affects the health of 43 percent of Americans.

Stress at work is of particular concern (Verespej, 2000):

1. The cost of stress at the workplace is estimated to be $200 billion annually.
2. Approximately 60 to 80 percent of all industrial accidents are due to worker stress.
3. In one survey, 46 percent of workers said that the level of stress at work had increased due to technology, specifically voice mail and e-mail.

College students are especially affected by stress. A fall 1999 survey of college freshmen (Cooperman, 2000) found that a record-breaking 30.2 percent of freshmen feel "frequently overwhelmed by all I have to do." In 1985, only 16 percent of survey respondents reported feeling stressed. In the 1999 survey, 38.8 percent of women said they feel frequently overwhelmed, compared to 20 percent of men. This finding is probably related to other survey findings showing that women spend more time than men studying, doing volunteer work, participating in student clubs or groups, and doing housework or child-care responsibilities. Meanwhile, men spend more time than women exercising or playing sports, partying, playing video games, or watching television.

The buffering effect of leisure on stress is documented in several studies (Siegenthaler, 1997), but unfortunately, instead of using leisure to relax and relieve stress, many Americans use their free time to engage in stressful activities they happen to like (Creekmore, 1994). Some of the other stress-related problems encountered during free time include bombardment of information from high technology devices (Carter, 1994) and having to make choices from too many options (Davidson, 1994). As an example, Keyes (1991) states that the average American supermarket stocked 3,000 items in 1946 and over 10,000 by 1990. He explains that choices do not make life easier, but rather tend to make people anxious.

What are the effects of all this stress on leisure? It can prevent people from experiencing pleasure from their recreational activities, as reported in a study on the effects of stress on hedonic capacity (Berenbaum and Connelly, 1993). Clearly, stress can have a negative impact on both leisure and health.

The purpose of this chapter is to examine the relationship between leisure and stress and to explore how leisure can prevent or reduce stress. The relevance of stress theory to recreation is much more heavily emphasized in this chapter than the physiological characteristics of stress are. More specifically, the learning objectives of this chapter are to

1. Identify statistics on the prevalence of stress as a societal problem.
2. Define stress.
3. Contrast the terms stress and stressor.

4. Contrast positive and negative stress.
5. Identify recreational activities that are positive stressors and those that are negative stressors.
6. Identify the stages of general adaptation syndrome (GAS) and the corresponding stages experienced in most recreational activities.
7. Describe how recreational activity can be utilized to balance the stress quotient equation.
8. Explain the implications of type A/B personality research for leisure.
9. Define relaxation.
10. Identify recreational activities that can facilitate relaxation.
11. State a minimum of three personal leisure goals related to stress reduction and relaxation.

STRESS THEORY AND CONCEPTS

Stress Defined

According to Hamberger and Lohr (1984), a universally acceptable definition of stress has not yet been formulated. However, Selye's definition of stress and his theories and concepts of stress are the most popular and comprehensive ones in the literature (Hamberger and Lohr, 1984). Selye (1956, p. 54) defines stress as "the state manifested by a specific syndrome which consists of all the non-specifically induced changes within a biologic system." Before explaining this definition in detail, several other terms should be contrasted.

Stress and Stressor

Stressors are what cause stress. Selye (1956, p. 64) defines a stressor as "that which produces stress." Therefore, financial problems, exams, and other anxiety-producing situations are examples of stressors, not stress.

Eustress and Distress

Not all stress is damaging to the body. *Distress,* or negative stress, is damaging, but *eustress,* or positive stress, is not. According to Allen (1983), eustress represents challenge and stimulation for healthy growth and development, whereas distress represents that which produces wear and tear on an organism. The following are examples of recreation-related stressors that would likely produce eustress: roller coasters, water slides, white-water rafting, sky diving, and skiing. The following are recreation-related examples of stressors that would likely produce distress: continuous interpersonal conflict at a party or other social recreation setting, an intense athletic competition with a negative outcome (e.g., losing an important match in a tennis tournament), and watching a captivating horror movie. However, whether an activity produces eustress or distress depends on the participant's perceptions of the activity (Selye, 1980). Charlesworth and Nathan (1981) quote Shakespeare in this regard: "Things are neither good nor bad, but thinking makes them so."

Exercise 8.1 is presented to facilitate a personal clarification of recreation-related eustress and distress. Based on Exercise 8.1, are you able to discern common characteristics that distinguish eustress-producing recreation from distress-producing recreation? In comparing your list of activities with those of others, what discrepancies in categorization do you notice? Were any activities sometimes eustress producing and sometimes distress producing? Are most of your recreational activities eustressful, distressful, or neither?

The eustress-distress relationship is analogous to the theory of optimal arousal discussed in Chapter 5. According to the theory of optimal arousal, an individual seeks an optimal (usually moderate) level of arousal in activities. When the arousal level is too low, the participant becomes bored and performs at a lower level; when the arousal level is too high, the participant becomes anxious and also performs at a lower level. Allen (1983) describes the relationship of performance and growth to level of stress in similar terms. At an optimal (moderate) level of stress, performance and growth are at a peak. At stress levels that are above or below this optimal level, performance and growth are lower. Allen (1983) categorizes *distress* as being

EXERCISE 8.1. Inventory of Recreation-Related Stressors

Instructions

In the first column list all recreation-related stressors in your life. In the second column, mark an "E" if you view it as being more as a eustress-producing stressor or a "D" if you view it as being more of a distress-producing stressor. In the last column, explain why you categorize the activity as eustress producing or distress producing.

Name of activity	Eustress = E Distress = D	Explanation of categorization

stress that is *above* the optimal level; *eustress* is viewed as stress that is at or near the optimal level. Therefore, like arousal, stress can be viewed as challenge or stimulation. In both cases, the key to optimal health is moderation.

Explanation of Selye's Stress Definition

Previously in this chapter, stress was defined as a *state* manifested by a *specific syndrome* that consists of all *nonspecifically induced changes* within a biologic system (Selye, 1956). To clarify the meaning of this definition, each of the italicized terms will be explained in detail.

1. *State:* Stress is characterized by a particular state of being. Selye suggests that if many people under stress are observed, common characteristics of their state of being can be identified. Stress produces physiological changes that are evident in most people under stress. This state of being is produced by nonspecifically induced changes.
2. *Nonspecifically induced changes:* In explaining the concept of nonspecific causation, Selye (1956) states that stress can be induced anywhere and by anything. Thus, stress is nonspecifically induced. However, stress is manifested by a specific syndrome called general adaptation syndrome (GAS).
3. *Specific syndrome (GAS):* According to Selye, stress is characterized by a specific pattern of changes or a syndrome, GAS. To better understand GAS, each word of this term is explained as follows:
   • GAS is a *general* syndrome in that it has a widespread effect on the biologic system. Many parts of the body are affected by GAS.
   • GAS is an *adaptation* syndrome in that it stimulates a defense or adjustment to a stressor.
   • GAS is a *syndrome;* a syndrome is a set of coordinated stages that are dependent on one another. GAS consists of three stages described in detail in the next section.

Stages of GAS

GAS consists of three stages: alarm, resistance, and exhaustion.

1. The *alarm stage* is the body's initial reaction to a stressor. In this stage, the body's adaptive defenses are activated (Hamberger and Lohr, 1984). According to Selye, the alarm stage is characterized by a loss of body weight and the blood becoming more concentrated (with hormones). This stage is short-lived and soon gives way to the stage of resistance (Hamberger and Lohr, 1984).
2. The *stage of resistance* is in many ways very different from the alarm stage (Selye, 1956). During this stage, the blood becomes diluted and body weight returns to normal. The organism is working at peak efficiency and is unlikely to succumb to the stressor (Rathbone and Rathbone, 1971). Depending on the nature of the stressor and strength of the organism, this stage can range in duration from a matter of seconds to a period of days, weeks, or even months. According to Rathbone and Rathbone, the stage of exhaustion occurs next, after the adaptive energy has been expended.
3. During the *stage of exhaustion,* the organism is in a weakened state and is vulnerable to the stressor (Rathbone and Rathbone, 1971). However, the damage inflicted on the organism again depends on the strength of the organism and the nature of the stressor. A very strong stressor could result in significant wear and tear on the body and produce a stress-related disease such as a heart attack. On the other hand, a mild stressor might only produce a very brief feeling of fatigue, with no significant damage to the body.

The relationship of the different stages of GAS to resistance level is summarized in Figure 8.1 (Schafer, 1987). As illustrated in the figure, before the stressor is perceived, an individual is at a normal level of resistance, but in the alarm stage, resistance falls below this normal level. In the stage of resistance, the level of resistance becomes higher than normal, then falls below normal in the stage of exhaustion.

General adaptation syndrome is one of the key elements of Selye's stress theory. The relevance of Selye's stress theory to recreation is explored in the next section.

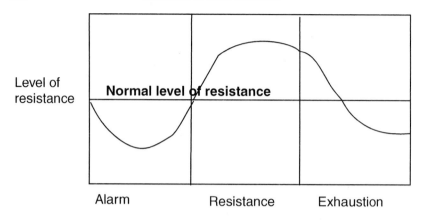

FIGURE 8.1. Stages of GAS and Resistance Level (*Source:* Adapted from Selye, 1956.)

APPLICATION OF STRESS THEORY TO RECREATION

GAS and Its Corresponding Stages in All Recreational Activities

According to Selye (1956), the three phases of the stress response are relevant in all activities. Selye states that in all activities (including recreational activities), the first stage is *surprise* (alarm stage of GAS), then *mastery* (stage of resistance), and finally *fatigue* (stage of exhaustion). Similar to the stages of GAS, the duration of the three phases (surprise, mastery, and fatigue) experienced during a recreational activity can vary. Surprise will usually be very brief, but mastery can range from a few seconds to weeks and months, and fatigue can also vary from just a few seconds to weeks or even months. The relevance of these stages to a variety of recreational activities is examined next.

Example 1: Baseball

The three stages (surprise, mastery, fatigue) seem to apply to the activity of being at bat.

1. *Surprise:* The pitch initially surprises the batter as it comes in. Even if the batter expected a particular type of pitch (e.g., fastball, curveball, or screwball), the exact velocity and direction of the ball is not predetermined. Therefore, at least for a short period of time, the batter can be said to be in a stage of surprise (similar to the alarm stage of GAS) as the ball comes in to home plate.

2. *Mastery:* The duration of this phase can vary in the situation of being at bat. If the batter swings and hits a home run, the mastery stage (similar to the resistance stage of GAS) lasts during the successful swing, the flight of the ball over the wall, and the batter's run around the bases. However, if the batter merely swings and hits a foul ball, then mastery is short-lived, just the few seconds of the swing, contact, and flight of the ball. If the batter swings and misses, it can be argued that the mastery stage is even shorter, lasting only for the few moments of the batter's swing and ending as soon as the ball lands in the catcher's glove.

3. *Fatigue:* This phase might last longer for a batter who has just hit a homer and run around the bases than for a batter who merely swings and hits a foul ball.

Therefore, Selye's notion of experiencing three stages that are similar to the stages of GAS (surprise equals alarm; mastery equals resistance; fatigue equals exhaustion) appears to be relevant to physically active sports such as baseball. However, does it accurately reflect a passive form of recreation, such as watching television?

Example 2: Watching Television

Surprise, mastery, and fatigue seem to occur even in this recreational activity, though their manifestation is vastly different from the baseball example.

1. *Surprise:* The surprise stage is brief if watching a rerun and longer in duration if flicking on the television for a new program. The surprise centers on adjusting to the initial volume of the sound and quality of the picture and trying to understand the program's content.

2. *Mastery:* The mastery stage varies according to the duration of the program as well as personal interest in the program. Once the initial surprise elements have been adapted to, the viewer is in control (mastery), watching and hopefully enjoying the show.

3. *Fatigue:* After a suspenseful drama or intense romantic story, the viewer might experience a period of fatigue. A boring program might also cause fatigue to set in. After a mildly entertaining show, the fatigue stage occurs but might be short (only a few seconds long) and barely noticeable.

Exercise 8.2 presents an opportunity to examine the relevance of Selye's concepts to personal leisure experiences. Based on Exercise 8.2, do you think Selye's stages are applicable to all of your recreational activities? Can you think of any recreational activities in which surprise, mastery, and fatigue would not occur?

Balancing the Stress Quotient Through Recreation

Another stress concept of Selye's that is relevant to recreation is deviation. Selye (1956) defines *deviation* as the act of turning something from its course. Deviation can be an effective means of counteracting purely mental stress. To fully understand the process of deviation and how recreation can assist in it, Selye's stress quotient must first be explained.

Selye defines the *stress quotient* as follows:

$$\frac{\text{local stress in any one part}}{\text{total stress in the body}}$$

Selye states that an imbalance in this equation should be corrected. Of particular concern is the situation in which local stress is much greater than total stress, as illustrated in the following example.

Two travelers each have 150 pounds of luggage to carry. Traveler A has all 150 pounds stuffed into one huge suitcase that is held in the right hand. Traveler B has the 150 pounds distributed evenly between a backpack and two suitcases. If numerical value could be computed for the stress quotient, traveler A's stress quotient would be much higher:

EXERCISE 8.2.
Applying Selye's GAS to Personal Leisure Activities

Instructions

Select two diverse activities for analysis. In the spaces provided, explain each of the three phases for each activity. Compare the duration of each phase for each activity.

Activity 1 _____ **Activity 2** _____

1. Surprise:

_____

_____

_____

_____

_____

_____

_____

1. Surprise:

_____

_____

_____

_____

_____

_____

2. Mastery:

_____

_____

_____

_____

_____

_____

_____

2. Mastery:

_____

_____

_____

_____

_____

_____

3. Fatigue:

_____

_____

_____

_____

_____

_____

_____

3. Fatigue:

_____

_____

_____

_____

_____

_____

Traveler A

$$\frac{\text{local stress}}{\text{total stress}} \quad \frac{\text{very high}}{\text{very low}} \quad \begin{array}{l}\text{(150 pounds of strain on the right arm and shoulder)}\\\text{(nothing being carried by other body parts)}\end{array}$$

Traveler B

$$\frac{\text{local stress}}{\text{total stress}} \quad \frac{\text{moderate}}{\text{moderate}} \quad \begin{array}{l}\text{(maximum 50 pounds of strain anywhere)}\\\text{(both arms and shoulders as well as back are}\\\text{working to carry the luggage)}\end{array}$$

As shown, traveler A's stress quotient is very high, because whenever the numerator of a fraction is much greater than the denominator, the value of the fraction is high (e.g., 150 divided by 1 = 150). Conversely, any fraction in which the numerator and denominator are fairly equal would have a relatively low value (e.g., 50 divided by 50 = 1).

Traveler A will experience much more wear and tear and fatigue than will traveler B. Even though they are both carrying the same number of pounds, traveler A's unbalanced stress quotient makes the luggage-carrying experience more fatiguing.

At the beginning of this section, *deviation* was defined as turning something from its course. More specifically, through deviation, general stress can be used to balance the stress quotient equation and thereby lessen the negative impact of local stress (Selye, 1956).

Selye discusses the example of how deviation can combat the mental stress of worrying about finances. Worrying about finances is a specific stressor. However, without enough general stress to counterbalance this specific stress, the financial worries can become all-consuming. Worrying can lead to severe physical problems such as ulcers and hypertension. However, as Selye discusses, mild forms of general stress from activities such as sports, dancing, music, and travel can help to restore a lopsided stress quotient to normal and thereby reduce the negative effects of the local stressor (worry). Interestingly, Selye uses recreation-related examples in explaining the concept of deviation. Several more examples are presented to clarify how recreation can help to balance a stress quotient through deviation, as well as how recreation can sometimes lead to an unbalanced stress quotient.

Example 1: Weight Lifting

Lifter A and lifter B each lift weights for forty-five minutes, at approximately the same pace and weight. However, lifter A works on the right and left biceps exclusively, whereas lifter B works out the biceps, triceps, hamstrings, quadriceps, abdomen, and pectorals. Imagine the fatigue and pain lifter A feels after such an unbalanced workout. In contrast, lifter B feels minimal pain, because of the balanced stress throughout the body. Lifter B utilizes the concept of deviation to make weight lifting a healthier experience, whereas lifter A's obsession with biceps creates an unbalanced stress quotient and likely a great deal of pain and fatigue.

Example 2: Tennis

After a strenuous match, a right-handed player might have an unbalanced stress quotient, a great deal of local stress having been produced on the right arm and shoulder. However, a recreational activity that produces general stress or places a more generalized demand on the body (e.g., swimming) can be employed to balance the stress quotient, thereby minimizing the negative effects of the local stress. Swimming after a tennis match is a good recreation-related example of using deviation to prevent local stress from producing harm.

Example 3: Watching a Horror Movie

Viewing an intense horror movie can create mental stress, manifested as a headache. The stress quotient can be balanced through recreation. Taking a long walk after the movie will produce general stress that will help to balance the stress quotient. Again, a recreational activity is employed to balance the stress quotient equation through deviation.

Thus far in this chapter, the stress-recreation connection has been clarified with respect to GAS, eustress versus distress, and deviation. As discussed in the next two sections, leisure philosophy and activities have important implications for determining the overall stressfulness of one's lifestyle.

TYPE A/B BEHAVIOR AND LEISURE

According to Allen (1983), Beech, Burns, and Sheffield (1982), Gherman (1981), and Gill (1983), type A and B individuals differ in many ways, as displayed in Table 8.1. The type A individual is far less likely to be able to enjoy leisure than is a type B individual. The type A individual is constantly hurrying from one activity to the next, preoccupied with accomplishments, material acquisitions, and work. The type B individual takes time to appreciate leisure and is a better observer of the surrounding environment. Imagine a type A and a type B individual taking a nature walk together. The type A individual would probably do the walk in half the time and notice half the scenery.

Allen (1983) points out that most of the research completed to date has found no significant differences in productivity between type A and type B individuals. Even though type A individuals seem to work harder and type B individuals seem to be more leisure oriented, the type Bs possibly work more effectively because of their superior vision of overall goals and purpose. Although the productivity level of type A and B does not seem to differ significantly, health status does.

TABLE 8.1. Contrast of Type A and Type B Behaviors

Type A individual	Type B individual
1. Feels guilty about relaxing	1. Takes the time to appreciate leisure and beauty; focuses more on the quality of life
2. Ambitious, hard worker	2. Less ambitious
3. Tries to do many things at once	3. Focuses on one thing at a time
4. Impatient and restless	4. Patient
5. Eats, walks, and talks hurriedly	5. Paces oneself effectively
6. Has poorly defined goals, which leads to unfinished work, errors, and frustration	6. More focused, less frustrated

Health Implications of Type A and Type B Behavior

Type A individuals have a much higher risk of coronary heart disease than type B individuals. Beech, Burns, and Sheffield (1982) cite a study by Friedman and Rosenman that provides compelling data on the much higher risk of coronary heart disease among type A individuals. In the Friedman and Rosenman study, 3,411 middle-aged men were initially assessed as having either a type A or type B personality. Approximately half of the men were classified as type A. Eight-and-one-half years later, the rate of coronary heart disease of the type A men was twice that of the type B men. Approximately 85 percent of the type A men aged thirty-nine to forty-nine developed coronary heart disease.

The reasons for these findings are clear. Type A individuals experience more distress than type B individuals. Beech, Burns, and Sheffield (1982) identify some of the negative health-related implications of distress: increased heart rate, increased blood pressure, increased muscular tension, slowing of the digestive system, and increased psychological anxiety.

Other research indicates that one particular difference between type A and type B individuals, not listed on Table 8.1, has an even greater impact on health. It seems that hostility and anger are the keys to the higher mortality rate for type A individuals. Angier (1990) cites a study in which women with long-term, suppressed anger were three times more likely to have died than women who did not have these hostile feelings. A study of 118 lawyers over a twenty-five-year period found that only 4 percent of those rated as easygoing had died, whereas 20 percent of those rated as most hostile had died (Angier, 1990).

In summary, distress can create serious health problems. The question is, what can be done to prevent or overcome distress? As discussed in the next section, leisure can play a major role in preventing and overcoming distress.

HOW LEISURE CAN HELP OVERCOME AND PREVENT DISTRESS

Leisure Philosophy

The most effective way to prevent an unhealthy accumulation of distress is to have a strong, sound philosophy of leisure and life. As discussed in Chapter 6, a sound philosophy of leisure involves having ultimate, long-range, and short-range goals.

Selye (1956) also emphasizes the importance of personal philosophy and having ultimate, long-range, and short-range aims ensuring maximum health and well-being. Selye states that having worthy aims provides a sense of security and peace of mind. He also states that feelings of insecurity, aimlessness, and frustration (which often stem from not having a sound philosophy of leisure and life) are perhaps the greatest sources of distress. It is interesting to note that although Selye is a physician and well known for his medical research on stress, he places the greatest emphasis on leisure and personal philosophy in dealing with the stress of life.

Selye (1956, p. 299) views humans' ultimate aim as expressing themselves "as fully as possible, according to their 'own lights.'" This view is strikingly similar to the self-expression theory discussed in Chapter 5.

Selye's view of long-range aims is that they should be designed to enable future gratification. Selye emphasizes that material aims are not worthy long-range aims and that attaining materialistic goals does not really lead to a happy and meaningful life. He sees long-range aims as being primarily interpersonal, one of the foremost considerations being to earn the gratitude of others.

Selye believes that short-range aims should be designed for immediate gratification. He emphasizes the importance of allowing oneself to enjoy the pleasures of life. Enjoying these pleasures seems to have a significant, positive effect on health. According to Goleman (1994), studies have shown that having pleasant leisure experiences such as fishing or jogging can lower stress and have a positive effect on the immune system.

Selye also warns of the unhealthiness of delaying leisure. He discusses how many people constantly put off leisure for the future, promising themselves more leisure at a later date, after they have accomplished a work project. However, the opportunity for more work and earning more money to purchase more material goods seems to always present itself, and so the promise of increased leisure in the future never comes true.

In summary, Selye's view of dealing with stress is remarkably leisure oriented. He places great importance on enjoying life's pleasures, planning for future gratification, seeking satisfaction through social interaction, and pursuing optimal self-expression. Selye's views seem to be well supported by research on the relationship of leisure attitudes and activities to physical and psychological well-being that was cited in Chapter 2. Perhaps the most important idea expressed by Selye (1956, p. 300) that pertains to leisure philosophy and goal setting is "Fight always for the highest attainable aim, but never put up resistance in vain." In other words, as discussed in Chapter 6, personal goals should be set as high as possible, so that goals are a source of inspiration to reach higher. However, goals must also be realistic, for if futile attempts are made to meet an unattainable goal, frustration will build up.

Research cited by Goode (1999) shows that a sense of control over life events is strongly related to stress. Those that feel less in control feel more stress. As discussed in Chapter 6, one of the benefits of goal setting is that it provides the opportunity to take personal responsibility for one's life. As discussed by Ardell and Tager (1982), one of the key variables in determining personal stress level is the extent to which personal responsibility is accepted for the stressors in life. They advocate assuming greater personal responsibility for the stress of life as a means of lessening the distress experienced in day-to-day life. Exercise 8.3, adapted from Ardell and Tager's (1982) book, is designed to facilitate the assumption of greater personal responsibility for stressors.

Reflect on Exercise 8.3 after it has been completed. Do you have more control over the stress in your life than you thought you had? Will your stress level now be lower, knowing that you have greater control over your life than you thought you had? Ultimately, the purpose of this exercise is to facilitate a greater awareness of the extent to which personal stressors can be controlled.

In addition to goal-setting and self-awareness exercises, many specific recreation-related behavioral methods of controlling stress are available. These methods are useful in stress reduction, but they cannot substitute for having a sound philosophy of leisure and life. The first method discussed, exercise, is particularly effective.

Stress Reduction Through Recreational Exercise

According to Allen (1983), physical activity has direct effects on the body that can reduce distress and the probability of psychoso-

EXERCISE 8.3. Assuming Personal Responsibility for Stressors

Instructions

1. In the first column, list and briefly describe all of the regularly occurring negative stressors in your life. Focus more on the leisure-related as opposed to work-related stressors in your life.
2. In the second column, identify the benefits of each negative stressor. Why do you let these stressors occur regularly? Some benefit or pay-off is probably connected with each stressor. Give this column a good deal of thought. Consider the following examples:

Stressor   *Benefits*

1. Riding bicycle in   Good exercise, more convenient than driving and
   heavy traffic   looking for parking, saves energy and money.

2. Waiting in line at The food is needed; if greater quantities were
   supermarket   purchased less frequently, it wouldn't be as fresh, or
                       if it was purchased at the small convenience store, it
                       would be more expensive.

As illustrated in the example, most regularly occurring negative stressors exist because of a decision to let them exist, in order to reap the benefits associated with the stressor.

3. In the third column, write in a "+" if you feel that the benefits of the stressor outweigh its costs or a "–" if you feel the costs outweigh the benefits.
4. In the last column, identify what action you intend to take. In cases where the benefits far outweigh the costs, perhaps no action is most desirable. However, in some cases where the benefits outweigh the costs, a small change in behavior could possibly reduce the negative effects of the stressor while still allowing you to derive the same benefits. For instance, in the supermarket example, the lines might be shorter at night than during the day.

Several courses of action are possible in situations in which the costs of the stressor are greater than its benefits:

1. Eliminate the activity associated with the stressor from your life. Either forego the benefits of the stressor or find an alternative means of deriving the benefits obtained from the stressor.
2. Continue the activity but change your perception of it (an activity acts as a stressor only if it is perceived as one). Knowing that you *can* eliminate the stressor from your life might reduce the level of stress it causes.
3. As discussed previously, modify the activity so that its costs are reduced and its benefits remain constant or increase.

Stressor description	Stressor benefits	+ or −	Action

matic disease. In fact, based on observation of animals, it seems that lack of physical activity is a major contributor to the high level of stress in modern society (Allen, 1983).

Research supports the claims of exercise being an effective stress reducer. Kelly's (1986) study of college students enrolled in a lifestyle intervention course indicated that the course contributed to significantly reduced stress levels. Exercise training was one of the three main components of the course. Berger's (1986) study found that swimmers reported less tension, anxiety, depression, anger, and confusion and more vigor after swimming than before swimming. In Berger's (1986) study, both beginning and intermediate swimmers reaped stress-reduction benefits, but exercise needed to be done regularly and good environmental conditions were important, such as not having uncomfortably hot or cold air or water temperatures. Similarly, studies by Fort (1986), Morgan (1980), Sachs and Buffone (1984), and Wilson, Berger, and Bird (1981) provide evidence that jogging and aerobic exercise in general help reduce many indices of physiological stress.

Other types of exercise can also be used to relieve stress. Callaman (1993) discusses a program called "Corporate Kicks, Inc." which helps employees relieve stress by providing instruction in martial arts and other forms of exercise.

Exercise is a positive force in stress reduction for several reasons. Everly and Rosenfeld (1981) explain that exercise causes a cooling of the skin, decreased blood pressure, striate-muscle relaxation, and decreased anxiety levels. Everly and Rosenfeld (1981) cite one study in which fifteen minutes of walking was found to be a more powerful muscle relaxant than 400 mg of meprobamate (a tranquilizer).

Unlike drugs, exercise usually has no harmful side effects. In fact, exercise can have a multitude of physical and mental benefits, as discussed in Chapter 7. Physical activity is a category of recreational activity that has an incredibly long list of different options for participation. Guidelines for selecting the best exercise for total well-being are included in Chapter 7. Another important consideration in preventing stress-related health problems discussed in Chapter 7 is nutrition. However, one topic related to health and fitness not discussed in Chapter 7 that is related to stress reduction is sexual activity.

The Role of Sexual Activity in Stress Reduction

Allen (1983) states that sexual activity is the nicest form of physical activity for controlling stress. On the other hand, some forms of sexual expression are not necessarily recreational or positive outlets (e.g., prostitution). The primary focus here is the impact of sexual activity on stress reduction.

Allen (1983) offers an explanation of the biological changes produced by sexual activity that contribute to stress reduction. For example, sexual activity can cause the release of endorphins within the brain. The release of endorphins can serve as an antithesis to the onset of psychogenic stress as well as a means for facilitating pain reduction.

However, Allen states that the psychosocial aspects of sexual activity are even more important than the biological aspects in facilitating stress reduction. For example, he cites social isolation as being one of the most significant psychosocial stressors. Sexual activity is perhaps the most powerful means of preventing feelings of social isolation. Of all forms of leisure activity, there are probably none that can reduce psychological distance between two individuals as powerfully and as quickly as sex.

However, it also seems that friendly relationships can help protect individuals from stress. Goleman (1992) cites a study on monkeys which found that the friendliest ones had stronger immune responses, while the hostile and aggressive ones had the poorest immune responses. Friendly intimacy seems to buffer the immune system from stress, whereas interpersonal conflict can strain the immune system.

Similarly, as discussed in the next section, music can either help to relieve stress or create stress.

Stress Reduction Through Music

Because music can be either a stressor or relaxer, Halpern (1978) says that every time people turn on the radio they are playing radio roulette, because they do not know if the sounds they will hear will affect them positively or negatively. Halpern advocates paying close attention to the sounds in one's life, noting which are pleasant and which are unpleasant, and then taking action to increase the positive ones and decrease the negative ones.

According to Halpern, popular music is sometimes stress producing rather than relaxing, because music is often out of harmony with the listener's biological needs. To counteract this problem, Halpern (n.d.) produced a record designed to get the seven chakras (energy centers) of the body in harmony with one another. He claims that through biofeedback testing, this music has been proven effective in stress reduction and relaxation. Therefore, to be guaranteed a relaxing experience when listening to music, it might be advantageous to carefully select music such as Halpern's instead of the usual popular or rock and roll music. Of course, some popular music, as well as classical, jazz, and new age, can also be very relaxing.

The idea of using music to reduce stress and promote relaxation is incorporated in a new device called RESPeRATE which uses music to lower blood pressure. Abramoff (2002) reports that this device is attached by wires to a small sensor and a set of ordinary earphones, and with the help of two computers inside the machine, it determines the wearer's breathing rate and composes a series of musical tones that the patient uses to guide and eventually lower the breathing rate. Slower breathing rates help to reduce blood pressure and lower the risk of heart disease and stroke. In summary, this invention is an example of how music can help to promote relaxation, which in turn can have a major impact on health. The concept of relaxation is discussed further in the next section.

Relaxation and Stress Contrasted

Beech, Burns, and Sheffield (1982) define relaxation as the lengthening of skeletal muscle fibers. In contrast, stress and tension cause the skeletal muscle fibers to contract or shorten. During contraction, glycogen is broken down, heat is produced, and fatigue products (e.g., lactic acid) are formed. On the other hand, during a period of relaxation, fatigue products are cleared away from the bloodstream. Therefore, relaxation can help to counteract the tiring effects of stress.

Beech, Burns, and Sheffield identify several benefits of deep relaxation:

1. Relaxation facilitates a better ability to deal with stressors.
2. Relaxation helps to eliminate many stress-related physical problems, such as hypertension and headaches. The pain associated with a headache is caused by the contraction of the skeletal muscle fibers of the head and back of the neck. Relaxation can lengthen the very muscle fibers that are causing the pain associated with the headache, thereby eliminating the pain.
3. Relaxation can help accelerate recovery from an illness.
4. Relaxation reduces psychological anxiety levels, thereby contributing to improved interpersonal relationships.

Thus, relaxation is beneficial in many ways. The next topic to be addressed is how to facilitate relaxation through recreation.

Relaxation Through Recreation

Exercise 8.4 is presented to facilitate self-awareness of recreation-related relaxation possibilities. To learn about new relaxing recreational activities, compare your list of activities and ratings with those of others. The following questions should be discussed:

1. Which activities seem to be rated highest in relaxation by most people?
2. Are there discrepancies in relaxation ratings? Discuss the possible reasons for these differences.
3. What leisure goals would you like to set, based on the discrepancies between your participation ratings and relaxation ratings?

Laughter and humor are particularly powerful recreational relaxants. The relationships between humor, laughter, stress, and relaxation are examined in the next chapter.

EXERCISE 8.4. Identification of Recreational Relaxation Activities

Instructions

1. In the first column, list all recreational activities that you think are relaxing, regardless of whether you regularly participate in the activities.
2. In the second column, identify your level of participation in each activity.
   0 = never participate
   1 = infrequent participation
   2 = occasional participation
   3 = frequent participation
   4 = very frequent participation
3. In the last column, rate each activity's effectiveness in promoting relaxation. Base your rating on personal opinions and experiences.
   1 = slightly relaxing
   2 = moderately relaxing
   3 = very relaxing
   4 = "ultimate" relaxation

Activity	Participation rating	Relaxation rating

Other effective relaxation techniques that can be easily incorporated into one's leisure are deep breathing, guided imagery, meditation, neuromuscular relaxation, and yoga. Allen (1983), Beech, Burns, and Sheffield (1982), Brown (1984), Charlesworth and Nathan (1981), Everly and Rosenfeld (1981), Gill (1983), and Hamberger and Lohr (1984) discuss a variety of these types of relaxation techniques. Beech, Burns, and Sheffield (1982) present some useful guidelines applicable to almost any self-administered relaxation technique:

1. Assume responsibility for the success or failure of the technique. If you do not give it a good try, it will not work.
2. Do not expect instant results. In the beginning, practice the technique regularly, perhaps thirty minutes each day. Like any new skill, relaxation techniques must be practiced to gain competence in them.
3. Let go and let it happen.
4. Set aside at least twenty minutes for each relaxation period. Allocating less time might cause a hurried attitude, preventing the achievement of true relaxation.
5. The environment should be conducive to relaxation: soft lighting, comfortable furniture, quiet, and freedom from distractions.
6. The use of an instructional tape can facilitate the success of the relaxation technique being attempted.

The following are some specific guidelines and instructions for the previously described relaxation techniques. Refer to the references listed at the end of this chapter for more detailed descriptions of each technique.

1. *Meditation.* Mental repetition is perhaps the simplest yet one of the most potentially powerful meditative techniques. Select a word or phrase (a mantra) to repeat silently over and over, and continue this mental repetition for at least twenty minutes. According to Everly and Rosenfeld (1981), research indicates that this type of meditation can help treat hypertension, phobias, drug and alcohol abuse, and anxiety, as well as increase positive mental health. However, although this technique seems uncomplicated, extensive training may be needed to be able to reach the highest levels of relaxation and insight.

2. *Neuromuscular relaxation.* Neuromuscular relaxation involves progressive tensing and loosening of muscles throughout the body. A possible sequence (pause twenty seconds in between each exercise) could be to do the following:

> Focus on the feet. Tense and contract the muscles in the feet for five seconds. Then relax the feet muscles and focus on further relaxing these muscles for another twenty seconds.
>
> Then do the same thing for the lower leg muscles.
>
> Continue to the thigh muscles.
>
> Focus next on the abdominal muscles.
>
> Move to the chest area next.
>
> Follow with the shoulders.
>
> Proceed to the hands.
>
> Finish with the neck, head, and face.

According to Everly and Rosenfeld (1981), research indicates that neuromuscular relaxation can help treat insomnia, hypertension, headaches, and anxiety.

3. *Deep Breathing.* Another simple yet effective relaxation technique is deep breathing. Inhale slowly through the nostrils, hold the breath for several seconds, then exhale slowly through the mouth. Continue this technique for twenty minutes and mentally concentrate on the breathing process the entire time.

4. *Guided imagery.* This technique also involves some deep breathing, but rather than mentally focusing on the breathing process, one's thoughts center on a detailed description of a relaxing image, such as relaxing in a beautiful meadow or sailing on a peaceful lake. A helpful image to begin the session with is stuffing all personal problems in a big suitcase and locking this suitcase in a closet, out of sight.

5. *Yoga.* Yoga cannot be adequately discussed in just one chapter, let alone a section of a chapter. Many excellent books on yoga techniques are available that would be very helpful, such as those by Christensen (1987), Finger and Guber (1984), Hittleman (1985), Isaacson (1986), Iyengar (1980), Lidell (1983), and Mishra (1987), but taking a yoga class would be much more desirable. As Allen (1983) discusses, yoga can have tremendous relaxation, stress-reduction, attitude, and fitness benefits.

One last word of caution regarding these relaxation techniques: Do not try to cram them into an already-busy schedule. The stress of modern life is to a large degree self-imposed. Instead of always rushing, people need to take time out to do nothing more often and let their rhythm slow down (Rechtschaffer, 1994). Devoting one day each week to leisure could be incredibly rejuvenating and stress reducing. Keyes (1991) describes with admiration a Jewish psychiatrist who observes the Sabbath faithfully, living simply, blocking out technology, and experiencing a day of being, not doing, once a week. In a related vein, relaxation techniques should not evolve into another activity to do, but should instead be used to help you become a more relaxed individual.

Paulsen (1994) offers some advice from some prominent individuals on how to feel more relaxed and lead a less-stressful life:

1. Try to find a way to work less, and then stop shopping as a leisure activity, because often all we are doing is buying things that require us to work long hours to pay for (social economist Juliet B. Schor).
2. People need to feel the support of others; become intimate with someone you can trust (stress researcher Robert M. Sapolsky).
3. Cut back on those activities that do not match up with what is really important to you and try to make even routine tasks such as cooking and cleaning more enjoyable by creating ways to do them more efficiently or artistically (psychologist Mihaly Csikszentmihalyi).

Related to this idea, Exercise 8.5 is presented to determine how to make routine tasks more enjoyable by making them either more artistic/fun or less time consuming by doing them more efficiently.

SUMMARY

Many recreational options exist for relaxation and stress reduction, many more than were discussed in this chapter. For example, outdoor recreation can be a very relaxing, stress-relieving outlet (Iso-Ahola, 1980). Many of the stress-reduction and relaxation-inducing activities described in this chapter can easily be incorporated into even a tight leisure schedule, as they require only a short block of time.

EXERCISE 8.5. Making Chores Less Stressful, More Recreational

Instructions

1. Identify routine chores (e.g., cleaning, laundry, cooking, washing dishes, etc.) that cause you stress.
2. For each of these chores, identify how you could make the chore more enjoyable or fun, even a recreational experience.
3. Alternatively, identify ways to do the chore more efficiently, with the idea that you will feel less stressed knowing that you created more leisure time by being able to do the chore in less time.
4. Some ideas are presented for the first chore. Continue with more ideas for that one and then identify some chores that cause you stress and describe how you can make them more fun or do them more efficiently.

Ways to make the chore more fun   **How to do the chore more efficiently**

Chore #1: Doing the Laundry

Ways to make the chore more fun	How to do the chore more efficiently
1. Plan a laundry night once a week with some friends. Bring games, snacks, drinks, etc., and transform laundry into a weekly "laundry party."	1. Do it less often.
	2. Study or read between cycles.
2. Alternatively, if doing the laundry alone, make it the time when you get to listen to your favorite music.	3. Have separate laundry baskets, one for whites and one for colors. Put dirty clothes in the appropriate basket as you put them in the dirty laundry during the week, thereby saving you the task of sorting.
3. _____ _____	4. _____ _____

Chore #2

_____   _____

_____   _____

_____   _____

_____   _____

Chore #3

_____   _____

_____   _____

_____   _____

_____   _____

However, as desirable as recreational stress-reduction and relaxation techniques may be, they are not the key to dealing effectively with stress. Of utmost importance is to have a strong philosophy of leisure and life. If you have not done so already, take the time to list your most important leisure goals, both long-term and short-term. In the long run, having well-defined goals will reduce your stress level even more than daily massages and hot tubbing.

REFERENCES

Abramoff, J.L. (2002). Not only the savage beast. *The Jerusalem Report,* October 21, pp. 33-34.
Allen, R.J. (1983). *Human stress: Its nature and control.* Minneapolis: Burgess.
American Institute of Stress (2000). Stress—America's #1 health problem. Available at <www.stress.org/problem.html>.
Angier, N. (1990). Anger can ruin more than your day. *The New York Times,* December 13, pp. B1, B9.
Ardell, D. and Tager, M. (1982). *Planning for wellness* (Second edition). Dubuque, IA: Kendall Hunt.
Beech, H.R., Burns, L.E., and Sheffield, B.F. (1982). *A behavioral approach to the management of stress: A practical guide to techniques.* New York: Wiley.
Berenbaum, H. and Connelly, J. (1993). The effect of stress on hedonic capacity. *Journal of Abnormal Psychology,* 103(3), 474-482.
Berger, B.G. (1986). Use of jogging and swimming as stress-reduction techniques. In J.H. Humphrey (Ed.), *Human stress: Current selected research,* Volume 1 (pp. 169-190). New York: AMS Press.
Brown, B.B. (1984). *Between health and illness: New notions on stress and the nature of well-being.* Boston: Houghton Mifflin.
Callaman, L. (1993). Stressbusters: Corporate kicks; When the karate master comes to your office. *Forbes,* 151(10), 541-545.
Carter, P. (1994). High-tech stress: Is technology making you crazy? *Essence,* 24(10), 26.
Charlesworth, E.A. and Nathan, R.G. (1981). *Stress management: A comprehensive guide to wellness.* Houston, TX: Biobehavioral Publishers and Distributors.
Christensen, A. (1987). *The American Yoga Association beginners manual.* New York: Simon and Schuster.
Cooperman, K. (2000). Record numbers of the nation's freshmen feel high degree of stress, UCLA study finds. University of California-Los Angeles School of Education and Information Studies, Higher Education Research Institute, Press release.
Creekmore, C. (1994). Theory of the leisure trap. *Utne Reader,* 61, p. 61.
Davidson, J. (1994). "Overworked Americans" or overwhelmed Americans? Learning to relax and choose which decisions to make and inputs to respond to is the key to getting rid of that overwhelmed feeling. *Business Horizons,* 37(1), 62-67.

Everly, G.S. and Rosenfeld, R. (1981). *The nature and treatment of the stress response: A practical guide for clinicians.* New York: Plenum Press.

Finger, A. and Guber, L.G. (1984). *Yoga moves.* New York: Simon and Schuster.

Fort, I.L. (1986). The immediate response of physiological and psychological stress measures to aerobic exercise. In J.H. Humphrey (Ed.), *Human stress: Current selected research,* Volume 1 (pp. 191-198). New York: AMS Press.

Gherman, E.M. (1981). *Stress and the bottom line: A guide to personal well-being and corporate health.* New York: AMACOM.

Gill, J.L. (1983). *Personalized stress management: A manual for everyday life and work.* San Jose, CA: Counseling and Consulting Services Publications.

Goleman, D. (1992). New light on how stress erodes health. *The New York Times,* December 15, pp. B5, B9.

Goleman, D. (1994). Life's small pleasures aid immune system. *The New York Times,* May 11, pp. B5, B7.

Goode, E. (1999). For good health, it helps to be rich and important. *The New York Times,* June 1, pp. D1, D9.

Halpern, S. (n.d.). *Spectrum suite* (sound recording). Palo Alto, CA: SRI Records and Tapes.

Halpern, S. (1978). *Tuning the human instrument: An owners manual.* Palo Alto, CA: Spectrum Research Institute.

Hamberger, L.K. and Lohr, J.M. (1984). *Stress and stress management: Research and applications.* New York: Springer.

Health Resource Network. (2000). Stress facts. Available at <www.stresscure. com/hrn/facts.html>.

Hittleman, R. (1985). *Introduction to yoga.* New York: Bantam Books.

Isaacson, C. (1986). *The here's health book of yoga for all ages.* Rochester, NY: Thorsons Publishing.

Iso-Ahola, S.E. (1980). *The social psychology of leisure and recreation.* Dubuque, IA: Wm. C. Brown.

Iyengar, B.K.S. (1980). *The concise light on yoga.* New York: Schocken Books.

Kelly, B.J. (1986). Lifestyle intervention and stress management: The effects of instruction on lifestyle survey scores, blood pressure, and heart rate. In J.H. Humphrey (Ed.), *Human stress: Current selected research,* Volume 1 (pp. 163-168). New York: AMS Press.

Keyes, R. (1991). *Time lock: How life got so hectic and what you can do about it.* New York: HarperCollins Publishers.

Lidell, L. (1983). *The Sivananda companion to yoga.* New York: Simon and Schuster.

Mishra, R.S. (1987). *Fundamentals of yoga: A handbook of theory, practice, and application.* New York: The Julian Press.

Morgan, W.P. (1980). Test of champions: The iceberg profile. *Psychology Today,* July, pp. 92-99, 101, 108.

Paulsen, B. (1994). A nation out of balance. *Health,* October, pp. 45-48.

Rathbone, F.S. Jr. and Rathbone, E.T. (1971). *Health and the nature of man.* New York: McGraw-Hill.

Rechtschaffer, S. (1994). Why an empty hour scares us. *Utne Reader,* 61, 64-65.

Sachs, M.L. and Buffone, G. (Eds.). (1984). *Running as therapy: An integrated approach.* Lincoln: University of Nebraska Press.

Schafer, W. (1987). *Stress management for wellness.* New York: Holt, Rhinehart and Winston.

Selye, H. (1956). *The stress of life.* New York: McGraw-Hill.

Selye, H. (Ed.). (1980). *Selye's guide to stress research,* Volume 1. New York: Van Nostrand Reinhold.

Siegenthaler, K.L. (1997). Health benefits of leisure. *Parks and Recreation,* 32(1) (January), pp. 24, 26, 28, 30, 31.

Verespej, M.A. (2000). Stressed out. *Industry Week,* 249(4), 30-34.

Wilson, V.E., Berger, B.G., and Bird, E.I. (1981). Effects of running and of an exercise class on anxiety. *Perceptual and Motor Skills,* 53, 472-474.

Chapter 9

The Use of Humor and Laughter in Coping with and Reducing Stress

Kelli Cliff McCrea

INTRODUCTION

A person without a sense of humor is like a wagon without springs—jolted by every pebble in the road.

Henry Ward Beecher

The idea that humor and laughter have therapeutic qualities is not a new one, for it is even mentioned in the Bible. Research on humor and laughter and their relationship to stress has become a serious area of study, as evidenced by increased quantity and quality of articles published in professional journals. The purposes of this chapter are to examine the benefits of humor and laughter in coping with and reducing stress and to provide information about how to incorporate more humor and laughter into everyday life. The learning objectives for this chapter are to be able to discuss the following as related to coping with and reducing stress:

1. The physiological benefits of laughter and humor.
2. The psychological and affective benefits of laughter and humor.
3. The social and interpersonal benefits of laughter and humor.
4. The cognitive benefits of laughter and humor.
5. The incorporation of humor and laughter into everyday life.

HUMOR, LAUGHTER, AND STRESS DEFINED

Humor and laughter are not one and the same. It is not necessary for one to be present to experience the other (LaFrance, 1983). Laughter is a complex physiological activity which involves the contraction of most of the muscles in the face and the abdomen and is manifested by physical changes such as flared nostrils, a vibrating jaw, teary eyes, blushing, and the head and torso bending forward and flexing backward. In most instances, laughter occurs when there is a sudden psychological or emotional shift due to being caught off guard (Morreall, 1983). However, laughter can occur when others laugh, without knowledge or awareness of why they are laughing; some say it is contagious.

Humor, on the other hand, is a cognitive activity. Ziv (1984) defines *humor creativity* as having the ability to perceive relationships between objects, ideas, or people incongruously and being able to communicate this perception to others verbally or nonverbally. *Humor appreciation,* on the other hand, is having the ability to enjoy and understand humor creativity messages and incongruous situations.

McGhee (1979) emphasizes that to perceive humor, an individual must have knowledge or an understanding of the normal scheme of things. Nerhardt (1977) further suggests that to evoke humor, the perception of incongruity must occur in a nonthreatening and safe environment. As might be expected, studies have found great variation in the type of humor and the rate and degree of laughter experienced by different individuals (McGhee and Goldstein, 1983). Among other reasons, this is a result of social influences such as family and friends' beliefs and lifestyles (McGhee and Goldstein, 1983).

There are various approaches to defining stress. For the purposes of this chapter, *stress* is defined as "a set of adverse physiological, emotional, cognitive and behavioral reactions to events or situations that are perceived by the individual as threatening to his/her well-being and taxing his/her coping abilities" (Martin, 1988, p. 137). According to Martin, people engage in three types of coping strategies. The first involves reappraising an intolerable situation as challenging, the second involves reducing physiological tension resulting from emotional stress, and the third involves actively altering the stressful situation.

THE BENEFITS OF HUMOR AND LAUGHTER

> Laughter is the sensation of feeling good all over, and showing it principally in one place.

> Josh Billings

So, why are humor and laughter important? Because we are constantly faced with minor setbacks such as failing an exam, getting a speeding ticket, or losing a wallet, and occasionally faced with major setbacks such as the death of a loved one or the loss of a job. With all the difficulties in life, it is no wonder that stress is so prevalent. While humor assists in emotionally coping with stress, laughter aids in relieving the negative physical effects when stress occurs (Fry, 1986; Peter and Dana, 1982; Cousins, 1979).

Humor and laughter are adaptive coping mechanisms that can moderate stress (Leftcourt and Martin, 1986). The real advantage that humor and laughter have over other stress management methods is that they are versatile; both can occur spontaneously anywhere at any time, thus increasing the potential for frequent stress-reduction "workouts." In general, other methods (i.e., jogging, yoga, meditation) require more preparation, time, money, and overall physical fitness. Laughter and humor are, indeed, the miracle drugs with no bad side effects (Peter and Dana, 1982).

Physiological Benefits

> [T]he old man laughed loud and joyously, shook up the details of his anatomy from head to foot, and ended by saying that such a laugh was money in a man's pocket, because it cut down the doctor's bills like everything.

> Mark Twain

The physiological benefits of laughter include (1) tension reduction (Fry, 1986); (2) stimulation of the sympathetic nervous system (Schachter and Wheeler, 1962); (3) an increase in respiratory activity (Moody, 1978); (4) stimulation of the circulatory system (Peter and Dana, 1982; Fry and Stoft, 1971); and (5) pain reduction (Cousins, 1979). Mestel (1998) cites a research study in which college students who were watching funny videos experienced an increase in disease-fighting antibodies and immune cells, as well as a decrease in cortisol (a stress hormone). Humor and laughter are being incorporated into medicine through a society called the Association for Applied and Therapeutic Humor (Mestel, 1998).

Muscle tension often accompanies stress. Many researchers have noted that there is an increase in muscle tension while laughing and a subsequent relaxation following laughter (Chapman and Foot, 1976; Fry, 1986; Deckers and Devine, 1981; Nerhardt, 1970). Those muscles not directly affected by the laughter response relax during laughter. During hearty laughter one might experience falling off of a chair onto the floor, eyes watering, loss of bladder control, or not being able to grasp an object tightly. These manifestations may be a result of a loss of conscious control due to the contraction of other muscle groups (Fry, 1986).

Exercise has been proven to be an effective means of stress reduction (Brooks and Fahey, 1985; Schafer 1978). In analyzing the body's physiological response to exercise and laughter, there appear to be several similarities. These similarities include increased ventilation, increased heart rate, increased cardiac output, increased catecholamine (hormonal) response, and increased systolic blood pressure (Brooks and Fahey, 1985; Peter and Dana, 1982). For this reason, laughter is often referred to as "internal jogging" (Cousins, 1979).

Stress can cause a breakdown between certain systems in the body, resulting in a disturbance of homeostasis that can lead to an increase in a diseased state (e.g., ulcers, cancer) (Peter and Dana, 1982). Laughter can counteract this stress response. There appears to be a correlation between laughter and the stimulation of the sympathetic nervous system and consequent release of the hormones norepinephrine and epinephrine (Averill, 1969; Levi, 1965; Sternbach, 1962; Schachter and Wheeler, 1962). The sympathetic nervous system is responsible for control of the sweat glands, blood vessels, eyes, heart, bronchi, kidneys, bladder, anal sphincter, and intestines (Brooks and Fahey, 1985). Frequent stimulation of the system increases overall functioning and enables the body to handle physical stress more effectively.

Laughter causes full action of the diaphragm (the main muscle of respiration situated between the chest and abdomen), thereby increasing respiratory activity. When the diaphragm contracts and expands it massages the other organs above and below it, including the lungs and stomach (Moody, 1978). During a bout of hearty laughter, an individual's heart rate and blood pressure increase (Averill, 1969) and then shortly thereafter fall below an individual's normal level, allowing the body to enter a state of relaxation. The decrease in blood pressure and heart rate can last up to forty-five minutes (Peter and Dana, 1982); the long-term effects are still being investigated.

Physical pain can increase physical and emotional stress, and occasionally, stress induces pain (e.g., headaches and backaches). Although the exact mechanism is unknown, laughter seems to reduce physical pain. It has been hypothesized that the pain reduction is a result of the release of endorphins (pain-reducing enzymes with morphine-like properties) that are present in the brain during laughter. It could also be a function of the individual's attention being diverted from the pain during and after laughter.

Norman Cousins (1979) credits his pain relief with laughter therapy. Cousins had a serious collagen disease that caused him great pain. He was told that he had a one in 500 chance to survive. Working from the notion that positive emotions might produce positive chemical changes in the body, Cousins began a therapeutic program of laughter using Marx Brothers and Candid Camera films. He found that ten minutes of sustained laughter gave him at least two hours of pain-free sleep. Laboratory tests revealed a positive physiological change as well.

Psychological and Affective Benefits

> We don't laugh because we're happy, we're happy because we laugh.
>
> William James

Psychological and affective benefits of humor and laughter include (1) a sudden shift in cognitive perspective (Leftcourt and Martin, 1986; Anderson and Arnoult, 1989); (2) reducing negative emotions such as anxiety, anger, and depression (Moody, 1978; Peter and Dana, 1982; Korotkov and Hannah, 1994; Fry and Salameh, 1993); (3) creating and maintaining a positive attitude (Moody, 1978); and (4) feelings of well-being and euphoria (McDougall, 1922; Moody, 1978; Peter and Dana, 1982).

Humor, by nature, playfully distorts or exaggerates reality. Data obtained from a long-term study of how men cope with life's difficulties indicate that one of the five strategies for coping with stress and life events was humor (Vaillant, 1977). Leftcourt and Martin (1986) studied the psychological effects of stress and found

> The negative effects of stress were less pronounced for individuals who tended to laugh and smile in a wide variety of situations, who placed a high value on humor, and who make use of humor as a means of coping with stress than for those to whom these descriptions did not apply. (p. 57)

Results of an experiment investigating the relationship between humor and coping with stress in a military combat course indicated that active humor (production) increased the quality of functioning during stressful events (Bizi, Keinan, and Beit-Hallahmi, 1988). Finally, in a study examining humor appreciation and creativity in college students, Overholser (1992) found that subjects who indicated that they use humor to cope with stressful situations were less depressed, less lonely, and had greater self-esteem than those who do not. However, he suggested that humor could become a form of denial if used excessively.

Changing or altering one's perspective can minimize stress. Distancing oneself from the stressor provides the opportunity to look at the problem objectively and identify possible resolutions. Humor and laughter can assist in this process. "Rather than feeling governed by the situation and obliged to look at it in only one way, we feel playful toward it and thus put ourselves in control" (Morreall, 1983, p. 122).

The ability to laugh at oneself is an indicator of a positive attitude. Being able to see the humor in a given situation reduces feelings of helplessness because it affirms that the individual, not the situation or emotion, is in control of his or her life. Moody (1978) writes, "Perhaps ultimately, and in the deepest sense, humor works by rallying, and by being a manifestation of the will to live" (p. 115).

Laughter has been associated with the secretion of the arousal hormones dopamine, norepinephrine, and epinephrine. The stimulatory influences of these hormones in the mind and body include the feeling of euphoria (McDougall, 1922; Moody, 1978). In summary, Peter and Dana (1982) state that

Even the most physically and mentally healthy individual has disappointments that trigger the blues. When seen with a sense of humor, these traumas and stresses tend to pass quickly, and the individual soon will return to the peak of wellness. Mentally healthy individuals accept unexpected setbacks as a part of life. They don't waste time and effort worrying that their circumstances are not ideal. They simply make the best of their circumstances. (p. 22)

Social and Interpersonal Benefits

Laughter is the shortest distance between two people.

Victor Borge

The social and interpersonal benefits of humor and laughter include (1) a means of breaking the ice and establishing communication (Moody, 1978; Morreall, 1983; Hertzler, 1970); (2) maintaining relationships (Moody, 1978; Hertzler, 1970; Graham, Papa, and Brooks, 1992); and (3) facilitating communication of sensitive issues (Peter and Dana, 1982; Hertzler, 1970).

Laughter is an indicator of attitude similarities. Attitude similarities have been proven to affect attraction among strangers (Gonzales et al., 1983). Laughter can lead to grouping of individuals due to shared interest in the laughter theme (Hertzler, 1970). In new social settings stress is common. Using humor or sharing laughter immediately reduces stress associated with meeting new people. It becomes a social lubricant (Moody, 1978; Blumenfeld and Alpern, 1986), giving people the feeling of being connected.

"Humor apparently helps people succeed in intimate relationships because it allows them to handle the stress within those relationships" (Hampes, 1992, p. 127). Hampes (1992) found that individuals measuring high in intimacy (Measures of Psychosocial Development) scored significantly higher on the Situational Humor Response Questionnaire than did the low-intimacy group. Hampes (1992) postulates that "if a person can laugh at stressful situations that arise in intimate relationships, it might allow that person to release physiological and psychological tension and thereby make it easier for intimacy to occur" (p. 129). Lynch (1979) cites several studies supporting the idea that one's longevity and health are influenced positively by interpersonal relationships. Unfortunately, there is always the potential for stress-producing situations in relationships. Laughing together about petty differences will minimize conflicts and, consequently, reduce stress. Humor and laughter discourage hostility and friction and help to maintain social and interpersonal unity (Hertzler, 1970).

Humor can facilitate communication of sensitive issues. A confrontational situation can be made easier if one person involved utilizes humor or laughter. This results in distancing people from the problem and allows the maintenance of a proper perspective. By reducing the stress and tension that often accompany a problem, any anger that exists can be deflected and the situation can be more readily resolved.

> In applying our rational powers, humor often can be the catalyst that makes the process work. In problem solving, humor isn't trivial. It should be used to deflate the over inflated, not to trivialize that which is genuinely important. (Peter and Dana, 1982, p. 139)

Hampes (1993) investigated the relationship between humor and generativity (promoting the welfare of other people), both of which are characteristics of psychologically well-adjusted adults. Those individuals who scored high on generativity scored significantly higher on two measures of humor than those with low generativity scores. Hampes (1993) conjectured that "humor may facilitate generativity through such mediating variables as intimacy and creativity as well as through stress reduction" (p. 131). Indeed, humor and laughter affect our lives more than we realize.

Cognitive Benefits

A content analysis of humor definitions and theories (Murdock and Ganim, 1993) revealed that "definitions of humor were highly integrated within the domain of creativity" (p. 61). Dacey (1989) found that trick playing, joking, and family "fooling around" take an important place in families of highly creative adolescents, particularly when compared with other families. Humor and creativity seem to have a reciprocal relationship, in which humor positively influences creativity and vice versa.

Humor and laughter have been found to positively affect brain functioning. In more than one study, researchers found that humor and the ensuing laughter heightened both hemispheres of the brain, resulting in an "unusually high level of consciousness and information processing," thus enabling the individual to see "both the abstract, subtle nuances of a problem and its more concrete, logical aspects at the same time" (Coleman, 1992, pp. 270-271).

Although the empirical evidence is inconclusive, it has been demonstrated that humor can positively affect recall of lecture and/or written material presented in the classroom (Ziv, 1984; Vance, 1987; Kaplan and Pascoe, 1977). This seems to be particularly true when the material to be learned is complex. For example, Ziv (1984) found a significant increase in scores on a statistics exam following the use of relevant humor to teach statistics. Many educators believe that the increase in test scores is a function of reducing test anxiety as well as making the classroom environment more conducive to learning. Kuiper, Martin, and Olinger (1993) also discovered that individuals who scored high on the Coping Humor Scale were more apt to appraise an exam as a positive challenge and would adjust their expectations for future performance based on previous performance, thereby reducing stress.

INCORPORATING HUMOR INTO EVERYDAY LIFE

The one thing all charming people have in common, no matter how they may differ in other respects, is an amused detachment from their commonplace troubles.

Sydney J. Harris

One explanation for an individual's ability to perceive and appreciate humor is reinforcement (McGhee and Goldstein, 1983). Humor is intrinsically reinforcing and enjoyable because new forms of stimulation are provided, thereby maintaining an optimally interesting environment (Singer, 1973). One probable source of external reinforcement is an individual's parents. Bell and McGhee (1982) found that college males whose fathers, and females whose mothers, frequently participated in clowning and joking rate themselves as initiating humor frequently.

In a study examining the relationships between children's humor, behavioral characteristics, acceptance by peers, and self-perceptions, Sletta and Sobstad (1993) discovered that for very young children, humor was not consistently related to peer acceptance or rejection while the opposite was true for adolescents. Canzler (1980) observed that elementary school age boys initiated humor much more frequently than girls, and while the girls were eager to laugh at boys' antics and jokes, boys did not respond to the girls' attempts to be funny. Numerous other studies cite differences in male and female humor (McGhee and Lloyd, 1981; Chaney, 1993). Although one can speculate that genetic differences exist between male and female humor, it is more likely a function of socialization at a very young age (Kuchner, 1991).

People are born with an unlimited capacity for laughter. "By about four months, infants laugh an average of once an hour and by four years may laugh as much as once every four minutes" (The Laughter Project, 1984, p. 11). In the process of growing up, laughter becomes a function of belief systems and social learning (The Laughter Project, 1984; McGhee and Goldstein, 1983). Children are told "That's not funny" or "Wipe that smile off your face." They are taught that laughter is undignified and disruptive, that life is serious and should be treated that way.

Several programs specifically designed to promote humor have achieved success in counteracting the negative effects of illness, aging, and general life stress (e.g., The Laughter Project at the University of California at Santa Barbara; The Living Room of the Stehlin Foundation for Cancer Research in Houston, Texas; and the Lively Room at De Kalb General Hospital in Decatur, Georgia). Frank J. Prerost (1993), a professor of psychology at Western Illinois University, developed a formal humor-production training procedure for older adults. "The goal of the Humor Production Project (HPP) is to enhance one's personal sense of humor which can release anxieties and provide assistance in the development of a sense of mastery over life event stresses" (p. 19). Unique programs such as this have enabled many individuals to cope with stressors in their lives, and in some cases, heal themselves.

Articles published in professional journals suggest that private corporations advocate the use of humor and laughter to increase employee job satisfaction and productivity (Boverie, 1994; Caudron,

1992; Gorkin, 1990; Morreall, 1991). A few corporations, such as Eastman Kodak, have designated "humor rooms" where employees can go to watch videos. In justifying their role as humor consultants, Metcalf and Felible (1992) cite statistics from a survey conducted by a life insurance company that 14 percent of U.S. workers quit their jobs in 1990 because of excess stress and 34 percent seriously considered quitting their jobs. An organization called FUNsulting, etc. tries to make work more enjoyable and less stressful by bringing humor and laughter into the workplace (Krebs, 1999).

Most people find humor in jokes, cartoons, and comedy routines. Unfortunately, they do not take the opportunity to find humor in the everyday "serious" parts of life such as deadlines, financial problems, relationships, and physical health. "Humor and the related laughter enable people to live with some of the most insistently tabooed realities of human life, however sinister, awesome, fearsome, obscene, indelicate, or contrary to the reigning conventions they may be believed to be" (Hertzler, 1970, p. 135).

> Relearning to laugh involves coming to the understanding that most of what happens in life is not so serious that it cannot be laughed about. It also means learning to laugh at the single thing most people take too seriously—themselves. (The Laughter Project, 1984, p. 12)

Because many individuals have been socialized not to laugh, it takes a considerable amount of practice to change behaviors and attitudes that inhibit laughter. People can choose to bring more laughter and less stress into their lives. The key is to practice.

Tips for Creating Healthy "Ha-Ha's"

- Share embarrassing moments with a friend.
- Start a comedy scrapbook (file) of jokes, anecdotes, and comics that reflect the ironic, weird, and funny things that happen while at school or work.
- Create a humorous environment by putting jokes and comics up on a bulletin board.
- Collect video/audio tapes of your favorite comedian or TV situation comedy.

- Look for humorous advertisements or humorous mistakes in the newspaper.
- Give humorous gifts to friends or family.
- Write down everything that amuses you.
- Take every opportunity to be with people who make you laugh.
- Keep "toys" around that can be used to alleviate a stressful situation (e.g., bubbles, puppets, joke-store items).
- Focus humor on yourself. Do not tell jokes that will offend others.
- Be childlike (not childish).
- Adopt a comic viewpoint.

Related to the last suggestion, to adopt a comic viewpoint, Exercise 9.1 is presented to help you identify some stressful situations in your life that can be dealt with in a humorous way by adopting a comic viewpoint.

Try to apply the ideas generated in Exercise 9.1 to the next stressful situation you encounter. Incorporating the comic viewpoint into your life can help you to turn many of the stressors in your life into humorous, laughter-inducing situations. In addition, if you are able to incorporate more laughter into your life, you will be a healthier, less stressful person. Exercise 9.2 asks you to examine what makes you laugh and how to incorporate more of your favorite laughter producers into your life.

For additional information and tips for increasing laughter in your life, contact the following people or organizations:

Fun Technicians, Inc.
Box 51160
Syracuse, NY 13215

Workshop Library on World Humor
Box 23334
Washington, DC 20024

Joel Goodman, PhD, Editor
Laughing Matters
c/o The HUMOR Project
480 Broadway, Suite 210
Saratoga Springs, NY 12866

Laugh Lovers News
Box 1495
Pleasanton, CA 94566

Laughmakers
PO Box 160
Syracuse, NY 13215

International Mirth Month, Whole Mirth Catalog
1034 Page Street
San Francisco, CA 94117

Hunter "Patch" Adams, MD
The Gesundheit Institute
<www.patchadams.org>

Annette Goodheart
Laughter Therapy
635 North Alisos Street
Santa Barbara, CA 93103

E. T. "Cy" Eberhart
3233 Sandalwood Lane NW
Salem, OR 97304

FUN-dynamics
c/o Dr. Mary-Lou Galician
Walter Cronkite School-ASU
Tempe, AZ 85287-1305

SUMMARY

The primary focus of this chapter was to support the idea that laughter and humor are effective tools for reducing negative stress. The research cited in this chapter clearly supports this idea and also documents the extensive benefits of laughter and humor.

EXERCISE 9.1.
Alternative Humorous Responses to Stressful Situations

Instructions

1. In the first column list some stressful situations that you encounter in your life. List all types of stressors, both those that are social/interpersonal (e.g., being interviewed as a prospective new member of a fraternity) and those that are not (e.g., being stuck in a traffic jam).
2. In the second column, list an alternative, feasible *humorous* response to that situation. For example, in a traffic jam, instead of getting angry and blowing your horn, would blowing bubbles out the window be a laughter-producing alternative response for you? How about listening to a comedy tape? Similarly, instead of getting nervous at the fraternity interview, how could you break the ice with humor and laughter?

Stressor	Alternative humorous response
Ex. Traffic jam	Blow bubbles; listen to a comedy tape

1. _____   _____
   _____   _____
   _____   _____

2. _____   _____
   _____   _____
   _____   _____

3. _____   _____
   _____   _____
   _____   _____

4. _____   _____
   _____   _____
   _____   _____

5. _____   _____
   _____   _____
   _____   _____

EXERCISE 9.2. Incorporating More Laughter into My Life

Instructions

1. In the first column, under each category, identify some of your favorite laughter producers.
2. In the second column, list ideas for increasing your exposure to some of these favorite laughter producers to bring more laughter and humor into your life.

Favorite laughter producers	**Ideas for increasing them**

People:

Ex. My brother   Invite him to visit more

_____   _____

_____   _____

Activities/situations:

Ex. Playing games such as charades   Have game nights with friends

_____   _____

_____   _____

Movies/TV/entertainment:

Ex. Seeing live stand-up comedy   Go to comedy clubs more

_____   _____

_____   _____

Cartoons/books:

Ex. Sunday comics   Buy the Sunday newspaper

_____   _____

_____   _____

Toys/games:

Ex. "Whoopie cushion"   Buy gag items at a novelty store

_____   _____

_____   _____

REFERENCES

Anderson, C.A. and Arnoult, L.H. (1989). An examination of perceived control, humor, irrational beliefs, and positive stress as moderators of the relation between negative stress and health. *Basic and Applied Social Psychology,* 10(2), 101-117.

Averill, J.R. (1969). Autonomic response patterns during sadness and mirth. *Psychophysiology,* 5, 399-414.

Bell, N.J. and McGhee, P.E. (1982). Social interaction implications of humor. Paper presented at a meeting of the Southwestern Society for Research in Human Development.

Bizi, S., Keinan, G., and Beit-Hallahmi, B. (1988). Humor and coping with stress: A test under real-life conditions. *Personality and Individual Differences,* 9(6), 951-956.

Blumenfeld, E. and Alpern, L. (1986). *The smile connection: How to use humor in dealing with people.* New Jersey: Prentice-Hall.

Boverie, P. (1994). Humor in human resource development. *Human Resource Development Quarterly,* 5(1), 75-91.

Brooks, G. and Fahey, T. (1985). *Exercise physiology: Human bioenergetics and its applications.* New York: Macmillan Publishing Company.

Canzler, L. (1980). *Humor and the primary child.* Technical report. ED # 191583.

Caudron, S. (1992). Humor is healthy in the workplace. *Personnel Journal,* 71, 63-78.

Chaney, C. (1993). Young children's jokes: A cognitive developmental perspective. Paper presented at the Annual Meeting of the Western States Communication Association, Albuquerque, New Mexico.

Chapman, T. and Foot, H. (Eds.) (1976). *Humour and laughter: Theory, research and applications.* New York: John Wiley and Sons.

Coleman, J.G. (1992). All seriousness aside: The laughing-learning connection. *International Journal of Instructional Media,* 19(3), 269-276.

Cousins, N. (1979). *Anatomy of an illness as perceived by the patient.* New York: W.W. Norton and Company.

Dacey, J.S. (1989). Discriminating characteristics of the families of highly creative adolescents. *The Journal of Creative Behavior,* 23(4), 263-271.

Deckers, L. and Devine, J. (1981). Humor by violating an existing expectancy. *Journal of Psychology,* 108, 107-110.

Fry, W.F. Jr. (1986). Humor, physiology and the aging process. In L. Nahemow, K.A. McCluskey-Fawcett, and P.E. McGhee (Eds.), *Humor and aging* (pp. 81-98). Orlando, FL: Academic Press, Inc.

Fry, W.F. Jr. and Stoft, P.E. (1971). Mirth and oxygen saturation levels of peripheral blood. *Psychotherapy and Psychosomatics,* 19, 76-84.

Fry, W.F. Jr. and Salameh, W. (Eds.) (1993). *Advances in humor and psychotherapy.* Sarasota, FL: Professional Resource Exchange.

Gonzales, M.H., Davis, J.M., Loney, G.L., Lukens, C.K., and Junghans, C.M. (1983). Interactional approach to interpersonal attraction. *Journal of Personality and Social Psychology,* 44, 1192-1197.

Gorkin, M. (1990). The higher power of humor. *Legal Professional,* 7, 48-51.

Graham, E., Papa, M., and Brooks, G. (1992). Functions of humor in conversation: Conceptualization and measurement. *Western Journal of Communication,* 56, 161-183.

Hampes, W.P. (1992). Relation between intimacy and humor. *Psychological Reports,* 71, 127-130.

Hampes, W.P. (1993). Relation between humor and generativity. *Psychological Reports,* 73, 131-136.

Hertzler, J.O. (1970). *Laughter: A socio-scientific analysis.* New York: Exposition Press.

Kaplan, R.M. and Pascoe, G.C. (1977). Humorous lectures and humorous examples: Some effects upon comprehension and retention. *Journal of Educational Psychology,* 69, 61-65.

Korotkov, D. and Hannah, T.E. (1994). Extraversion and emotionality as proposed superordinate stress moderators: A prospective analysis. *Personality and Individual Differences,* 16(5), 787-792.

Krebs, B. (1999). Reporting to the bored. *The Sacramento Bee,* April 11, p. E2.

Kuchner, J.F. (1991). The humor of young children. Paper presented at the Meeting of the National Association for the Education of Young Children, Uniondale, New York.

Kuiper, N.A., Martin, R., and Olinger, L. (1993). Coping humour, stress, and cognitive appraisals. *Canadian Journal of Behavioural Science,* 25(1), 81-96.

LaFrance, M. (1983). Felt versus feigned funniness: Issues in coding smiling and laughing. In P.E. McGhee and J.H. Goldstein (Eds.), *Handbook of humor research,* Volume 1 (pp. 1-12). New York: Springer-Verlag.

The Laughter Project (1984). *Laughter and stress.* Santa Barbara: The University of California Press.

Leftcourt, H.M. and Martin, R.A. (1986). *Humor and life stress.* New York: Springer-Verlag.

Levi, L. (1965). The urinary output of adrenalin and noradrenalin during pleasant and unpleasant emotional states. *Psychosomatic Medicine,* 27, 80-85.

Lynch, J. (1979). *The broken heart.* New York: Basic Books, Inc.

Martin, R.A. (1988). Humor and the mastery of living: Using humor to cope with the daily stresses of growing up. *Journal of Children in Contemporary Society,* 20(1/2), 135-154.

McDougall, W. (1922). A new theory of laughter. *Psyche,* 2, 289-300.

McGhee, P.E. (1979). *Humor: Its origin and development.* San Francisco: Freeman.

McGhee, P.E. and Goldstein, J.H. (Eds.) (1983). *Handbook of humor research,* Volume 1. New York: Springer-Verlag.

McGhee, P.E. and Lloyd, S.A. (1981). A developmental test of the disposition theory of humor. *Child Development,* 52(3), 925-931.

Mestel, R. (1998). The best medicine. *The Los Angeles Times,* December 28, pp. S1, S5.

Metcalf, C.W. and Felible, R. (1992). Humor: An antidote for terminal professionalism. *Industry Week,* 241, 14-19.

Moody, R.A. (1978). *Laugh after laugh: The healing power of humor.* Jacksonville, FL: Headwaters Press.

Morreall, J. (1983). *Taking laughter seriously.* Albany: State University of New York Press.

Morreall, J. (1991). Humor and work. *Humor: International Journal of Humor Research,* 4, 359-373.

Murdock, M.C. and Ganim, R.M. (1993). Creativity and humor: Integration and incongruity. *The Journal of Creative Behavior,* 27(1), 57-70.

Nerhardt, G. (1970). Humor and inclinations of humor: Emotional reactions to stimuli of different divergence from a range of expectancy. *Scandinavian Journal of Psychology,* 11, 185-194.

Nerhardt, G. (1977). Operationalization of incongruity in humour research: A critique and suggestions. In A.J. Chapman and H. Foot (Eds.), *It's a funny thing, humour* (pp. 185-195). London: Pergamon Press.

Overholser, J.C. (1992). Sense of humor when coping with life stress. *Personality and Individual Differences,* 13(7), 799-804.

Peter, L.J. and Dana, B. (1982). *The laughter prescription.* New York: Ballantine Books.

Prerost, F.J. (1993). A strategy to enhance humor production among elderly persons: Assisting in the management of stress. *Activities, Adaptation and Aging,* 14(4), 17-24.

Schachter, S. and Wheeler, L. (1962). Epinephrine, chlorpromazine, and amusement. *Journal of Abnormal and Social Psychology,* 65, 121-128.

Schafer, W. (1978). *Stress, distress and growth.* Davis, CA: Responsible Action.

Singer, J.L. (1973). *The child's world of make believe.* New York: Academic Press.

Sletta, O. and Sobstad, F. (1993). Social competence and humor in pre-school and school-aged children. Paper presented at the Biennial Meeting of the Society for Research in Child Development, New Orleans.

Sternbach, R. (1962). Assessing differential autonomic patterns in emotions. *Journal of Psychosomatic Research,* 6, 87-91.

Vaillant, G.E. (1977). *Adaptation to life.* Boston: Little Brown and Company.

Vance, C. (1987). A comparative study on the use of humor in the design of instruction. *Instructional Science,* 16(1), 79-100.

Ziv, A. (1984). *Personality and sense of humor.* New York: Springer Publishing Company.

Chapter 10

Recreation and Social Development

INTRODUCTION

Some forms of recreation have a positive effect on social development, others have a negative effect, and some have a questionable effect. The main thrust of this chapter is to analyze the effects of various types of leisure activity on social development.

Social development is an important concern because social activity is an important determinant of quality of life. The psychological and physiological effects of social activity are explored in this chapter. Recreational means of enhancing social activity and social development are also examined. In addition, friendships, a vital aspect of a satisfying leisure lifestyle, are discussed. Practical tips for improving social skills and making friends are presented.

More specifically, the learning objectives for this chapter are to

1. Identify psychological and physiological benefits of social interaction.
2. Contrast positive and negative effects of watching television and playing video games on social development.
3. Contrast positive and negative effects of listening to popular music on social development.
4. Identify and describe three different levels of friendship.
5. Identify considerations in attempting to improve social development and in attempting to initiate, maintain, and enhance friendships.
6. Identify recreational activities that can enhance social development.

IMPORTANCE OF RECREATIONAL SOCIAL INTERACTION

Psychological and Physiological Benefits

It is difficult to separate the psychological and physiological benefits of social interaction. However, it is easy to contrast the physiological and psychological states of loneliness with those of positive social interaction, as shown in Table 10.1.

As shown in the table, loneliness is characterized by negative psychological and physiological states, whereas positive social interaction leads to desirable psychological and physiological states. Leisure provides both the greatest opportunity for positive social interaction and the greatest potential for feelings of isolation and loneliness. Societal trends such as high divorce rates, high crime rates and fear of crime, and reduced opportunities for social interaction at work due to increased reliance on technology (e.g., communicating with co-workers via e-mail instead of personal contact) are shutting people off from one another and depriving them of social contacts. It is even more imperative to have social interaction during leisure if it is not present at work or in the home environment. In light of the significant physiological and psychological effects of social interaction, it is important to explore how to maximize socialization through recreation. This examination should involve a review of both the positive and

TABLE 10.1. Loneliness versus Social Interaction

Loneliness—physical/psychological states	States during positive social interaction
Feeling sad, depressed	Happy
Lethargic	Energized
Stress	Relaxed
Low self-esteem	High self-esteem
Confused	Alert
Unmotivated	Motivated
Vulnerable	Confident
Detachment	Feelings of warmth, closeness with others

negative implications of various forms of recreational activity on social development.

TELEVISION, MOVIES, AND VIDEO GAMES AND THEIR EFFECTS ON SOCIAL DEVELOPMENT

As mentioned in Chapter 4, watching television is the most heavily participated in leisure activity among Americans. Playing video games has also become an increasingly popular recreational activity, particularly among youth. The positive and negative implications of these recreational activities on social development are explored in this section.

Winn (1987) and Pawlowski (2000) highlight some of the negative effects of television on socialization. For example, television prevents families from doing other activities and sharing more meaningful experiences together. Studies show that when the television is on, little or no conversation takes place among family members. According to Winn, television is a hidden competitor for all other activities. The activities that television replaces, such as play, conversation, or reading, are better learning tools or socialization practices.

Even educational television tends to break down the ability to do sequential thinking and disrupt the overall sensory organization of the child (Stockbridge, 1994). Unfortunately, studies show that young children have already watched 1,500 hours of television before they start school and will have spent 18,000 hours watching television by the time they graduate from high school, as opposed to 12,000 hours in school (Pawlowski, 2000).

Another problem with watching television and movies is that it distorts reality. One government study found that people were doing drugs, drinking, or smoking in 98 percent of the top movie rentals (Riechmann, 1999). Bufkin (2000) reports that teenagers, one of the main age groups that watch a great deal of television, rely more on the media than on their parents for education on sensitive topics such as sex, sexually transmitted diseases, drugs, and alcohol. Thus, teenagers are particularly vulnerable to the reality distortions of movies and television shows.

Another concern is the excessive violence shown on television. Carlsson-Paige and Levin (1992) state that during the approximately seven years of time spent watching television by age eighteen, 26,000 murders would have been witnessed. However, as discussed by Kellerman (1999), although many studies show a correlation between media violence and aggression, a causal link has not been established. For example, in Japan, where the level of media violence is much higher than in the United States, the level of violent crime among both children and adults is much lower than it is in the United States. Television is apparently only one of many factors related to violent behavior.

According to Mander's (1978) analysis, it seems that watching television can seriously harm interpersonal communication skills and overall functioning, at least temporarily. Mander explains that brainwave patterns go into a smooth, steady rhythm and thinking processes dim while watching television. The reasons for this are lack of eye movement, visual fixation on a specific object (the television screen), idleness, inactivity, and body inertness while watching television. According to Mander, studies show that when the eyes are not moving, instead are just staring, thinking diminishes. Mander asserts that television trains people to be zombies. He explains that television is a form of sensory deprivation, causing confusion and disorientation because it is constantly placing images in the viewer's brain. When coupled with the viewer's susceptibility to television's images and ideas resulting from the almost hypnotic state that it creates, watching television has the potential to create confusion and difficulty in distinguishing between reality and the images implanted artificially by programs and commercials. How does this confusion affect socialization? Ever try socializing with a confused individual? It's not easy!

Furthermore, the distortion of reality can be transferred to interpersonal interactions. Mander states that people sometimes act out the images they have seen on television without realizing it. Therefore, the interactions of two avid television viewers can sometimes really be largely the product of a Hollywood scriptwriter's mind!

Yet another disturbing effect of watching television is the apparent diminishing of sexual activity among males who watch sports on television. One theoretical explanation for this phenomenon is that a process called cathexis takes place, whereby viewers release so much energy and emotion during a televised sporting event that they do not have enough energy remaining for sex (Levy, 1983).

Another apparent problem is that overexposure to sex in television and other media might be contributing to sexual dissatisfaction (Albers, 1990). The television shows most often watched by the average college student contain 2,000 references to sex (on an annual basis), with most of this sexual content being unrealistic and leading to unrealistic expectations and dissatisfaction with their own sex lives (Albers, 1990).

There is also special concern for television's effect on children's socialization, especially with regard to hyperactivity. Television's images of action and violence stimulate the child to imitate these behaviors while simultaneously cutting the child off from activity and real sensory stimulation. Watching television is a very passive activity, yet it implants images of high adventure, excitement, and violence in the mind. In this way, watching television can cause not only hyperactivity, but frustration as well (Mander, 1978).

If television has such a negative effect on people, why not simply stop watching television? According to Mander, television seems to be addictive. It is very difficult to get out of the trancelike state induced by the passive fixation on the television set and its flickering lights. This can help explain why it is so popular, even though studies such as Sahin's and Robinson's (Lodziak, 1986) indicate that television is the least enjoyable of all leisure activities. After watching television, people report being less relaxed, less happy, and less able to concentrate, compared to how they feel after participating in sports or other leisure activities (Goleman, 1990). Given these negative effects of television on socialization and its immense popularity, it seems that something must be done. In this regard, a "television turn-off week" has become an annual event; the one that occurred in April 2001 had six million participants (Anonymous, 2001). The purpose of this effort is to redirect attention away from television and toward leisure activities such as sports, volunteerism, gardening, music, reading, and other more productive and healthy activities. Winn (1987) advocates "unplugging the plug-in drug" and offers the following suggestions for eliminating or cutting down on television viewing (also see the suggestions for reducing television viewing time in Chapter 6):

1. Have all family members sign a contract to eliminate or reduce television viewing.
2. Make special plans for individual and group activities to replace television, especially during times when it will be missed the most.
3. Before beginning the television reduction/elimination program, assess how many hours of television are actually viewed. Keep a one-week log of viewing time describing personal feelings during and after the shows that were viewed.
4. Then, after reducing or eliminating television viewing, write about the effects of this change on day-to-day life and mention what activities have taken the place of watching television.
5. Create a special reward for totally eliminating television viewing.
6. To ease the process of reduction/elimination, take out interesting books from the library to fill in the small blocks of free time normally devoted to television.

Another suggestion for reducing the television viewing time of children is to resist the temptation to use television as a baby-sitter. Get your children together with other children. It is amazing how even a three-year-old can be so much easier to care for and entertain when another child (though not necessarily a sibling) is around. Think how much better it is for the child's social development to play with other children than to be glued to the television.

If all else fails, some devices are available to help parents wean their children from television. These "black box" gadgets, which enable parents to program a daily or weekly viewing time budget, seem to be fairly effective (Silver, 1993).

It is also interesting to examine the effects of video recorders on television viewing patterns and socialization. Video recorders on the one hand allow more control over program viewing, providing the opportunity for more discrimination in viewing choices. However, watching videos can also create another form of addiction. Unfortunately, video viewing habits might even be more harmful to socialization than watching television. Spouses often watch videos *separately*. Whereas a VCR is often used to entertain when it is first purchased, within a few months it is used primarily for family or individual use, leaving little or no opportunity for socialization.

Television is not the only form of recreational visual media that might have a negative impact on socialization. Video games have also come under scrutiny. Playing video games can be viewed as anti-social behavior, because it involves a human being interacting with a machine rather than with people. Many of the solitary video games are violent in nature, which might lead to inappropriate aggressive behavior.

Provenzo (1992) believes that the social and educational impact of video games must be confronted. He views them as being based on violence, aggression, and gender bias, encouraging behavior that is immoral. However, Nagourney (1984) concludes that overall, the advantages of video games outweigh their disadvantages. One impressive advantage is that they can help bridge racial difficulties. Nagourney quotes a Boston video-game player who points out the racial diversity of the players interacting (without problems) at local arcades. Nagourney also cites research which indicates that video games do not cause increased violent behavior. In fact, video games can be viewed as a substitute for undesirable group behavior, such as recreational drug use, because video games provide the stimulation teens would otherwise be seeking through alcohol and drugs.

Still, a big controversy regarding video games is whether the violent war simulation games cause youth to be more violent. It is possible that, in some cases, playing these games provides skills, training, and motivation for young killers to carry out deadly attacks. Even if the counterargument is true, that video games do not turn good kids bad (Kellerman, 1999), in what ways are these violent games beneficial? Wouldn't it be better if youth were spending more time playing sports, reading, and doing other leisure activities, as opposed to playing violent video games? Hopefully, through enhanced leisure education efforts, the leisure behavior patterns of youth can be directed away from playing video games and toward more physically, socially, and emotionally beneficial leisure activities.

In summary, visual media, such as watching television or movies and playing video games, can have negative implications for social development. These pastimes are all popular leisure activities in the United States, especially among youth. Another common leisure activity, listening to popular music, can also greatly affect social development, as discussed in the next section.

POPULAR MUSIC AND ITS EFFECTS
ON SOCIAL DEVELOPMENT

Listening to music can be an activity that either promotes socialization or inhibits it. On the positive side, listening to live music provides an opportunity for people to congregate. Music can foster group harmony and reduce social distance among group members, because everyone in the group is sharing a common experience. When people clap, sing, or sway in unison to music, an atmosphere very conducive to socialization is created.

However, listening to music can sometimes deter socialization. For example, loud music at bars and at other gathering places can make conversation extremely difficult, to the point where people stop trying to socialize because it is difficult to hear and be heard above the noise. Another way in which listening to music can be a social deterrent is the use of headphones. People enter their own private space when listening to music on headphones, oblivious to everything and everyone around them. It is daunting to approach someone or to try to have a conversation with someone who is wearing headphones.

Another concern with popular music's effect on social development relates to the messages relayed in the lyrics of popular songs. There are concerns that popular music is having a negative impact on the social development of youth, that it promotes teen drug use, pregnancy, crime, suicide, and violent behavior.

In summary, as with visual media, there are concerns regarding the potentially negative impact of popular music on social development. Exercise 10.1 presents an opportunity to evaluate whether visual media and popular music have a more positive or more negative impact on your social development.

Your answers to Exercise 10.1 will probably show you that the popular media have a significant and sometimes negative impact on socialization. The next section examines how to incorporate activities into your leisure that can have a more positive impact on socialization than watching television, listening to music, and playing video games.

EXERCISE 10.1.
Evaluating the Impact of Popular Culture on Social Development

Instructions

1. In the first column, list and briefly describe recent examples of personal participation in watching television shows or movies, playing video games, or listening to popular music.
2. In the second column, for each example listed, determine if the activity had a positive or negative impact on your social development. Explain the positive and negative implications of each activity on your social development (discuss the reasons why you think the activity had either a positive or negative effect on socialization).

Recent examples of participation   **Perceived effects on socialization**

FACILITATING SOCIAL DEVELOPMENT THROUGH LEISURE AND ENHANCING LEISURE THROUGH SOCIALIZATION

One of the most important factors in having an enjoyable leisure lifestyle is having friends with whom to share recreational experiences. Conversely, one of the best ways to meet people and make new friends is through participation in recreational activities. This section begins with an examination of different types of friendship and then explores ideas for initiating, maintaining, and enhancing friendships.

Defining Friendship

Reisman (1979) defines a friend as someone who likes and wishes to do well by someone else and believes these good feelings and intentions are reciprocated. Reisman identifies three types of friendships as follows:

1. *Reciprocal:* This relationship involves equal giving and receiving. The friends have equal status and both give love and loyalty to each other.
2. *Receptive:* In this relationship, only one person gives love and loyalty. The friends have unequal status.
3. *Associative:* The loyalty and fondness in this relationship are not deep. The relationship is based on a situation or an acquaintance.

Exercise 10.2 is designed to help clarify personal definitions of friendship.

After completing this exercise, answer the following questions:

1. Under which category did you label most of the people on your list?
2. Do you have any receptive friendships in which you are the giver? Why do you desire these relationships? Conversely, if you have a receptive friendship in which you are the receiver, why do you think that the other person desires this relationship?

3. Do any names on the list not fit into any of the three categories? Should any names be deleted from the list? Do any of the names on your list not meet the criteria for friendship identified in this definition? According to this definition, the recipient of love and loyalty in a receptive friendship would not be considered a friend.
4. Describe how your reciprocal friendships evolved. How many of them began as associative relationships? What do you do to maintain these relationships?

The last question leads to the next topic in this section, namely how to initiate, maintain, and enhance friendships.

Initiating, Maintaining, and Enhancing Friendships

A person can never have too many friends or, as Pliskin (1983) suggests, never stop seeking to increase the number of friends you have. Exercise 10.3 is intended to help clarify ways to increase the number of friendships in your life.

Making new friends is only half of the battle. Maintaining and enhancing friendships requires constant attention. Pliskin (1983) offers several suggestions for maintaining and enhancing friendships.

1. Recognize that *how you behave affects how others behave toward you.* If you behave in a positive manner, others are likely to reciprocate, but acting cold, hostile, or aggressive can turn a friend into an enemy.
2. *Instead of complaining* about someone's behavior, *take positive steps* to encourage the other person to improve his or her behavior toward you. If it is difficult to behave kindly when the other person is not behaving that way, pretend you are an actor and the role you have been assigned is to act kindly to this person. It is likely that your kindness will cause the other person to behave better toward you. However, if this technique does not produce the desired effect, try a different tactic.

3. *Greet people with a smile.* Smiles help generate positive feelings, which in turn facilitate friendliness.
4. *Treat others with honor and respect.*
5. *Offer* others signs of *recognition and affection.*
6. When meeting people for the first time, try to *look for their virtues rather than focus on their faults.*
7. *Be flexible in your demands and expectations of others.* If you are too rigid, your disappointment in people for not meeting your expectations or demands will prevent you from forming friendships.
8. *Avoid* the following behaviors: *insulting others, talking negatively about others, lying, deceiving others in financial matters, and getting angry easily at others.*
9. *Try to get to know specific information about prospective friends.* It is not sufficient to have only general impressions of how people behave and react. It is essential to know others' specific personality traits and needs in order to develop pleasurable relationships.
10. *Be willing to self-disclose personal information,* although discretion should be used. Self-disclosure indicates to others that you feel positively about them, which in turn creates positive feelings toward you.

In addition to these suggestions, Waitley (1983) offers several suggestions for improving interpersonal communication, which, if followed, will facilitate friendships:

1. Try to *look at yourself through others' eyes.*
2. Try to *be open-minded.*
3. *Take full responsibility for success in the communication process.* If you are the listener, take full responsibility for understanding what has been said, or if talking, take full responsibility for being sure others understand what you are saying.

In summary, having friends is a key element of a satisfying leisure lifestyle. In addition to the aforementioned suggestions for initiating, maintaining, and enhancing friendships, recreational activities can play a major role in socialization.

EXERCISE 10.2. Friendship Defined

Instructions

1. In the first column, simply list as many of your friends' names as you can. Do not pay any attention to ranking their names.
2. In the second column, categorize your friends as being reciprocal, receptive, or associative friends.
3. Reexamine your list of *associative* friends and place an "X" in the last column for those friends with whom you wish to terminate an association because of the lack of satisfaction derived from the relationship. Place a "√" next to the names of those friends with whom you believe there is the potential to have reciprocal relationships. Identify steps you can take to upgrade these relationships.

Name	Type of friend	Evaluation/actions to take

EXERCISE 10.3. Initiating Friendships

Instructions

1. In the first column, list all of the places, activities, and programs that would provide an opportunity to make new friends.
2. In the second column, list all of the people you know with whom you would like to become friends. Next to each person's name, identify an act of kindness you could do for that person to foster the development of a friendship.
3. In the last column, list, in priority order, the specific actions you plan to take to increase the number of friends in your life.

Where/how to make new friends	New friends desired and how to win them over	Plan of action for increasing friendships

SOCIALIZATION IN RECREATIONAL ACTIVITIES

Although the "singles industry" (e.g., bars, dating services, spas) leads people to believe it costs money to make friends, there are really many alternatives. The following is a list of recreational activities that can facilitate making new friends:

1. Joining clubs and organizations
2. Doing volunteer work
3. Entering a tournament in a particular sport
4. Participating in a special event, such as a race, march, or fund-raising dance
5. Enrolling in a recreational class, such as art, dance, music, or sports through a university, community college, municipal parks and recreation department, or privately run facility
6. Becoming a member of a sports facility
7. Joining a team in any sport
8. Joining a performing group (e.g., a band, drama group, chorus)

Each of these options is very broad and encompasses a wide range of choices. For example, in any community, dozens of viable options for doing volunteer work probably exist. The beauty of doing volunteer work, as well as the other options listed, is that not only do these activities provide an opportunity to meet people, but they also are enjoyable and rewarding by themselves. Furthermore, participation in special events (#4) or a performing group (#8) can help to foster positive feelings between people of different racial and ethnic groups and thereby facilitate establishing friendships with a wider range of people. For example, in Scher's (2001) study in Israel on the effects of participation in a theater group on the attitudes of Jewish and Arab youth, it was found that the theater program helped to improve the level of trust and readiness to undertake social relationships between the two groups. Similarly, research on Jewish and Arab elders in Israel found that participation in a program of recreational activities improved their attitudes toward each other (Leitner, Scher, and Shuval, 1999; Leitner and Scher, 2000).

Regarding sports facilities (#6), an attractive facility, such as a "leisure pool" (Hunsaker, 1989) can greatly encourage socialization as well as exercise. The leisure pool consists of a free-form body of shallow water, featuring waterfalls, bubble benches, spiraling water tubes, and whirlpools. Several universities are drawing up plans for such facilities on their campuses. The leisure pool can be an excellent alternative to bars or alcohol-saturated parties that college students might otherwise flock to as a place to meet people.

To conclude this chapter, Exercise 10.4 is presented to facilitate a self-evaluation of how personal social development can be enhanced through leisure activities. Hopefully, Exercise 10.4 will help to clarify both the negative and the positive aspects of present recreational activities with respect to socialization and to identify new activities or changes in participation patterns that can enhance socialization. It is interesting that although socializing is often cited as one of the most desirable forms of leisure activity, the leisure habits of many people detract from socializing. Burns (1993) has some observations in this regard:

1. People seem to prefer to watch a movie alone at home on a VCR rather than in theaters with others.
2. People exercise at home alone on their own exercise equipment instead of exercising with others at a club or recreation center.
3. People play games with computers instead of with a partner.
4. People walk on a treadmill instead of taking a walk in the park.

Do any of these observations hold true for you? Hopefully the suggestions offered in this chapter can be put into action to improve the social component of your leisure.

SUMMARY

Leisure activities can enhance social development, but in some cases they can actually detract from it. It is important to carefully consider activity choices so as to maximize social development.

EXERCISE 10.4.
Enhancing Social Development Through Leisure Activities

Activity	Current participation status and its impact on socialization	Desired change in participation
1. Membership in clubs and organizations and at sports facilities		
2. Volunteer work		
3. Participation in tournaments		
4. Participation in special events		
5. Recreational classes enrolled in		
6. Memberships in sports teams and/or performing groups		

276LEISURE ENHANCEMENT

REFERENCES

Albers, J. (1990). Study says media sex overload creates frustration. *Colorado Daily,* December 12, p. 13.

Anonymous (2001). T.V. turnoff week 2001 earns IRA support. *Reading Today,* 18(3), 42.

Bufkin, J. (2000). The images of sex and rape. *Violence Against Women,* 6(12), 13-28.

Burns, L. (1993). *Busybodies: Why our time-obsessed society keeps us running in place.* New York: W. W. Norton and Co.

Carlsson-Paige, N. and Levin, D.E. (1992). A big upsurge in war-toy marketing and kid violence. *Sacramento Bee,* May 3, pp. F1, F2.

Goleman, D. (1990). How viewers grow addicted to watching TV. *The New York Times,* October 16, pp. B1, B10.

Hunsaker, J. (1989). A new splash at colleges. *Athletic Business,* October, pp. 55-58.

Kellerman, J. (1999). Violence doesn't begin in the theater. *The Wall Street Journal,* June 9, p. B4.

Leitner, M.J. and Scher, G. (2000). A follow-up study to peacemaking through recreation: The positive effects of intergenerational recreation programs on the attitudes of Israeli Arabs and Jews. *World Leisure and Recreation,* 42(1), 33-37.

Leitner, M.J., Scher, G., and Shuval, K. (1999). Peace-making through recreation: The positive effects of intergenerational activities on the attitudes of Israeli Arabs and Jews toward each other. *World Leisure and Recreation,* 41(2), 25-29.

Levy, J. (1983). *Leisure today.* Guelph, Ontario: Backdoor Press.

Lodziak, C. (1986). *The power of television: A critical appraisal.* New York: St. Martin's Press.

Mander, J. (1978). *Four arguments for the elimination of television.* New York: Morrow Quill Paperbacks.

Nagourney, E. (1984). Video games: Consuming free time? *World Leisure and Recreation Association Journal,* 26(3), 23-27.

Pawlowski, C. (2000). *Glued to the tube: The threat of television addiction to today's family.* Naperville, IL: Sourcebooks, Inc.

Pliskin, Z. (1983). *Gateway to happiness.* Brooklyn, NY: Aish Hatorah Publications.

Provenzo, E.F. Jr. (1992). What do games teach? *Education Digest,* 58(4), 56-59.

Reisman, J.M. (1979). *Anatomy of friendship.* New York: Irvington Publications.

Riechmann, D. (1999). U.S. checks entertainment's influence on drug use among youth. *The Boston Globe,* April 29, p. A13.

Scher, G. (2001). Attitudes, national stereotypes and preparedness for social interaction of Jewish and Arab youth who participated in the joint theatrical project in Tel Aviv-Jaffa. Master's thesis (abstract), Haifa University, Haifa, Israel.

Silver, M. (1993). What's your password? Gadgets that help parents wean kids from TV-itis. *U.S. News and World Report,* September 20, p. 79.

Stockbridge, J. (1994). The big picture: Television's effect on children, families and society. *Shasta Parent,* February, pp. 14-15.

Waitley, D.E. (1983). *Seeds of greatness.* New York: Pocket Books.

Winn, M. (1987). *Unplugging the plug-in drug.* New York: Viking Penguin Press.

Chapter 11

Gambling and Recreational Drug Use: Analysis of Two Prevalent Leisure-Related Problems

INTRODUCTION

In the discussion of the importance of leisure education in Chapter 2, reference was made to the existence of leisure-related problems in society as evidence that many people need help and direction in creating positive leisure lifestyles. In this chapter, two of these leisure-related problems, gambling and recreational drug use, are discussed in depth. The term *recreational drug use* is used in this chapter to refer to the consumption of alcohol and the use of other drugs (e.g., marijuana) as a leisure activity or as an aspect of a leisure activity (e.g., binge drinking at a party).

Gambling and recreational drug use were chosen for discussion because they are widespread activities, especially among college students, are clearly leisure related, and can have negative consequences. For each activity, statistics are presented on its prevalence in society and the problems it causes. Theoretical explanations are offered as to why these activities should be considered problems, why people engage in these activities for recreational purposes, and how these problems can be overcome. Special attention is devoted to the participation patterns of and problems caused to college students (e.g., binge drinking).

The learning objectives for this chapter are to

1. Cite statistics on the prevalence of gambling in society.
2. Contrast different types of gambling.
3. Identify problems of gambling.
4. Identify theoretical explanations of gambling as a leisure activity.

5. Identify leisure activity alternatives to gambling.
6. Cite statistics on the prevalence of recreational drug use in society.
7. Cite statistics on the prevalence of problems related to recreational drug use.
8. Identify theoretical causes of recreational drug use.
9. Identify theoretical and practical solutions to the problems of recreational drug use.

GAMBLING

Prevalence of Gambling

Annual spending on legal gambling in the United States is over $600 billion (Nelson, 2000). Betting on sports is legal only in Nevada and remains a major activity of organized crime, with estimated business of $80 to $380 billion per year (Nelson, 2000). According to Platz and Millar (2001), more money was spent on gambling than on tickets to sports events, movies, theme parks, video games, and recorded music combined. Casinos alone earned over $20 billion in 1999 (Davis and Elkin, 2001). Approximately 30 percent of U.S. households visited a casino in 1999, making an average of 5.4 trips per year.

Evidence suggests that college-age gamblers are more likely to have problems related to gambling than are adults (Platz and Millar, 2001). Most pathological gamblers begin gambling at this age. As discussed in the next section, there are different types of gamblers, with pathological or obsessive gamblers being the ones whose lives are at greatest risk of being destroyed by gambling.

Types of Gamblers

Abt, Smith, and Christiansen (1985) identify several different types of gamblers:

1. *Casual (recreational) gamblers:* Those who gamble because of curiosity or for social reasons, usually on impulse.
2. *Occasional gamblers:* On predetermined special occasions or as an escape, these gamblers spend a great deal of time and money when they gamble.
3. *Risky gamblers:* People who seek risk, rather than enjoyment, from particular gambling games.
4. *Professional gamblers:* Those who gamble for economic gain, not for enjoyment.
5. *Habitual gamblers:* Those who integrate gambling into their real life and gamble without giving it much thought.
6. *Serious gamblers:* Those who have an intrinsic interest in gambling yet are able to control it and stick to predetermined limits.
7. *Obsessive (pathological) gamblers:* People who seek an escape from the real world and become preoccupied with gambling.

Although there are many different kinds of gamblers, all have the potential to become obsessive or pathological gamblers because gambling is addictive (Dickerson, 1984). Furthermore, in a study of almost 1,000 college students (Platz and Millar, 2001), pathological and recreational gamblers shared seven of the top ten motives for gambling: to win, excitement, risk, autonomy, escape daily routine, exploration, and to be with friends. Therefore, it is understandable that so many recreational gamblers become problem gamblers. In all cases except for professional gamblers, gambling is considered a leisure activity. Unfortunately, it is a leisure activity that causes many problems, as discussed in the next section.

Problems of Gambling

Over 5 million Americans are pathological gamblers, and approximately 15 million more are at risk of falling into that category. Over 5 percent of the population has a gambling problem at some time, twice the rate of cocaine addiction. Adolescents have a rate of problem gambling of 9.4 percent, compared to 3.8 percent for adults. The American Psychiatric Association defined gambling as an addiction problem comparable to alcohol and drug abuse (Brody, 1999).

The addictive nature of gambling is illuminated by research showing that gambling activates the same regions of the brain as snorting cocaine (Wen, 2001). Compulsive or pathological gamblers seem to have vulnerable dopamine systems that cause them to keep gambling even though they are losing money and have conscious knowledge that they will lose in the long run (Blakeslee, 2002).

Kong (1997) reports that gambling disorders increased by more than 50 percent since the mid-1970s, due to the growth in lotteries, casinos, charitable bingo, and other forms of legalized gambling. People with mental disorders or substance abuse problems are more likely to also have a gambling problem (Pulley, 1997).

One positive development in gambling is a new device that utilizes the addictive nature of slot machines to get gamblers to exercise. The "Pedal 'N Play" contraption is a recumbent exercise bicycle that is connected to a slot machine (Jacobs, 2001). Gamblers are thus able to get exercise while they gamble.

Theoretical Causes of and Leisure Alternatives to Gambling

Before discussing the relationship of specific play theories and concepts of leisure to gambling, it is interesting to note that gambling casinos are actually utilizing theories of psychological needs and behavior modification techniques to manipulate people to spend more money. According to Popkin (1994), casinos have experimented with using various scents and colors to subconsciously influence gamblers to spend more time (and lose more money) in their casinos. Positive reinforcement (occasional winning) is also used to draw people to gamble more. Making alcohol (the bars will serve a generous shot and a half) and money (ATMs at most casinos) readily available also encourages more gambling. Martinez (1983) identifies two motives that underlie gambling: a need to confirm one's existence and a need to confirm one's self-worth or self-esteem. These motives relate directly to several of the theories discussed in Chapter 5.

The competence-effectance theory (Kraus, 1984) is relevant to the motive of needing to confirm one's existence. The competence-effectance theory states that play is motivated by a desire to produce an effect on the environment. When the desired effect is produced, it confirms the player's existence and promotes feelings of competence. In gambling, the desired effect of betting is usually winning money. Producing the desired effect confirms the player's existence and can lead to feelings of enhanced self-esteem.

Maslow's hierarchy (Maslow, 1971) identifies self-esteem as an important human need. Winning a bet against all odds can be a self-esteem booster. Furthermore, gambling can be an easy way to enhance self-esteem, because winning is largely dependent on luck rather than skill or stamina.

However, trying to confirm one's existence and self-esteem through gambling is foolish, because in most gambling situations the odds are stacked against the gambler. Continuous losing in a gambling situation can lower self-esteem rather than raise it. Because the odds are usually in favor of losing, gambling is not a good leisure activity to choose to enhance self-esteem and confirm one's existence.

Many leisure activity alternatives to gambling would be more effective at confirming one's existence or enhancing self-esteem. For example, participation in art, music, and writing activities are definite ways to confirm one's existence, because participation results in outcomes that can easily be validated. Similarly, the end products of art, music, or writing activities usually are effective self-esteem enhancers. Another excellent self-esteem enhancer is exercise, because of the positive effects it has on physical appearance.

Another motivation for gambling is that it is an escape from reality. Abt, Smith, and Christiansen (1985) state that gambling provides an opportunity to break away from the routine of life and lets people feel they are in control of their own fate. Wagner states that gamblers are unable to accept reality (Eadington, 1976), and gambling is an escape that protects or prevents people from dealing with reality. The need to break away from social reality was identified by Erikson (Kraus, 1984) as a primary motivation for play. Gambling is an example of a leisure activity pursued as a means of breaking social reality. However, it is not a good leisure activity choice for breaking from reality and gaining control of one's fate, because a gambler is *not* in control of the outcome of gambling activity. The gambling outcome depends on luck and on the odds fixed by the gambling establishment.

Numerous leisure alternatives to gambling more effectively provide escape and put participants in control of their own fate. For example, outdoor recreation activities such as boating, hiking, and fishing are great escapes from the routine of urban life, and participants are much more in control of their own fate than they are when gambling in a casino.

Another motive for gambling is thrill seeking (Downes et al., 1976). The risk and stimulation of gambling are an antidote to boredom (Abt, Smith, and Christiansen, 1985). As explained in the theory of optimal arousal (Iso-Ahola, 1980), seeking optimal psychological stimulation is a major motivation for participation in recreational activities. Compulsive gamblers seem to seek higher levels of arousal than casual gamblers, because they take greater risks when they gamble (greater potential for financial losses).

The problem with gambling is that unlike other high-risk recreation activities such as skydiving, the likelihood of the negative outcome occurring (losing money) is very great. The nonprofessional gambler is more likely to lose than to win, but the skydiver is more likely to land safely than to have an accident.

The arousal theory can help explain why so many people become addicted to gambling. At the beginning, gambling, like any activity, can be very arousing even in a small dose because of its novelty. However, once the novelty wears off, more stimulation (different circumstances, higher stakes) is needed to attain the optimal level of arousal. In gambling, as the stakes increase so does the possibility of financial ruin and other problems.

Better alternatives to gambling exist for those seeking high-risk or high-arousal recreation. For example, amusement rides provide a high level of physical stimulation with a very low risk of physical harm. Similarly, outdoor high-risk activities such as mountain climbing provide a high level of mental and physical stimulation yet, if done properly, have a relatively low risk of harm.

A simpler motive for gambling offered by Abt, Smith, and Christiansen (1985) is that it is fun. Fun, enjoyment, and pleasure are certainly important benefits of recreation. But does gambling really provide these benefits? It would be interesting to compare the fun and enjoyment aspect of gambling with that of other recreational activities. Observing people in casinos gives the impression that gambling is less enjoyable than most other recreational activities. Exercise 11.1 provides the opportunity for you to do your own experiment.

Select two activities for observation, one being a gambling activity, the other a nongambling activity, and note the frequency of behaviors listed on the chart for both activities. One interesting way to conduct this experiment is to observe the same group of people play a nongambling game on one occasion (e.g., charades) and watch them

EXERCISE 11.1.
Assessing Enjoyment of Gambling and Nongambling Activities

Behavior*	Gambling activity	Nongambling activity
Laughter		
Smiles		
Verbal exclamations of enjoyment		
Happy conversation		
Facial expressions of tension		
Verbal expressions of tension		

*While observing the activities, simply mark each time you observe one of the behaviors listed. Later, add a description of the prevalence of each behavior during the activities.

gambling (e.g., poker) on another occasion. Alternatively, it is fascinating to observe the behavior of gamblers at a casino and compare it to the behavior of a group of people playing softball or volleyball or enjoying a day at the beach. Most likely, you will find that gambling is less enjoyable than other recreational activities.

Another criticism of gambling is its position on Nash's pyramid of leisure (Nash, 1960). The most appropriate levels on the pyramid in which to classify gambling are entertainment and simple amusement (level 1) and retardation of self-development (level 0). As discussed in Chapter 5, the lower levels of Nash's pyramid (levels 1, 0, and –0) represent low-value and undesirable categories of recreational activities. Therefore, based on Nash's pyramid, it is highly desirable to replace gambling with other recreational activities that can be classified on the higher levels of the pyramid and may be even more enjoyable than gambling.

In summary, although gambling is a popular form of recreation, it is also an undesirable activity, especially from a theoretical viewpoint. Similarly, recreational drug use is immensely popular but also is undesirable for many reasons.

RECREATIONAL DRUG USE

Recreational alcohol consumption (especially binge drinking) is the main topic discussed in this section because it is the most widely used and damaging (in terms of deaths caused and economic costs) of any drug. Statistics are also more readily available on alcohol than other drugs because alcohol is legal. Statistics related to alcohol consumption among college students are highlighted in this section.

The phrase "alcohol and other drugs" is used throughout this section. Achenbach (1994) points out the ludicrousness of the often-used expression "drugs and alcohol." Alcohol *is* a drug. However, it is legal and has been part of American culture for a long time. Nevertheless, it must be recognized that it is indeed a drug.

In discussing alcohol, the primary focus in this chapter is on its consumption as a recreational activity, not the disease of alcoholism or incidental light drinking (e.g., sipping a glass of wine with dinner). Again, Achenbach (1994) points out the absurdity of attitudes toward alcohol in that even people who do not drink much will have an occasional drink or two. Imagine someone saying that they were not into cocaine, but they liked to sometimes snort a line or two with dinner.

Binge Drinking Among College Students

Binge drinking is the most problematic form of recreational drinking. It can be defined as five consecutive drinks for a man and four for a woman. In common terms, it means drinking a great deal in order to get drunk. It is what students do when they say, "I'm going to get wasted tonight!"

Binge drinking is prevalent among college students. Approximately 44 percent of college students binge drink, and 23 percent are frequent binge drinkers (Schemo, 2002). The Centers for Disease Control reported that from 1993 to 2001, the rate of binge-drinking episodes among drinkers ages eighteen to twenty increased by 56 percent (Markel, 2003). Problems related to binge drinking among college students are serious.

1. Drinking among college students contributes to 1,400 deaths, 500,000 injuries, and 70,000 cases of sexual assault annually (Branch, 2002). That means that on an average day, four college students die in alcohol-related accidents, 1,370 suffer injuries, and 192 are raped or sexually assaulted (Schemo, 2002).
2. Approximately 600,000 (13 percent of college students) reported having been assaulted by classmates who drank too much (Schemo, 2002).
3. Approximately 400,000 (8 percent of college students) admitted to having unprotected sex when drinking (Schemo, 2002).
4. Drinking games that college students play for recreational reasons are closely related to future problematic alcohol use (Adams, 2000).

A study of about 14,000 students at 119 four-year colleges nationwide (Hsu, 2000) provides some interesting statistics on how problematic frequent binge drinking is. Table 11.1 compares the incidence of various problems among nonbinge drinkers, occasional binge drinkers, and frequent binge drinkers. The nonbinge drinkers had not binged in the past year; the occasional binge drinker binged once or twice in a two-week period, and the frequent binge drinker

TABLE 11.1. Comparison of Alcohol-Related Problems Among Non-, Occasional, and Frequent Student Binge Drinkers

Problem	Nonbingers (%)	Occasional bingers (%)	Frequent bingers (%)
Miss class	8.8	30.9	62.5
Argue with friends	9.7	23.0	42.6
Unprotected sex	3.7	9.8	20.4
Trouble with police	1.4	5.2	12.7
Drive after drinking	18.6	39.7	56.7
Damage property	2.3	8.9	22.7

Source: Hsu, 2000.

binged three or more times in a two-week period. In this study, there were 5,063 nonbingers, 2,962 occasional bingers, and 3,135 frequent bingers.

As shown in Table 11.1, college students who are frequent binge drinkers are much more likely to miss class, argue with friends, engage in unprotected sex, have trouble with the police, drive after drinking, and damage property than are other students. Binge drinking leads to trouble.

The following are some other interesting statistics related to recreational drinking among college students (Anonymous, 1994):

1. The average college student drinks thirty-four gallons of alcoholic beverages per year.
2. Three of five college women were drunk when they became infected with sexually transmitted diseases.
3. Approximately 95 percent of violent campus crime and 90 percent of campus rapes involve alcohol.
4. Drinking more appears to be related to lower grades. "A" students only averaged 3.6 drinks per week, while "D" and "F" students averaged 10.6 drinks per week. This statistic is surely related to the figures in Table 11.1 that show that frequent binge drinkers miss class more often than other students.

Where students live seems to affect their drinking habits. Approximately 75 percent of students living in fraternity or sorority houses binge drink, compared to 51 percent of those living in dorms, 50 percent of those living in off-campus housing, 36 percent of those living in substance-free housing, and 25 percent of those living at home with their parents (Powell, 2002).

Another interesting statistic related to college students' alcohol consumption is that students spend $5.5 billion annually on alcohol, far more than the cost of books (Wolburg, 2001).

In summary, alcohol consumption is a major problem among college students. However, it is not just a problem among college students but among the general population as well. For example, the rate of binge-drinking episodes among all American adults increased by 35 percent from 1993 to 2001 (Markel, 2003). In addition, the use of other drugs for recreational purposes (e.g., marijuana) is widespread and causes significant problems for people of all ages. In the next section, problems in the general population associated with the use of alcohol and other drugs are examined.

Problems Related to Substance Abuse in the General Population

Substance abuse is the number one health problem in the United States in that more deaths and disabilities are associated each year with substance abuse than with any other cause (National Council on Alcoholism and Drug Dependence [NCADD], 2002). Substance abuse is also a major problem in other countries, as indicated in some of the following statistics:

1. *Deaths:* Approximately 55,000 young Europeans die each year due to alcohol (Weber, 2001). In the United States, 100,000 alcohol-related deaths are estimated to occur annually. For example, the 17,448 individuals killed in alcohol-related crashes in 2001 represented 41 percent of the 42,116 traffic deaths in 2001 (Mothers Against Drunk Driving [MADD], 2002).
2. *Accidents/illnesses:* According to Reynaud (2001), most of the patients admitted to hospital emergency services are drunk.
3. *Economic costs:* The costs associated with substance abuse in the United States are approximately $276 billion/year (NCADD, 2002).

4. *Family problems:* More than 50 percent of all adults have a family history of alcohol-related problems. More than 50 percent of cases of domestic violence are alcohol related.

In the statistics cited, alcohol is the substance contributing the most to the problems associated with substance abuse. Therefore, it is important to place great effort into attempting to reduce substance abuse in general and alcohol abuse in particular. A significant effort has been made in recent years in campaigning against drunk driving. However, the emphasis on reducing drunk driving might be misleading people to believe that consuming alcohol is okay as long as you do not drive. Discussions with my college classes indicate that almost all students believe drinking and driving is dangerous but that drinking and using other drugs is safe as long as you do not drive.

However, drinking *is* dangerous, even if you do not drive. Yes, drinking and driving is especially dangerous, but alcohol-related crashes account for only 17,448 of the approximately 100,000 alcohol-related deaths in the United States annually. Domestic violence occurs in the home, not in cars. Approximately 33 percent of all suicides, 48 to 64 percent of deaths in fires, and more than 50 percent of homicides are alcohol related (NCADD, 2002). It is not even safe to walk and drink! Almost one-third of all pedestrians age sixteen and over who were killed in traffic accidents in 2000 were intoxicated (MADD, 2002). The message is clear: Drinking is dangerous, whether you drive or not. You can stay at home and drink and cause harm to yourself and others in many different ways. Alcohol encourages aggression by disrupting normal brain mechanisms that restrain impulsive behavior (MADD, 2002).

Another problem with some of the advertising campaigns against alcohol abuse is the slogan "drink responsibly." Yes, light or moderate consumption of alcohol is better than heavy or binge drinking. However, it is difficult to consume alcohol in light or moderate amounts. Fox (2002) cites a study in which drinking just two glasses of wine or two small beers was found to impair judgment. People with alcohol in their bloodstream make more mistakes and are less aware of the mistakes that they are making. Therefore, even if a person decides at the beginning of the night that they want to "drink responsibly," it can be difficult to stick to this decision, because after two drinks inhibitions are lowered and judgment is impaired. In addition, if others around you are drinking heavily and seem to be having fun, the temptation to drink more can be irresistible. If the goal is to avoid the pitfalls of drinking heavily, it is easier to accomplish this goal by not drinking at all and surrounding yourself with others who are also not drinking.

Marijuana is the second-most popular recreational drug and has been considered by some people to be relatively harmless. For example, although my students almost unanimously agree that drinking and driving is unsafe, a majority of my students seem to think that it is safe to drive while under the influence of marijuana. Actually, it is unsafe to drive while under the influence of marijuana. Among male drivers age fifteen to thirty-four killed in car crashes, alcohol was involved in 70 percent of the fatalities, and the second-most common substance found in the bloodstream (among 37 percent of the victims) was marijuana (Bayer, 1996).

Marijuana use is rising among youth. From 1991 to 2001, the percentage of U.S. students who have used marijuana increased from 10 percent to 20 percent among eighth graders, from 23 percent to 40 percent among tenth graders, and from 37 percent to 49 percent among twelfth graders (Carroll, 2002). Because the marijuana used today is anywhere from ten to twenty times as potent as what was being passed around in the 1960s, there is a greater risk of daily dependence and physical addiction to it (Markel, 2002). Another problem related to marijuana use is that it is strongly related to the use of other, more dangerous drugs. Teens who smoke marijuana are more likely to use drugs such as cocaine, heroin, and LSD (Califano, 1999). According to University of Michigan researchers, at least 53 percent of American adolescents have tried an illicit drug by the time they finish high school (Markel, 2003).

In summary, the use of alcohol and other drugs for recreational purposes is harmful in many ways and is widespread. Many drugs used for recreational purposes were not discussed here. Trends in drug use change constantly. Occasionally, new drugs that are supposedly "safe" become popular, but after a while, the dangers of the drugs become more widely known and a different new drug becomes the "in drug," the one that supposedly makes you high without harming you. However, there is no "recreational" drug that is not harmful. The safest, healthiest way to "get high" is through recreational activities. Leisure education is needed to help people understand how to obtain the "high" feeling they seek through drugs from other recreational activities instead.

One of the keys to understanding why recreational drug use is so widespread and to determining how to reduce it is to examine it as a leisure activity choice, utilizing various theories and models of leisure behavior that were discussed in previous chapters. It is possible to reduce the recreational use of alcohol and other drugs, but not through stricter law enforcement or legalization of drugs. In fact, Walters (2002) reports that in countries where drugs were legalized, use increased consistently and sharply. The most effective way to reduce the use of alcohol and other drugs is by reducing people's desire to use these substances. The next section focuses on exploring the needs people seek to fulfill through recreational drug use and alternative recreational activities that can better meet these needs, without harmful side effects.

Theoretical Causes of and Alternatives to Recreational Drug Use

Similar to gambling, the simplest explanation of why people use recreational drugs is that it is fun and enjoyable. For example, cocaine's appeal stems from its reputation to be able to provide a uniquely pleasurable experience. However, a study by Byck and Van Dyke indicates that its ability to produce a "high" is overrated (Long, 1986). Similarly, people claim that alcohol consumption leads to feelings of happiness and relaxation, although alcohol's positive effects are vastly exaggerated, especially by the media (Kilbourne, 1982).

Relaxation is an important value of recreation, as identified in the relaxation theory (Kraus, 1984). However, relaxation can be achieved effectively by a variety of recreational activities that have none of the harmful consequences of recreational drug use. For example, listening to music, getting a massage, or taking a swim are just a few examples of recreational activities that can have a relaxing effect.

College students often justify getting drunk on the weekends as a means of letting loose, releasing pent-up emotions from a week of stressful studying, examinations, and writing papers. The catharsis theory (Ellis, 1973) recognizes the value of recreation as a safe outlet for the release of pent-up emotions. However, as the statistics in the previous section indicate, drinking is an unsafe outlet. Participation in sports is a safer outlet for pent-up emotions than getting intoxicated.

Another justification for getting drunk is that it is an escape. For college students, it means escaping from the realities of educational, parental, and social pressures. However, drinking can make these realities even more difficult to face. After a night of drinking and a hangover the morning after, life's problems are often even more difficult to confront. Erikson recognized the value of play as a means of breaking from social reality (Kraus, 1984), but much better means of escape than getting drunk are available. Recreational activities such as watching a good movie, participating in outdoor recreation, and traveling help people escape from the pressures of life without the negative side effects of drinking.

Furthermore, drinking is as much an act of giving in to social pressures as it is a means of escape. Peers often exert a great deal of pressure to drink. Teens are receiving a powerful message from their peers that using alcohol and other drugs is "cool," as indicated by a study of wealthy suburban teens which found that boys who drank alcohol had a higher social status than those who did not (Wen, 2001). Another study found that if adolescents associated with peers who used alcohol and other drugs, and if they perceived a low level of parental monitoring, they were more likely to use these substances (Caldwell and Darling, 1999).

Another form of social pressure leading people to drink more is the glorification of alcohol in the media. Printed and televised advertisements, as well as the portrayal of drinking on television shows, in the movies, and in popular music, portray a distorted image of alcohol as an enhancer of power, wealth, sexual prowess, and friendship and have a profound effect on encouraging people to drink (Kilbourne, 1982).

Another justification for recreational drug use revolves around the fulfillment of the third level of needs on Maslow's (1971) hierarchy: love and belongingness. In particular, drinking and getting drunk are commonly viewed as experiences shared by close friends or as an experience that draws people closer together. Burda and Vaux's (1988) study found that drinking plays a significant role in the social support processes of college males. One explanation for this phenomenon is that alcohol is a social lubricant, that it makes people less inhibited.

Unfortunately, alcohol's effect on lowering inhibitions in general apparently also lowers people's inhibitions to perform harmful acts, such as violent crimes and suicide attempts.

Other recreational ways to lower inhibitions and decrease social distance exist, such as laughter and playing fun games. However, the most powerful (but also most difficult) way to lower inhibitions and facilitate socialization is through a positive outlook and self-image. Chapter 12 presents a variety of ideas for enhancing self-esteem and fostering positive attitudes about leisure and life.

In fact, a negative attitude toward leisure appears to be a characteristic of alcoholic men. In Berg and Neulinger's (1976) study of 183 alcoholic men and 335 working adults, it was found that the alcoholics differed from the nonalcoholics in that they saw themselves as having more leisure than they wanted, being more work oriented, preferring highly structured free time, and viewing leisure negatively. Based on these findings, leisure education should be an integral component of treatment programs for alcoholics. Furthermore, leisure education should be an integral component of alcohol-abuse prevention programs, because boredom relief is a commonly identified motive for recreational drug use (Weil, 1975).

Similar to gambling, recreational drug use is an activity that is classified as a lower-level activity on Nash's pyramid of leisure (Nash, 1960). Recreational drug use is often even lower than the zero level (retardation of self-development) and instead rates as a subzero-level activity (acts performed against society). The subzero rating is easily justified by the prevalence of problems associated with recreational drug use (particularly alcohol) cited previously in the chapter. It is desirable to replace recreational drug use with recreational activities equally as enjoyable but which fit into the higher levels of Nash's pyramid.

Exercise 11.2 provides an opportunity to explore alternative leisure activities to recreational drug use. If you personally do not drink or take other drugs, then complete the exercise by interviewing someone who does.

Hopefully, Exercise 11.2 will yield the insight that far better ways exist to meet personal needs than through recreational drug use. The next step is to actually replace recreational drug use with these better leisure alternatives.

EXERCISE 11.2. Leisure Alternatives to Recreational Drug Use

Instructions

1. In the first column, list all those needs which you feel are met through recreational drug use.
2. In the middle column, for each need listed, identify one or more alternative activities which can meet the same needs, and explain how well the activity meets the needs.
3. In the last column, compare/describe the aftereffects of recreational drug use with the aftereffects of the alternative activity chosen.

Needs fulfilled by recreational drug use	Alternative leisure activities that meet these needs and a description of how these needs are met	Comparison of aftereffects of drug use versus that of alternative activity

In summary, recreational drug use is a negative use of free time, but nevertheless is a popular form of recreation. The most effective way to alleviate this problem is through education. It is hoped that this section will contribute significantly to education about and prevention of the problems of recreational drug use.

There is reason to be optimistic that progress can be made in encouraging people to drink less. The statistics on the reduction in smoking are a good indicator of how education, awareness, and legislation can combine to change behavior in a positive way. According to Schafer (1989), the percentage of adults who smoke has been almost cut in half since 1965 (from 40 percent to 22 percent). Nearly half of Americans who ever smoked have quit. It is estimated that between 1964 and 1985, 750,000 deaths were prevented by decisions to quit smoking or not start. If so much progress can be made in reducing cigarette smoking, the same kind of progress is possible with regard to alcohol and other drugs. In fact, some progress has been made in reducing binge drinking among teens. The percentage of boys ages twelve to seventeen who engaged in binge drinking dropped from 19 percent to 11 percent between 1988 and 1998, and the percentage of girls who engaged in binge drinking dropped from 11 percent to 6.6 percent (Lewin, 2002). So, there is cause for optimism.

SUMMARY

Gambling and recreational drug use are not the only negative uses of free time in society, but they are two of the most prevalent. Although these activities can help fulfill legitimate needs such as relaxation, escape, and fun, numerous alternative recreational activities can also fulfill these needs. Individuals and society cannot afford to continue paying the price of the problems associated with gambling and recreational drug use. Expanded leisure education efforts can help alleviate these and other leisure-related problems in society.

REFERENCES

Abt, V., Smith, J.F., and Christiansen, E.M. (1985). *The business of risk: Commercial gambling in mainstream America.* Lawrence: University Press of Kansas.
Achenbach, J. (1994). None dare call it a drug. *The San Francisco Chronicle,* January 2, p. 3.

Adams, C.E. (2000). Changes over one semester in drinking game playing and alcohol use and problems in a college student sample. *Substance Abuse,* 20(6), 97-106.

Anonymous (1994). Campus drinking: Who, why, and how much? *U.S. News and World Report,* June 20, p. 21.

Bayer, L. (1996). The White House's war on drugs. *The Wall Street Journal,* November 4, p. A18.

Berg, C. and Neulinger, J. (1976). Alcoholics' perceptions of leisure. *Journal of Studies on Alcohol,* 37, 162-163.

Blakeslee, S. (2002). Hijacking the brain circuits with a nickel slot machine. *The New York Times,* February 19, p. D1.

Branch, S. (2002). College alcohol abuse injures, kills thousands, the NIH says. *The Wall Street Journal,* April 9, p. D14.

Brody, J.E. (1999). Compulsive gambling: Overlooked addiction. *The New York Times,* May 4, p. D7.

Burda, P.C. and Vaux, A.C. (1988). Social drinking. *Journal of Youth and Adolecence.* 17(2), 166-171.

Caldwell, L.L. and Darling, N. (1999). Leisure context, parental control, and resistance to peer pressure as predictors of adolescent partying and substance use: An ecological perspective. *Journal of Leisure Research,* 31(1), 57-77.

Califano, J.A. Jr. (1999). The grass roots of teen drug abuse. *The Wall Street Journal,* March 26, p. A22.

Carroll, L. (2002). Marijuana's effects: More than munchies. *The New York Times,* January 29, p. D6.

Davis, W. and Elkin, T. (2001). Harrah's ads accentuate the positive. *Advertising Age,* 72(12) (March 19), 49-54.

Dickerson, M.G. (1984). *Compulsive gamblers.* New York: Longman.

Downes, D.M., Davies, B.P., David, M.E., and Stone, P.E. (1976). *Gambling, work, and leisure: A study across three areas.* Boston: Routledge and Kegan Paul.

Eadington, W.R. (1976). *Gambling and society: Interdisciplinary studies on the subject of gambling.* Springfield, IL: Charles C Thomas.

Ellis, M.J. (1973). *Why people play.* Englewood Cliffs, NJ: Prentice-Hall.

Fox, M. (2002). 2 glasses of wine may hurt judgment. *The Boston Globe,* November 8, p. A19.

Hsu, K. (2000). Campus survey finds no cut in binge drinking. *The Boston Globe Nation,* March 15, pp. A1, A7.

Iso-Ahola, S.E. (1980). *The social psychology of leisure and recreation.* Dubuque, IA: Wm C Brown.

Jacobs, A. (2001). One-armed bandits and 2 tired legs: Burning fat (and cash) at the casino. *The New York Times,* January 7, p. 17.

Kilbourne, J. (1982). *Calling the shots: The advertising of alcohol* [Film]. Cambridge, MA: Cambridge Documentary Films.

Kong, D. (1997). Gambling ills surge, study finds. *The Boston Globe,* December 5, p. A22.

Kraus, R.G. (1984). *Recreation and leisure in modern society* (Third edition). Glenview, IL: Scott, Foresman.

Lewin, T. (2002). Teenage drinking a problem but not in way study found. *The New York Times,* February 27, p. A19.

Long, R.E. (Ed.) (1986). *Drugs and American society.* New York: H. Wilson.

Markel, H. (2002). For some, marijuana grows mean. *The New York Times,* April 30, p. D5.

Markel, H. (2003). Tailoring treatments for teenage drug users. *The New York Times,* January 7, p. D6.

Martinez, T.M. (1983). *The gambling scene: Why people gamble.* Springfield IL: Charles C Thomas.

Maslow, A. (1971). *Toward a psychology of being.* New York: Van Nostrand Reinhold.

Mothers Against Drunk Driving (MADD) (2002). Stats and resources. Available at <www.madd.org/stats>.

Nash, J.B. (1960). *Philosophy of leisure and recreation.* Dubuque, IA: Wm C Brown.

National Council on Alcoholism and Drug Dependence (NCADD) (2002). Alcoholism and drug dependence are America's #1 health problem. Available at <www.ncadd.org/facts/numberoneprob.html>.

Nelson, M. (2000). Morality, politics, and gambling. *Vital Speeches of the Day,* 66(13) (April 15), 406-410.

Platz, L. and Millar, M. (2001). Gambling in the context of other recreation activity: A quantitative comparison of casual and pathological student gamblers. *Journal of Leisure Research,* 33(4), 383-395.

Popkin, J. (1994). Tricks of the trade. *U.S. News and World Report,* March 14, pp. 48-52.

Powell, A. (2002). Binge drinking holds steady. *Harvard University Gazette,* April 4, p. 13.

Pulley, B. (1997). Compulsion to gamble seen growing. *The New York Times,* December 7, p. A22.

Reynaud, M. (2001). Patients admitted to emergency services for drunkenness: Moderate users or harmful drinkers? *American Journal of Psychiatry,* 158(1), 96-99.

Schafer, W. (1989). Progress against smoking. *Stress and Health Report* (Enloe Hospital Stress and Health Center, Chico, CA), November/December, pp. 1-2.

Schemo, D.J. (2002). Study calculates the effects of college drinking in U.S. *The New York Times,* April 10, p. A16.

Walters, J.P. (2002). Don't legalize drugs. *The Wall Street Journal,* July 19, p. A18.

Weber, W. (2001). Young people's alcohol consumption reaches alarming levels in Europe. *Lancet,* 357(2), 617.

Weil, A. (1975). Why people take drugs. In M. Wilson and S. Wilson (Eds.), *Drugs in American life* (pp. 23-35). New York: H. W. Wilson.

Wen, P. (2001). An addictive thrill. *The Boston Globe,* May 24, p. A1.

Wolburg, J. (2001). The risky business of binge drinking. *Journal of Advertising,* 30(4), 23.

Chapter 12

Personal Leisure Philosophy

INTRODUCTION

The importance of having a well-defined philosophy of leisure and life was mentioned in Chapter 8 as a key to being able to deal effectively with stress. Another reference to the importance of developing a strong leisure philosophy was made in Chapter 6 in relation to the role of goal setting and prioritization in leisure planning and time management. The purpose of this chapter is to stimulate thought on developing a comprehensive personal leisure philosophy. More specifically, the learning objectives of this chapter are to

1. Describe the role of ethics in defining a personal leisure philosophy.
2. Define ethics and identify criteria for determining the morality of a leisure activity.
3. Identify major internal obstacles to leisure fulfillment and ways of overcoming these obstacles.
4. Describe the importance of positive thinking as a basic element of a personal leisure philosophy.
5. Identify ways to stimulate the production of positive-thinking chemicals.
6. Contrast right- and left-brain functions.
7. Describe the importance of cultivating the right brain as part of a philosophy that fosters maximal leisure well-being.
8. Describe the importance of self-esteem in a sound leisure philosophy.
9. Identify ways to enhance self-esteem.

10. Incorporate ideas about ideal leisure into a personal philosophy of leisure and life.
11. Write a comprehensive statement of a personal leisure philosophy.

THE ROLE OF ETHICS IN DEFINING
PERSONAL LEISURE PHILOSOPHY

Why consider ethics in defining personal leisure philosophy and determining leisure activity choices? Why not base leisure activity choices and personal leisure philosophy entirely on the criteria of enjoyment and psychological/physical benefits? The answers to these questions will become more clear after examining exactly what ethics and ethical behavior involve.

First, ethics are personal, not clearly defined in the way that laws are. Ethics go beyond laws in defining proper behavior and conduct. For example, cutting in front of someone in a checkout line may not necessarily violate any laws, but most people already in line would view the behavior as wrong. Ethical conduct involves more than just refraining from actions that offend people. It also involves being sensitive to how a situation would be viewed if others knew about it. Ethics and laws together form the code of acceptable behavior that makes it possible for people to live together in this world. A society in which people are law abiding but oblivious to morals and ethics would be a miserable place to live.

Therefore, whether people consider ethics when choosing leisure activities can have a significant impact on the overall well-being of a society. For this reason, it is important to address ethical concerns in developing a philosophy of leisure and in selecting leisure activities.

The question arises about how to determine whether particular leisure activities are ethical. Discussions with college students over the years usually seem to conclude with the issues of causing physical and/or emotional harm to oneself and others and causing general harm to society as valid criteria for determining whether leisure activities are ethical. If harm is caused, even though it may be unintentional, an activity is viewed as being unethical. Furthermore, even if harm is not caused but the activity creates a high risk for harm to occur (e.g., drunk driving), an activity is viewed as unethical.

It is essential to periodically reevaluate one's personal code of ethics, because it is so easy to rationalize immoral behavior and incorporate it into a supposedly ethical way of life. In addition, the media, peers, and sometimes even parents and teachers can have a negative influence on a person's sense of ethics by participating in or condoning unethical behavior. Therefore, maintaining a high standard of ethics in leisure requires constant attention.

An analysis of the morality of a common leisure activity among college students is presented in Table 12.1. The activity, binge drinking, is unethical if judged on the basis of the information in Table 12.1 (based on statistics cited in Chapter 11). However, this activity continues to be popular among college students and other people as well. If people considered ethics when they chose their leisure activities, then binge drinking would not be as popular and many lives would be saved.

Exercise 12.1 is presented to shed light on how ethical your personal leisure behavior has been. The key to the exercise is to be hon-

TABLE 12.1. The Ethics of Binge Drinking As a Leisure Activity

Criteria for determining ethics	Information related to the criteria
1. Likelihood of physical harm to others	Very high. Approximately 50 percent or more of fatal automobile accidents, murders, spouse abuse, child abuse, and accidental deaths and injuries involve alcohol.
2. Likelihood of emotional harm to others	High. The lowered inhibitions brought about by heavy drinking can also bring about behavior that is loud, obnoxious, and offensive to others. Also, alcohol is a common source of problems in marriages and family life.
3. Likelihood of physical harm to self	Very high. Aside from the high risk of automobile and other accidents, the medical harm caused by alcohol is enormous. Heavy alcohol consumption is related to hypertensive diseases, many forms of cancer, liver problems, and other serious illnesses.
4. Likelihood of emotional harm to self	High. Alcohol is an addicting drug. Alcohol dependence is destructive to self-esteem.
5. Likelihood of negative impact on society in general	Very high. The economic cost of alcohol-related car crashes alone is over $100 billion annually.

EXERCISE 12.1.
Examining the Ethics of Various Leisure Activities

Instructions

1. List your ten favorite leisure activities and then exchange lists with someone.
2. Select an activity from your friend's list that does not appear on your list and that you feel is unethical. Following the same format as Table 12.1, examine the ethics of that activity. Your partner will do likewise.
3. Give each other an opportunity to justify the activities that were under scrutiny.
4. Reexamine your favorite activities and assess which ones you would now consider to be unethical.
5. Describe how a greater concern for ethics might affect your leisure behavior. Try to be as specific as possible.

Part I: List of My Ten Favorite Leisure Activities

1. _____   6. _____
2. _____   7. _____
3. _____   8. _____
4. _____   9. _____
5. _____   10. _____

Part II: Examining the Ethics of a Leisure Activity of My Friend

Activity chosen for analysis _____

Criteria for determining ethics	Information related to the criteria
1. Likelihood of physical harm to others	
2. Likelihood of emotional harm to others	
3. Likelihood of physical harm to self	
4. Likelihood of emotional harm to self	
5. Likelihood of negative impact on society in general	

est. Unethical behavior can be continued indefinitely unless there is an honest confrontation with ethics, which is the purpose of Exercise 12.1. Hopefully, this exercise is just the beginning of a reinforced awareness of ethical concerns in leisure behavior. Consideration of ethics should be an integral element of a personal leisure philosophy.

In summary, many widely practiced leisure activities are unethical. Given the importance of ethical behavior for the well-being of society, it is imperative that ethics be an integral consideration in determining leisure behavior.

OVERCOMING OBSTACLES TO LEISURE FULFILLMENT

As discussed in the previous section, ethics may be viewed as an obstacle to leisure fulfillment, because considering ethics could prevent participation in enjoyable activities. However, in reality, other, more powerful obstacles to leisure fulfillment exist, some of which are self-imposed. This section will examine some of the most common obstacles to leisure fulfillment and some ways to overcome these obstacles.

First, it is important to recognize that there are two kinds of obstacles: internal and external. External obstacles are circumstances beyond our control, such as the weather, work commitments, and family obligations. Internal obstacles are ones that can be controlled, such as guilt, lack of free time, lack of motivation, and inadequate knowledge of leisure resources. This section focuses exclusively on internal obstacles. The following is a discussion of major internal obstacles to leisure fulfillment and how they can be overcome.

Guilt

Guilt can prevent participation in a leisure activity or detract from the enjoyment of it. Guilt feelings about enjoying leisure can be caused by a strong work ethic, parental or peer influence, or disorganization (not knowing if you can get your work done). Do the following to prevent guilt from being an obstacle:

1. Reinforce a strong leisure ethic as part of a comprehensive personal philosophy.
2. Write daily time-management plans that allow visualization of work-related activities being accomplished.
3. Complete important work tasks before recreating, so you can recreate with a clear mind and feel that you "deserve" a leisure break. However, if taken to the extreme, this principle can prevent an individual from ever recreating.

Lack of Free Time

Lack of free time is one of the most commonly mentioned barriers to participation in recreational activities. However, as discussed in Chapter 6, it is possible to create more free time through improved time-management skills, sleep reduction, and other methods.

Lack of Motivation

One way to become motivated to participate in recreational activity is to believe that participation has an important effect on personal well-being. Understanding the specific benefits of participation in particular activities can instill this belief. For example, fully understanding the psychological and physiological benefits of recreational exercise (as discussed in Chapter 7) will help to increase motivation to participate in fitness-related activities. Understanding the general benefits of leisure activity (see Chapter 2) and theoretical explanations of leisure needs and satisfactions (see Chapter 5) will help motivate an individual to participate in leisure activities.

Poor Knowledge of Leisure Resources

Not knowing where and how to fulfill leisure interests can be a barrier to leisure activity participation. To overcome this obstacle, a variety of information resources should be consulted, such as municipal parks and recreation departments, libraries, telephone books, newspapers, magazines, the Internet, schools, local chambers of commerce, and sports clubs. Numerous state, regional, national, and international leisure activity organizations (e.g., United States Tennis Association) can also provide helpful information on specific activities. This obstacle can easily be overcome by taking concrete action to acquire information.

Lacking a Partner

Sports such as tennis and racquetball require a partner. Some ways to meet potential partners for recreational activities are to enroll in a class, join a club, or post a notice at a nearby facility. Also, simply joining any organization or going to public community events (e.g., a race) will broaden the possibilities of meeting people who share similar leisure interests.

If you are a college student, try to create new ways to meet new people and find partners for your favorite activities by taking advantage of some of the unique opportunities available at universities. For example, join intramural tournaments or participate in activities sponsored by the campus recreation and intramurals department. Perhaps you can even encourage one or more of your instructors to make an announcement or pass around a phone list to form a softball team, volleyball team, or some other activity for which you need other participants.

Outside Influences

Peers, parents, social norms, and the media can influence leisure behavior to a greater extent than people realize. Unfortunately, outside influences often prevent individuals from pursuing recreational activities they really desire and can instead lead them to participate in more socially accepted activities. The important philosophical principle to remember in order to avoid undue influence of others on leisure behavior is that leisure needs vary greatly from person to person, and we must all personally design our leisure to fulfill our most important needs and desires.

Habits/Set Patterns

It is easy to get into a "leisure rut." Once a pattern of leisure behavior is established, whether it is optimally satisfying or not, people stick with it, leaving no room for new and possibly better activities. Exercise 12.2 is designed to help create a greater awareness of personal leisure habits and desirable changes in established patterns of leisure behavior.

EXERCISE 12.2. Breaking Out of a Leisure Rut

1. List the leisure activities you participated in during the past week and how much time you devoted to each one. _____

   _____

2. List the leisure activities that you would love to do but have not been able to engage in lately. _____

   _____

3. Rate the desirability of last week's leisure activities on a scale from 1 to 10 (10 being the most desirable). _____

   _____

4. How much time was spent in activities that were rated 5 or lower?

   _____

5. Examine if some of your most desired activities could have been participated in instead of the lower-rated activities. _____

   _____

6. Devise a loose plan for next week's leisure activities, trying to eliminate the lower-rated activities and including as many of the more highly desired activities as possible. _____

   _____

7. Answer the following questions:

   Which of the lower-rated activities have been frequently participated in for more than six months? _____

   Why do you think you continued to participate in these activities if they were not very satisfying? _____

   Why did you not replace these activities with more desirable ones sooner? _____

   _____

The purpose of Exercise 12.2 is to facilitate identification of undesirable personal leisure habits and provide motivation for breaking out of these habits. If you know an individual who you feel is stuck in a leisure rut, why do you think he or she does not do anything about it? Probably the greatest enemy to positive change is laziness. Leisure, like work, requires constant attention and effort if it is to continuously improve and not stagnate.

Likewise, overcoming obstacles to attaining leisure goals can require a great deal of effort. Exercise 12.3 is presented to facilitate the identification of obstacles to leisure goal attainment and to develop ways of overcoming these obstacles. One generally applicable suggestion for overcoming obstacles is to think positively and focus on success. As discussed in the next section, positive thinking can be a powerful tool in promoting maximal leisure well-being.

THE POWER OF POSITIVE THINKING

Positive thinking can be a beneficial element of a personal leisure philosophy. It can turn bad situations into good ones and can enhance psychological and physical well-being. Positive thinking and leisure are closely interrelated in that positive thinking can enhance leisure well-being and leisure activities can elicit positive thoughts.

Furthermore, being optimistic seems to have important implications for health. In one study, Harvard researchers found that men in their sixties were less likely to develop coronary heart disease if they had optimistic outlooks on life (Wen, 2001). Similarly, a study by Carnegie Mellon University researchers found that angioplasty patients who were more pessimistic were nearly three times as likely to have a recurrence of arterial blockage than were the more optimistic patients (De Las Nueces, 1999). A study on the effects of optimism on illness found that optimism seems to help prevent people from getting sick during stressful times (Gilbert, 1998). Other health-related benefits of optimism reported by Dorsey (2000) are that HIV patients who were optimists showed fewer symptoms and coped better than other HIV patients, and in another study at Cornell University, positive mood seemed to be related to heightened creativity and greater mental agility. Researchers at the Mayo Clinic, in a study spanning three decades and involving 839 people, found that optimistic people

EXERCISE 12.3.
Overcoming Obstacles to Leisure Goal Attainment

Instructions

1. In the first column, list three personal leisure goals (refer to the leisure goal-setting exercise in Chapter 6).
2. In the second column, identify the internal obstacles to meeting each goal.
3. Exchange papers with someone else.
4. In the last column, partners will try to identify ways to overcome each of the obstacles listed in the second column.
5. Exchange papers again and discuss the feasibility of the ideas for overcoming the obstacles.
6. Did your partner come up with any suggestions for overcoming your obstacles that you had not thought of?

Leisure goal	Internal obstacles to goal attainment	Ideas for overcoming the obstacles
1. _____	1. _____	1. _____
_____	_____	_____
_____	_____	_____
_____	_____	_____
_____	_____	_____
2. _____	2. _____	2. _____
_____	_____	_____
_____	_____	_____
_____	_____	_____
3. _____	3. _____	3. _____
_____	_____	_____
_____	_____	_____
_____	_____	_____
_____	_____	_____

lived 19 percent longer than pessimists (Reuters, 2000). Unfortunately, pessimism seems to be on the rise. According to Schafer (1992), the rate of depression in America has increased *tenfold* in recent decades, largely due to a greater prevalence of pessimism.

Leisure activity is the key to reducing pessimism and depression and increasing positive thinking and happiness. Meyers (Carrol, 1992) discusses the factors that promote happiness, and most of them are related to leisure: fitness and health; realistic goals and expectations; positive self-esteem; feeling of control; extrovertedness; friendships; intimate, sexually warm marriage of equals; spiritual faith; challenging work; adequate rest and retreat, with active leisure; and optimism/positive thinking. According to Cook (2000), psychologists say that the things many people think would make them happy, such as money, beauty, or social prominence, do not seem to matter. A 1998 study found no relationship between salary and ultimate happiness, and a 1995 study found that physical attractiveness had little or no effect on happiness. A study involving college students found that students who were already relatively high in the attainment of appearance, financial success, and popularity were lower in well-being and self-esteem (Kohn, 1999).

Positive thinking is a key to happiness, because happiness is controlled by thoughts. People choose to think either positive or negative thoughts and in this way are in control of their happiness. Pliskin (1983) recognizes that people do not always have complete control over their thoughts, that negative thoughts sometimes seem to automatically pop into the mind. However, negative thoughts can be removed by making a conscious effort to eliminate them. Pliskin explains that a person cannot think two thoughts at the same time. Rather than fighting negative thoughts, the most effective way to make negative thoughts disappear is to make an effort to think positive thoughts. The positive thoughts will replace the negative ones.

The leisure-related implications of positive thinking are enormous. Even though events that occur during a leisure activity are sometimes beyond our control (e.g., an unexpected thunderstorm comes along to interrupt a picnic), we are in control of our attitudes toward a situation. It is an individual's choice to be upset about the storm, focus on thoughts on how to improve the situation (e.g., move the picnic indoors), or try to find positive aspects of the situation (e.g., being together with friends despite the storm). The picnic/thunderstorm example illustrates how people have control over their happiness. As Pliskin states, it is foolish to use your mind to make yourself miserable when you have the potential to use your mind to make yourself happy.

According to Foreman (1981), research indicates that mood swings affect the brain's release of neurotransmitters, which in turn affect a variety of bodily functions, including sleep inducement and appetite control. These neurotransmitters also affect moods. Therefore, the mind/body connection works in both directions: positive attitudes help to elicit the secretion of positive-thinking chemicals such as norepinephrine, and higher levels of norepinephrine help bring about an elevated mood. O'Connor (1986) identifies several recreational ways to increase norepinephrine levels:

1. *Laughter:* Ever notice the euphoric mood a good hearty laugh brings about?
2. *Rapid physical movement:* Any sustained (for at least ten minutes) aerobic type of activity (see Chapter 7) can raise the level of positive-thinking chemicals in the body. This pleasant mood-changing effect of vigorous exercise is known as a "runner's high" (Foreman, 1981).
3. *Risk recreation:* Notice the euphoria people seem to be experiencing on thrill rides in an amusement park. Their norepinephrine levels must be extremely high. However, when the perceived risk of an activity exceeds the optimal level of arousal, the activity will have a negative, not positive, effect on one's mood.
4. *Experiencing something beautiful:* Whatever it may be—a painting, a song, a sunset, or a person—dwelling on the beauty of something can elevate norepinephrine levels.
5. *Receiving compliments:* Ever notice the positive mood swing caused by a compliment? When was the last time you received a compliment? How did it make you feel?
6. *Loving anything:* Whether it be a person, place, or object, dwelling on loving feelings about something helps to raise norepinephrine levels.
7. *Volunteering:* Luks (1988) states that studies indicate most volunteers report feeling a physical sensation similar to a "runner's high." This sensation seems to be caused by the release of endorphins.

Unfortunately, seeking increased norepinephrine levels through risk recreation does involve some real danger. For example, thrill rides such as modern roller coasters have been linked to brain trauma and other injuries (Gilbert, 2002). New rides are even bigger, faster, and more jolting. Injuries on amusement park rides in the United States increased 60 percent from 1996 to 2000, when 10,580 injuries needed emergency room treatment (Gilbert, 2002).

Increased injuries and fatalities are also related to increased participation in extreme sports. Greenfeld (1999) reports that snowboarding has grown 113 percent in five years, and mountain biking, skateboarding, scuba diving, and other extreme sports have also grown in popularity. Corresponding to the increased participation figures for these activities are the statistics indicating increased hospital emergency room visits for skateboarding-related injuries (up 33 percent), snowboarding (up 31 percent), and mountain climbing (up 20 percent). BASE jumping has one of the highest fatality rates of all sports, with forty-six participants being killed in the first eighteen years of its existence (Greenfeld, 1999). Despite its high fatality rate, its popularity seems to be constantly growing.

A safer, yet perhaps equally or more effective way to increase norepinephrine levels seems to be singing in a choir. Fisher (2001) reports one research study which found that singers in a choir described themselves as feeling happy or euphoric when rehearsing or performing. A protein used by the immune system called immunoglobulin A increased 150 percent during rehearsals and 240 percent during performance.

Another recreational way to stimulate the production of positive-thinking chemicals and put people in a good mood seems to be eating certain "good-mood foods." Carper (1999) cites research indicating that eating chocolate, fish, foods high in vitamin D (such as milk, salmon, and fortified cereal), and B vitamin foods (such as dried beans, whole grains, fish, bananas, avocados, eggs, poultry, and dairy products) can help to prevent depression and improve people's moods.

It seems that the less intense, longer lasting mood boosters have a greater impact on overall happiness than do the more intense, faster ones such as thrill rides. Diener (Wen, 2000) reports that happy people have mild-to-moderate pleasant emotions most of the time, rather than intense positive moments some of the time.

Therefore, one of the important aspects of leisure activities to which we should be attuned is the emotional state they create. Exercise 12.4 asks you to examine how various recreational activities affect your mood and to identify recreational ways to increase the time during which you experience pleasant emotions in your life.

In summary, recreational activities can have a positive physiological effect, stimulating the brain to produce positive-thinking chemicals, which in turn affect emotions. Incorporating positive thinking into a personal leisure philosophy is a sure path to a happier life. Another possible connection of leisure philosophy to personal well-being concerns the theory of right- and left-brain functioning.

THE RIGHT BRAIN AND LEISURE

The neocortex of the brain has two hemispheres (left and right), each one governing its own functions (Geba, 1985). Left-brain functions include verbal, writing, math, and analytical skills; the right-brain functions include artistic, creative, spiritual, and intuitive processes. According to Geba, industrial societies are left-brain oriented, at the expense of not fully cultivating right-brain functions. In Geba's view, recreation is more of a right-brain process. Therefore, because industrial societies are left-brain oriented, they have difficulty being fully receptive to leisure. Until the right brain is "freed," Geba contends that people cannot truly recreate.

Geba's assertions support the arguments made in Chapter 2 on behalf of enhancing leisure education efforts in schools. The educational system seems to emphasize developing left-brain skills (verbal, math, and analytical skills), while paying much less attention to developing right-brain skills (art, music, and other creative activities are usually considered "frills"). Through leisure education, right-brain functions will have an opportunity for greater development. If Geba's assertions regarding right- and left-brain functioning are correct, development of the right brain is essential if people in modern society are to break away from a pattern of rational, analytical thought and become immersed in the intuitive, creative, and spiritual side of life that is associated with recreation.

The purpose of Exercise 12.5 is to assess how neglected your right hemisphere is and to develop ways to cultivate this hemisphere. First list the major tasks or activities you engaged in yesterday and identify

EXERCISE 12.4. Leisure and Moods

Instructions

1. In the first column, identify recreational activities that put you in a bad mood. Think about this carefully. For example, do certain "friends" put you in a bad mood? Do certain types of television shows or movies or music make you feel down?
2. In the second column, list those recreational activities that put you in a good mood. Include leisure activities that give you an intense norepinephrine boost and also those that create mild-to-moderate, lasting pleasant emotions.
3. In the last column, identify ideas for increasing your "good-mood time" through recreational activities. List ideas for increasing current or occasional activities that put you in a good mood, ideas for new activities that you think would put you in a good mood, and ideas for eliminating or cutting down on recreational activities that seem to put you in a bad mood.

"Bad mood" leisure	"Good mood" leisure	Ways to increase "good mood" leisure

EXERCISE 12.5. Freeing the Right Hemisphere

Yesterday's right-brain activities and tasks	**Yesterday's left-brain activities and tasks**
1. Morning	1. Morning
2. Afternoon	2. Afternoon
3. Evening	3. Evening

Right-brain activities that could be incorporated into my life

1. _____ 6. _____

2. _____ 7. _____

3. _____ 8. _____

4. _____ 9. _____

5. _____ 10. _____

whether they were right-brain or left-brain functions. Then make a second list of right-brain activities that you feel could be incorporated into your life. The intent of this exercise is to stimulate thought on how to cultivate the right brain to enable you to have a more recreational lifestyle. Self-esteem, discussed in the next section, is also a vital prerequisite for maximal leisure well-being.

SELF-ESTEEM

Leisure and self-esteem are closely interrelated. High self-esteem facilitates participation in and enjoyment of a wide variety of leisure activities; low self-esteem can be a major obstacle to leisure fulfillment. On the other hand, positive leisure experiences can greatly enhance self-esteem.

A few thought-provoking questions are presented to emphasize the interrelatedness of leisure and self-esteem:

I. What recreational activities have you dreamed about doing but have not tried because you do not think you are capable?

II. Have you ever had the frustrating experience of trying to convince a friend or relative to attempt a recreational activity he or she was needlessly afraid of but obviously was capable of doing?

III. How do you feel about yourself after an especially enjoyable recreational activity?

IV. Are you more willing to try new things when you are feeling good about yourself?

V. How can people improve their self-esteem? Pliskin (1983) offers some answers to this question.

   A. Make a clear determination of what is important in your life. Then the numerous but relatively insignificant failures in day-to-day life will not affect your feelings of self-worth, because you will recognize their insignificance in the greater scheme of things.

   B. Realize your values and skills and take pride in them.

   C. Recognize that material wealth is not a valid criterion of self-worth.

   D. Do not compare yourself with others.

E. Do not allow other people's evaluations of you to affect your self-esteem.
F. Do not allow your mistakes to rob you of feelings of self-worth. Keep your mind focused on your potential for positive action.
G. Work at improving yourself. As Waitley (1983) suggests, seek personal growth through classes, seminars, fitness programs, reading, and other means. Waitley also offers several other self-esteem tips:
   1. Always greet people with a smile; it helps make you feel good about yourself.
   2. Accept compliments by saying "thank you." Do not play down or play up the value of a compliment.
   3. Do not brag. Bragging is a sign of needing attention and perhaps having feelings of inferiority.
   4. Talk affirmatively about progress you are making rather than dwelling on problems.

These suggestions for enhancing self-esteem can be incorporated into a personal philosophy of leisure and life. Remembering these principles and tips in every situation will not only help improve self-esteem but will also help make all activities, especially leisure activities, more enjoyable. High self-esteem is needed to feel able to reach for one's leisure dreams, to try to make the ideal a reality.

VISUALIZING AND REACHING FOR THE IDEAL

A positive element of a personal leisure philosophy is to constantly strive for maximal leisure well-being. In order to strive for maximal leisure well-being, a vision of personal maximal leisure well-being is necessary. A first step in defining your personal maximal leisure well-being is to fantasize about your ideal leisure lifestyle. Exercise 12.6 is intended to facilitate envisioning an ideal leisure lifestyle.

The intent of this exercise is to facilitate the identification of feasible activities that could enhance personal leisure well-being. If it was difficult to envision an ideal leisure lifestyle or your ideal leisure lifestyle was very similar to your present one, then try fantasizing a bit more. True, your present leisure might be wonderful, but everyone has room for improvement. To help stimulate imagination, try to vi-

EXERCISE 12.6. My Ideal Leisure Lifestyle

Imagine you have won the lottery and are now financially independent for life. You no longer have to work or attend school. You can spend your time precisely as you please. Describe how you would spend your time in the space below. Do not focus on how you would spend your money; rather, stay focused on what your typical day-to-day activities would be. Begin by describing what you would do with your life shortly after winning the lottery, and then delve into what your daily life would be like after you adjusted to your newly found financial freedom.

After writing this essay, answer the following questions:

1. How difficult was it to identify what you would want your new leisure lifestyle to be like? _____
_____

2. How similar is your ideal leisure lifestyle to your present leisure lifestyle? _____
_____

3. What leisure activities identified in your ideal leisure lifestyle could you try to incorporate into your life, even if you never win the lottery?
_____
_____

4. Did you include work in your ideal lifestyle because having nothing but leisure seemed like it would be boring after a while? _____
_____
_____

sualize the leisure lifestyle of highly esteemed others, whether they be people you know who are exceptionally happy or celebrities you greatly admire.

Another way to stimulate imagination is to read leisure-related books and magazines. Such literature will surely present ideas on enticing activities you have never even heard of before. Even with limitless free time, it seems that boredom is unnecessary, given the diversity of leisure pursuits that are available.

Having a clear vision of the ideal leisure lifestyle is a key element of a personal leisure philosophy, because without this vision, it is difficult to know how to approach leisure enhancement. Constantly reaching for the ideal prevents individuals from falling into the pitfalls of stagnation or boredom.

SUMMARY

Previous chapters pointed out the importance of laughter and other recreational stress-reduction activities, recreational exercise to promote fitness, and leisure planning and time management in attaining maximal leisure well-being. This chapter focused on key elements to consider in developing a personal leisure philosophy for maximizing leisure well-being.

These key elements are summarized as follows:

- Be optimistic; practice positive thinking in all aspects of life.
- Enjoy leisure without feeling guilty; recognize the necessity of leisure for physical and mental well-being.
- Take adequate time for leisure, make it a top priority.
- Maximize intrinsic motivation for leisure activities by making sure that your activities are fun and enjoyable.
- Determine what activities feel best for you personally and plan your leisure accordingly; do not let activity choices be controlled by others.
- Always try new activities, avoid falling into a leisure rut.
- Visualize the ideal and reach for it.
- Consider ethics in choosing activities for participation.
- Recognize the value of active recreation in promoting happiness and the pitfalls of sedentary, unchallenging leisure.
- Be flexible, open-minded to change.

To conclude this chapter, you are asked to incorporate the information presented in this chapter and in previous chapters in writing a statement of your personal leisure philosophy (Exercise 12.7). Included in this personal philosophy should be a clear identification of ultimate, long-term, and short-term leisure goals.

EXERCISE 12.7. My Personal Leisure Philosophy

Instructions

Save this statement, write another one a year from now, and compare the two.

_____

_____

_____

_____

_____

_____

_____

_____

_____

_____

_____

_____

_____

_____

_____

_____

_____

_____

_____

_____

_____

_____

_____

REFERENCES

Carper, J. (1999). 5 good-mood foods. *USA Weekend,* January 1-3, p. 22.

Carrol, J. (1992). So is anyone happy? The key to happiness is a sense of control and (surprise) humor. *The San Francisco Chronicle,* August 24, pp. D3, D5.

Cook, G. (2000). Happy hunting: Researchers delight in determining what brings us joy. *The Boston Globe,* October 1, pp. A1, A6.

De Las Nueces, D. (1999). Expecting the best is good for the heart. *The New York Times,* August 10, p. D8.

Dorsey, G. (2000). Cheer up—Make way for the happiness revolt. *The Jerusalem Post,* July 2, p. 18.

Fisher, M. J. (2001). Joy of singing in a choir could be preventive medicine, researchers say. *The Boston Globe,* March 31, p. A5.

Foreman, J. (1981). Mind-body separation has become obsolete. *Los Angeles Times,* December 27, pp. 24-26.

Geba, B. H. (1985). *Being at leisure, playing at life.* San Diego, CA: Leisure Science Systems International.

Gilbert, S. (1998). Optimism's bright side: A healthy, longer life. *The New York Times,* June 30, p. C7.

Gilbert, S. (2002). When brain trauma is at the other end of the thrill ride. *The New York Times,* June 25, p. D5.

Greenfeld, K. T. (1999). Life on the edge. *Time,* September 6, pp. 28-36.

Kohn, A. (1999). In pursuit of affluence, at a high price. *The New York Times,* February 2, p. D7.

Luks, A. (1988). Helper's high. *Psychology Today,* October, pp. 39, 42.

O'Connor, C. (1986). Lifestyling. Course packet formerly used for Recr 10 at Chico State, Chico, CA.

Pliskin, Z. (1983). *Gateway to happiness.* Brooklyn, NY: Aish HaTorah.

Reuters (2000). Longer life? Put on a happy face. *The Boston Globe,* February 8, p. E5.

Schafer, W. (1992). Depression, pessimism, and choice. *Stress and Health Report* (Enloe Hospital Stress and Health Center, Chico, CA), July/August, pp. 1-2.

Waitley, D. (1983). *Seeds of greatness.* New York: Pocket Books.

Wen, P. (2000). Happiness is a positive thought. *The Boston Globe,* March 14, p. F1.

Wen, P. (2001). Doctors seek insight into our outlook. *The Boston Globe,* November 27, pp. C1, C4.

PART III:
EXPANDING LEISURE HORIZONS

Chapter 13

Leisure Throughout the Life Cycle

INTRODUCTION

Being able to adapt to change is cited several times in this book as one of the keys to happiness and well-being. This chapter examines some of the major changes that typically occur throughout the life cycle and their implications for leisure. Hopefully, the information provided in this chapter can be utilized to facilitate a smooth adjustment to life-cycle changes. Leisure, similar to other aspects of life, must adapt appropriately to changes encountered throughout the life span in order to maintain the highest possible level of happiness and well-being.

This chapter is not intended to be a comprehensive overview of leisure in the different stages of the life cycle. Rather, it seeks to foster a better understanding of some of the similarities and differences in leisure at different stages in the life cycle and some of the special leisure-related concerns of different age groups. The main purposes of this chapter are to learn how the past (childhood and adolescence) affects leisure in the present (adulthood) and to explore what can be done to ensure maximal leisure well-being in the future (later life).

The learning objectives for this chapter are to

1. Identify stages of development in childhood and their implications for children's play.
2. Identify special concerns regarding leisure in childhood.
3. Cite research on the relationship of leisure in childhood to leisure and well-being in adulthood.
4. Identify special concerns regarding leisure in adolescence.
5. Contrast characteristics of leisure throughout various stages of life.
6. Identify significant milestones throughout the life cycle and their implications for leisure.
7. Identify ideas for ensuring maximal leisure well-being in later life.

LEISURE IN CHILDHOOD

The different stages of childhood can be categorized as follows (Cordes and Ibrahim, 2003):

1. *Infancy (birth to eighteen months):* Through play experiences, infants experiment with and learn to master motor skills such as hand-eye coordination.
2. *Toddlerhood (eighteen months to three years of age):* Play experiences provide opportunities for pretend play and imaginative role-playing and the development of gross motor skills such as running, jumping, and throwing. The attention span is short and planned activities are easily disrupted. Toddlers play side by side in activity known as parallel play, as they are not yet capable of interactive play.
3. *Preschool (three to five years of age):* In this stage there is a decrease in egocentricity, an increased ability to reason, and increased awareness of relationships with others and gender differences. Play is still unstructured, but by age five, children are beginning to enjoy some competition.
4. *Middle childhood (five to twelve years of age):* Children in this stage continue to develop physically, mentally, and emotionally, but at a slower, steadier pace. Through leisure activities, children can form their first close relationships outside their family. This stage can be further divided into younger children, ages five to eight, and older children, ages nine to twelve (Edginton et al., 2002). Younger children are more interested in having fun and learning skills, whereas older children are more interested in competition.

Before further exploring childhood leisure, it would be useful to look back on personal childhood leisure experiences. Exercise 13.1 is presented to provide an opportunity to examine the relevance of some of the research on children's play to personal childhood leisure experiences.

Next, work on Exercise 13.2 with the help of some classmates and friends of the opposite sex. The purpose of this exercise is to examine male/female differences in leisure in childhood and their effects on male/female differences in leisure interests and activities of college students.

EXERCISE 13.1. Examining Personal Childhood Play Experiences

Answer the following questions in the spaces provided.

1. Describe a typical personal play day (Saturday, Sunday, or holiday) at any time from age five to twelve. _____

_____

2. In what leisure activities did your parents most frequently participate?

_____

3. What were your parents' favorite leisure activities? _____

_____

4. What messages did your parents convey to you regarding leisure?

_____

5. In retrospect, was your childhood play most affected by your parents' leisure activities attitudes or their satisfaction with activities? _____

_____

6. In what ways are your present leisure activities influenced by your childhood play experiences? _____

_____

7. In what ways are your present leisure activities similar to those of your parents? _____

_____

8. Based on this exercise, how would you approach trying to influence your children's leisure? _____

_____

_____

EXERCISE 13.2. Exploring Male/Female Differences in Leisure

Instructions

1. In the first column, based on the answers to Exercise 13.1, list some of the main differences you found in comparing the childhood leisure experiences of males and females. Underneath the list of differences, make a second list of similarities that you found.
2. In the second column, list some of the main differences you found in comparing the leisure interests and activities of male and female college students. Underneath the list of differences, make a second list of similarities that you found.
3. At the bottom of the page, write your conclusions regarding your perceptions of the similarities and differences in the leisure interests and activities of male and female college students.

Childhood leisure comparisons	College students' leisure comparisons
Differences	*Differences*
Similarities	*Similarities*
Conclusions	

Refer back to your answers to Exercises 13.1 and 13.2 as you read about the research on male/female differences in childhood play experiences and their implications for leisure in adulthood. Determine if the research cited from the 1970s is still relevant today. For example, according to Greendorfer (1977), even at six months of age males are given more freedom to explore and are less restricted in crawling; later in childhood, boys play rougher with toys, more frequently play outdoors, and play farther from home than girls. Did you find these differences in comparing your answers to Exercises 13.1 and 13.2 with those of classmates?

Some might argue that even if these differences in childhood lead to differences in leisure pursuits in adulthood, there is no problem with males and females having different leisure interests. However, one problem encountered by many married couples is a discrepancy in leisure pursuits that can drive couples to spend much of their free time apart and consequently become more distant. According to Shaw (1992), joint activities (those including interaction) increase marital satisfaction, whereas individual or parallel activities (e.g., watching television) do not. If males and females are encouraged to develop *similar* interests in childhood, it is likely that adult males and females will share more common interests, which will undoubtedly bode well for marital relationships. Isn't it more enjoyable to be in a relationship with someone with whom you share many common interests than to have a partner with whom you feel unable to participate in your favorite activities?

Are concerns about gender inequality outdated? Aren't men and women of the twenty-first century more equal in terms of sharing similar interests and more evenly dividing household and child-rearing responsibilities? Apparently not as much as many people would think. According to an eleven-nation study, preschoolers worldwide are alone with their fathers less than one waking hour per day (Sobieraj, 1995). While American mothers spend almost eleven waking hours as sole supervisors of their preschoolers each day, American fathers average only forty-two minutes per day. Fathers in Thailand spend the most time with their preschoolers, just over three hours per day, while fathers in Hong Kong spend the least time, just six minutes per day. Meanwhile, mothers around the world spend much more time with their preschoolers. Belgian mothers are with their children the least, but still average 5.2 hours daily.

Another inequality between men and women is in providing care for elderly parents. Bedini (2002) reports that 75 percent of family caregivers are female. Providing care to an elderly parent presents a challenge in terms of leisure, as 81 percent of caregivers say that it restricts their personal free time and 62 percent say that it restricts family free time.

In summary, gender differences in childhood play are important to consider, as they can lead to significant leisure-related differences in adulthood. Since the 1960s, emphasis has been placed on encouraging females to participate more in aggressive, physically demanding sports that were traditionally dominated by males. Perhaps more effort needs to be placed on encouraging males to participate in cooperative activities and activities that foster the development of caring and nurturing behavior which have been traditionally associated with females. Hopefully, these efforts can have positive effects on adult leisure.

A related concern is American society's emphasis on competitive and organized sports for children. Is it possible that the immersion of American children in competitive, organized activities causes problems later in adulthood, such as having difficulty being able to enjoy spontaneous leisure experiences, to create and improvise activities, and to de-emphasize goal-oriented activities and focus on interpersonal interactions? Would a greater emphasis on noncompetitive play for children help socialize them into becoming more sociable, less goal-oriented adults?

Research indicates that childhood leisure behavior can have a significant effect on adult life. Brooks and Elliott (1971) found that leisure activities and satisfactions in childhood correlated positively with psychological adjustment at age thirty. Their study involved seventy-four persons who were assessed at less than two years of age, then reassessed at age thirty.

Yoesting and Burkhead (1973) found that childhood outdoor recreational activities were an important predictor of adult recreational activities. Approximately 40 percent of the thirty-five activities examined in this study were participated in similarly in childhood and in adult life. In a study of adults aged twenty-one to sixty-one, Kelly (1974) found that almost 50 percent of recreational activities participated in as an adult were initiated in childhood.

Parents seem to have a significant effect on children's play. In Barnett and Chick's (1986) study of ninety-seven preschoolers, it was found that the leisure satisfaction of parents was a better predictor of children's play than were the parents' leisure attitudes or activities. For example, the more playful children tended to have mothers with higher leisure satisfaction. In addition, social play was related to parents' satisfaction with social leisure activities. However, strong relationships were not found in comparing the leisure activities of parents and children.

Another area in which parents have a great influence on children is fitness. In a study by the Boston University School of Medicine (Schafer, 1991), children with active mothers were twice as likely themselves to be active; those with active fathers were 3.5 times more likely to be active.

Parents' influence on childhood leisure is especially important, given the variety of potentially negative influences on childhood leisure. For example, Kutner (1994) feels that the primary message to be deduced from watching the Olympics is that in sports, winning is all important, that dedication, grace, sacrifice, talent, and sportsmanship do not count.

Kutner reports that sports psychologists and coaches are concerned about the effects of the media's negative messages on children, because studies show that children do not automatically develop good sportsmanship, that it must be taught to them specifically. Duret's (1994) study of 263 children, ages eight, ten, and twelve, in forty-six volleyball clubs in France provides evidence to support these concerns. In Duret's study, the children seemed to have more of a scoffing and derisive attitude toward the other players. Those with an encouraging, cooperative attitude were in the minority.

Another area of concern related to influences on children's play is the proliferation of war toys. According to Zur (1990), sales of such toys have risen 800 percent in the United States since 1982. Opponents of war toys claim that such toys prepare children for war and other kinds of violence. Sweden and Finland have banned the sale of war toys entirely. On the other hand, proponents of war toys feel that they provide an acceptable way of harmlessly releasing aggressive behavior and an outlet for imaginative play. Others argue that children must be allowed to play as they choose. Zur feels that the key is to let children play as they choose, for freedom is the essence of play, but to minimize the negative impact war toys and violent television shows can have, parents should think of their home as a classroom. In families in which members are treated with respect and dignity, children will learn to relate to others similarly, whereas children growing up in an abusive environment will more likely take on these negative behavior patterns.

Perhaps the greatest concern regarding childhood leisure is too much television. Children spend more time watching television than they do reading or studying and are less likely to play outdoors once television is introduced into their lives (Pawlowski, 2000). It is hypothesized that extensive television watching in early childhood is related to the rise in attention disorders and learning disabilities. Spending a great deal of time watching television also seems to be related to the rise in obesity among children (Shell, 2000).

The following list summarizes some of the main concerns regarding the current and future status of leisure in childhood.

1. Providing *safe play environments* for children is essential. Over 200,000 children per year receive emergency medical care for playground-related injuries, at a cost of over $1 billion (Hudson, Mack, and Thompson, 2000).
2. Related to the issue of safety is *violence and fear of violence*. As discussed by Kelly and Freysinger (2000), the problems of crime and violence can prevent children from feeling that it is safe to play outdoors.
3. The *proliferation of war toys and violent video games* is a possible cause of the increase in violence among children.
4. The *negative influence of the media* might be partly responsible for the increase in violence among youth and is also seen as glorifying unhealthy behavior such as using alcohol and other drugs.
5. The media has also been blamed for contributing to the *overemphasis on competition* in children's leisure activities.
6. The *sedentary nature* of childhood leisure has a negative impact on fitness and has led to an increasing incidence of obesity among U.S. children.
7. Watching *too much television* seems to have a negative impact on thought processes.
8. Meanwhile, *increasing exercise* is seen as being able to boost children's brain functioning (Kong, 1999). In particular, *spontaneous exercise and play* seems to be best at providing brain connections that stimulate learning (Meltz, 1998).

9. *Reduction in recess time and in physical education programs* is creating challenges to allowing adequate time for children to play and exercise.
10. *The high divorce rate and rise in single-parent families* creates numerous challenges for childhood leisure and social development.
11. *The overstructuring of children's time* is seen as infringing on children's opportunities to engage in healthy, beneficial, spontaneous, creative play (Holmes, 1998).
12. *Sex-role stereotyping* in children's play is hypothesized to accentuate leisure-related differences between males and females, leading to potential conflicts in marriage in adulthood.

LEISURE IN ADOLESCENCE

For numerous reasons, adolescence is a difficult period of the life cycle. Evidence of its difficulty is the high incidence of negative behavior among adolescents, such as substance abuse, vandalism, and violent crimes. American youth are in greatest danger of being victims of violence, with nine out of ten young people murdered in industrialized nations slain in the United States (Reaves, 1993). Another major problem among youth is suicide; from 1960 to 1990 the rate of reported suicides among young people nearly tripled (Wartik, 1991). It is estimated that three out of four youth suicide victims have abused alcohol or other drugs (Wartik, 1991). Free time can either provide the opportunity to engage in these negative activities or it can be utilized to prevent problematic behavior.

In discussing the importance of leisure activity in preventing negative adolescent behavior patterns, Hamilton (1983) states that when adolescents are bored, they often resort to activities with negative consequences. According to Yin, Katims, and Zapata (1999), leisure boredom is a factor to consider in explaining the development of delinquency, and participation in various conventional organized leisure activities can reduce delinquency and increase positive social control. Therefore, a key to preventing adolescent delinquent behavior is to prevent boredom.

However, a problem is that some of the most common leisure activities of adolescents actually cause boredom. For example, Hamilton states that video games are ultimately boring because they do not involve interpersonal interaction and therefore lack a connection to real life. In addition, Hamilton expresses concern that watching television, the second most frequently participated in activity of adolescents, has a negative effect on adolescents. He cites a study which found that adolescents reported feeling worse when they watched television than when they did anything else. Not spending much time watching television has been identified as a factor related to belonging to educational tracks (college-bound programs) with good social prospects in adulthood (Koivusilta, Rimpela, and Rimpela, 1999).

Leisure activity can be a positive force in the lives of adolescents. Kleiber and Larson (1986) found that the seventy-five adolescents in their study experienced greater freedom and intrinsic motivation from their leisure activities than in other daily life activities. Witt and Crompton (1999) discuss the emergence of teen centers, run for and by youth, as a setting for adolescent leisure activities that can help give adolescents a feeling of empowerment. Family leisure experiences can also be beneficial, and a lack of shared leisure experiences with parents can be detrimental (Robertson, 1999). In addition, participation in sports can enhance feelings of self-worth, but males are more likely than females to feel competent in the physical domain and derive enhanced self-esteem through sports (Trew et al., 1999). James (2001) reports that teenage girls are considerably less fit than boys and are generally less physically active. A large number of teenage girls quit playing sports and never take them up again.

Although leisure activities such as exercise and sports can be beneficial for adolescents, encouraging them to participate in activities can be challenging. Interestingly, Willits and Willits (1986), in their study of 3,294 eighth and eleventh grade students in Pennsylvania, found that adolescents more involved in work and other obligatory activities also tended to seek out greater leisure participation (e.g., socializing, reading, and participating in clubs and organizations). Meanwhile, less work time was related to more time spent watching television. It seems that up to a point, keeping adolescents as busy as possible with work and other activities fosters greater participation in leisure activities. Interestingly, in Gagnon's (1994) study of adolescents ages twelve to seventeen, the most often cited barrier to leisure activity participation was lack of time. However, based on the Pennsylvania study, it appears that lack of time might be more of an excuse than a genuine constraint. Gagnon's study also found that the two main motivations for leisure activities were having pleasure and being with friends.

Rickards and Glesne (1984) discuss two vastly different functions that adolescent leisure activities can serve: easing the transition to adulthood or prolonging adolescence. Based on their observations of the leisure behavior of American and Caribbean youth, Rickards and Glesne (1984) felt that the leisure activities of the American youth tend to be the type that prolong adolescence, whereas those of the Caribbean youth tend to be the type that foster socialization into adult roles.

Exercise 13.3 is presented to examine this concept on a personal level. In the first column, list and briefly describe your most prominent forms of recreation as an adolescent. In the second column, identify for which adult roles the activities helped prepare you. In the last column, explain how these activities helped prepare you for these roles. Leave the second and third columns blank for those activities you feel were the type that helped prolong adolescence.

Based on your answers to this exercise, would you say that your adolescent leisure activities were more of a help or a hindrance to socialization into adult roles? Do you feel adolescent leisure activities should facilitate socialization into adult roles, or should they help enable the adolescent to delay growing up?

LEISURE IN ADULTHOOD

Some researchers believe that after leaving adolescence and acquiring different life roles in young adulthood, people in midlife (approximately ages thirty-five to fifty-five) resume the identity struggles of adolescence. Le Shan (1973) states that in middle adulthood, as in adolescence, people are free to pursue activities that are self-satisfying and help answer personal questions regarding the meaning of life. In early adulthood, financial constraints and child-rearing responsibilities tend to inhibit such leisure pursuits.

Osgood (1987, p. 3) states that "middle age can be referred to as a leisure renaissance because of the greater freedom to pursue activities of individual choice." Osgood also emphasizes the need to pro-

EXERCISE 13.3. Assessing Adolescent Leisure

Adolescent leisure activities	Related adult roles	How socialization into the adult roles was fostered by the activities

vide leisure opportunities that can help middle-aged adults find answers to their questions about self-worth and the meaning of life.

Rather than being a leisure renaissance, middle age can also be the beginning of a period of boredom. Mobily (1987) states that the greater freedom middle-aged adults acquire once child-rearing and financial responsibilities have lessened sometimes results in boredom, especially if an individual has neglected the leisure self earlier in life. Because chronic boredom can cause depression and anxiety, it is important to prevent excessive boredom from setting in when free time increases in middle age. One means of prevention is to cultivate a variety of leisure interests in early adulthood that can be pursued vigorously in later adulthood, when free time is more abundant. However, it is easy to neglect the development of leisure interests in early adulthood because of preoccupation with establishing a career and raising a family.

Participation in recreational activities need not decline as one ages, and it can even increase. Warnick's (1987) data on adult involvement in water-based activities, travel, and other forms of recreational activity support this assertion.

Unfortunately, one form of recreational activity that often declines with age is exercise. Summerfield and Priest (1987) advocate using play as a motivational tool to encourage adults to exercise. According to Summerfield and Priest, exercise is often not as pleasurable for adults as it is for children because adult exercise is usually more structured and less play oriented. One way to encourage greater adult involvement in exercise programs is by highlighting the play aspects of the programs.

Encouraging adults to exercise is a critical concern because of the strong relationship between exercise and well-being (see Chapter 7). Maintaining a high level of participation in exercise through adulthood can help ensure a happier and healthier life in late adulthood.

LEISURE IN LATER LIFE

The topic of leisure and aging is important because of the growth of the older population, the increased free time usually associated with advanced age, and research showing the strong connection between leisure activity and life satisfaction in later life (Leitner and Leitner, 2004). The challenge is to ensure that elders participate in appropriate and stimulating recreational activities. Active and social recreational activities are the most beneficial, but the leisure activities of elders tend to be sedentary and solitary. Leisure is a key to making later life a happy time of life. A positive attitude and some planning and preparation for leisure in later life can help to maximize leisure well-being in this stage.

Exercise 13.4 is presented to facilitate an exploration of personal beliefs about leisure in later life. In the first column, list your present leisure activities. In the second column, list what you believe are the most popular leisure activities of elders today. In the last column, list what you predict will be your favorite leisure activities at age seventy-five.

Referring to Exercise 13.4, were your predicted leisure activities at age seventy-five more similar to those of elders today or to your present activities? Explain the rationale for your answers. If you predicted a more active lifestyle for yourself at age seventy-five than that of today's elders, what action do you plan to take to ensure that this positive scenario unfolds?

The following are some suggestions for ensuring maximal leisure well-being in later life, based on material covered in previous chapters:

1. Constantly remind yourself of the benefits of leisure activity and make leisure a high priority in your life.
2. Do not neglect the leisure aspects of life, even during busy periods during the life cycle.
3. When leisure is neglected for a period of time, it can be difficult to adjust to increased free time in later life.
3. Cultivate new leisure interests throughout the life cycle.
4. Remember that leisure education is a lifelong process. It is always useful to be aware of new leisure activity opportunities and leisure resources in the community.
5. Be adaptable and flexible, to be able to deal effectively not only with societal changes but also with personal changes and significant life events encountered during the course of a lifetime.

EXERCISE 13.4. Leisure in Later Life

My current leisure activities	Today's elders' leisure	My leisure at seventy-five

SIGNIFICANT LIFE EVENTS/MILESTONES

According to Neulinger (1981), some of the major milestones in the life cycle are starting school, first date, first car, first job, career choice, marriage, first child, widowhood, retirement, and the "empty nest" phenomenon (when children are grown and leave home). Each milestone has a significant impact on leisure. Exercise 13.5 is designed to help you explore the personal ramifications of these milestones.

In the first column, circle those milestones that you have already reached. List additional milestones that have occurred in your life or that you expect will occur. In the second column, describe the implications for leisure of each milestone. For milestones that have not yet been reached, project what you think the implications of the milestone will be for your leisure behavior.

In reviewing Exercise 13.5, which milestones do you view as the most important ones in terms of their leisure-related implications? Which ones do you view as negative milestones and which as positive ones? Do you view retirement as a negative or positive milestone?

SUMMARY

Presently, the life cycle is segmented into periods for education (approximately the first twenty to twenty-five years), work (ages twenty or twenty-five to sixty or sixty-five), and leisure (approximately age sixty-five and beyond). Is this segmentation really necessary? As discussed by Mobily (1987), other life-cycle options are possible. Would it not be better if work, education, and leisure were interspersed throughout the life cycle? In other words, working years could be extended well beyond age sixty-five, and instead there could be years off work for leisure and for education interspersed throughout the life cycle. Does this life pattern seem more appealing than the present life-cycle segmentation? It is important to consider the alternative life patterns carefully, for if the present education/work/leisure life-cycle segmentation is not the best possible system, efforts should begin immediately to change it.

EXERCISE 13.5. Personal Milestones and Leisure

Milestones	Leisure-related implications
Starting school	
First date	
First car	
First job	
Career choice	
Marriage	
First child	
Widowhood	
Retirement	
"Empty nest" phenomenon	
Others:	

REFERENCES

Barnett, L. and Chick, G. (1986). Chips off the ol' block: Parents' leisure and their children's play. *Journal of Leisure Research,* 18(4), 266-283.

Bedini, L.A. (2002). Family caregivers and leisure: An oxymoron? *Parks and Recreation,* 37(1), 25-31.

Brooks, B. and Elliott, D.M. (1971). Prediction of psychological adjustment at age thirty from leisure time activities and satisfactions in childhood. *Human Development,* 14(1), 51-61.

Cordes, K.A. and Ibrahim, H.M. (2003). *Applications in recreation and leisure for today and the future* (Third edition). New York: McGraw-Hill.

Duret, P. (1994). Leisure, physical activities, and sense of justice in children. *World Leisure and Recreation,* 36(1), 16-18.

Edginton, C.R., Jordan, D.J., DeGraaf, D.G., and Edginton, S.R. (2002). *Leisure and life satisfaction: Foundational perspectives* (Third edition). New York: McGraw-Hill.

Gagnon, P. (1994). Leisure activities of the young adolescents (age: 12-17). *World Leisure and Recreation,* 36(1), 19-21.

Greendorfer, S.L. (1977). Role of socializing agents in female sports involvement. *Research Quarterly,* 48, 304-310.

Hamilton, J.A. (1983). Development of interest and enjoyment in adolescence. Part II. Boredom and psychopathology. *Journal of Youth and Adolescence,* 12(5), 363-372.

Holmes, S.A. (1998). Children study longer and play less, a report says. *The New York Times,* November 11, p. A18.

Hudson, S.D., Mack, M.G., and Thompson, D. (2000). Play it safe: Steps to keeping playground surfacing safe for our children. *Parks and Recreation,* 35(4), 78-87.

James, K. (2001). "I just gotta have my own space!" The bedroom as a leisure site for adolescent girls. *Journal of Leisure Research,* 33(1), 71-90.

Kelly, J.R. (1974). Socialization toward leisure: A developmental approach. *Journal of Leisure Research,* 6, 181-193.

Kelly, J.R. and Freysinger, V.J. (2000). *Twenty-first century leisure current issues.* Boston: Allyn and Bacon.

Kleiber, D. and Larson, R. (1986). The experience of leisure in adolescence. *Journal of Leisure Research,* 18(3), 169-176.

Koivusilta, L., Rimpela, A., and Rimpela, M. (1999). Health-related lifestyle in adolescence—Origin of social class differences in health? *Health Education Research,* 14(3), 339-355.

Kong, D. (1999). Exercise seen boosting children's brain function. *The Boston Globe,* November 9, pp. A1, A9.

Kutner, L. (1994). Parent and child. *The New York Times,* February 17, p. B4.

Le Shan, E. (1973). *The wonderful crisis of middle age.* New York: Warner Books.

Leitner, M.J. and Leitner, S.F. (2004). *Leisure in later life* (Third edition). Binghamton, NY: The Haworth Press.

Meltz, B.F. (1998). Better thinking through playing? *The Boston Globe,* December 31, pp. C16, C19.

Mobily, K.E. (1987). Leisure, lifestyle, and life span. In R.D. MacNeil and M.L. Teague, *Aging and leisure: Vitality in later life* (pp. 155-180). Englewood Cliffs, NJ: Prentice-Hall.

Neulinger, J. (1981). *To leisure: An introduction.* Boston: Allyn and Bacon.

Osgood, N. (1987). The mid-life leisure renaissance: A developmental perspective. *Leisure Today,* October, pp. 3-7.

Pawlowski, C. (2000). *Glued to the tube: The threat of television addiction to today's family.* Naperville, IL: Sourcebooks, Inc.

Reaves, G. (1993). U.S. rated dangerous for young people. *San Francisco Examiner,* September 26, p. A4.

Rickards, W.H. and Glesne, C. (1984). Free time and the transition to adulthood: A cross-cultural examination of American and Caribbean youth. In *Abstracts from the 1984 Symposium on Leisure Research* (p. 56). Alexandria, VA: National Recreation and Parks Association.

Robertson, B. (1999). Leisure and family: Perspectives of male adolescents who engage in delinquent activity as leisure. *Journal of Leisure Research,* 31(4), 335-359.

Schafer, W. (1991). Parents influence children's fitness. *Stress and Health Report* (Enloe Hospital Stress and Health Center, Chico, CA), November/December, pp. 1-2.

Shaw, S.S. (1992). Family leisure and leisure services. *Parks and Recreation,* 27(12), 13-16, 66.

Shell, E.R. (2000). The childhood obesity epidemic. *The Boston Globe,* October 3, pp. E1, E5.

Sobieraj, S. (1995). "In absentia" fatherhood. *The Jerusalem Post,* January 23, p.7.

Summerfield, L.M. and Priest, L. (1987). Using play as motivation to exercise. *Leisure Today,* October, pp. 24-26.

Trew, K., Scully, D., Kremer, J., and Ogle, S. (1999). Sport, leisure, and perceived self-competence among male and female adolescents. *European Physical Education Review,* 5(1), 53-73.

Warnick, R.B. (1987). Recreation and leisure participation patterns among the adult middle-aged market from 1975 to 1984. *Leisure Today,* October, pp. 17-23.

Wartik, N. (1991). Jerry's choice. *American Health,* October, pp. 73-76.

Willits, W.L. and Willits, F.K. (1986). Adolescent participation in leisure activities: "The less, the more" or "The more, the more?" *Leisure Sciences,* 8(2), 189-206.

Witt, P. and Crompton, J. (1999). A paradigm of the times. *Parks and Recreation,* 34(12), 66-75.

Yin, Z., Katims, D., and Zapata, J. (1999). Participation in leisure activities and involvement in delinquency by Mexican American adolescents. *Hispanic Journal of Behavioral Sciences,* 21(2), 170-186.

Yoesting, D.R. and Burkhead, D.L. (1973). Significance of childhood recreation experience on adult leisure behavior: An exploratory analysis. *Journal of Leisure Research,* 5(1), 25-36.

Zur, O. (1990). Rethinking the war on war toys. *The Quest,* Winter, pp. 28-37.

Chapter 14A

Recreation for Special Populations: An Overview

Laura J. McLachlin
Tracy M. Claflin

INTRODUCTION

Why is learning about special populations important? Because anyone can experience an accident, emotional stress, or an addiction. Temporary or permanent, these conditions can occur at any point in life. Whether it be a friend, lover, parent, co-worker, or child, it is helpful to have a basic understanding of what the individual is experiencing and the recreational opportunities available.

This chapter strives to create a better understanding of people with special needs. It will examine the value of recreation for members of special populations, the characteristics of special populations, therapeutic recreation services, and recreational opportunities available to special populations.

The learning objectives of this chapter are to

1. Define special populations.
2. Cite statistics on the prevalence of special populations.
3. Explain the value of recreation for special populations.
4. Define the characteristics of several special populations.
5. Define therapeutic recreation services.
6. Identify recreational opportunities available to special populations.
7. Describe the Americans with Disabilities Act and the implications it has on recreation programs and services for people with disabilities.

8. Discuss the role of attitudes in the provision of recreation services for special populations.

SPECIAL POPULATIONS DEFINED

The term "special populations" encompasses a broad range of groups, including but not limited to the following: people with disabilities (such as arthritis, visual impairment, deafness, emotional disturbance, and paraplegia); people who abuse drugs; people who have eating disorders; people who are social offenders; the elderly; minority populations; refugees and immigrants from many countries; and the homeless (California Department of Education, 2002). Special populations does not mean disabled. The term special populations will be used throughout this chapter as a label for a group of people. Although labeling individuals can be useful at times, it often results in creating false or deceptive images of people. For example,

PHOTO 14.1. Road racing is one of the many recreational activities special populations can enjoy.

think of all of the terms or characteristics that come to mind when you hear the term senior citizen. Perhaps negative characteristics such as bad drivers, slow, senile, or weak come to mind. These perceptions may stem from personal experiences, parental influence, or simply ignorance about the group of people. However, when a person is given a label, such as "crippled," "handicapped," "crazy," or "drunk," the focus tends to be directed toward the label or disability, rather than toward the ability of that person. Recreation therapists work hard at attempting to dispel myths and reduce negative stereotypes. It is hoped that throughout this chapter the reader's attention will be directed toward the strengths and abilities of those who are categorized as special populations.

PEOPLE WITH DISABILITIES

Overview

Approximately 20 percent of noninstitutionalized Americans have a disability, and over 75 percent of these people have an activity limitation which restricts their ability to participate in various activities ranging from recreation to education and employment to marital and family involvement (Edginton et al., 2002). Approximately 10 percent of the population has a severe disability (McNeil, 1997), but only a small fraction of people with disabilities live in institutions (LaPlante, 1992).

This section presents an overview of the major groups within the broad category of special populations. It is important to note that acute and chronic conditions can be either emotional, social, physical, intellectual, or a combination. Individuals with the same disability can vary considerably. For example, a developmental disability may cause one child to have difficulty only with motor tasks, whereas another child may be totally dependent on others for all daily living needs.

Another significant factor in understanding disabling conditions is the time the disability occurred. For example, an individual who becomes deaf at the age of ten possesses a well-developed oral vocabulary. An individual born deaf, however, may never acquire verbal conversation skills.

Developmental Disabilities

A developmental disability means a severe, chronic disability of an individual that is attributable to a mental or physical impairment or combination of mental and physical impairments. It is manifested before the age of twenty-two, is likely to continue indefinitely, and results in substantial functional limitations in three or more of the following areas of major life activity: self-care; receptive and expressive language; learning; mobility; self-direction; capacity for independent living; and economic self-sufficiency. In addition, a developmental disability can reflect an individual's need for special services or support (Developmental Disabilities Assistance and Bill of Rights Act, 2000).

Down's syndrome, which was referred to in the past as mongolism, is a commonly known developmental disability. However, individuals with developmental disabilities fall within a wide range of functioning levels, varying from mildly disabled to profoundly disabled. Although people might usually think of a developmental disability as being associated with below-average intellectual functioning, some physical disabilities fall under this category because they occur during the developmental period (e.g., cerebral palsy and spina bifida). It is important to note that many physical disabilities do not affect mental functioning at all.

An individual with a mild developmental disability may be completely independent, possessing all necessary daily living skills with the exception of handling vocational and financial matters. Sheltered workshops (work-oriented facilities which provide controlled working environments and individual vocational goals to assist the disabled person to progress toward normal living) offer the necessary opportunities to maximize independence and to instill a sense of accomplishment (Goldenson, 1978).

People with developmental disabilities may have short attention spans, impaired memory, and limited motor skills. Speaking in simple sentences, changing the activity frequently, and demonstrating as much as possible can assist them toward successful recreational experiences.

PHOTO 14.2. Traveling continues to be a popular pastime for many people.

Physical Disabilities

The term physical disabilities refers to physical degeneration or loss to an individual that has been caused by congenital (prior to or during birth) or adventitious (traumatic or after birth) factors. Physical disabilities may stem from a variety of sources:

1. Chronic health-related conditions such as diabetes, asthma, and cystic fibrosis.
2. Congenital malformations such as heart defects and spina bifida.
3. Muscular-skeletal system disorders such as muscular dystrophy, arthritis, and scoliosis which affect the ability to use muscles, joints, and skeletal structure.
4. Nervous system impairments such as cerebral palsy, stroke, multiple sclerosis, spina bifida, spinal cord injury, and epilepsy (Howe-Murphy and Charboneau, 1987).

Symptoms of these disabilities may include weakness of limbs, paralysis, and uncontrollable muscles. The symptoms differ dramatically in each individual. For example, the location on the spinal column where an injury occurs will determine the amount of paralysis and/or weakness. An individual may injure the spinal cord and still possess the ability to walk with assistance from crutches. An injury to the upper back or neck region may leave a person completely paralyzed from where the injury occurred down to his or her toes.

Recreational activities may require minimal modification in the rules or equipment. For example, in wheelchair tennis two bounces are allowed instead of one. For people with upper-body weakness, lightweight softball equipment, such as a plastic bat and ball, is available.

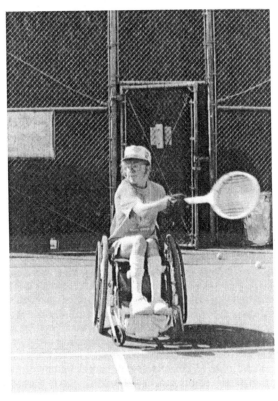

PHOTO 14.3. Physical challenges do not prevent people from enjoying activities such as tennis.

Hearing Impairments

Hearing impairments are the most common physical disability in the United States. The estimated demographic figure has ranged from 22 million to as high as 28 million deaf and hard-of-hearing children and adults. Of these, only a few million are considered "deaf" and the remainder are hard of hearing (Berke, 2001). This significant range of occurrence is due to the fact that some "deaf" people may actually be hard of hearing, and some of those people categorized as "hard of hearing" may actually be deaf. Furthermore, many individuals choose not to identify themselves as having a hearing loss, thus causing statistics to be difficult to collect. Hearing impairments range from mild to profound. A mild hearing loss involves hearing that is defective but functional with or without a hearing aid. A profound hearing loss, or deafness, is when the sense of hearing in the best ear is nonfunctional for communication.

The primary obstacle facing individuals with hearing impairments is communication. Because of language deficits, a person with a hearing impairment falls behind in many fundamental cultural skills. Assistive devices and techniques are available that help to facilitate communication and independence among people with hearing impairments. Hearing aids, sign language, lipreading, and teletypewriters (a device that connects a telephone to a keyboard and screen) are all used as methods of communication. Deaf individuals may also use interventions such as interpreters.

Recreational activities for people with hearing impairments require minimal modification. The leaders should position themselves to be seen clearly by participants, demonstrate as much as possible, and use visual aids.

Visual Impairments

The terms partially sighted, low vision, legally blind, and totally blind are all considered visual impairments. "Partially sighted" indicates some type of visual problem has resulted in a need for special services. "Low vision" generally refers to a severe visual impairment, not necessarily limited to distance vision. This term applies to all individuals with sight who are unable to read the newspaper at a normal viewing distance, even with the aid of eyeglasses or contact lenses.

"Legally blind" indicates that a person has less than 20/200 vision in the better eye or a very limited field of vision. "Totally blind" indicates very little or no vision at all. Visual impairment is the consequence of a functional loss of vision, rather than the eye disorder itself. Eye disorders, which can lead to visual impairments, can include retinal degeneration, albinism, cataracts, glaucoma, muscular problems that result in visual disturbances, corneal disorders, diabetic retinopathy, congenital disorders, and infection (National Information Center for Children and Youth with Disabilities, 2002).

Most people with visual impairments are not completely blind; rather, they are usually able to make use of residual vision or light perception. Often they will require assistance in transportation, reading, and other daily living tasks. Guide dogs, white canes, tape-recorded books, large-print books, and voice-controlled calculators and computers are available to increase independence and mobility for people with visual impairments.

Recreational considerations include using a partner if requested by the individual, allowing the person to feel the leader's movements when a skill is being demonstrated, and speaking clearly.

Emotional Disabilities

Emotional disability means a condition in which the person exhibits one or more of the following characteristics over a long period of time which adversely affects daily performance: inability to build or maintain satisfactory interpersonal relationships with peers and teachers; inappropriate types of behavior or feelings under normal circumstances; a general pervasive mood of unhappiness or depression; a tendency to develop physical symptoms or fears associated with personal, school, or work problems. This term includes neuroses, psychoses (i.e., schizophrenia), and personality disorders (Fairfax County Public Schools, 2002). There are commonalities among these classifications. All human beings attempt to function in their society to maximize satisfaction and minimize stress. Coping mechanisms are identified, developed, and practiced throughout life. At times, individuals may experience difficulty in dealing with the day-to-day stresses of life. These difficulties may manifest themselves as symptoms of emotional disabilities.

Anxiety, phobias (uncontrollable fears), hysterical displacements (converting anxiety into physical symptoms), and unrealistic com-

PHOTO 14.4. Waterskiing for people with physical disabilities is possible with a Kan Ski.

pulsions (repeating a behavior inappropriately) are examples of behaviors that people develop to compensate for malfunctioning personalities. These types of disabilities can occur at any time in a person's life and may be either acute or chronic. One-on-one counseling, crisis centers, stress-management classes, support groups, medication, residential treatment, and hospitalization are currently the most common forms of treatment.

People with emotional disabilities usually do not require modifications in recreational activities. The leader should be sensitive to the emotional state of the person and not place the individual into situations that may create feelings of intimidation or discomfort.

Substance Abuse

Abuse of alcohol and prescribed or illegal drugs is one of the nation's fastest-growing problems. Nearly half of all Americans ages twelve and older reported being current drinkers of alcohol. Interestingly, 62 percent of young adults aged eighteen to twenty-two enrolled full-time in college reported any use, binge use, or heavy use of alcohol, while 50.8 percent of their peers not enrolled full-time reported using alcohol. In terms of other forms of drug use, approximately 14 million Americans (6.3 percent of the population age twelve and older) use illicit drugs (Substance Abuse and Mental Health Services Administration, 2000).

Substance abuse involves several dimensions of the social structure of our society. It affects not only the life of the abuser, but also the lives of family and friends and those in the workplace and school. Because of this multifaceted impact, a vast array of programs and services are offered to individuals affected by substance abuse. Alcoholics Anonymous, Adult Children of Alcoholics, Al-Anon, Alateen, Alatot, Narcotics Anonymous, private physicians, counselors, clergy, and other related support services can be found throughout the country.

Because misuse of leisure time is prevalent among people who abuse substances, proper use of free time needs to be encouraged. Leisure education and participation in recreational activities should be fostered to create a healthy balance in life.

Elders

Elders (age sixty-five and over) comprise a unique special population because it is one category that nearly everyone will eventually join. Therefore, leisure services for elders should be of special concern because of the personal ramifications. It is also the fastest-growing portion of the population. Among the older population, the fastest-growing segment is the eighty-five and over age group (Leitner and Leitner, 2004).

Recent research shows that the best prescription for a long and happy life is physical exercise and plenty of social opportunities. Recreation therapists and activity directors working with elders can focus on meeting their social and physical needs through recreation.

Depending on where elders reside, they can enjoy a wide variety of recreation, but those in residential facilities may need assistance in order to participate. The traditional stereotype of senior citizens seems to be weak elderly persons in nursing homes. However, it is important to note that only 3.4 percent of the nation's older population live in nursing homes (Leitner and Leitner, 2004). This population is also discussed in Chapter 13.

PHOTO 14.5. Intergenerational activities offer benefits for both elders and children.

Eating Disorders

Eating disorders, such as anorexia nervosa, bulimia nervosa, and binge eating, are becoming increasingly prevalent throughout Western countries. According to U.S. estimates from the National Institute of Mental Health (2002), approximately 5 to 10 percent of girls and women and 1 percent of boys and men suffer from eating disorders. Eating disorders are not illnesses in themselves but become a problem when they interfere with the person's physical or mental well-being, disorganize the person's life to a marked degree, or distort the person's self-image.

Anorexia and bulimia are viewed as psychiatric or emotional disorders, whereas obesity involves a self-destructive impulse-control problem. Individuals with eating disorders tend to misuse their leisure time. Chronic thoughts of food, excessive exercise, starving, purging (self-induced vomiting), and/or gorging are examples of activities that dominate the free time of someone with an eating disorder.

Treatment of eating disorders involves developing healthy leisure activity skills, counseling, stress management, behavior modification, biofeedback, and/or medication.

Social Disabilities

Social disabilities are social behaviors that have been identified as delinquent or unacceptable to society. Vandalism, theft, obsessive gambling, gang affiliation, and truancy are examples of socially inappropriate behaviors. Most delinquent behavior occurs during free time. The behavior may meet a leisure need, but it is usually detrimental to society. Thus, the notion of delinquency as a leisure activity suggests the need for a leisure-oriented treatment approach.

A growing body of evidence suggests that after-school programs have more crime-reduction potential than juvenile curfew. Juvenile violence peaks in the after-school hours on school days and in the evenings on nonschool days. In addition, juveniles are at the highest risk of being victims of violence at the end of the school day (Snyder and Sickmund, 1999).

To address these concerns, a concerted effort within a variety of states is being discussed. For example, in a 2001 survey, 80 percent of California voters expressed that they wanted the state to provide more funding to local communities for youth violence prevention (Rothhaar, 2001). Respondents favored programs that provide youth with structured, supervised activities during nonschool hours, such as tutoring and mentoring, job and vocational training, organized sports, and arts programs. Seventy percent of the respondents thought that after-school programs would be extremely effective in reducing youth violence, compared to just 46 percent who thought that teaching violence prevention in the classroom would be extremely effective.

These types of concerns provide a timely opportunity for the parks and recreation profession to promote itself as a leader in the related fields of youth development and violence prevention. Recreation programs are being used not only with juvenile offenders but also with youth who are labeled "at risk" of becoming delinquent. Through these types of efforts, sustained public support, and committed professionals, perhaps a decline in socially inappropriate and self-destructive behaviors is possible.

PHOTO 14.6. Swimming is wonderful exercise for people of all abilities.

All of the aforementioned populations are unique in their own ways. They all use different and sometimes creative methods to accomplish daily tasks and to participate in leisure activities. Whether it be through the use of an adaptive ski to race down the face of a mountain or the assistance of a sighted guide to navigate a nature trail through a national park, every individual can achieve a successful leisure experience. These are only a few examples of what therapeutic recreation offers to special populations to enhance the quality of their lives.

THE VALUE OF RECREATION FOR SPECIAL POPULATIONS

People who are physically or mentally disabled, elderly, social offenders, substance abusers, or sensory impaired have the same needs for, and the same human rights to, leisure involvement as other individuals. However, they may encounter limitations in experiencing full participation in the normal social structure of society. These limitations go beyond their disabling conditions. For example, people with disabilities seem to face greater financial constraints in selecting leisure activities. According to one survey, people with disabilities are more likely to be unemployed or to receive lower than average wages. They work in comparatively poor conditions with less access to senior and managerial posts (Jones, 1985). A problem related to financial constraints is the cost of some of the adaptive equipment which enables people with physical disabilities to enjoy recreational experiences. For example, the "surf wheelchair," a wheelchair outfitted with huge balloon tires that will not get stuck in the sand, ranges in price from $1,300 to $2,600 (Montague, 2000). People have successfully lobbied some municipalities to provide surf wheelchairs at public beaches.

Another barrier relating to leisure for special populations is provision of community recreation programs. A study by Vaughan and Winslow (Kennedy, Austin, and Smith, 1987) concluded that transportation, budget allocations, identification of members of special population groups, insufficient numbers of program personnel, and architectural barriers were the primary obstacles in providing recreation to people with special needs. This group of people has more free time than any other segment of the population and often experiences "forced leisure," that is, free time imposed by the conditions of society.

How does the concept of "forced leisure" fit into your philosophy of leisure? Is it actually leisure? If you imagine yourself as a person with a disability who was unable to find employment, lived on a restricted income, and had a large amount of free time every day, would your perception of leisure change from what it is now? How?

Traditionally, special populations have been excluded from finding fulfillment within the context of leisure. They were expected to gain acceptance from "normal" people, acquire a job, and attain functional levels of behavior. Minimal effort was made toward assisting this group to achieve the social and leisure skills considered so essential to the rest of society. Now, through public awareness and legislation, more recreational services and programs are provided for individuals with special needs. These programs create meaningful experiences through leisure activities that are essential for human development.

For example, Porter (1975) discovered that when a group of emotionally disturbed youth participated in an eight-day wilderness experience program, their levels of self-esteem, social acceptance, and self-control were higher than those of a similar group who did not participate in the program. Risk recreation, such as camping, skiing, and kayaking, has the same intrigue, stimulates the same level of interest, and is as beneficial for special populations as it is for the rest of the population (Arthur and Ackroyd-Stolarz, 1979).

Sports in general are beneficial for people with disabilities. A study of women with physical disabilities who participated in an elite-level sport (Ashton-Shaeffer et al., 2001) found that the women saw their involvement in high-level sports as a way of regaining control over their bodies which empowered them both physically and mentally. They also felt that their mastery of skills gave them an identity based on the role of athlete, not the role of "disabled person." Similarly, Hendrick (1985) found that adolescents in a wheelchair tennis program experienced increased self-perception of physical competence as a result of participation. In addition, several studies have shown that creative arts such as music, movement, and drama have a positive effect on individuals with developmental disabilities (Hayes and Crain, 1979; Stensrud, 1976; Wingert, 1972). Patterson (2000) discusses the special benefits of serious leisure activities (see Chapter 1) for people with disabilities. Because many people with disabilities may never be able to find a suitable job, Patterson advocates that serious leisure activities can provide challenge, status, and a set of colleagues which people might otherwise have at a place of employment. Furthermore, Patterson believes that leisure education and counseling services need to be implemented with people with disabilities in order to support their participation in serious leisure activities.

The preceding studies are only a few examples that illustrate the benefits of recreation for special populations. A general conclusion can be drawn that recreational experiences can meet the same needs and provide the same benefits for both special populations and the general public.

PHOTO 14.7. Musical performances can provide outlets for self-expression and creativity.

THERAPEUTIC RECREATION

What types of leisure activities can special populations participate in? Exercise 14.1 asks you to imagine what your leisure activities would be if you became disabled.

In completing this exercise, what were your feelings? Typically, an individual who experiences a traumatic disability or any type of loss (e.g., loss of a limb, mental capacity, sight) progresses through five stages of coping mechanisms. These stages are denial, anger, bargaining, depression, and acceptance (Kübler-Ross, 1969). Perhaps while you completed Exercise 14.1 you experienced one or more of these stages. When a person is encountering one of these stages, it can be difficult to motivate that individual toward participation in leisure activities.

Exercise 14.1 was intended to stimulate thought about recreational activities for special populations. The fact that an individual has a

EXERCISE 14.1.
My Leisure Pursuits As a Person with a Disability

Imagine yourself waking up tomorrow morning with a serious disabling condition. How would your life be different? How would your new condition affect your recreational pursuits? This exercise is designed for you to become more familiar with recreation opportunities for special populations. You will be asked to imagine that you have a disability. You must then imagine how you will continue to participate in your favorite leisure activities.

1. Column one identifies your new disabling condition.
2. Column two identifies recreational activities which you participated in prior to your disability.
3. In the third column you are to decide how you could continue to participate in the same activity with your new disability. For example, what if your favorite activity was cycling and you became blind? How could you continue to enjoy this activity? The modification or change in this example would be to switch to a tandem bicycle. You would then be able to enjoy your favorite leisure activity.

Disabling changes	Recreational activities	Modification to activity
Blind	Baseball	_____
		_____
Deaf	Dancing	_____
		_____
Paraplegic	Tennis	_____
		_____
Senile	Bingo	_____
		_____
Lack of speech	Current events group	_____
		_____
Amputee	Bowling	_____
		_____

physical, mental, or social limitation does not imply an inability to partake in leisure activities. In this chapter, a variety of recreational opportunities available to special populations are identified.

Therapeutic recreation is the professional field that provides leisure services to special populations. Therapeutic recreation offers outdoor activities (such as camping, rafting, and skiing), dance, music, art, drama, competitive sports, and community outings to special populations. Through the provision of recreational activities, therapeutic recreation professionals assist individuals in leading a healthy leisure lifestyle. Therapeutic recreation is defined as a process that uses recreation to bring about a desired change in behavior to promote the growth and development of an individual (Gunn and Peterson, 1984).

Therapeutic recreation specialists (also called recreation therapists) possess an assortment of skills and knowledge. They conduct leisure assessments and evaluations, select and modify activities, and design and implement recreation programs for special populations. Approximately 39,000 recreation therapists are employed in the United States, with almost 40 percent of them employed in hospitals and just over 25 percent working in nursing and personal care facilities. Recreation therapists are also employed in correctional facilities, substance-abuse treatment centers, community programs for special populations, adult day-care programs, community mental health centers, and residential facilities (Edginton et al., 2002).

Although recreation therapists can provide a variety of activities, the majority of special populations provide their own programs. Recreation offers opportunities to overcome negative attitudes for both special populations and the general public. Participation in recreation contributes to a positive psychological state by increasing confidence and self-esteem (Howe-Murphy and Charboneau, 1987). Several other methods can also assist in changing attitudes toward special populations. These include the following:

1. Volunteering with special populations.
2. Increasing contact with or exposure to special populations.
3. Eliminating physical and social barriers that prevent access to recreational activities for special populations.
4. Integrating recreational and educational experiences with special populations and the general public.

PHOTO 14.8. Golf is a popular sport for people of varying abilities and disabilities.

THE AMERICANS WITH DISABILITIES ACT

The Americans with Disabilities Act (ADA), passed in 1990, guarantees equal opportunity for individuals with disabilities in public- and private-sector services and employment. Broadly, the ADA bans discrimination on the basis of disability. A comprehensive anti-discrimination law for persons with disabilities, the ADA extends to virtually all sectors of society and every aspect of daily living—work, leisure, travel, communications, and more. It provides basic civil rights protection to persons with disabilities. Simply stated, the ADA is about changing attitudes; it is about assuring the inclusion of people with disabilities into the social, political, and economic mainstream of society. The ADA attempts to change the way we think about people with disabilities. No longer is it appropriate to focus on what people cannot do, but rather on what they *can* do. Recreation agencies, both private and public, are adopting several strategies to comply with the requirements of the ADA (Tainter, 1993).

SUMMARY

The primary focus of this chapter was to present an overview of recreation for special populations. Throughout the chapter you have been encouraged to move away from traditional views of special populations and to accept and appreciate these conditions as natural variances. The need to play and recreate remains essential for all human beings. The only differing element is the method people choose to achieve those leisure experiences. Therapeutic recreation assists in providing leisure opportunities to people with special needs to facilitate personal growth and development. Developing an awareness of special populations and instilling a positive change in attitudes toward them can serve as one of the most powerful tools in the process of integration and equality.

REFERENCES

Arthur, M. and Ackroyd-Stolarz, S. (1979). *A resource manual on canoeing for disabled people.* The Canadian Recreational Canoeing Association.

Ashton-Shaeffer, C., Gibson, H., Holt, M., and Willming, C. (2001). Women's resistance and empowerment through wheelchair sport. *World Leisure,* 43(4), 11-21.

Berke, J. (2001). Demographics of hearing loss—Statistics on deafness. Available at <http://deafness.about.com/library/weekly/aa062001.htm>.

California Department of Education (2002). Carl D. Perkins Vocational and Technical Education Act (PL 105-332). Available at <www.cde.ca.gov/perkins/about.html>.

Developmental Disabilities Assistance and Bill of Rights Act (DD Act) (2000). P.L. 106-402. Available at <www.nau.edu/ihd/aztap/ddabra.shtml>.

Edginton, C.R., Jordan, D.J., DeGraaf, D.G., and Edginton, S.R. (2002). *Leisure and life satisfaction: Foundational perspectives* (Third Edition). New York: McGraw-Hill.

Fairfax County Public Schools (2002). Department of Education, Office of Special Education. Available at <http://www.fcps.k12.va.us/DSSSE/index.htm>.

Goldenson, R.M. (Ed.) (1978). *Disability and rehabilitation handbook.* New York: McGraw-Hill.

Gunn, S.L. and Peterson, C.A. (1984). *Therapeutic recreation program design: Principles and procedures.* Englewood Cliffs, NJ: Prentice-Hall.

Hayes, G.A. and Crain, C. (1979). Music and movement activities for the multihandicapped mentally retarded in a residential camping environment. *Therapeutic Recreation Journal,* 13(1), 14-20.

Hendrick, B.N. (1985). The effects of wheelchair tennis participation and mainstreaming upon the perceptions of competence of physically disabled adolescents. *Therapeutic Recreation Journal,* 19(2), 34-36.

Howe-Murphy, R. and Charboneau, B. G. (1987). *Therapeutic recreation intervention: An ecological perspective.* Englewood Cliffs, NJ: Prentice-Hall.

Jones, J. (1985). A positive approach to the employment of disabled workers. *Personnel Management,* 17, 21-22.

Kennedy, D.W., Austin, D.R., and Smith, R.W. (1987). *Special recreation: Opportunities for persons with disabilities.* Philadelphia, PA: Saunders.

Kübler-Ross, E. (1969). *On death and dying.* New York: Macmillan.

LaPlante, M.P. (1992). *How many Americans have a disability?* Disability Statistics Abstract No. 5. San Francisco: Disability Statistics Programs, University of California.

Leitner, M.J. and Leitner, S.F. (2004). *Leisure in later life* (Third edition). Binghamton, NY: The Haworth Press, Inc.

McNeil, J.M. (1997). *Americans with disabilities: 1994-1995.* Current Population Reports, U.S. Department of Commerce, Bureau of the Census, Economics and Statistics Administration (P70-61). Washington, DC: Government Printing Office.

Montague, R. (2000). Surf wheelchairs help disabled enjoy the beaches once again. *The Boston Globe,* August 21, pp. B1, B4.

National Information Center for Children and Youth with Disabilities (2002). Visual impairments. Fact sheet 13 (FS13). Available at <http://www.nichcy.org/pubs>.

National Institute of Mental Health (2002). Statistics on eating disorders like anorexia, bulimia and binge eating disorder, short collection of statistics on eating disorders. Available at <www.annecollins.com/eating-disorders/statistics.html>.

Patterson, I. (2000). Developing a meaningful identity for people with disabilities through serious leisure activities. *World Leisure,* 42(2), 41-51.

Porter, W. (1975). The development and evaluation of a therapeutic wilderness program for troubled youth. Unpublished thesis, University of Denver, Denver, CO.

Rothhaar, J. (2001). More recreational activities to prevent violence. *California Parks and Recreation,* 57(3), 20-21.

Snyder, H.N. and Sickmund, M. (1999). *Juvenile offenders and victims: 1999 national report.* Washington, DC: National Center for Juvenile Justice, Office of Juvenile Justice and Delinquency Prevention.

Stensrud, C. (1976). Creative drama and the multiply handicapped. *Journal of Leisurability,* 3, 17-26.

Substance Abuse and Mental Health Services Administration (2000). *Summary of findings from the 2000 National Household Survey on Drug Abuse.* Washington, DC: Department of Health and Human Services.

Tainter, W. (1993). *Americans with Disabilities Act: A comprehensive overview.* Sacramento: Department of Rehabilitation, California.

Wingert, L. (1972). Effects of music: An enrichment program on the education of the mentally retarded. *Journal of Music Therapy,* 9, 13-22.

Chapter 14B

Recreation for Special Populations: A Wheelchair Athlete's Perspective

William Bowness

Imagine yourself alone, late at night, driving across a barren desert. You look up and see a brilliant light falling from the sky. As you watch, you see the object is not really falling but flying . . . no, hovering, directly in front of you. You find yourself mesmerized by the huge oval shape. Staring at the object, you can feel yourself being lifted from your car, not out the door but vaporizing through the steel roof.

Once inside the alien craft you notice that your body has not made the journey. You are inside a different body, an alien body! You can hear the rhythmic breathing and feel the pulse of this strange shell that traps you. The shell you now inhabit has arms and legs (at least that is what they look like), but you cannot make anything move! There you are, the same person that was driving in the desert just moments earlier, but now entrapped within an alien body.

This story could have been written in a less sci-fi fashion by substituting the space craft with an oncoming drunk driver. Instead of being transported to the alien craft you are taken to the nearest emergency room. Even though your strange body is not an alien form in appearance, it may as well be the Martian body mentioned in the story. A doctor informs you that your neck and spinal cord are broken and you will not be able to move anything below your shoulders. There is little chance to reverse the damage.

Just because you are "trapped in a strange body" does not mean the "inside you" has changed. Your favorite pizza, baseball team, and television show are still the same. In fact, all of your likes and dislikes remain unchanged. A physical disability does not mean the end of your life. The interests of the disabled are as far-reaching as those of their "able-bodied" peers. Virtually every aspect of recreation and play found in the able-bodied world is evident in the world of the disabled. There are wheelchair tennis players, water-skiers, sky divers, and white-water rafting guides. A traumatic injury or disabling disease does not reduce the desire (or need) for competition, high risk, physical challenge, and outdoor adventure. If you liked to snow ski before your injury, chances are you will enjoy the thrill of skiing afterward.

The following is the account of my personal experiences with having a traumatic disabling injury and becoming involved in wheelchair sports. I hope that by sharing a small part of my life, the reader will gain a better insight into the abilities and capabilities of physically challenged people. Further, I hope my story helps people understand just how important recreation is for all people, regardless of their physical or mental limitations.

I can remember the day I went to the veterans hospital to visit a friend who had fought in Vietnam. I had once watched him play high school football, and now he was a triple amputee. He was in terrible shape, taking all sorts of pain medication, and he barely recognized me when I came in. On my way home I thought to myself that if anything like that happened to me, I would not want to live.

This was my first experience with a handicapped individual, and I had no way of knowing it would become a lifelong endeavor for me. Three years later, at the age of eighteen, I was involved in an automobile accident that left me with a broken spinal cord and paralysis from the hips down. There was never a lingering thought about anything except continuing with my life.

Even before the dust settled at the scene of the accident I had a good idea of what had happened to my legs. Having extensive training in emergency first aid, I knew I had a spinal cord injury. At the time I did not really think about the implications this injury would have for the rest of my life. Besides the back injury, I also had several broken ribs, which made breathing almost impossible and very painful, internal bleeding, a severed index finger, and several deep cuts on my legs. My immediate concern was not whether I would ever walk again, but rather if I would make it to see the next day.

I was taken to the nearest hospital and placed in the intensive care unit. One of the doctors called my parents and instructed them to catch the first plane possible because he could not guarantee how long I might live. The first two days after my accident were just a drug-induced dream. I can remember waking up suspended in air, looking at the floor, sandwiched within a rotating "bed" called a Stryker frame. Every two hours a nurse would turn the frame over, and I would go from looking at the floor to looking at the ceiling. After seven days in the intensive care unit I was stable enough to be transported. I was flown via an air ambulance to a large urban hospital in southern California.

After twenty days of stabilization, an operation was performed to fuse my broken vertebrae. (The twenty-nine vertebrae of the spinal column encase the spinal cord and keep your shoulders from resting on your hips.) Two stainless steel rods called Harrington rods were placed along the broken segment of my back. Bone chips from my pelvis were introduced to start calcification and ultimately fused five vertebrae together. This process was solely to give support to my back, without which I would have been no better off than a jellyfish. The doctors later told me it was apparent that one vertebra had twisted and slipped back, cutting the spinal cord laying directly behind. There would be no hope of any return, since they could see where the cord had been cut in two.

The spinal cord is the telephone cable of the human body. It carries messages to and from the brain and all the major organs and extremities in the body. The spinal cord is part of the central nervous system (CNS), which consists of the brain, brainstem, and spinal cord. You may have heard about a person who had a finger severed in an accident. The person is rushed to the hospital and the finger is surgically attached. After a brief healing process, the finger works just as well as before the accident. The CNS lacks the enzymes that are in the rest of the body which enable nerves to rejoin after they are cut. When damage to the spinal cord occurs it usually causes a permanent, irreversible impairment. Nothing is wrong with my brain or legs; simply, the communication between them has been cut.

Two days after the Harrington rods operation I was encased in a plaster cast that went from under my arms and collarbone down to my hips. A hole about the size of a soccer ball was cut out for my belly. Although I did not know it at the time, I was going to wear this shell for three and a half months! By the third month you could smell me before you saw me. The cast was supposed to keep me immobile for the time it took the back to completely fuse. After the plaster cast was removed, I was fitted with a removable aluminum and plastic "jacket." I could remove it when I went to bed but had to wear it at all other times.

Thirty days after my accident I was transferred again, this time to a small hospital for rehabilitative medicine. "Rehab" is where you are taught how to live in our stand-up society as a sit-down person. This is where you are taught to use your "Martian body." Many people do not realize that a traumatically disabled person has to go to school to learn about being disabled. There is not a special Gimp Fairy that comes along and taps you on the head and says, "You now know everything you need to about being disabled." I knew virtually nothing about the world of the disabled, and rehab is where I learned. My teachers were a team of dedicated medical professionals that specialized in rehabilitative medicine. My team was headed by a doctor of physiatry (physiatry is the specialization specific to rehabilitative medicine). She oversaw the progress I made while working with physical (PT), occupational (OT), and recreational therapists, psychologists, social workers, and nurses.

At the hospital where I was treated, the PTs worked on strength and wheelchair mobility. The OTs taught activities of daily living (ADL). ADLs are such tasks as getting dressed (try dressing without standing up—it is not impossible, just different), cooking, driving a car, and maneuvering a cart in a crowded grocery store.

The social worker was the liaison between the hospital and my family. She made sure I had a place to go when I was discharged and was helpful in filling the gap between me and the real world. The psychologist was there to help lead me through the natural grieving process that follows a loss. I had lost the use of part of my body and needed to deal with that loss.

Of all the therapies I had contact with, recreational therapy stands alone as the most helpful one. When I first arrived at the hospital, "rec" therapy was solely diversional. Table games and an occasional movie were the extent of it. By the time I was discharged I was attending baseball games and day fishing trips and playing basketball at the park across the street.

I had always been an athletic person, and the spinal cord injury did not change my desire or need for high risk, competition, and vigorous exercise. While I was still in the hospital I can remember getting my father to take me to the trap and skeet range to shoot. I still had my support jacket, and I am sure the doctor would not have seen any humor in this outing. Within weeks of my discharge from the hospital I was on a wheelchair basketball team near my parents' home. I was still the same person I had always been, and that lifestyle included the world of athletics.

I enjoyed the profession of recreation so much that I volunteered at the rehab hospital as a recreation aid. Six months later the recreation therapist on the spinal cord unit suddenly left for another position. I was hired as an interim recreation therapist. I worked several months in this position, long enough to decide this was the profession I wanted to pursue. I moved to the small university town of Chico, located in northern California, and enrolled in their recreation administration program.

I brought with me the knowledge and experience of almost two years of individual and organized team sports. Chico in the late 1970s had very little to offer the active disabled individual in the way of organized recreation. Within the year I had assembled a small core of disabled and able-bodied people to play basketball. That year I was the first wheelchair individual to run in the local marathon. In September 1980, an energetic assistant professor in the recreation department and I organized a wheelchair tennis tournament that still continues as an annual event.

Recreation has always been an outlet for me. The tenth anniversary of my auto accident was marked in 1987, and I am doing more in the world of sports than ever before in my life. I am currently the world record holder for sit waterskiing in the slalom event off (6 @ 40' at 36 mph, which means I made six buoys behind a forty-foot rope with a boat speed of 36 miles per hour). I won first place for slalom in the first World Trophy for waterskiing held in London, England. I have pushed in over fifteen marathons. (My best time is 2 hours, 28 minutes. The record for the Boston Marathon is 1 hour, 40 minutes!) Before I started waterskiing, I was a nationally ranked open-division wheelchair tennis player. I still play for the local basketball team and was chosen for the all-league team in 1986. I have qualified to go to nationals in sit snow skiing and still enjoy snow skiing as a recreational sport. I was a member of (and helped start) the Casa Colina Condors wheelchair basketball team that went on to the Final Four of the National Wheelchair Basketball Association in 1978.

On a recreational level, I enjoy hunting, fishing, racquetball, all-terrain vehicle (ATV) riding, and camping. I have enjoyed white-water rafting, flying, and skin diving. I am currently learning how to fly an ultralight. I honestly believe that I can do anything I set my mind to—I just need to adapt some of the activities to my abilities. However, I must admit that sometimes I get myself in some pretty sticky situations because of this attitude.

For example, one summer I drove from California to Chicago, Illinois, for a tennis tournament. I had loaded my van with all the sports equipment I might need. After the tennis tournament I volunteered at a wheelchair basketball camp that a friend held at the University of Wisconsin–Whitewater. I had brought my marathon chair just in case I might enter a race somewhere along the way. As it turned out the marathon chair came in handy when I went to visit an old friend in Madison, just thirty miles north.

Madison is a city built on rolling hills around a lake. That evening my friend and I went for what was supposed to be a leisurely jog around her neighborhood. I had broken one of the sacred rules of road racing by not wearing gloves on this push. My marathon chair has no brakes, and the only way to stop is to use your hands (that is why gloves are so important).

Whenever we came to the top of a hill I found it easier to speed to the bottom and wait rather than trying to hold my chair back with un-protected hands. This worked well enough until we came to the top of a particularly long, steep hill.

Once more I headed off, calling back over my shoulder to my friend that I would see her at the bottom. I thought I heard my running partner call out, "by the way," and thought it was a strange time to tell me a story. It was just going to have to wait until she caught up to me. Using the steering device on the front casters of my chair, I was slaloming back and forth across the street, trying to control my speed. This worked fine until three cars slowly drove past, forcing me to the side of the road and also forcing me to give up my zig-zag style of speed control.

I began to realize that I was gaining too much speed to be consid-ered under control. To make matters worse, I finally figured out what my friend had tried to tell me at the top. She had not said, "by the way" but "HIGHWAY!" Sure enough, at the bottom of the hill was a six-lane highway full of rush-hour traffic. It was so congested that the cars that had passed me were now backing up at the corner. I tried to brake, but the high rate of speed caused a smoky smell to come from my hands. The seriousness of the situation was pointed out by a child looking out the back window of the last car waiting to enter the highway. His face was contorted in a fiendish grin as he pointed out the oncoming runaway to the other occupants of the car.

There was no way I was going to make it across the highway without becoming a spot on the road. I had one last chance to save myself. Once again I reached down to the steering controls, and just before passing the car with the child-sadist I turned a hard left. My chair raised up onto the two right wheels and I flew across the street into the driveway of a church (it must have been fate). I became airborne for a couple of seconds, finally ending my flight in a planter of ivy. There I was, still in my chair, sitting in the middle of the ivy. People on the street started applauding as I dusted myself off. I am sure that I am one disabled person that Madison will not soon forget.

I hope my story does not encourage anyone to jump into a track chair without brakes and speed down hills. However, I do hope my personal experiences have helped the reader appreciate that whether in a wheelchair or not, it is up to the individual to make the most of life and that recreation is a vital component of an exciting, rewarding, and fulfilling existence.

Chapter 15

Outdoor Recreation
and Natural Resource Lands

David E. Simcox

INTRODUCTION

This chapter addresses a particular type of leisure activity known as outdoor recreation. More specifically, the chapter explores the relationship between natural resource lands such as forests, deserts, mountains, beaches, rivers, lakes, and oceans and the leisure experiences and activities that are enjoyed in such places. In addition, the values associated with natural resource lands and how these lands are managed to provide multiple benefits that include wildlife, scenery, and outdoor recreation activities are examined. Americans are privileged to have a wealth of natural resource lands available for outdoor recreation. Various concepts regarding protection of and responsible behavior in these lands will be discussed. The learning objectives for this chapter are to

1. Define and discuss the term *outdoor recreation.*
2. Identify resources for outdoor recreation participation.
3. Define the term *natural resource lands* and discuss the relationship between outdoor recreation and natural resources.
4. Define both physical and social-psychological carrying capacity and discuss the relationship between these concepts, outdoor recreation, and appropriate personal behavior on natural resource lands.
5. Discuss the physiological, sociological, and psychological benefits of outdoor recreation on natural resource lands.

6. Discuss the need for stewardship of natural resource lands so as to protect outdoor recreation values and opportunities now and in the future.

DEFINITIONS

Outdoor Recreation Defined

For the purposes of this chapter, *outdoor recreation* is defined as the interaction between an activity and an outdoor natural environment that recreates an individual physically, psychologically, emotionally, and socially. Outdoor recreation is a unique form of recreation because of the importance of the interaction between the recreation activity and the natural environment. For example, in picnicking (an outdoor recreation activity), the natural environment is critical to the enjoyment of the activity. In an activity such as table tennis (not considered outdoor recreation), the natural environment has little or no impact on the enjoyment of the activity.

The natural outdoor environment significantly influences people. Although downhill skiing can be simulated with plastic ski runs and surfing can be simulated with wave-making machines, these substitutes fall far short of the real experience. The natural outdoor recreation environment adds richness to experiences and provides a wide variety of opportunities for new knowledge, scenic beauty, solitude, challenge, and excitement.

The rates of participation shown in Table 15.1 are particularly meaningful in considering how important outdoor recreation is for people. In 2000, nineteen out of twenty Americans over sixteen years of age participated in outdoor recreation. The media can create the impression that outdoor recreation is dominated by high-tech and sensational activities such as extreme skiing, parasailing, and rock climbing. In fact, the top four outdoor recreation activities are nature observation, walking/hiking, sight-seeing, and picnicking.

All of these activities are enjoyed by more than 100 million Americans each year, are inexpensive, and promote relaxation and family togetherness. The high participation in nature observation represents a significant trend over the past two decades. Participation rates in wildlife-related activities have increased fourfold over this time. The popularity of camping is also important. Approximately 53 million

TABLE 15.1. Outdoor Recreation Participation: Sixteen Years Old and Older

Type of outdoor activity	Percent of population sixteen years or older	Number in millions
Any outdoor recreation activity	94.5	189.3
Observing nature	76.2	152.6
Walking/hiking	66.7	133.7
Sight-seeing	56.6	113.4
Picnicking	50.1	103.8
Fishing	28.9	57.9
Bicycling	28.6	57.4
Camping	26.3	52.8
Canoeing/kayaking/white-water rafting	15.9	31.9
Downhill skiing/snowboarding	10.7	21.3
Hunting	9.3	18.6
Waterskiing	8.9	17.9
Horseback riding	7.1	14.3
Sailing	4.8	9.6
Snowmobiling	3.6	7.1
Cross-country skiing	2.7	5.4

Source: Cordell et al., 2000.

Americans went camping in 2000. When the length of camping season is considered (typically only about five months), the great popularity of camping becomes evident. Snowmobiling and cross-country skiing are activities that are greatly limited. The ability of Americans to participate in these activities is limited by geography, climate, and affordability. Even with these limitations, 7.1 and 5.4 million Americans enjoy snowmobiling and cross-country skiing, respectively, each year.

Natural Resources Defined

Often people associate outdoor recreation more with places than with activities. Frequently, a place may be more important to a person than the activity done there. For example, many backpackers claim that it is the wilderness environment that makes the experience so pleasing, not the actual hiking. Because outdoor recreation is inherently tied to outdoor places, a definition for such environments is needed. For the most part, this chapter addresses outdoor recreation engaged in on public natural resource lands. Natural resource lands are defined as those places that provide a wide variety of resources utilized to the benefit of people both economically and experientially.

Approximately one-third of the lands in the United States are public natural resource lands. The term public is used because these lands are owned by federal, state, city, or county governments. More specifically, these lands include national parks, national forests, wilderness areas, state parks or beaches, city parks, or even such places as desert conservation areas. A more liberal definition would even include the ocean and sky as recreational natural resources. Because natural resource lands are government owned, people are free to use these lands for outdoor recreation. Although many natural resource lands are owned privately, especially such places as ski and vacation resorts, this chapter focuses primarily on public natural resource lands.

One of the benefits of natural resource lands is the ability to accommodate recreation activities in a pleasing environment. However, natural resource lands provide many other benefits. Forest lands provide timber and wood products, forage for livestock, sources of water, wildlife habitats, and minerals such as gold, silver, and copper. The ocean is a natural resource that provides commercial fishing, oil, and transportation. The desert is a natural resource that provides minerals, forage for livestock, and wildlife habitats.

Conflicts arise when natural resource lands are utilized for multiple benefits. For example, harvesting the timber needed to build houses, school desks, and pencils can adversely impact recreation because of diminished scenic beauty, loss of water quality, and disruption of wildlife and their habitat. What is more important, wood products or recreation? It is a difficult question. Because of these and many other conflicts, agencies exist to manage natural resource lands.

Through effective natural resource management, these lands are able to offer a wide range of uses and benefits. Congress has established very specific laws and mandates to govern the use and management of forests, mountains, deserts, and oceans to ensure a sustained yield of benefits from all the potential uses of the land.

Many different agencies manage natural resource lands, and each has a different purpose. The National Park Service oversees the national parks. These lands are managed primarily to preserve their natural characteristics, scenery, and recreation opportunities. The U.S. Forest Service manages the national forests. These lands produce multiple benefits and products, including wood, water, forage, wildlife, minerals, and recreation. Such multiple-use lands are administered in a way aimed at providing opportunities to develop all of these uses without diminishing the value of any individual use.

LEISURE IMPLICATIONS

In terms of your own outdoor recreation opportunities, it is interesting to consider that the types of activities and experiences you desire are greatly influenced by three important factors associated with natural resource lands:

1. Certain activities are available to you only if you live in proximity to natural resource lands that provide an environment conducive to your activity.
2. The need to develop natural resources for uses other than recreation may have an impact on your recreation activities and experiences.
3. The way that an agency manages its natural resource lands affects the quality of your outdoor recreation.

These elements have specific implications for leisure. It is important for people to assess their resources for participating in outdoor recreation activities. In particular, the ability to fully enjoy outdoor recreation is dependent on an understanding of natural resource lands and the opportunities they provide. Furthermore, it is important to understand that natural resource lands are managed. The way in which lands are managed influences outdoor recreation experiences. Having an understanding of these relationships is an integral part of being an informed citizen. Consider the following questions:

1. Why do you think people like to recreate outdoors?
2. What specific benefits do people gain by recreating outdoors?
3. Why would people choose to recreate outdoors when they might be able to do the same activities indoors?

As you continue reading this chapter, think about your answers to these questions. The following sections will help you to solidify your thoughts. Next, take a few minutes to complete Exercise 15.1.

This exercise allows you to assess your outdoor recreation opportunity resources. You should have identified a number of outdoor recreation activities and a number of resources or opportunities where you might enjoy these activities.

THE ROLE OF OUTDOOR RECREATION IN DAILY LIFE

The most important role of outdoor recreation in the daily lives of most people is the opportunity provided to interact with natural environments. Some authors have suggested that people have an inherent, genetically encoded need to interact with the natural environment because humans evolved and developed in a natural setting (Dubos, 1968; Kaplan, 1977). This reasoning suggests that by living in a built or urban environment, people disassociate themselves from their own native habitat and therefore have a need to return to a more natural environment.

This idea is only scientific conjecture, but it is interesting to consider. Many people do feel a strong attraction to the beauty of the natural world. At the same time, people have shown the ability to adapt well to urban living (Wohlwill and Kohn, 1976). Although many individuals do appear to need some contact with nature, some authors propose that humans have actually feared nature from the very beginning of their existence (Tuan, 1979). The fear of the unknown, wild animals, and wilderness may still influence people. Could this be why people build urban areas that seem to exclude nature? For some people, a fear of nature may be based on the fact that they are so urbanized that they have never had contact with natural wildlands at all.

EXERCISE 15.1. Identifying Resources for Outdoor Recreation

Instructions

1. Review the list of activities. Think about your experiences with each of these activities. For those activities you have no experience with, think about where you might try them if you had the opportunity.

2. In the column labeled "Nearest location for participation," write down a specific location where you could engage in each activity. If you have never participated in the activity, where do you think you might be able to try the activity?

3. In the column labeled "Favorite location for participation," write down the name of your favorite place for participating in the activity. If you have never attempted the activity, leave the space blank.

4. In the column labeled "Agency," give the name of the agency, group, or organization that operates or manages the area you described under "nearest" location. Some possible organizations might be the National Park Service, U.S. Forest Service, a state parks department, a city parks department, or maybe even a private resort or company.

5. Finally, look back at the activity list and ask yourself these questions: Do I regularly participate in many of these activities? If I wanted to, is there an area close by where I could participate? How could I find out where I could participate in these activities?

Activity	Nearest location for participation	Favorite location for participation	Agency
Hiking			
Bicycling			
Horseback riding			
Backpacking			
Nature observation			

(continued)

(continued)

Activity	Nearest location for participation	Favorite location for participation	Agency
Photography			
Canoeing			
Hunting			
Waterskiing			
Fishing			
Off-road vehicles			
White-water rafting			
Picnicking			
Rock climbing			
Nature walks			
Sailing			
Camping			
Cross-country skiing			

Do people *need* to have some type of contact with the natural environment? Has the urban environment become the natural habitat of humankind?

Whether nature is needed or not, it is known that the natural environment creates wonderful opportunities for individual satisfaction and benefit. The natural resource lands where outdoor recreation occurs provide not only playgrounds for activity but also tremendous resources for knowledge and exploration into the science of nature. Natural resources provide excellent opportunities for environmental education, study of natural science and history, and in many places, the chance to learn about ancient and historic cultures.

Beyond these opportunities for contact with nature, exploration, knowledge, and education, participation in outdoor recreation on natural resource lands provides direct personal benefits to the individual that are of tremendous importance. Many authors and researchers have studied the positive attributes associated with recreation activities on natural resource lands (for an overview, see Knopf, 1983; Kaplan and Talbot, 1983). Their findings indicate that natural resource lands are sources of physiological, psychological, and sociological benefits.

Physiological Benefits

The opportunities for physiological improvement through outdoor recreation are diverse. For example, Bailey (1978) explains that activities such as cross-country skiing and backpacking are among the best forms of aerobic exercise. The fact that these activities take place in interesting and beautiful environments makes them both beneficial and pleasurable. Bicycling, rowing, and running are also excellent aerobic outdoor recreation activities. Rock climbing is great for developing muscular strength. Even a simple activity such as walking has become extremely popular for outdoor enjoyment and aerobic development in recent years. For most people who participate in these activities, their personal focus is on the enjoyment of the experience. Improvement in health and fitness is an added bonus. Once fitness is achieved, people find they are better able to participate in a wider variety of outdoor recreation activities.

Aside from the fitness benefits of outdoor recreation, research is beginning to reveal that outdoor recreation can help promote many positive chemical/physiological conditions. Experiencing the beauty of nature, the excitement of accomplishment, or the exhilaration of physical activity promotes the release of hormones such as norepinephrine and endorphins. These physiological responses to beauty, achievement, and exercise have a tremendous effect in reducing the symptoms of stress and negative emotions.

Psychological Benefits

The psychological benefits of human interactions with natural environments are varied and well documented by researchers (Kaplan, 1983; Kaplan and Talbot, 1983; Knopf, 1983; Rossman and Ulehla, 1977; Shafer and Mietz, 1969; Ulrich, 1983; Wohlwill, 1976). Of all the psychological benefits gained through outdoor recreation, escape is perhaps mentioned most often in the literature (Driver and Tocher, 1970; Knopf, Driver, and Bassett, 1973). Natural resource lands provide opportunities to escape the rigors of daily life. They allow the individual to cope with such stressful conditions as noise, crowding, and the complexity, unpredictability, and high stimulus of urban living. Natural environments offer alternative mental stimuli because of their uniqueness compared with the daily living and working environment. These alternative mental stimuli provide psychological benefits in terms of learning opportunities, exploration, inquiry, and an increase in mental and emotional resources. It is thought that natural landscapes are among the best learning environments because they provide a setting where wonderment and fascination are more prevalent (Kaplan, 1978).

Another psychological benefit of outdoor recreation on natural resource lands is enhanced self-esteem. Many outdoor recreation activities are associated with some type of achievement. Reaching the top of the mountain, getting up on one water ski, catching a trophy-size fish, or successfully running the white-water rapids of a river are all achievements. To many people, these achievements are the most important forms of personal testing and confidence building in their lives. Compared with the routine tasks of most jobs where compliments and encouragement are rarely given, achievements in outdoor recreation can be a much greater source of self-esteem (Kaplan, 1977).

Outdoor recreation also has an important relationship to personality (Knopf, 1983; Wiggins, 1973). People are given the ability to express their unique personality traits through specific outdoor recreation activities. For example, high-arousal-seeking personalities may participate in more complex and stimulus-oriented activities (Mehrabian and Russell, 1974). Competitive personalities may prefer highly socialized activities to allow competition, whereas noncompetitive personalities may prefer activities oriented toward solitude. It is possible that a recreation activity or environment may in fact influence an individual's personality, causing the person to adopt certain lifestyle traits to match that of the activity or environment.

Many outdoor settings provide opportunities for privacy, security, and solitude. Proshansky, Ittleson, and Rivlin (1976) claim that these are among the most valuable psychological benefits available from any environment. Many people, especially urban dwellers, experience a lack of privacy, serenity, and solitude in daily life. It is often impossible to cope with other problems until these elements are obtained. Many natural environments, especially wilderness and backcountry settings, are tremendous resources for privacy, security, and solitude. Once these important psychological feelings are gained by an individual, the natural environment becomes a supportive setting for personal introspection, self-appraisal, and restoration. The ability of natural environments to provide solitude and privacy and thereby allow personal introspection and restoration has played an important role in the development of policies for the protection of parklands and wilderness. Many basic philosophies about the value of protecting the environment are built around these psychological conditions.

Finally, outdoor recreation on natural resource lands can play an important role in the way frustrations are released. Often, excessive frustration in daily life leads to aggressive behavior. In extreme cases, this behavior may be displayed negatively through such activities as vandalism, crime, or other depreciative acts. Outdoor recreation offers an alternative to negative aggression. It allows people to have an activity and environment that is safe for the release of aggression in an appropriate manner. This release may be achieved in a positive way through risk-recreation activities such as downhill skiing, whitewater rafting, or even strenuous hiking and climbing (Kraus, 1984; Menninger, 1960). Outdoor recreation and natural resources provide an atmosphere for positive releases of aggression outside of school, the workplace, or the home environment.

Social Benefits

Many outdoor recreation activities have a high socialization level by their very nature. Activities such as picnicking and camping are obvious examples. Some activities are highly socialized because they have a level of risk or danger. Good examples are rock climbing or white-water rafting. Because of the danger involved, it is wise never to participate in these activities alone.

By building on the concept of socialization, a tremendous range of benefits in outdoor recreation associated with the sharing of experiences with others are identified. Participation in an outdoor recreation social group allows people to test themselves against the norms and standards of others who share in the same activities, experiences, and environments (Lee, 1972). These standards of achievement or prestige (Kretch, Crutchfield, and Ballachey, 1962) can be positive substitutes for the more stressful achievements demanded in the workplace and may be the only source of recognized achievement in a person's life.

Recreation group interactions also help in developing confidence in interpersonal relationships. Outdoor recreation activities help to form a meaningful bond or affiliation between group members (Cheek and Burch, 1976; Kraus, 1984; Kretch, Crutchfield, and Ballachey, 1962), especially when all members of the group are testing themselves against a common environment. This "common cause" allows people to become more comfortable with others and to learn different perspectives and ideas. For example, youth summer camp programs and adult retreat programs use outdoor recreation as a source of learning and development of interpersonal relations (Hanson, 1977; Kaplan, 1977).

Outdoor recreation provides many opportunities for cooperative efforts. Activities such as rock climbing and white-water rafting require a great deal of cooperation and group effort for the experience to be a success. Even activities such as setting up a campsite or sailing a boat require a unique level of cooperation. Many outdoor programs such as Outward Bound and the Wilderness Education Association use backpacking, rock-climbing, boating, and mountaineering experiences to teach cooperation. These programs have been useful in helping delinquent youth to overcome social problems and in teaching professionals how to cooperate with co-workers to meet common goals (Hanson, 1977; Kaplan, 1977).

Outdoor recreation provides opportunities for people to play new and different roles in a group. Typically, group activities such as backpacking, summer/winter camping, cross-country skiing, and bicycle touring require that group members perform certain tasks for the experience to be successful. These tasks include opportunities in organization, leadership, first aid, logistics, and provision of food and supplies. Many benefits are associated with taking responsibility for these tasks. Life's daily routine usually relegates people to one type of role at home or in the workplace. By playing different roles during recreational experiences, people have the opportunity to expand and grow confident in new roles. The low-level employee learns what it is like to have a leadership role, while the executive learns something about taking orders instead of giving them.

It is important to consider that outdoor recreation provides opportunities for individuals to more clearly define and understand themselves through an affiliation with other people who have similar recreational interests. This benefit may be the most important one of all. Outdoor recreation social groups provide opportunities for the development of a rich, positive lifestyle outside of the daily routine and supported by others with similar goals.

MANAGEMENT OF OUTDOOR RECREATION LANDSCAPES

Because outdoor recreation provides so many benefits, it is important that the values associated with such benefits are preserved for future generations. In order to preserve these values, the landscapes upon which outdoor recreation occurs must be managed and protected. This section addresses the issue of managing and protecting natural resource lands. The protection of these lands is the responsibility of all people who enjoy the privilege of outdoor recreation.

Diversity of Opportunities and Landscapes

Different types of outdoor recreation activities require unique landscapes for participation: white-water rafting requires free-flowing rivers; hunting requires lands with healthy wildlife habitats; backpacking requires wilderness landscapes; waterskiing requires lakes or reservoirs; and car camping requires highly developed sites with parking and sanitation facilities. Because of these requirements for participation, outdoor recreation landscapes must be managed to provide for a diversity of activities and landscapes rich in recreational value.

Intensive management is often required to help lands accommodate all of the activities that people desire. For people to enjoy fishing, lakes and streams are managed by fisheries experts to promote the health of fish and their aquatic habitat. For people to enjoy hiking, horseback riding, or mountain bike riding, land managers must build and maintain trails. Wilderness experiences are promoted when lands are managed to exclude any human influences. Wilderness management may be the most difficult form of management because it requires the elimination of logging, grazing of livestock, mining, aircraft noise, air pollution, and the effects of acid rain.

Beyond the national land-management agencies and organizations identified in Table 15.2, many state and local agencies and organizations also manage natural resource lands. All of these agencies take a very active part in manipulating, regulating, and managing lands for the benefit of all Americans. Three land-management concepts generally used by natural resource agencies are the recreation opportunity spectrum (ROS), the physical carrying capacity concept, and the social-psychological carrying capacity concept.

Recreation Opportunity Spectrum (ROS)

The ROS is a system and philosophy for managing diverse recreation activities on natural resource lands (Driver and Brown, 1978). It is a philosophy based on the idea that the most important value in outdoor recreation is the feeling of freedom obtained from a variety of activity choices. At the same time, it is a system that dictates how landscapes are to be modified or designed to allow for diverse experiences.

To explain the ROS, the management of a national forest is discussed. The national forests are managed by the U.S. Forest Service. A forest service planner must provide as many diverse recreation opportunities as possible by making accessible a number of environments and places that promote different uses. A typical forest has mountains,

TABLE 15.2. Natural Resource Management Agencies

Agency	Types of lands	Management philosophy
U.S. Forest Service (public)	National forests, wilderness areas	Multiple use: the concurrent management of recreation, wildlife, timber, livestock, water, and minerals
National Park Service (public)	National parks, monuments, and historical sites	Preservation and use: the protection of landscape scenery, areas of historical importance, and preservation of ecological conditions
Bureau of Land Management (public)	Forests, deserts, and rangelands	Multiple use: the concurrent management of recreation, wildlife, timber, livestock, water, and minerals
U.S. Fish and Wildlife Service (public)	Lands with important fish and wildlife habitats	Protection and enhancement of fish and wildlife habitats to yield numerous values and activities including hunting, fishing, and aesthetic uses
Bureau of Reclamation and the U.S. Army Corps of Engineers (public)	Reservoirs and waterways	Development of water projects that provide agricultural and urban water sources, control of flooding, and recreational opportunities
Nature Conservancy (private)	Diverse landscapes of ecological value and diversity	Landscape preservation and protection from significant human intrusions; recreation limited to hiking, viewing, and nature study
Ducks Unlimited (private)	Wetlands and waterfowl habitats	Protection, preservation, and enhancement of waterfowl habitats so as to increase opportunities associated with wildlife values, including hunting, bird-watching, photography, and aesthetics

timbered lands, grassy meadows, lakes, running streams, and open rangelands. Managing the land to promote a range of activities from wilderness backpacking to recreational-vehicle camping while accommodating other uses such as timber harvest is a challenging task.

The ROS system helps a planner to meet this challenge. The system designates six land-management classifications under which nearly all possible outdoor recreation uses could occur. These classifications are as follows:

1. *Primitive*—areas more commonly known as wilderness areas. They are managed to prevent the intrusion of human progress with the exception of recreation use. Typical activities in this type of area might include backpacking, mountaineering, cross-country skiing, or canoeing and rafting. Although mountainous landscapes are typically associated with wilderness areas, such places as wild and scenic rivers, deserts, and coastline wilderness areas are included.

2. *Semiprimitive, nonmotorized*—areas very similar to wilderness areas but may contain some human influences such as cabins, livestock ranching, or small reservoirs.

3. *Semiprimitive, motorized*—areas natural in appearance but where some roads and trails have been provided to allow better access. Typical activities might include fishing, hunting, off-road vehicle use, and nature study.

4. *Roaded, natural*—areas providing free access to any motorized vehicle and having facilities that are developed for specific uses. Such facilities include campgrounds, launch ramps and parking areas, picnic sites, small marinas, lodges, and ski areas.

5. *Rural*—areas showing signs of significant environmental modifications but with some natural elements still evident. Such areas may have small towns, clusters of lodges and restaurants, and service businesses in a seminatural setting.

6. *Urban/city park*—heavily modified, man-made environments that retain little evidence of natural processes. These lands often have extensive facilities to promote sports and picnicking activities in a setting dominated by exotic vegetation (Benjamin, 1987).

A forest service planner probably would not consider including opportunities offered in the sixth category and would leave such planning to city recreation departments.

The U.S. Forest Service relies heavily on the ROS in its planning and manages lands across a wide range of ROS designations. Other agencies focus more on some categories than others because of their management philosophy (see Table 15.2). The National Park Service focuses primarily on the first three categories but does provide some areas from categories four and five. City and county parks departments typically focus on the fourth and sixth categories. Agencies that manage large lakes and reservoirs focus more on categories four and five. Through this mixture of agencies and their respective emphasis on different ROS categories, all of the needs of people are met by providing diverse environments that accommodate many activities. Without natural resource agencies, such a diversity of activities and environments would not be available.

Physical Carrying Capacity

Carrying capacity is an extremely simple yet critically important concept in terms of managing natural resource lands (Chubb and Chubb, 1981; Knudson, 1980). People deal with carrying capacity in everyday life. For example, when too much milk is poured into a glass, the carrying capacity of the glass is exceeded and the result is spilled milk. When too many cars are put onto a road, the carrying capacity of the road is exceeded and the result is a traffic jam. In terms of natural resource lands, *physical carrying capacity* is defined as the point at which the impacts of use and activity on the land damage or exceed the land's natural ability to heal and regenerate itself. Perhaps there is a place on campus where so many people have walked on the lawn that the soil is too damaged and compacted for the grass to grow back. In this case, the physical carrying capacity of the lawn has been exceeded. Just as with a glass of milk or a road, the natural environment can withstand only so much use before its physical capacity to handle or absorb that use is exceeded. The result of exceeding physical carrying capacity is often an environmental mess.

To fully understand this concept, it is important to realize that nature has a wonderful ability to regenerate and restore itself. Trees are harvested from the forest, but new trees regenerate and grow to take their place. People hunt and fish, yet fish and wildlife reproduce to maintain their populations. Often, natural resource managers will set controlled, low-intensity forest fires knowing that nature will reproduce a healthier forest in the following year.

However, nature is also fragile. If too many trees are cut, forests cannot regenerate without additional help from people. If too many fish are caught, there will not be enough left to reproduce and repopulate a lake or a stream. When this happens, fish must be artificially grown and restocked into lakes and streams at a high cost. If a fire burns too intensely, the soil will be sterilized and the forest will not regenerate without human intervention. In these latter cases, physical carrying capacity has been exceeded and nature cannot readily heal itself. Physical carrying capacity is an important concept in natural resource management because lands are managed best when people can allow nature to do the work of growing and replenishing itself. However, it is possible only if the carrying capacity of the land is not exceeded.

The concept of physical carrying capacity has an important relationship to outdoor recreation. Natural resource managers find that excessive recreation use has the potential to severely exceed physical carrying capacity. In some areas, the trampling of wildflowers and vegetation around picnic areas and campgrounds has degraded the environment to the point where vegetation will not grow back. Excessive fishing can literally "fish out" a lake or stream. In Yosemite National Park, visitors to the giant redwoods have compacted the soil at the base of many trees, causing them to die. In some areas, trails that receive heavy horseback, mountain bike, and foot use have become knee-deep ditches in the ground. In other areas, the irresponsible use of off-road vehicles has caused soil erosion resulting in vegetational loss, loss of wildlife habitats, and water pollution. Careless recreationists have caused the loss of entire forests through wildfire.

Although the recreation behavior of any one individual may seem to be of little consequence, the collective behavior of the millions of recreation users of natural resource lands may have serious impacts. Natural resource managers often have no choice but to limit the number of people who can hunt, fish, camp, hike, or picnic in popular areas so that the natural setting can be saved or rehabilitated. Sadly, such limitations on people's freedom to enjoy outdoor recreation are necessary in order to maintain high-quality parks, forests, rivers, lakes, and beaches.

Social-Psychological Carrying Capacity

The psychological benefits associated with outdoor recreation are many. The ability to escape to a restorative environment in relative solitude from others is arguably among the most important psychological benefits of outdoor recreation. Unfortunately, with so many people enjoying outdoor recreation, escape is becoming increasingly difficult. The concept of social-psychological carrying capacity addresses this issue (Knudson, 1980; Shelby and Heberlein, 1986). Natural resource managers define social-psychological carrying capacity as the point at which people's recreational experiences are negatively impacted by the actions, behavior, and presence of other people. Individual perceptions vary in regard to this form of carrying capacity. For some people, the mere sight of another person in a wilderness area exceeds their social-psychological carrying capacity and they perceive their experience to be ruined. For other people, the sight of another person may be a welcome addition to the experience. Many examples of social-psychological carrying capacity are experienced in day-to-day life. People who smoke in crowded restaurants may negatively impact the dining experiences of others. People who play their stereo too loud impact the solitude and privacy of their neighbors.

Natural resource managers deal with social-psychological carrying capacity through many methods. One method is simply to limit the number of people who are allowed to use an area. Another method is to try to change the behavior of people using an area. Behavior modification is typically achieved either by educating and informing people of appropriate behavior or by designing facilities that discourage certain types of uses. A third method is known as use zoning. This is a management technique that designates certain uses in certain places. Uses that are incompatible, such as hunting and bird-watching, are designated for specific areas. Hunters are not allowed in bird-watching areas and bird-watchers are not allowed in hunting areas.

The management of a campground is a good example of how these methods might be used. Often, conflicts arise in campgrounds that are being used by both tent campers and people camping in large recreational vehicles. Tent campers often complain that recreational vehicles are too large and noisy to allow enjoyment of their camping experience. Recreational vehicle owners often claim that tent campers are merely jealous of all the amenities contained in a recreational vehicle. How might a natural resource manager resolve these conflicts?

One solution is to limit the number of campsites that are open for use. This would disperse campers across a larger area so that conflicting uses are not in contact with one another. Another solution might be to design either campsites that cannot accommodate large recreational vehicles or facilities without good, flat tent sites thus encouraging only vehicle camping. This action would effectively modify camping behavior and cause one group to go elsewhere while encouraging the other group to remain. Certain rules could be imposed to modify behavior. For example, a noise curfew of nine p.m. could be enforced to eliminate the use of radios, generators, televisions, and appliances in recreational vehicles, thus preserving the solitude of the camping experience for all campers. Finally, use zoning could be enforced. Tent camping could be limited to one part of the campground and recreational-vehicle camping to another. Another solution might be to design an additional campground that is best suited to recreational-vehicle camping and restrict recreational vehicles to that campground.

There are many methods for managing carrying capacity. The three methods discussed (limiting numbers, behavior modification, and use zoning) are common methods and can be used to solve both physical and social-psychological carrying-capacity problems. Take a few minutes to complete Exercise 15.2. Use your knowledge of the three carrying-capacity management methods to create solutions to the problem that is presented.

In terms of limiting user numbers, you might have suggested that a permit system be developed that allows only a certain number of people to use the park each day. A ranger could be assigned to each park entrance, and once a certain number of cars, bicycles, motorcycles, or horses have entered, no more would be allowed in. Some solutions based on behavior-modification methods might include designing the trail with barriers so that users could not get off the trail; building additional trails to eliminate the number and frequency of conflicts; designing trails with bumps and dips so that riding bicycles, motorcycles, and horses would not be encouraged; putting turnstiles at trailheads to prevent access to motorcycles; educating users of the dangers involved in traveling at high rates of speed on the trail or road; limiting automobile use of the park road to only certain hours of the day, and creating a bicycle lane on the park road. Use zoning could provide a number of solutions such as creating specific trails for specific types of transportation, limiting some uses to the road and other

EXERCISE 15.2. Solutions to Carrying-Capacity Problems

Problem

Imagine a parkway that follows a beautiful, tree-lined creek for many miles. Within the parkway is a one-lane road that follows the creek the entire length of the parkway. This road is heavily used by people in automobiles and on bicycles. Also within the parkway is a trail that follows the creek. This trail is heavily used by walkers, joggers, horseback riders, bicyclists, and occasionally by people on motorcycles. The trail is only four feet wide. Recently, a number of accidents and incidents have occurred which indicate that the carrying capacity of the park's transportation routes is being exceeded. Hikers, bicyclists, horseback riders, and motorcyclists are starting to get off the trail and are destroying the park's vegetation. A number of traffic accidents have occurred between people in automobiles and bicyclists. People on bicycles have scared horses and their riders, causing many riders to fall. Walkers and joggers have complained about horse manure on the trails. Many people have complained about motorcycles on the trail making too much noise, raising dust, and traveling at dangerously fast speeds. People on bicycles have surprised walkers and joggers coming around corners and have collided with them.

Now imagine that you are the superintendent of the park just described. Based on your knowledge of the methods for dealing with carrying-capacity problems (limiting numbers, behavior modification, and use zoning), list a number of solutions to the problems discussed. Remember, you want to avoid conflicts while still allowing all of the uses to occur. Use the following form.

Method	Solutions
Limiting numbers	1. _____
	2. _____
	3. _____
	4. _____
	5. _____
Behavior modification	1. _____
	2. _____
	3. _____
	4. _____
	5. _____
Use zoning	1. _____
	2. _____
	3. _____
	4. _____
	5. _____

uses to the trail, and limiting transportation uses between mileposts on the trails or road.

Exercise 15.2 raises a number of important issues. Often decisions and policies that are made to solve carrying-capacity problems end up restricting the freedom of park users. The reason for these restrictions is, ironically, to protect both the park and its users. Such decisions are rarely made without some form of citizen input. Informed citizens who understand carrying-capacity issues can play a valuable role in helping to overcome outdoor recreation conflicts.

To summarize, managing natural resource lands is difficult and complicated. Managers must try to provide people with the entire spectrum of outdoor recreation opportunities (ROS), minimize conflicts between people and their desired activities (social-psychological carrying capacity), and make sure that the environment will remain as natural as possible for the enjoyment of future generations (physical carrying capacity). It is quite a challenge!

PROTECTION, STEWARDSHIP, AND RESPONSIBILITY

Think of your favorite outdoor recreation activities. For each activity, what would be the ultimate or best experience for that activity? For downhill skiers, being the first skier cutting turns down the hill after an overnight snowfall has dropped a foot of new, powdery snow might be the ultimate experience. For rock climbers, being the first to climb and master a particular face of a rock or mountain might be the best experience. For fishing enthusiasts, being all alone and casting into a lake full of hungry trout who have not seen another lure all year might be the ultimate experience. What are the chances of being able to have these ultimate experiences? Not very good. Surprisingly, only a few decades ago, people could easily attain these ultimate experiences. To achieve such experiences today would probably require a great deal of money, travel, luck, and timing. Why did things change?

The simple answer to this question is that more people are recreationally using natural resource lands than ever before. Cordell and colleagues (2000) report that federal lands in the United States (national parks, forests, and refuges) receive about 1.6 billion visits each year. The same report reveals that state parks in the United States receive about 730 million visits each year. Since 1960, outdoor resources have become more accessible, technology has made participation safer and more comfortable, and a tremendous boom in information has increased awareness of the opportunities. Technology has also created many new forms of participation including hang gliding, mountain biking, scuba diving, and recreational ballooning. The economics of this growth in activity are strong and assure continued growth.

In addition to these factors, probably the most important reason for a growth in outdoor recreation use is demographics. The past twenty years were a period when the largest subpopulation in the United States, the World War II baby-boom generation, became active adults. As the population grows, the demand on natural resource lands for outdoor recreation will become more competitive. Pressures on the physical carrying capacity of the land and conflicts over social-psychological carrying capacity issues will increase. In addition, no significant additions have been made to the amount of natural resource lands available for outdoor recreation since the 1970s, nor does the future look bright for such additions. It is a problem known all too well—too many people, not enough room.

Solutions to this problem do exist. The keys to these solutions lie in the words *protection, stewardship,* and *responsibility.* The purpose of discussing the concept of carrying capacity was to illuminate the fact that personal behavior can have a tremendous impact on both the environment and the experiences of others who use natural resource lands. Some people believe that technology or the government will solve problems of overcrowding. However, the solution really depends on each individual who uses natural resources for recreation. Each individual is responsible for protecting the natural resource lands he or she uses. Everyone is responsible for being a good steward or caretaker of the land. The old phrase "take only pictures, leave only footprints" may sound trite, but it is more important now than ever before. The ability to enjoy outdoor recreation activities will become increasingly dependent on how well people accept personal accountability to the land and to others.

Americans are fortunate to have a wealth of public natural resource lands that is unmatched anywhere else in the world. Nearly one-third of all the land in the United States is available for public use. Consider what life would be like if there were no public lands. Outdoor recreation might be available only to those who could afford it. National parks would be more like private country clubs with excessive membership dues. In places where little public land is available today, people pay tremendously high prices to ski, fish, and even camp.

The fact that national parks and forests, state parks and beaches, lakes, reservoirs, and wild rivers exist and are essentially free for public use is truly one of the great *privileges* of being an American. The only means of retaining that privilege for present and future generations is to responsibly protect these lands, become good stewards, and respect the rights of others to enjoy them with us.

Future Trends in Land Use and Activities

Beyond the fact that more people will be competing for the use of public natural resource lands, there are other predictions for the types of activities and land-management practices of the future. Interviews with managers and leaders in the field of outdoor recreation reveal some interesting projections, such as more restrictions being imposed on the number of people using areas (Shafer, Moeller, and Getty, 1977). Use zoning will likely become more extensive so that incompatible uses and groups will be separated. Reservation and permit systems currently exist for popular campsites, back-country trails, and for many hunting opportunities. Competition for permits to climb Mount Whitney in California or raft the Rogue River in Oregon has become as fierce as getting tickets to the Super Bowl. In the future, people might have to compete for a use permit to fish in certain lakes, sit on the beach, or even swim in the ocean.

Sound farfetched? Some experts predict that within the next century, fish and wildlife will be so threatened that the taking of fish and game will be eliminated. All fish will have to be released back to the water and hunters will have to use tranquilizer darts instead of bullets. Predictions for beyond the year 2050 include heating of man-made lakes for swimming, development of underwater resorts, rivers constructed strictly for recreation, and the first park established on the moon (Shafer, Moeller, and Getty, 1977).

The opportunities of new technology will undoubtedly expand the range of outdoor recreation activities. Experts predict such innovations as personal submarines, jet-pack backpacks, hovercrafts, laser weapons for hunting, and indoor "natural" campsites in an environmentally controlled urban setting will be commonplace by the year 2060 (Shafer, Moeller, and Getty, 1977). Remember, it took only eight years to build a ship that could land a person on the moon.

SUMMARY

Technology may modify the way in which natural resource lands are used, but one fact will always hold true: the physiological, sociological, and psychological benefits associated with recreational uses of natural resource lands will always be in high demand. People will always desire close personal contact with nature. As stewards of the land, it is our responsibility to protect and maintain the quality of outdoor recreation and the environments where it occurs, both for ourselves and for future generations.

REFERENCES

Bailey, C. (1978). *Fit or fat*. Boston, MA: Houghton Mifflin.

Cheek, N.H. and Burch, W.R. (1976). *The social organization of leisure in human society*. New York: Harper and Row.

Chubb, M. and Chubb, H.R. (1981). *One third of our time? An introduction to recreation behavior and resources*. New York: Wiley.

Cordell, H.K., McDonald, B.L., Teasley, R.J., Bergstrom, J.C., Martin, J., Bason, J., and Leeworthy, V.R. (2000). Outdoor recreation participation trends: National survey on recreation and the environment: 2000. In H.K. Cordell, *Outdoor recreation in American life: A national assessment of demand and supply trends* (pp. 219-321). Champaign, IL: Sagamore Publishing.

Driver, B.L. and Brown, P.J. (1978). The opportunity spectrum concept and behavioral information in outdoor recreation resource supply inventories: A rationale. In G. H. Lund, V.J. LaBau, P.F. Ffolliott, and D.W. Robinson (Eds.), *Integrated inventories of renewable natural resources: Proceedings of the workshop* (pp. 24-31). General Technical Report RM–55. Rocky Mountain Forest and Range Experiment Station, Fort Collins, CO.

Driver, B.L. and Tocher, S.R. (1970). Toward a behavioral interpretation of recreation, with implications for planning. In B.L. Driver (Ed.), *Elements of outdoor recreation planning* (pp. 9-31). Ann Arbor, MI: University Microfilms International.

Dubos, R. (1968). *So human an animal*. New York: Charles Scribner's Sons.

Hanson, R.A. (1977). An outdoor challenge program as a means of enhancing mental health. In *Children, nature, and the urban environment: Proceedings of a symposium fair* (pp. 171-173). USDA Forest Service General Technical Report NE–30. Northeastern Experimental Station, Upper Darby, PA.

Kaplan, R. (1977). Summer outdoor programs: Their participants and their effects. In *Children, nature, and the urban environment: Proceedings of a symposium fair* (pp. 175-179). USDA Forest Service General Technical Report NE–30. Northeastern Experimental Station, Upper Darby, PA.

Kaplan, R. (1983). The role of nature in the urban context. In I. Altman and J.F. Wohlwill (Eds.), *Behavior in the natural environment: Human behavior and environment* (Vol. 6) (pp. 127-161). New York: Plenum Press.

Kaplan, S. (1978). Attention and fascination: The search for cognitive clarity. In S. Kaplan and R. Kaplan (Eds.), *Humanscape: Environment for people* (pp. 84-90). North Scituate, MA: Duxbury Press.

Kaplan, S. and Talbot, J.F. (1983). Psychological benefits of a wilderness experience. In I. Altmati and J.F. Wohlwill (Eds.), *Behavior in the natural environment: Human behavior and environment* (pp. 163-203). New York: Plenum Press.

Knopf, R.C. (1983). Recreational needs and behavior in natural settings. In I. Altman and J.F. Wohlwill (Eds.), *Behavior in the natural environment: Human behavior and environment* (pp. 205-240). New York: Plenum Press.

Knopf, R.C., Driver, B.L., and Bassett, J.R. (1973). Motivations for fishing. In *Transactions of the 28th North American Wildlife and Natural Resources Conference* (pp. 191-204). Washington, DC: Wildlife Management Institute.

Knudson, D. (1980). *Outdoor recreation*. New York: Macmillan.

Kraus, R. (1984). *Recreation and leisure in modern society* (Third edition). Glenview, IL: Scott, Foresman.

Kretch, D., Crutchfield, R.S., and Ballachey, E.L. (1962). *Individual in society*. New York: McGraw-Hill.

Lee, R.G. (1972). The social definition of outdoor recreation places. In W.R. Burch, N.H. Cheek, and L. Taylor (Eds.), *Social behavior, natural resources, and the environment* (pp. 68-84). New York: Harper and Row.

Mehrabian, A. and Russell, J.A. (1974). *An approach to environmental psychology*. Cambridge, MA: MIT Press.

Menninger, W.C. (1960). Recreation and mental health. In *Recreation and psychiatry* (pp. 8-17). New York: National Recreation Association.

Proshansky, H.M., Ittleson, W.H., and Rivlin, L.G. (1976). Freedom of choice and behavior in a physical setting. In H.M. Proshansky, W.H. Ittleson, and L.G. Rivlin (Eds.), *Environmental psychology: People and their physical setting* (Second edition) (pp. 170-180). New York: Holt, Rinehart and Winston.

Rossman, B.B. and Ulehla, Z.J. (1977). Psychological reward values associated with wilderness use: A functional-reinforcement approach. *Environment and Behavior, 9*, 41-66.

Shafer, E.L. and Mietz, J. (1969). Aesthetic and emotional experiences rank high with northeast wilderness hikers. *Environment and Behavior, 1*, 187-197.

Shafer, E.L., Moeller, G.H., and Getty, R.E. (1977). Future recreation environments. USDA Forest Service Research Paper NE–301. Northeastern Forest Experiment Station, Upper Darby, PA.

Shelby, B. and Heberlein, T.A. (1986). *Carrying capacity in recreation settings.* Corvallis, OR: Oregon State University Press.

Tuan, Y.-F. (1979). *Landscapes of fear.* New York: Pantheon Books.

Ulrich, R.S. (1983). Aesthetic and affective response to natural environments. In I. Altman and J.F. Wohlwill (Eds.), *Behavior in the natural environment: Human behavior and environment* (Volume 6) (pp. 85-125). New York: Plenum Press.

Wiggins, J.S. (1973). *Personality and prediction: Principles of personality assessment.* Reading, MA: Addison-Wesley.

Wohlwill, J.F. (1976). Environmental aesthetics: The environment as a source of affect. In I. Altman and J.F. Wohlwill (Eds.), *Human behavior and environment,* Volume 1 (pp. 37-86). New York: Plenum Press.

Wohlwill, J.F. and Kohn, I. (1976). Dimensionalizing the environmental manifold. In S. Wapner, S.B. Cohen, and B. Kaplan (Eds.), *Experiencing the environment* (pp. 19-53). New York: Plenum Press.

Chapter 16

Leisure in Selected Countries

INTRODUCTION

This chapter presents information on interesting aspects of leisure in selected countries around the world. The purpose of this chapter is to learn about different leisure activities and concerns in various countries that can provide insight into improving leisure on both a personal and a societal level. The chapter is not intended to be a comprehensive overview of leisure around the world. That could be the topic of a two- or three-volume book! Only a select number of countries are discussed in this chapter. The discussions of each country are not in-depth descriptions of the countries, but instead are concise summaries of leisure-related trends, concerns, or activities in those countries. Even the sections on Egypt, Saudi Arabia, India, Nepal, Russia, and Australia and New Zealand, although they are very brief, provide some useful information and insight into leisure that can be applied to life and leisure in the United States. Obviously, many countries are not discussed in this chapter, not because they are any less interesting, but due to limited space or lack of accessibility to information.

A benefit of studying and comparing leisure of various nations is that it facilitates a greater understanding of leisure in the United States in the past, present, and future. For example, many similarities exist between the leisure activities of people in undeveloped countries and those of preindustrial America. Being able to get a taste for leisure in the United States in the past facilitates a clearer understanding of why and how leisure in this country became what it is today. Viewing other cultures also aids in evaluating the positive and negative aspects of leisure in the United States today. Finally, the leisure behavior patterns of other countries can help predict the future leisure behavior patterns of Americans. In particular, leisure innovations in countries such as Japan, Sweden, and Great Britain often are adopted in the United States several years later.

The learning objectives for this chapter include the following:

1. Identify similarities in the leisure of selected countries to that of the United States in the past.
2. Identify similarities and differences in the leisure of selected countries to that of present American society.
3. Predict future changes in leisure in the United States based on leisure activities and attitudes in other countries.
4. Identify interesting aspects of leisure in Western Europe, Israel, Egypt, Saudi Arabia, India, Nepal, Thailand, Japan, Hong Kong, China, Russia and countries of the former Soviet Union, and Australia and New Zealand.
5. Identify desirable and undesirable characteristics of leisure in selected countries.
6. Identify ideas for improving the leisure well-being of American society based on leisure activities and attitudes in other nations.
7. Identify leisure activities and ideas that could be adapted successfully in the United States.

This chapter has been organized into separate sections for each country or region. The information presented is based on a review of literature, interviews with foreigners living in the United States, personal observations during visits to various countries, and interviews with recreation professionals and the people of various nations. This version of the chapter is different from the one that appeared in the second edition of the book, because the world has changed a great deal. In particular, it was amazing to see, firsthand, the changes in China from our first visit there in 1987 to our most recent visit in 2001. Similarly, significant changes in leisure in Israel have occurred in recent years that we have been able to experience in person (our latest visit there was in the summer of 2001). Some of the photographs included in this chapter were taken during the authors' five-month world tour in 1987 and 1988 and appear in the chapter because they are still relevant. Included at the end of some of the sections are descriptions of games from other countries. These games and many more can be found in the book by Jernigan and Vendien (1972). Before discussing specific countries, some global comparisons related to leisure are presented in the next section.

GLOBAL COMPARISONS

Among industrialized countries of the world, it appears that Americans have the least leisure and work the longest hours.

Annual Number of Hours Worked (Sancton, 1999)

United States	1,966
Japan	1,889
Britain	1,731
France	1,656
Norway	1,399

According to Olson (1999), work hours have decreased in most countries since 1980 but seem to have increased in the United States. For example, the annual number of hours worked by the Japanese went down from 2,121 in 1980 to 1,889 in 1995, while in the United States, the number of hours worked went up from 1,883 in 1980 to 1,966 in 1997. Greater disparity in leisure and number of hours worked is likely to develop as countries such as France enact legislation to reduce the workweek to thirty-five hours (Sancton, 1999).

Combining statistics on productivity and wealth with statistics on happiness reinforces the truth of the adage that "money can't buy happiness." Americans are the wealthiest, but not the happiest. Workers in the United States produced a per capita average of $49,905 of goods in 1996, more than workers of any other country (Olson, 1999), yet the United States ranked only tenth among nations in "number of expected happy years" (Cook, 2000). In a global study of happiness, Iceland ranked first with an average of 62.04 "happy years," whereas Americans average only 57.76 "happy years." However, other countries had much lower figures for number of happy years than the United States. Among the bottom ten countries were India at 36.44 years, Russia at 34.48 years, and in last place, Bulgaria at 31.57 years (Cook, 2000).

WESTERN EUROPE OVERVIEW

Industrialization and urbanization are almost inescapable in developed nations. Crowded living conditions in big cities require creative solutions to the problem of providing adequate recreational opportunities in limited space. The photograph of half-court tennis in Paris (Photo 16.1) illustrates one solution to the challenge of providing recreational facilities in limited space. The game of half-court tennis is played on a court literally half the size of a regulation-size tennis court.

Another aspect of leisure that seems to be similar in most Western European nations is the concern for moral order among youth. Personal conversations with residents of various countries indicated that as in America (though not necessarily on the same level as the United States), people are concerned that teenagers and young adults are taking drugs, consuming alcohol, and indulging in other potentially harmful activities during their free time. Another general observation based on the authors' world travels is that the people of Westernized developed nations seem to have less free time than people in undevel-

PHOTO 16.1. One advantage of half-court tennis: Twice as many people can play in the same space required for regulation tennis.

oped countries. Godbey (1981) states that a study comparing free time of the French and a primitive Peruvian indigenous tribe found that the Peruvian natives have approximately four hours of more free time per day than the French. Who is happier? It is a difficult question to answer. However, based on personal observations, it seems that in some cases, people in poorer countries are happier than people in affluent nations. As Godbey (1981) writes, there are two ways to reach affluence—one is to produce more (what developed nations do), the other is to be satisfied with less (which is exemplified in many undeveloped nations). This philosophical point will be applicable in the discussion of other countries later in the chapter.

Looking at some specific countries in Western Europe, a leisure-related difference between American and French workers is the structure of the workday. Especially in the small cities and rural areas of France, people take a two- to three-hour break in the middle of the day. Unlike Americans grabbing fast-food lunches, many of the French enjoy a leisurely midday meal followed by a nap. According to N. Samuel (personal communication, 1987), the French place great importance on meals as a form of recreation. Carey (1986) writes that most Europeans are more dedicated to relaxation in everyday life than are Americans. Greeks, similar to the French, take a long midday break. Most stores and businesses are closed for three hours in the middle of the day. Napping is a common activity during this time.

Some French companies have begun to provide recreational activities for their employees, such as yoga, swimming, calisthenics, reading, and music. Many employers provide inexpensive lunches for their employees. Another leisure-related benefit that some French employers offer is the use of company-owned vacation homes for inexpensive rates (based on a sliding fee scale). According to Dimanche (1995), nearly 60 percent of the population leaves home each year for a vacation that lasts fifteen days on the average. The guaranteed five weeks of paid vacation time each year for French wage earners (Samuel, 1993) helps make these lengthy vacations possible. Because so many people take vacations during the summer months, nearly all businesses close in July or August (Dimanche, 1995).

A similarity between France and Great Britain has been a shift toward greater flexibility in work-time organization creating enhanced synchronization of time schedules among family members (Hantrais, 1987). According to Hantrais, Clark, and Samuel (1984), in both France and Britain, family and leisure are perhaps more important than work. Instead of work schedules dictating free time and family leisure activities, family and leisure shape work schedules.

A difference between the two countries is climate. The cool, wet climate throughout most of Britain severely limits outdoor recreation opportunities. The British complain of the unpredictability of even the summer weather in England, making favorite activities such as barbecues and picnics difficult to plan.

Sugden and Bairner (1986) state that the British government uses leisure as a means of social control in Northern Ireland. They claim that when a greater degree of public disorder exists, the government provides more leisure services to distract and control people. In this way, the government utilizes recreation as a tool for maintaining law and order.

A significant leisure-related social disorder problem in England is violence at soccer matches. According to Pratt and Salter (1984), "football hooliganism" perhaps stems from the origins of the game in the nineteenth century in which football was a game for entire villages. Rules were loose and the games would often lead to full-scale rioting and violence. In modern society, the problem of spectator violence at soccer games is magnified by the media recognition it receives. Fortunately, spectator sports and violence at spectator events constitutes but a small portion of leisure activities in Great Britain.

Leisure is the largest category of expenditure in the United Kingdom. The average family spends the most money on leisure, followed by food, housing, and cars (Gunnell, 2000). McCabe (1993) reports that the most popular sport activities in the United Kingdom are walking, swimming, darts, cycling, running, snooker, and badminton. Other popular sports for males include football, squash, and weight training. Women show a preference for tennis, ice-skating, table tennis, bowling, and "keep-fit." According to Parker (1985), the most popular leisure activities in Great Britain are (in order) visits with friends and relatives; visits to pubs and restaurants; bathing or sunbathing; walking, hiking, and rambling; and visits to shows, fairs, carnivals, and theme parks. Parker (1985) also states that most free time is spent in the home and garden, this tendency being especially relevant for women.

McGillivray, Maxwell, and Foley (2000) report that in the 1990s, there was an increase in the number of employers providing health and fitness facilities for staff in their workplaces. However, they express concerns that female employees may be disadvantaged in workplace fitness provision because of the emphasis on a traditional facility-based model as opposed to promoting low-intensity physical activity.

This section concludes with a few ideas for recreational programs and activities from Western European nations that could be successfully adopted in the United States. One such idea is the Danish senior citizens study group program. According to Gregersen (1986), this highly successful program involves elders participating in study circles to pursue in-depth topics of interest. The study circles take trips related to what they are discussing, and some become involved in programs with school children. Gregersen (1986) states that the program is beneficial because all participants are involved in the learning process and people learn from one another.

Bauman, Marchlowitz, and Palm (1985) describe Germany's successful Spielfests. Spielfests are games festivals that can involve as many as 65,000 participants. Games played are primarily ball and movement games that can be organized on the spot (e.g., volleyball, relay races, tug of war, Earth ball). The games serve to break down social barriers and help people recognize that playing games is a basic lifelong need. Germany holds approximately 1,000 Spielfests annually. The Spielfest concept has spread to Switzerland, Austria, Brazil, Argentina, Israel, Portugal, and France.

Finally, some activity ideas from Western European countries are presented.

Cloche-Pied Collectif (Belgium)

Preparation: Form two or three rows (teams) of five to ten players each. Separate the rows by ten to fifteen feet.

Starting position: Team members line up behind one another. Players place their right hand on the shoulder of the person in front of them and their left hand on the bent left leg of the person behind them.

Action: Teams progress by successive hops without loosening their hold.

Objective: The first team to cross the finish line wins.

La Poste Court (Belgium)

> *Preparation:* Chairs for each player, arranged in a square. Each side of the square represents a particular city.
>
> *Starting position:* Players are seated, the leader is standing.
>
> *Action:* When the leader calls out the name of two cities, the two sides of the square must exchange seats. The leader tries to take one of the empty seats.
>
> *Objective:* To not get caught without a seat. The person left standing becomes the new leader.

Robin's Alive (Denmark)

> *Preparation:* Blow up a balloon and leave it untied at the mouthpiece.
>
> *Starting position:* Players sit or stand in a circle.
>
> *Action:* Pass the balloon from player to player, grasping the open end and trying not to let air escape.
>
> *Objective:* To pass the balloon without air escaping. Player who gets the balloon with no air in it has to do a stunt.
>
> *Variations:* Form teams of eight to twenty players each, in lines. First team to pass its balloon up and back with air left in the balloon wins.

String and Hat Contest (Greece)

> *Preparation:* One long rope or heavy string, ends tied together, and one hat for each player.
>
> *Starting position:* Stand in a circle around the rope, equal distance apart, holding onto the rope with the left hand. Hats are behind each player on the floor, out of reach.
>
> *Action:* Players try to reach their hats and put them on their heads without letting go of the rope.
>
> *Objective:* Succeed in getting a hat and prevent others from reaching their hats by pulling on the rope.

PHOTO 16.2. An unfinished tennis court on Crete. Without fences, stray balls can travel quite a distance.

ISRAEL

Introduction

The section on Israel is the longest one of this chapter. Israel is a small country, with a population of just over 6 million, so why give so much attention to this country? One reason is a great deal can be learned in the United States about terrorism and its effects on leisure by studying Israel. Concerns about terrorism have dominated the news in the United States since 9/11/01. Terrorism has affected leisure, in particular, travel and tourism, perhaps more than any other factor at the start of the twenty-first century. Israel, unfortunately, has had more experience in dealing with terrorism than any other democratic country in the world. By studying Israel, insight can be gained into how to deal with terrorism as a factor to be considered in planning and participating in leisure activities. Another reason why studying leisure in Israel is important is that Israel is one of America's strongest, closest allies in the world. American trends have a great deal of influence on leisure in Israel, but in some cases, trends in Israel have an effect on leisure in the United States.

Although Israel is a small country, a great deal has been written about leisure in Israel. One of the world leaders in the area of leisure education, Hillel Ruskin, was a professor at Hebrew University in Jerusalem and the chair of the education commission of the World Leisure and Recreation Association. Some of the information in this section is based on his writings and those of his colleagues. There is also a great deal of information in this chapter based on firsthand experiences with life in Israel, as the authors lived there in 1994-1995, 1997-1998, and the summers of 1996, 1999, 2000, and 2001.

Israel is a country of contrasts. Modern Israeli cities are similar to American or Western European cities. However, within a short distance of many of these cities are Orthodox Jewish settlements and Arab villages where people seem to be living a lifestyle from times long past. Despite the challenges posed by a diverse population and the upsurge in terrorist attacks in Israel since September 2000, provision of leisure services in Israel has been making significant progress. This section has been divided into the following sub-sections: terrorism and leisure; making peace through recreation; religion and leisure; modernization of leisure; kibbutz life and leisure; and general trends.

Terrorism and Leisure

Before discussing terrorism in Israel and its effects on leisure, think about how terrorism has affected leisure in the United States since 9/11/01. Air travel plummeted. Hotels and resorts, airlines, car rental companies, and other businesses related to travel and tourism have gone through tough times. People became afraid to travel. Security has been tightened not only at airports but also at sporting events and other large-scale recreational events.

Now, imagine the situation in Israel. The climate is warm and people like to go out at night, not just on the weekends. There are outdoor cafes where people like to sit and socialize at all hours of the day and night. Israelis like to celebrate, and weddings and bar and bat mitzvah events tend to be on a large scale. Event halls are filled with celebrants most any night of the week, not just on weekends. Similar to the United States, indoor shopping malls can get pretty crowded.

There are also outdoor pedestrian malls and the old-fashioned outdoor *shuk,* a crowded but great place to buy fresh produce at reasonable prices. Many people rely on public transportation to get from place to place. Because of the low rate of violent crime, children, teenagers, and women seemed to have a freedom that exists in few places in the United States. Children in Israeli cities could walk about without an adult escort. Teenage girls and women could be out at night without a male companion, without fear. Unlike the United States, it would not be unusual to see a woman walking by herself on the beach late at night.

Since September 2000, homicide bombers have blown themselves up at the outdoor cafes, event halls, shopping malls, pedestrian malls, and shuks with frightening regularity. Terrorists have blown up numerous buses. Security has been tightened and many terrorist attacks have been prevented. Nevertheless, numerous attacks have still taken place. Given the size of Israel in relation to the United States, the number of dead and wounded Israelis from terrorist attacks since September 2000 is the equivalent of many times that of the 9/11/01 attacks. Imagine the effects of these attacks on life and leisure. After all, many of these attacks are actually occurring at places of leisure. How do Israelis cope with this situation? Interesting examples of Israeli creativity could be copied in the United States.

For example, downtown Jerusalem experienced several horrific terrorist bombings from September 2000 to 2002, and businesses such as restaurants and other places of entertainment suffered greatly because people were staying away from the area. However, Silver (2002) reports that in August 2002, the municipality decided to turn downtown into a protected pedestrian mall with several entrances guarded by security personnel. To attract people back to the area, several fairs were held, such as a food fair one week and a fashion fair another. By the end of September, it was estimated that almost half a million people had attended the various festivals. Amazingly, it seems that Israelis were able to use recreation as a means to overcome the fear of terrorism in order to breathe life back into downtown Jerusalem.

On a smaller scale, individual restaurants and cafes have hired their own security guards to give their patrons a greater feeling of security. The enhanced security has helped business at many establishments. In addition, places of entertainment that already had security, such as country clubs and fitness clubs, became even more popular with Israelis who were seeking recreational opportunities that they perceived as being safe. Yoga classes, folk dancing, and other activities at these clubs experienced increased participation during periods when the security situation seemed to be at its worst.

Another important characteristic of Israelis is their resiliency and courage. Terrorists want to kill people, but more than that, they seek to terrorize the general population. The terrorists behind the 9/11/01 tragedy are undoubtedly delighted over the general feeling of terror that they created in the United States in the aftermath of the attacks. Israelis understand that the terrorist groups launching attacks against them want to instill fear among the general population of Israel, and one of the ways Israelis defy the terrorists is through leisure. For example, at the height of a wave of terror attacks against Israelis in the summer of 2001, the annual dance festival in the town of Karmiel (in the northern part of the country) was held, and approximately 250,000 people enjoyed the three-day dance marathon.

Similarly, in the south of the country, at the resort city of Eilat, tens of thousands of vacationers could be seen walking along the Red Sea promenade at night, with scarcely a soldier or policeman in sight, as if no terrorist threat existed. Also in the summer of 2001, the Maccabiah Games were held in Israel. The Maccabiah Games are an athletic competition, similar to the Olympics, for Jewish athletes all over the world. Despite the threat of terrorist attacks, the games were held, involving over 3,000 athletes from over forty different countries. However, at the opening ceremony in Jerusalem, over 1,000 security personnel were deployed to protect the stadium filled with over 20,000 spectators and athletes. The opening ceremonies went off smoothly without an incident, although two terrorists did blow themselves up less than a mile away from the stadium in an aborted homicide bombing attack.

Ultimately, enhanced security can prevent many attacks, but not all of them. The only real way to defeat terrorism is through peace. Recreation can play a significant role in efforts to make peace, as explained in the next section.

Making Peace Through Recreation

The genuine hope of most Israelis is that one day a true and lasting peace between Arabs and Jews will bring prosperity and security to all people in the region. During the summer of 2000, the Israelis and Palestinians were involved in intensive negotiations to reach a permanent peace agreement. The breakdown of these negotiations in September 2000 led to the spate of terrorist attacks that have plagued the country since that time. Despite all of these attacks, many Israelis are still working hard to improve relations and build bridges to peace with their Arab neighbors.

Making peace involves making compromises. Neither side can have everything that they want. In order to make compromises, there needs to be some trust and mutual understanding. If you hate and distrust the other party, you are less likely to be willing to make compromises. Research on the topic of Arab-Jewish relations (Gal, 1996) indicated that negative attitudes were prevalent among Arabs toward Jews and vice versa.

I conducted research in Israel from 1997 to 1999 designed to examine the effectiveness of an intergenerational recreational activities program on improving the attitudes of Jewish and Arab elders toward one another. Statistical analysis of the data indicates that the recreational program was effective in improving the attitudes of elderly Israeli Arabs and Jews toward one another (Leitner, Scher, and Shuval, 1999) and that the positive effects of the program on attitudes remained even one year later (Leitner and Scher, 2000). My personal experiences with those involved in the study are even more compelling in leading me to conclude that it is possible to improve relations between Arabs and Jews through recreational activities. Improving relations between Arabs and Jews makes peace more possible. In several programs in Israel Arabs and Jews are participating together in recreational activities. These programs will hopefully contribute toward improved relations, helping to bring peace closer and eventually defeat the extremist forces behind terrorism.

Religion and Leisure

Terrorism and making peace with its neighbors are not the only challenges facing Israel. Internal conflicts relating to the role of religion in society center around leisure-related issues. One of the main issues is the nature of the Sabbath and how much the leisure activities on Saturdays of the general population can be restricted by the religious establishment. First, some background is necessary to understand this conflict.

Israel, unlike the United States, does *not* have separation of church and state. Judaism is the state religion and it influences the government and life in general in Israel. For example, Friday afternoon and Saturday have been the traditional day and a half off from work and school in Israel, because the Jewish Sabbath is on Saturday. Similarly, the public holidays when schools and government institutions are closed are based on the Jewish holidays that occur throughout the year. Although most Israelis are Jewish (among the 20 percent of Israelis who are Arabs, most are Muslim and a minority are Christians), most of them are *not* ultra-Orthodox Jews. The ultra-Orthodox Jews take a strict interpretation of religious laws and want the government of Israel to apply these religious laws tightly. Consequently, conflicts arise that are related to how these laws affect the leisure and life of the general population. Some examples of these conflicts are listed as follows:

1. Suppose that your only day off from work is Saturday and you want to go to the beach, but you do not have a car and buses are not operating.
2. Again, suppose that Saturday is your only day off from work, and you want to go shopping, but all stores in your town are closed on Saturdays.
3. Similarly, suppose that most restaurants and other places of entertainment that you wish to visit on Saturday are closed.
4. Conversely, suppose that you are an ultra-Orthodox Jew and here you are, living in the only Jewish nation in the world, and the peacefulness of your day of rest is disturbed by traffic going through your neighborhood, making it unsafe for your children to play in the streets even on this day of the week.
5. Again, imagine being an Orthodox Jew, trying to maintain a traditional lifestyle and to some extent trying to shelter your children from what you see as some of the negative influences of the media and hedonism in general, and being confronted every day with posters of seminude women plastered on the bus stop shelters.

Obviously, Israel faces some difficult dilemmas with regard to religion's influence on leisure. Currently, most places of entertainment, such as movie theaters, are open on Saturdays, but stores in cities and towns are not. However, shopping areas located outside of municipalities are permitted to be open, as are stores in Arab towns and villages. Public buses in most cities do not operate on Saturdays, but taxis are generally available. Traffic has been blocked off from many Orthodox Jewish neighborhoods, enabling residents of these neighborhoods to walk the streets on Saturdays, unimpeded by traffic. To some extent, these compromises are working. However, some secular Israelis are upset that they face too many restrictions imposed on them by the religious establishment, and some Orthodox Jews are upset that the Sabbath is desecrated by the activities of the secular Jews.

One interesting development in this battle between the religious and secular Jews is the movement toward a two-day weekend. Of course, this development would have major implications for leisure in Israel. Some Israelis see the two-day weekend as an answer to many of the conflicts between religious and secular Jews. It would enable Israelis to enjoy one day off per week that was free of restrictions, theoretically enabling the Orthodox to more strictly enforce religious restrictions on the Sabbath. Certainly, the two-day weekend would increase leisure opportunities for Israelis, especially travel.

Modernization and Leisure

Modernization in Israel has influenced leisure and life of Israelis greatly. For example, car ownership has increased greatly since 1980, creating more opportunities for domestic travel and tourism. However, some of the other aspects of modernization might be having negative effects on leisure in Israel.

It seems that leisure in Israel has become more sedentary because of the proliferation of sedentary entertainment such as cable television and computers. In terms of computer and television ownership, Israel has become more similar to the United States. Cable television did not become established in Israel until the 1990s and has greatly increased viewing options. Based on personal observations in Israel since 1987, it seems that children in Israel are spending more time at home in front of their computers and televisions, and as a result, more children are overweight. Nevertheless, O'Sullivan (1997) reports that the number of Israelis doing physical exercise doubled from 1992 to 1997.

In terms of home computers and television, Israelis are catching up to Americans, but in terms of cellular phone usage, Israel has been far ahead of the United States for years. However, the proliferation of cellular phones is perhaps one of the most negative aspects of leisure in Israel. In restaurants and cafes, museums, at the beach, in movie theaters, at concerts, on buses—almost everywhere—cellular phones are ringing and people are talking loudly on their phones. Even on a hike in a beautiful national park, the use of cellular phones can be loud and obnoxious. As cellular phones become more popular in the United States, the interruption to leisure that they create is more closely resembling life and leisure in Israel.

Kibbutz Life and Leisure

Cellular phones are used throughout the world, but the *kibbutz* is unique to Israel. The kibbutz is a communal living arrangement in which residents work together in a particular industry (e.g., agriculture) and use all income generated by the industry for the welfare of the collective settlement. In a "traditional" kibbutz, most meals are eaten together, women work while their children are in day care, and residents use the recreational facilities of the kibbutz (which sometimes include a swimming pool, sports facilities, library, music room, etc.) during their free time.

From a leisure perspective, the most fascinating aspect of kibbutz life is the greater amount of free time kibbutz residents (kibbutzniks) have compared with typical urban dwellers. Although kibbutzniks work as many or more hours than their urban counterparts, they are free from the following obligations that usurp so much of an average person's time: food shopping; cooking; daytime child care responsibilities; dealing with personal finances; most home and yard maintenance chores; and commuting to work (residents usually work at the kibbutz). Imagine how much more time Americans would have for leisure activities if they were free from these obligatory chores. Presently, only a small percentage of Israelis live on a kibbutz. Gorenberg (2002) reports that a few kibbutzim are working hard to preserve the communal vision of kibbutz life, but many of the 270 kibbutzim in Israel are gradually moving toward privatization. Despite fewer communal meals being offered, different salaries to workers becoming more commonplace, and some kibbutz members commuting to jobs located outside the community, the kibbutz still offers a unique way of life that has some leisure-related advantages.

General Trends

Ruskin (1984) identifies factors that have shaped leisure in Israel and are still relevant in the twenty-first century.

1. The amount of free time has grown steadily because of longer vacations, retirement policies, and national holidays.
2. Judaism instills cultural values that support leisure, such as the Sabbath (one day of rest from work per week) and numerous traditional holidays.
3. It is important that leisure provide relaxation to counteract the tension and anxiety that exists because of the constant threats to national security.
4. Recreation for special populations is a concern, especially in light of the significant number of soldiers disabled in combat.
5. Because of economic pressures, many Israelis work at more than one job. Leisure is needed to restore energy.
6. As Israel's population grows and cities expand, leisure programs become more important in combating the stress of urban life. In addition, special attention must be devoted to preserving outdoor recreation areas.

Ruskin (2002) compared the results of survey research conducted in Israel in 1970, 1990, and 1998, and reports the following developments in leisure:

1. Free time increased due to a shortened workweek.
2. Time spent watching television increased.
3. Participation in the arts (movies, theaters, museums, and classical music) decreased.
4. Social gatherings, going out to pubs and restaurants, trips in Israel and abroad, active sports, listening to popular music, and watching videos increased.

5. Computer use increased (18 percent of the population surf the Internet). Over 50 percent of all homes have a computer.
6. Approximately 80 percent of the population visits shopping malls, not only to shop but also for entertainment.
7. Hedonistic values have increased, and people seem to be increasingly interested in more intimate ways to spend free time, as opposed to more collective ways.

The last point is partly mirrored in developments in Israeli folk dancing. The popularity of Israeli folk dancing is unique in the world. According to Siegel (1994), approximately 200,000 Israelis folk dance regularly, and new dances are being choreographed every day. It is an activity popular with people of all ages. During the week, thousands of Israeli children and adults dance in schools, country clubs, and community centers. On the weekends, large-scale folk dancing events involving hundreds of people occur in big halls and gymnasia, outside on beach promenades, and in the main square of towns and cities. In part, folk dancing's continued popularity defies the trend away from collective leisure activities, because it is a collective activity involving many people gathered to participate together in a shared experience. However, the trends in Israeli folk dancing, in which couple dancing and line dancing are becoming more popular and circle dancing less popular, do in fact reflect the societal trend toward seeking more intimate, individualistic leisure experiences.

The Israeli family orientation to leisure is strong. The emphasis on family is most obvious during religious holidays, which usually center on family celebrations. Every week on the Sabbath, families can be seen strolling about, day and night. Fortunately, Israelis do not have a crime problem like Americans do, and the streets in many neighborhoods are filled on warm summer nights with children playing.

Another American problem that has not yet hit Israel is teenage drug and alcohol use/abuse. Unlike the beer-drinking, semidelirious groups of teenagers seen hanging out on Saturday nights in many American cities, Israeli youth fill the streets on Saturday nights with a more wholesome excitement. Street musicians play as young Israelis enjoying ice cream, pizza, or *falafel* (the national snack) sit and talk in cafes or promenades closed to traffic. However, there is concern that the use of alcohol and other drugs is rising. For example, per capita consumption of alcohol among Israelis doubled since 1980, to two liters per year (Siegel, 1995), but this rate of consumption is still far less than it is in countries such as Germany (twelve liters/year) or Great Britain (seven liters/year).

A popular way for Israelis to spend their free time is in organized mass events such as marches and competitive and noncompetitive running and swimming events. Gonen (1985) states that marches involving 2,000 to 10,000 people are held almost every weekend. The marches are free, are open to people of all ages, are noncompetitive, and provide an excellent opportunity to socialize, exercise, and get some fresh air. The largest and most famous march is the annual Jerusalem march (see Photo 16.3). This march involves up to 15,000 people, including tourists and representatives of other countries.

According to Gonen (1985), foot races are held every other weekend, except during the winter. Swimming events are also popular, the most popular being the Sea of Galilee event (4 km) in which 10,000 people swim across at their own pace and ability.

PHOTO 16.3. The annual Jerusalem march is a joyous event, enjoyed by many thousands of people.

In many ways, America seems to influence leisure and recreation in Israel. For example, Rebibo (1987) describes a fourteen-team youth baseball league organized by an American immigrant. The league has been especially beneficial for Ethiopian immigrants. According to the founder of the league, baseball not only helps fill the free time in the afternoons at the immigrant absorption centers, it also helps build the Ethiopian children's confidence because they are on equal footing with most Israeli children who also have never been previously exposed to the game.

Another popular American sport used as a social development tool is tennis. Kedar (1983) explains that Israeli tennis centers try to give children of all socioeconomic and ethnic backgrounds an equal opportunity to enjoy a lifelong sport in an educational environment. The underlying aims of the tennis programs are to promote social integration of immigrants from different countries, build understanding among children of different ethnic and cultural backgrounds, and provide an outlet for constructive behavior. Many of the 100 all-weather courts are located in poor neighborhoods and have helped to diminish juvenile delinquency problems in these neighborhoods. As Kedar (1983, p. 18) states, "Give the child the best and he will do the utmost to cherish it."

Yet another example of American influence in Israel is the system of parks and nature reserves in Israel. Even though Israel is a small country (the size of New Jersey), dozens of parks and nature reserves are scattered throughout the country. Camping is a popular activity for Israelis.

Hamat Gader is one of Israel's most unique national parks. Hamat Gader offers an unusual conglomeration of attractions: ruins of ancient Roman hot springs; enormous, beautiful natural hot mineral pools; a crocodile farm; water slides; and a trampoline where children can unleash their surplus energy to the beat of rock and roll music (see Photo 16.4).

In summary, leisure in Israel reflects a strong American influence yet has a unique flavor of its own. Lessons can be learned from Israel in terms of how to deal with terrorism. On a lighter note, Americans should also not follow in the footsteps of Israelis and allow cellular phones to disrupt otherwise peaceful and relaxing leisure activities. This section concludes with an Israeli game.

PHOTO 16.4. A unique Israeli innovation: a trampoline in a national park.

Leg Relay (Israel)

Preparation: One volleyball needed per team. Each team should have an equal number of players (six to twelve is best). No limit on the number of teams that can play.

Starting position: Team members sit in a line, close together, side by side, on benches or armless chairs, legs extended.

Action: The ball is passed from one person's legs to the next, without using hands. If the ball hits the floor, start from the beginning again.

Objective: The first team to pass the ball to the end of the line and back to the front wins.

EGYPT

Although a neighbor of Israel, Egypt seems worlds apart. The poverty and poor condition of many buildings set it apart from its modern neighbor. However, it is the people that make Egypt so different from Israel and just about every other nation that the authors have visited.

Egyptians, from our experiences, are a sensitive, caring people. Being in Egypt makes a Westerner realize how obsessed modern individuals have become with material possessions, at the expense of human relationships. Egyptians seem to be more sensitive to the moods and feelings of total strangers than many Americans are with friends and acquaintances. Egyptians can be understood better by examining the history of the country and its people.

Having large blocks of leisure time has been an accepted way of life in Egypt for hundreds of years. The agricultural people who lived along the fertile Nile Delta were unable to control the flooding of the Nile. The presence or absence of flooding determined whether the people had land to farm (which was their primary form of work). Thus, unemployment was a frequent occurrence and beyond the control of the people. This situation led to a passive attitude and an acceptance of large blocks of free time. A related outgrowth of this situation was the development of a greater orientation to people than to material goods. It will be interesting to see how these attitudes change now that Egyptians do have control over the flooding of the Nile since the Aswan High Dam was built (Fedden, 1977).

The leisurely attitude of Egyptians is apparent in the city as well as the country. Even at the airport, a place where most Westerners would expect to find tense workers, an arriving tourist finds the workers constantly stopping to talk to one another and share funny comments. However, Egyptians' leisurely orientation to life is most obvious in the countryside. Interpersonal interaction seems to take precedence over production. As illustrated in Photo 16.5 of the *felucca* (sailboat) operators, there is a strong element of leisure incorporated into most work.

Despite the seemingly stable, leisurely attitude of Egyptians, urbanization has brought changes to Egyptian life. One change is an increase in sports facilities, partly related to the growth of schools. The growth in sports participation is facilitated by government financial support (Ibrahim and Asker, 1984). According to Ibrahim and Asker, the most popular sport is soccer, followed by basketball and volleyball. Over a quarter of a million Egyptians are members of clubs or youth and community centers (Ibrahim and Asker, 1984).

PHOTO 16.5. These felucca operators manage to take many leisurely breaks during their typical workday.

Nevertheless, the leisure behavior of contemporary Egyptians is largely sedentary in nature. In a survey of 216 female and 162 male residents of Cairo and Giza (Ibrahim and Asker, 1984), the five most common leisure activities were (in order) watching television, visiting, talking, listening to the radio, and reading.

One reason for the low rate of participation in sports and other physically active recreational activities is the lack of facilities. According to H. M. Ibrahim (personal communication, 1988), even private sports clubs are overcrowded. In Ibrahim's view, overpopulation is the major problem confronting recreational services in Egypt. Related to the overpopulation problem is a shortage of open space for recreation and overcrowding of existing facilities. The need for more classrooms for children has even caused some existing recreational facilities at schools to be replaced by additional classrooms.

In summary, although Egyptians have a great deal of free time because of underemployment, their recreational opportunities are greatly limited by poverty, lack of facilities, and overcrowding. However, the positive side to these unfortunate circumstances is that it forces the Egyptians to spend more time together with their families and socializing with friends, which ironically are two highly desired activities for which many Americans claim to not have adequate time.

The following is an active Egyptian game.

Egyptian Stick Game (Egypt)

Preparation: One stick needed for each person (four- to five-feet high).

Starting position: Circle, each person seven to nine feet apart from his or her neighbors. Players hold their sticks upright, touching the ground directly in front of them.

Action: When leader says "change," players leave their sticks upright and race to the next stick on the right, trying to catch it before it hits the ground. If the stick hits the ground, the player is eliminated.

Objective: To be the last person left in the circle.

SAUDI ARABIA

In contrast to Egypt, Hunnicutt (1985) describes Saudi Arabia as a country experiencing a recreational metamorphosis. Petrodollars fueled massive construction of recreational facilities. Hunnicutt disagrees with those who say that the massive construction is a haphazard show of wealth. Rather, it is a well-planned program stemming from genuine concern for the people's welfare, a traditional interest in sports, internal social forces, and external cultural pressure from Western nations.

According to Hunnicutt, the Saudis seem to be concerned with developing almost every aspect of recreation in their country: sports facilities for competitive athletics as well as for public recreation; recruitment of coaches to train competitive athletes as well as recreation professionals who can help meet the leisure needs of the people; and the provision of outdoor recreation opportunities, such as camping. Today, Saudis in RVs visit a countryside not long ago inhabited by nomadic tribes.

Despite the rapid changes in the country in recent years, religious influence is still strong. Insight into Islamic customs and how they affect leisure and life in general is discussed in depth in Ibrahim's (1982) article on leisure and Islam. The Islamic people seem to have a more relaxed attitude toward life and leisure than do people in Western society. Ibrahim attributes this difference to the contrasts in Islamic versus Judeo-Christian theology. He compares the Islamic Sabbath to the Judeo-Christian Sabbath as an example of the Islamic religion's more relaxed attitude about life and leisure. According to Ibrahim, the only obligation on the Muslim Sabbath is a community noon prayer at the mosque, which lasts about an hour. The rest of the day is spent however one wishes. The Sabbath day (Friday) gets off to an early start on Thursday evenings, when coffeehouses are usually filled with customers (Ibrahim, 1982).

Ibrahim also points out that Islam never sanctified time or frowned on leisure activities, unlike other religions. He states that the only constraints on recreation have been the segregation of the sexes and the loss of open space since the 1930s. These two constraints are quite apparent in Kashmir, which is a predominantly Muslim state.

INDIA

Kashmir

Although it is officially a state in India, Kashmir is vastly different from the rest of India, which is why it is being discussed in a separate section. Similar to Saudi Arabia, Kashmir is primarily Muslim, whereas the rest of India is predominantly Hindu. The authors had the opportunity to spend a great deal of time with Kashmiri families during a visit to this beautiful state and were able to gain insight into Islamic customs, family life, and leisure.

The most striking difference between Kashmiri life and Western culture is the leisure and life of women. Kashmiri women have only a fraction of the freedoms Western women take for granted. According to the Kashmiri men the authors spoke with, women must ask their husbands for permission even to go to the grocery store. In other words, women have virtually no freedom to pursue leisure activities of their choosing, and therefore female participation in sports, music, and the arts is meager. However, there would be little time to pursue these activities even if the women had greater freedom. Because of the responsibilities of caring for a home and raising a large family, Kashmiri women have very little free time.

Meanwhile, Kashmiri men have more free time than women and total freedom to do what they wish. Favorite sports are soccer and cricket. Music, reading, and art are not as popular as they are in Western societies. Sitting and relaxing, conversing with friends, and drinking are how most free time is spent. Some men are able to take pleasure trips, though often without their families. The authors were told by several Kashmiris that men who are in the tourist industry (Kashmir is a favorite tourist spot because of its beautiful lakes, houseboat accommodations, and hiking opportunities) sometimes travel alone to foreign countries to visit tourists they met in Kashmir. When the Kashmiri men take these pleasure trips, they leave their wives behind to care for the children and their home. Fortunately, the situation for women is not the same in the other areas of India.

India Overview

It is difficult to describe India in general, because each state is so different. However, some general characteristics apply to most areas. One is the disparity in leisure opportunities among socioeconomic classes. Rough estimates are that 10 percent of the population would be classified as wealthy, 30 percent to 40 percent as middle class, and 50 percent to 60 percent as lower class. These terms are deceiving, because many middle-class Indians live by what Americans would perceive as lower-class standards. The term lower class is not really strong enough to describe the poverty in which so many Indian people live.

According to Gulshetty (1991), the majority of people in India live in villages, where poverty, unemployment, and illiteracy are rampant. In his study of families on small farms in a rural Indian village, most of the interviewees were initially baffled when asked about their use of leisure time, for the terms free time and leisure were so foreign to them. Gulshetty explains that with living conditions being as miserable as they are, the farmers in a village keep busy with work-related activities even after the workday is over. However, time is occasionally found for traditional recreational activities such as folk songs, dancing, storytelling, participating in drama, cockfighting, and bull races. Singh, Gupta, and Aggarwal (1994) examined the leisure activities of older adults in two rural Indian villages in the Punjab State, and found that the most frequently participated in pastimes are playing cards, discussion and talking, tending animals, walking, gossiping, reading newspapers, and watching television.

The wealthy class lives a different life than the rest of the population. Even though the wealthy class is a small minority (approximately 10 percent), they number tens of millions of people (India's total population is approximately 800 million). They enjoy abundant leisure opportunities such as tennis, golf, polo, cricket, swimming, music, art, and travel. The middle class, though not able to pursue as many activities because of monetary and time constraints, for the most part do have televisions, go to the movies, and own sound equipment and listen to music. According to Sharma (1991), popular activities of middle-class residents of the city of Guwahati (state capital of Assam) are reading books, magazines, and newspapers; discussions; writing; television; radio; movies; theater; gossiping; playing games; social visits; attending clubs and social gatherings; and visiting friends. In this study, there were major differences among various occupations in the priority given to different types of leisure activities. For example, intellectual activities were of highest priority to teachers (81.2 percent) and lawyers (73.3 percent) but were only of highest priority to 20 percent of shop owners. Meanwhile, only 6.3 percent of teachers and 6.7 percent of lawyers gave highest priority to audio-visual leisure activities, whereas 65 percent of shop owners rated it highest.

Singh (1994) states that the introduction of satellite television in India has affected leisure behavior patterns of Indian urban middle-class youth. It has reduced the frequency of radio listening and cinema going. However, it has not had an impact on VCR watching or on reading newspapers.

Gulshetty (1994) offers some insight into the caste system and its influence on leisure in rural India. Shukla (Gulshetty, 1994, p. 11) states that "Caste is hereditary and fixes one's position and status in the community. It serves as an agency of transmitting culture and skills to each of its group to which are also tied separate occupation." Gulshetty (1994) compared the leisure activities of households in the following castes: Hindu; Muslim; "Scheduled caste"; and "Backward caste." Gossiping with friends and relatives was the most popular leisure activity of all castes. The Hindu caste participated in listening to the radio and watching television (25 percent) and reading and writing (10 percent) more than any of the other castes did, and the Muslims participated more in celebrating social festivals and rituals (27 percent) more than any other caste.

Many Indian workers, especially shopkeepers, have a tremendous amount of leisure interwoven with work. Shopkeepers can be idle for much of the day. Much of a "work" day can actually be spent taking naps, relaxing, and talking with friends and neighbors. According to Professor Tej Vir Singh (personal communication, 1987), one reason leisure is not a major field of study in India is that Indians are indifferent to leisure because so many are idle and without work and thus unable to enjoy leisure.

At the other extreme are laborers who literally slave away all day for small wages. The fifteen-year-old *rickshaw* (bicycle taxi) operator in Photo 16.6 claims to work from five a.m. to eleven p.m. every day. He says that he never takes a day off and never has time to play. Although there are many lapses in his work during the day, he has virtually no leisure by Western standards. The life of this teenager seems pathetic when compared with the wealth of leisure activities a typical American fifteen-year-old enjoys. But, which teenager is happier? The young rickshaw operator seemed to be very happy to have customers to pedal around, even though the work is exhausting. He also seemed to enjoy his work breaks, chatting and laughing with other rickshaw operators. It is probably incomprehensible to this teenager how so many middle-class American teens with so much going for them could be suffering from psychological problems or substance abuse.

PHOTO 16.6. For some Indians, free time is virtually nonexistent, although a great deal of leisure is fused into the workday.

Another general characteristic of life in India is crowded living conditions. There is little space for outdoor recreation areas or sports facilities within cities. Nevertheless, children who are not working or begging are able to use their ingenuity to design soccer or cricket playing fields on narrow streets or to invent their own games and toys from rocks, empty containers, and other seemingly useless materials. This ingenuity is also characteristic of Nepalese children.

NEPAL

Nepal, similar to India, is primarily Hindu.* It shares a border with India and is a favorite spot for tourists wishing to see breathtaking views of the Himalayas. Photos 16.7 and 16.8 illustrate the ingenuity of the Nepalese children at play.

PHOTO 16.7. Nepalese children, lacking toys, busy themselves with games they create with stones and dirt.

---

*Special thanks for contributions to this section from Erin Angel, MA, a health and safety specialist with the American Red Cross of Boulder/Broomfield, Colorado. Erin lived in Nepal in the spring of 2001, helping to train people in Tibetan refugee camps in first aid/CPR.

PHOTO 16.8. Nepalese teenagers play a game called careboard, similar to billiards, but much less elaborate.

According to Hari Pokhrel (personal communication, 1987), although Nepalese villagers work hard and have few modern comforts, they are basically happy. Pokhrel grew up in a small village but lived in the city for many years, working in the tourist industry since 1972. Because he has traveled extensively in his work as a travel agent, Pokhrel is well aware of Nepal's relatively small variety of recreational opportunities. However, the Nepalese seem content to spend much of their free time chatting with friends. As illustrated in Photo 16.9, much of this socializing is done in a squatting position on city streets.

Changes are taking place in Nepal. The growth in the population of middle-class urban dwellers has led to Western-style developments such as radio, television, and health clubs (Photo 16.10). Television and radio have also become more popular in rural areas, with most villages having at least one radio. Every village has a teahouse where adults gather in an indoor/outdoor porch area and chat for hours. Men and women seem to go there at different times. In general, Nepali women recreate separately from men, especially in the case of swim-

PHOTO 16.9. Squatting and socializing is a common sight on streets and public squares in Nepal.

PHOTO 16.10. The fitness craze has even reached Nepal.

ming. In Pokhara, the pool has one day per week designated for women and small children only. However, most children are very poor and do not even have access to donated equipment, so they play made-up games that use little equipment (Angel, personal communication, 2003).

In summary, although changes are taking place in Nepal, leisure and life there are very different from that in the United States.

THAILAND

Recreation in Thailand is as rich and colorful as its friendly people, beautiful landscape, exotic foods, and magnificent Buddhist monasteries. Similar to other developing nations, it is a fascinating mixture of old and new, traditional and modern.

According to *Thailand in Brief* (Tourism Authority of Thailand, n.d.), the following international sports are popular among the Thai people: golf, soccer, badminton, tennis, bowling, basketball, and snooker (billiards). Day and night, Thai youth can be seen in the streets or in courtyards practicing badminton or soccer. Unlike the more sedentary nature of leisure in other developing nations, avid sports enthusiasm is evident. Swimming also seems to be a popular activity. Even in Bangkok, where the main river is as congested with boat traffic as Los Angeles freeways are with cars, youth frequently jump off the boat docks for a quick swim.

The Thais also have their own version of some international sports. For example, Thai boxing is very popular. In Thai boxing, the contestants can kick, shove, push, and use their bare feet, legs, elbows, and shoulders as well as their fists to batter their opponent.

Another unique Thai version of an international sport is Thai chess. According to Rice (1987), almost all Thais play chess; it is not only for the intellectual elite. Rice describes the great passion Thais have for chess. Huge crowds hover over street games, and the spectators as well as the players make noise to distract their opponent. Large sums of money are sometimes wagered.

The Thais also play a game similar to Hackey Sack, called *takrao*. In takrao, players in a loosely formed circle use all body parts (except hands) to pass a woven rattan ball to one another, trying to prevent it from hitting the ground. Eventually, the players try to kick the ball into a basket suspended above their heads (Tourism Authority of

Thailand, n.d.). In another version of this game, players try to kick the ball over a 5'2"-high net, similar to volleyball (Swift, 1988).

Yet another fascinating Thai activity is kite flying. In the summer months, it is a competitive activity in which one team flies male kites that try to ensnarl the opposing team's female kites and drag them into male territory. Meanwhile, the female kites try to bring down the male kites. This activity has its roots in the thirteenth century, when kites were used by the Thais in warfare (Tourism Authority of Thailand, n.d.).

Probably the most fascinating recreational activities to observe in Thailand are the games and spontaneous play of children. As depicted in Photo 16.11, children have a great time with their homemade toys. The hill tribe children, though poor, seem to be content without expensive toys.

In Thailand, all people play, including elders. There seems to be an awareness of the physical and psychological benefits of recreational activity. Photo 16.12 of senior citizens playing a bowling game similar to boule was taken at an athletic field/fitness facility that is part of a hospital/medical school complex in Chiang Mai, Thailand's second largest city.

PHOTO 16.11. Thai hill tribe children, busy at play with small plastic figures.

PHOTO 16.12. Thai elders playing boule, trying to protect themselves from the hot sun.

Eating does not seem to be the time-consuming, relaxing activity for Thais that it is for so many Europeans and Americans. Food is very abundant, with almost anything imaginable being prepared and sold from street stalls. Walking through the streets, it seems as though everyone is eating in a somewhat hurried fashion. The Thais appear to view food more as a necessity than a major recreational activity.

Art, music, and dance are also popular activities in Thailand. Much of the artwork is geared toward commercial products such as silk fans, parasols, and lacquerware. The Thais listen to Western music, locally produced Western-style music, as well as traditional Thai music.

In summary, the Thais enjoy a diversity of recreational activities more similar to the variety Westerners enjoy than to the limited activities of other developing nations. Perhaps the leisure activities of the Thai people contribute to their exceptionally friendly and happy demeanor.

JAPAN

In contrast to Thailand, Japan is a completely modern, Westernized country. The Japanese know all too well about the problems of urban congestion, but they have some interesting innovations to meet the challenge of providing recreational activities for people living in congested areas.

One aspect of recreational services in which the Japanese have been progressive is the provision of sports and recreation opportunities within industries. Guidelines and legislation for industrial recreation in Japan date back to 1951. According to Ebashi (1983), most large companies provide sports and recreation facilities for their workers. For example, the Matsushita Electric Company has forty-seven sports fields, seventy-five volleyball courts, nine swimming pools, twenty-one training rooms, forty-five clubhouses, sixty-eight tennis courts, twenty-two basketball courts, 189 Ping-Pong tables, and four gymnasiums for its 69,000 employees. Other companies also offer extensive recreational facilities and programs, the intent being to improve employees' quality of life, enhance employee fitness and health, foster the development of friendships among workers, and boost morale (Ebashi, 1983). Given the impressive productivity of Japanese industry, it seems that American companies might benefit from devoting greater attention to the provision of recreational facilities and programs for their employees.

It is interesting to note that the impressive productivity of Japanese industry is not necessarily due to long working hours. According to Kinsley (1990), Japanese workers are entitled to an average of sixteen days of paid vacation (compared to five to ten days for many American workers) and another twenty days off per year that are labeled holidays, of which eleven are national celebrations, the rest being vacation days grouped at summer's and the year's end.

Japanese men still seem to be clinging to a strong work ethic, and Japan's Economic Planning Agency is trying to convince workers to take their vacations and work fewer hours (Freeman, 1993). Attitudes seem to be changing among younger workers, but nevertheless, there is pressure to work long hours.

In a totally different realm, there has been a *Sonso boomu* in Japan, that is, a rapid growth in oxygen bars. For less than a dollar, a customer can inhale flavored oxygen for three minutes. The customer can choose from coffee, mint, lemon, and mushroom. Business in oxygen inhalation grew almost fivefold from 1986 to 1987. Oxygen inhalation originally began as a refresher in clubs following physical exertion, but it is now widely used as an energizing, effortless substitute for exercise. Especially in crowded and polluted cities, it is the easiest way to get a breath of fresh air (Boyer, 1987).

According to Nishino and Takahashi (1988), congestion and pollution create problems in providing outdoor recreation opportunities. Because of rising land costs, it is difficult to acquire land for recreational purposes. Also, the careless behavior of citizens has been harming outdoor recreation areas. Consequently, the Japanese are now moving some of their sports indoors (Anonymous, 1993). Incredible as it may sound, the Japanese have built successful (heavily used) indoor facilities for surfing and snow skiing. These facilities are popular because they enable participants to avoid the risks of running into bad weather, sickness from polluted waters, and cancer from ultraviolet radiation of the sun. Ideas for new indoor sports to develop include mountaineering, scuba diving, and even "body flying."

Another concern expressed by Nishino and Takahashi is that leisure education is needed to help the Japanese people deal with the increased free time brought about by a shorter workweek and increased life expectancy. The Japanese have the longest life expectancy in the world, and their workweek was shortened from six days to five days. Wysocki (1986) states that the Japanese do not have a strong sense of the importance of leisure and have difficulty taking leisure time. Therefore, leisure education seems to be essential if the Japanese are to deal successfully with increased free time.

Another leisure-related problem that leisure education could help to alleviate is surging alcohol consumption, particularly among youth. Fears of rampant alcoholism and underage drinking (the legal drinking age is 20) have led to a ban on using vending machines to sell beer (Coleman, 2000). It has become common to see intoxicated people on nighttime streets and in subways, and it is hoped that the effort to ban beer vending machines will help to reduce the problems of underage drinking and alcoholism (Coleman, 2000). Perhaps removing beer from vending machines will help, but as discussed in Chapters 2 and 11, leisure education is really the best way to help people discover alternative, healthier leisure activities that can meet the needs people seek to meet through alcohol consumption.

The following Japanese games are fun and easy to play.

Ichi-Ni-San (One-Two-Three) (Japan)

Preparation: Each player needs a partner. Draw a line between the partners. Partners cannot cross the line.

Starting position: Partners stand back to back, bending forward, hands on knees, rear ends touching.

Action: Partners bump each other with their rear ends.

Objective: Players who get their partner off balance are winners.

Furoshiki Mawaski (Scarf Passing Game) (Japan)

Preparation: One scarf for every three players. Fast-tempo music is desirable.

Starting position: Stand in a circle.

Action: Players with a scarf tie it around their neck, nod their head twice, clap hands twice, untie the scarf, and pass it to the next player on the right.

Objective: To avoid being caught with two scarves at once and to try to make someone else have two at once. Players caught with two scarves at once are eliminated. The last two players left are the winners.

HONG KONG

Hong Kong, like Japan, is ultramodern and densely populated. Also similar to Japan, Hong Kong's recreational services and facilities are progressive and extensive. In the previous edition of this book, this section of the chapter posed the question of what would happen to Hong Kong after the People's Republic of China (PRC) took control in 1997. Actually, as discussed in the section on the PRC, it is the PRC, not Hong Kong, that has changed drastically.

According to Dicken Yung (personal communication, 1988), the director of the Hong Kong Government Recreation and Culture Department and president of the Hong Kong Special Olympics Committee, the government policy maintains that mass participation in recreation and sports is more important than training athletes for competition. The government's emphasis on activities for all people includes the disabled and the elderly, as illustrated in Photos 16.13 and 16.14.

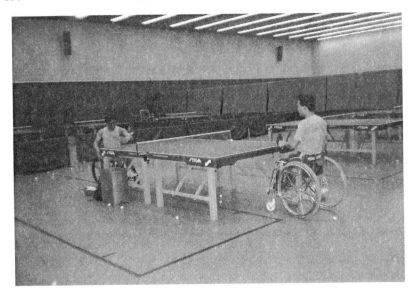

PHOTO 16.13. One example of recreation for special populations in Hong Kong.

PHOTO 16.14. Tai chi is a form of exercise enjoyed by many elders early in the morning.

The government's policy of encouraging mass participation in sports and recreation has paid dividends. Participation in activities increased from 47,248 in 1974-1975 to 773,763 in 1983-1984. There are approximately fifty sports organizations, one for each different sport. The government provides funding to these organizations, which coordinate the sports programs (Yung, personal communication, 1988). One organization, called TREATS, integrates children and youth with and without disabilities through recreation and play. In 1996, they provided over 100 different programs that integrated nearly 13,000 children and young people from over 200 groups, including sixteen day camps and eighteen overnight camps (Anonymous, 1997).

The government has built excellent facilities to enable greater participation in sports. An example of one of these facilities is shown in Photo 16.15. It is remarkable that the government has been able to set aside land for recreational use, given the high population density and astronomical land values in Hong Kong.

In addition to the excellent low-cost facilities and programs provided by the government, Hong Kong boasts some fabulous commercial recreation attractions. Ocean Park is a huge, sprawling area of

PHOTO 16.15. A beautiful new athletic field, set amid Hong Kong's skyscrapers.

land on Hong Kong Island's southern coast. The park has one of the world's largest aquariums, outdoor theaters for aquatic and animal shows, gardens, an aviary, and thrill rides.

In many ways, the leisure behavior patterns of Hong Kong residents are similar to those of Americans. Sivan (2000) conducted research on adolescent leisure in Hong Kong and found that similar to American teenagers, Hong Kong adolescents are increasing their use of electronic media and telecommunication technology. However, Hong Kong adolescents seem to be different from American teenagers in terms of the significant role of family in leisure companionship and the popularity of some instrumental and intellectual activities such as specific hobbies and going to public libraries (Sivan, 2000).

In summary, leisure in Hong Kong is in many ways similar to leisure in the United States. As discussed in the next section, leisure and life in the PRC has been modernized greatly and now more closely resembles Hong Kong and the United States.

PEOPLE'S REPUBLIC OF CHINA (PRC)

In the previous edition, this section ended with the sentence, "It will be interesting to see just how Westernized the PRC will become in the future." Seeing is believing! It was absolutely amazing to see and experience the extensive modernization of the PRC in April 2001, having not been in that country since 1987. The progress is evident both in the government-run facilities and in the new leisure opportunities available as an outgrowth of experimentation with capitalism.

The most striking difference in the PRC in 2001 as compared to 1987 is the explosion of wealth in the major cities. Walking through the streets of Beijing and Shanghai, it is obvious that many people are wearing nice, new, fashionable clothes, as opposed to the drab navy blue uniforms/outfits that were so common in 1987. Whereas in 1987 many Chinese people could only gawk at the store windows of the tourist department stores, today it seems that most people are walking around carrying shopping bags with items that few Chinese people could afford to purchase in 1987. Another difference is many more cars in the streets, although many people still get around by bicycle.

Based on simply observing people walk by on the streets, it seems that the Chinese are happier than they were in 1987. Now the people are able to enjoy the luxuries that they used to only be able to observe tourists enjoy or see on television shows or in movies from the United States.

On the surface, it seems that leisure in the PRC has been greatly Americanized. On most major streets of Beijing and Shanghai are an abundance of American fast-food restaurants, patronized by local people. The buildings are as modern and impressive as those found in any American city. However, despite all of this modernization and change, differences in leisure between the United States and the PRC exist.

According to Freysinger and Chen (1993), a major difference in the leisure activities and motivations for leisure of the Chinese as compared to Westerners is that the most important or favorite leisure activities of the Chinese are likely to be pursued alone or with friends, whereas in Western cultures, family leisure is frequently reported as being most highly valued. Freysinger and Chen's explanation is that in the Western world, family is seen as a haven from the larger world, whereas in Chinese society the family *is* the social system. Obedience and respect are the basis of family relationships; many parents do not play or joke around with children after the age of seven. Consequently, the Chinese would feel a greater sense of freedom in leisure activities pursued alone or with friends. In Freysinger and Chen's study of 100 adults in the Guangxi Province, the most important leisure activities identified were watching television; hobbies; exercise, sports, and other physical activities; reading; and socializing with friends.

Another difference between the PRC and the United States are the extensive leisure activities of elders. Municipal parks in major cities are filled most mornings with groups of older adults participating in a variety of exercise activities ranging from tai chi to ballroom dancing to badminton to exercising with swords. In addition, many elders attend classes at "Universities for the Long-Living," or through other programs sponsored by the government. It seems that more recreational and educational services are provided for elders in the PRC than in the United States, and the activity level of elders in the PRC is greater.

One similarity between the PRC in 1987 and 2001 is the congestion and pollution that plague the major cities. At many of the main tourist sites, it was difficult to walk around due to the hordes of people at the sites. Also, the foul-smelling air caused by pollution was at times sickening. In the winter in Beijing, the air is said to be even worse due to the smoke from all of the coal-burning heaters.

In summary, the PRC has modernized greatly since our first visit in 1987. One of the significant challenges it faces is how to deal with the pollution and overcrowding that can have serious negative consequences for leisure.

RUSSIA AND THE FORMER SOVIET UNION

To say that Russia and the rest of the former Soviet Union have undergone great changes is an understatement. Much of the literature on Soviet–American differences no longer applies, now that Russia and its neighboring countries formerly in the Soviet Union have abandoned communism. However, one interesting aspect of leisure and work in the Soviet Union was the use of short exercise periods prior to and during work hours at many factories in order to increase productivity and alleviate worker fatigue (Serguiff, 1976). Many industrial factories and cooperative farms had facilities for workers to play volleyball. The Soviet five-minute exercise break seems to be an idea worth trying in the American workplace.

One of the major changes in post-Soviet Russia is the influx of Western culture and proliferation of social indulgences. According to Burkard and Viviano (1994), prostitutes, black market luxury items, trash rock and roll, and violent crime have invaded the Russian society, which was once based on collective sacrifice and frugality. Pope (1992) writes that many Russians are horrified by the growing acceptance of Western popular culture and the eroding financial support for traditional Russian high culture.

Russia and the former members of the Soviet Union are in a period of transition. It will be interesting to see if the leisure activities of these nations continue to become more similar to those of Americans and Europeans, or if the backlash against Western cultures is strong enough to reverse this trend.

AUSTRALIA AND NEW ZEALAND

Different from the former Soviet Union and similar to the United States, Australia and New Zealand share many common leisure characteristics. Both countries have abundant outdoor recreation resources and high participation in sports such as rugby, cricket, and soccer. Both countries seem to have a stronger leisure ethic than the United States. Although the combined population of the two countries is much smaller than that of the United States, there seem to be many more world travelers from Australia and New Zealand than from the United States. One reason is the more liberal extended vacation policy prevalent in these countries. The authors met many Australians and New Zealanders in the course of their world travels who had been granted six months or a year off by their employers. Not many Americans would have a job to return home to after being away for a year.

Another reason for the large number of Australians and New Zealanders traveling for extended periods of time seems to be their stronger leisure ethic. In conversation with Americans about their usual two-week vacations, a common attitude expressed by Americans was "I couldn't imagine not working for six months!" On the other hand, Australians and New Zealanders seem to be comfortable with the idea of not working for a year or more, even if they do not have a job waiting for them when they return home.

Reflective of the strong leisure ethic in Australia and New Zealand is the large number of leisure studies programs in their colleges and universities. Furthermore, both governments promote recreation and sports participation, an example being New Zealand's "Come Alive" program (Stothart, 1984).

Overall, Australia and New Zealand share common concerns with the United States, as evidenced by Cushman's (1986) identification of major factors influencing recreation in Australia:

1. Smaller family size, more single-parent families, and dual-career households
2. Growth in the older population
3. Growth in profit-seeking leisure industries
4. Conservation groups fighting to preserve natural areas of beauty
5. Increased demand for recreation close to home or in the home

Clearly, these factors are applicable to America as well. Because of the great similarities the United States, Australia, and New Zealand share, it is especially beneficial for recreation professionals and academicians to share ideas on how to solve common leisure-related problems. In addition, much can be learned through travel to these countries. For example, in terms of conserving natural resources, much can be learned from Australia, which has become a world leader in ecotourism. Dowling (2000) defines ecotourism as a form of environmental tourism conducted in natural areas that incorporates ecologically sustainable activities, conservation supporting measures at the local level, active interpretation and/or education about the local region, and involvement of the local community. Ecotourism accounts for perhaps as much as 25 percent of all leisure travel.

To close this section, a fun game from New Zealand is presented.

Folding Arms (New Zealand)

Preparation: One large, soft ball is needed; eight to twenty participants work best.

Starting position: All players stand in a line, several feet apart, with arms folded. Leader faces the line.

Action: Leader either throws ball at a particular player or fakes throwing the ball. Players try to catch the ball or not be faked into unfolding their arms.

Objective: To remain in the game, players need to catch any balls thrown at them and not unfold their arms if a ball is not actually thrown at them. The last person left in the line is the winner and becomes the new leader.

SUMMARY

The world has become a smaller place as a result of improved communication systems and increased international tourism. Knowing more about leisure in other countries fosters a better understanding of leisure possibilities, as well as a greater appreciation for other cultures. Information that can facilitate leisure enhancement in the United States can be gleaned from an examination of leisure in other countries, including undeveloped nations. Much can be learned from reading this chapter, but it is no substitute for the ultimate learning experience—*travel*. As opposed to tourism, which might involve going to another country and simply staying at a beautiful resort and doing a little bit of sightseeing or shopping in tourist areas, travel involves becoming integrated into the local culture, staying and eating at locally operated establishments, and interacting with the local people. It is a better learning experience than staying at a fancy resort and can ultimately be more enjoyable, too. Talk to others first and plan your trip carefully. Have fun!

REFERENCES

Anonymous (1993). Surfing indoors. *The Economist,* December 15, p. 86.

Anonymous (1997). More fun for more children. *TREATS News,* July, p. 1.

Bauman, W., Marchlowitz, K.H., and Palm, J. (1985). Spielfest—Germany's games festivals: Where recreation and sport compose a new type of social event. *WLRA Journal,* 27(5), 8-11.

Boyer, J. (1987). A dose of flavored oxygen for exhausted customers. *The Rising Nepal,* December 3, p. 4.

Burkard, H.J. and Viviano, F. (1994). Mother Russia: In 1994, every hedonistic fantasy and natural resource is for sale. *Mother Jones,* 19(3), 48-55.

Carey, S. (1986). Joie de leisure. *Wall Street Journal,* April 21, pp. 9D, 14D.

Coleman, J. (2000). Beer gets a little scarcer in Japan. *The International Herald Tribune,* June 3-4, p. 16.

Cook, G. (2000). Happy hunting. *The Boston Globe,* October 11, pp. A1, A6.

Cushman, G. (1986). Trends and issues in leisure and recreation: An Australian perspective. *WLRA Journal,* 28(1), 26-31.

Dimanche, F. (1995). Factors impacting leisure in middle-aged adults throughout the world: France. *World Leisure and Recreation,* 37(1), 32-33.

Dowling, R.K. (2000). Global ecotourism at the start of the new millennium. *World Leisure,* 42(2), 11-19.

Ebashi, S. (1983). Japan: Sports and recreation within industries. *WLRA Journal,* 25(6), 4-8.

Fedden, R. (1977). *Egypt: Land of the valley.* Southampton, Great Britain: Camelot Press.

Freeman, A. (1993). The harried quest for a leisure class: Can the Japanese learn to enjoy life? *World Press Review,* 40(9), 11-14.

Freysinger, J. and Chen, T. (1993). Leisure and family in China: The impact of culture. *World Leisure and Recreation,* 35, 22-24.

Gal, R. (1996). *Summary of 1994 attitudinal research.* Zichron Yaacov, Israel: The Carmel Institute.

Godbey, G. (1981). *Leisure in your life: An exploration.* Philadelphia: Saunders.

Gonen, I. (1985). Popular mass events in Israel. *WLRA Journal,* 27(5), 23-25.

Gorenberg, G. (2002). Requiem for a dream? *The Jerusalem Report,* August 12, pp. 18-21.

Gregersen, U.B. (1986). Development work with senior citizens in Denmark. *WLRA Journal,* 28(2), 22-25.

Gulshetty, B. (1991). Leisure and small farmers in rural India. *World Leisure and Recreation,* 33(4), 7-8.

Gulshetty, B.S. (1994). Castes and leisure in rural India. *World Leisure and Recreation,* 36(3), 11-13.

Gunnell, B. (2000). Pleasure is such hard work. *New Statesman,* 129(4516), December 11, pp. 11-12.

Hantrais, L. (1987). Time, the family, and leisure in France and Britain: A report on an international research seminar. *WLRA Journal,* 29(2), 16-22.

Hantrais, L., Clark, P.A., and Samuel, N. (1984). Time–space dimensions of work, family, and leisure in France and Great Britain. *Leisure Studies,* 3, 301-317.

Hunnicutt, B. (1985). Recreation among the oil wells: Saudi Arabia develops its leisure services. *Parks and Recreation,* July, 50-55.

Ibrahim, H.M. (1982). Leisure and Islam. *Leisure Studies,* 1, 197-210.

Ibrahim, H.M. and Asker, N.F. (1984). Ideology, politics, and sport in Egypt. *Leisure Studies,* 3(1), 97-106.

Jernigan, S.S. and Vendien, C.L. (1972). *Playtime: A world recreation handbook.* New York: McGraw-Hill.

Kedar, R. (1983). Tennis booms in Israel communities. *WLRA Journal,* 25(5), 18-19.

Kinsley, M. (1990). You must be very busy. *Time,* August 20, p. 82.

Leitner, M.J. and Scher, G. (2000). A follow-up study to peacemaking through recreation: The positive effects of intergenerational activities on the attitudes of Israeli Arabs and Jews. *World Leisure and Recreation,* 42(1), 33-37.

Leitner, M.J., Scher, G., and Shuval, K. (1999). Peace-making through recreation: The positive effects of intergenerational activities on the attitudes of Israeli Arabs and Jews toward each other. *World Leisure and Recreation,* 41(2), 25-29.

McCabe, M. (1993). Family leisure budgets: Experience in the UK. *World Leisure Report,* pp. 30-34.

McGillivray, D.G., Maxwell, G., and Foley, M.T. (2000). UK workplace fitness provision and women: Missing opportunities? *World Leisure,* 42(4), 14-23.

Nishino, J. and Takahashi, K. (1988). Current leisure and recreation research in Japan. Paper presented at World Congress on Free Time, Culture, and Society, Chateau Lake Louise, Alberta, Canada, May 18.

Olson, E. (1999). Americans lead the world in hours worked. *The New York Times,* September 7, p. C9.

O'Sullivan, A. (1997). IDF seeks victory in battle of the bulge. *The Jerusalem Post,* November 16, p. 10.

Parker, S. (Ed.) (1985). *International handbook of leisure studies and research.* East Sussex, England: M. McFee, LSA Publications.

Pope, V. (1992). Madonna takes Moscow: The end of communism means hard times for Russian artists. *U.S. News and World Report,* September 28, pp. 55-58.

Pratt, J. and Salter, M. (1984). A fresh look at football hooliganism. *Leisure Studies,* 3, 201-230.

Rebibo, J. (1987). Play ball! *Baltimore Jewish Times,* July 24, pp. 50-51.

Rice, C. (1987). The mating game, Thai style. *Sowasdee,* December, pp. 79-82.

Ruskin, H. (Ed.) (1984). *Leisure: Toward a theory and policy.* London: Associated University Presses.

Ruskin, H. (2002). Past, present and future trends of leisure in Israel. In Ruskin, H. (Ed.), *Active leisure: Concepts and perspectives* (pp. 163-174). Jerusalem, Israel: The Hebrew University.

Samuel, N. (1993). Vacation time and the French family. *World Leisure and Recreation,* 35(3), 15-16.

Sancton, T. (1999). French revolution: A proposed 35-hour workweek infuriates bosses. *Time,* October 18, p. 76.

Serguiff, A.G. (1976). *Recreation and sports in the Soviet Union.* Los Angeles: A.G. Serguiff.

Sharma, D.B. (1991). Leisure pattern in an urban middle class in developing society: A study of Guwahati city. *World Leisure and Recreation,* 33(4), 9-11.

Siegel, J. (1994). Not a Hora story. *The Jerusalem Post* (Entertainment supplement), October 14-20, p. 2.

Siegel, J. (1995). Per capita consumption of pure alcohol doubles since 1980. *The Jerusalem Post,* June 20, p. 3.

Silver, E. (2002). Upbeat downtown. *The Jerusalem Report,* October 21, p. 13.

Singh, H., Gupta, M., and Aggarwal, B.K. (1994). Leisure among rural aged people in India. *World Leisure and Recreation,* 36(2), 29-31.

Singh, V.P. (1994). Satellite television and leisure activities of youth in an Indian city. *World Leisure and Recreation,* 36(3), 24-29.

Sivan, A. (2000). Global influence and local uniqueness: The case of adolescent leisure in Hong Kong. *World Leisure,* 42(4), 24-32.

Stothart, B. (1984). Recreation and sport: The New Zealand experience. *WLRA Journal,* 26(2), 5-8.

Sugden, J. and Bairner, A. (1986). Northern Ireland: The politics of leisure in a divided society. *Leisure Studies,* 5(3), 341-352.

Swift, E. M. (1988). Sport in the land of Sanuk. *Sports Illustrated,* February 15, pp. 112-132.

Tourism Authority of Thailand (n.d.). *Thailand in brief.* Bangkok, Thailand: Tourism Authority of Thailand.

Wysocki, B. (1986). Lust for labor. *Wall Street Journal,* April 21, pp. 10-12.

Chapter 17

Leisure in the Future

INTRODUCTION

The main purpose of this chapter is to clarify the importance of taking a proactive approach to leisure in the future and to facilitate a better understanding of factors that will cause changes in leisure in the future. This chapter does *not* intend to be a definitive source of predictions of future leisure changes, because such changes are difficult to predict. A current trend can sometimes be reversed instead of continued into the future. For example, the energy crisis in the 1970s led to dire predictions for the future of leisure activities such as nighttime sports played on lighted fields and most any recreational activity involving significant travel by private automobile. Some writers predicted that these activities would be banned by the 1980s, but in the twenty-first century, these activities are still going strong. Since 9/11/01, gloomy predictions have been made for travel and tourism because of terrorism. However, just as the energy crisis of the 1970s did not continue through the 1980s, perhaps it is possible that terrorism will not continue to be the major concern that it has been in the first few years of the twenty-first century. This point leads to another major theme of this chapter, which is to keep a positive attitude about the future because present-day problems and trends can be reversed even though they might seem unsolvable. Optimism helps to create positive energy to make good things come true in the future. Bearing this philosophy in mind, the learning objectives of this chapter are to

1. Identify the benefits of examining the future and of writing scenarios.
2. Identify the major factors influencing leisure in future society.
3. Identify likely future changes in leisure based on current trends.

4. Identify innovations that might create significant changes for leisure in the future.
5. Critique the scenarios of leisure in the future of other writers.
6. Write a scenario for leisure in the future.

WHY STUDY THE FUTURE?

If accurately predicting the future is difficult, why even bother? Why not just let the future happen? Several excellent reasons exist for studying the future:

1. It helps create a greater awareness of potential problems, thereby making people better prepared to deal with future problems.
2. Studying the future facilitates a clearer understanding of the impact of present behavior on future society, thereby motivating individuals to alter current behavior problems that, if continued, would have a negative effect on future society.
3. If people are cognizant of potential problems in the future, mobilization of resources and planning can begin today to ward off these problems.
4. Studying the future makes people take greater control of their lives and not merely be victims of future changes.
5. Studying the future also facilitates a clearer understanding of the interrelatedness of factors and events in producing change.
6. This greater understanding of the change process can be utilized in attempting to make positive changes occur. Rather than being reactive (responding to changes that appear), people can be more proactive (initiate desired changes).

In summary, the main reason for studying future leisure is that by doing so, people can act now to make the future better. The first step in this process is to understand the many factors that influence future leisure in society.

FACTORS AFFECTING FUTURE LEISURE

The following is an overview of factors that need to be considered before making predictions about leisure in the future:

1. *Attitudes toward leisure and work:* Will the work ethic weaken further or will it be revived?

2. *Religious influence:* It weakened in the United States in the 1960s and early 1970s and experienced a revival in the 1980s. How strong an influence will religion have on leisure behavior in the future?

3. *Population trends:* Demographic data indicate that people sixty-five and over will comprise a much greater percentage of the population in the future (Leitner and Leitner, 2004). What effect will this trend have on leisure services?

4. *Education:* Educational levels have been improving, and if this trend continues, leisure interests of the population might become even broader.

5. *Natural resources:* Outdoor recreation resources are finite, but whether they will be destroyed and become more scarce or will actually improve as a result of better conservation and preservation will be determined by government policy and the behavior of society.

6. *Energy resources:* Will the energy crisis of the 1970s return, or do people need not worry about limiting recreational usage of energy resources? Will technology such as solar energy be able to keep up with expanding energy needs and desires?

7. *Technology:* What amazing technological advances will revolutionize leisure in the future? What inventions will create new leisure opportunities?

8. *Influential people:* This is an impossible factor to foresee. Who could have predicted the impact that people such as the Beatles had on the leisure behavior of millions of youth in the 1960s? Who are the most influential people in today's society?

9. *Social norms:* Family structure, sex roles, and mores of sexual conduct underwent a metamorphosis from the 1960s to the 1980s. Will social norms swing back to more "traditional" values or continue to drift farther from the accepted norms of past generations?

10. *The economy:* Is disaster or prosperity impending? Will the workweek decline further or will people need to work more if economic times get rough?

11. *Consumption:* Will materialism and consumerism continue to grow, or will values shift to a more humanistic, environmen-

tally conscious orientation? According to Briscoe (1992), the richest fifth of the world is responsible for most of the environmental damage being caused in the world. Durning (1993) states that a shift from materialistic to non-materialistic goals needs to occur in order to protect the environment.

12. *The decline of work and the rise of leisure:* Will work hours really decline as predicted, and if so, how will the limited work and increased leisure be distributed? According to Veal (1987), the average worker toils 86,400 hours in a lifetime, but this figure would decline to 73,440 if work were distributed evenly and a 15 percent unemployment rate was avoided.

There are several different *ways to reduce lifetime work hours,* such as

- Give all workers seven years of sabbaticals during their career;
- Lower the retirement age to fifty-five;
- Continue full-time education to age twenty-four;
- Shorten the workweek to thirty-four hours; or
- Increase annual holidays to eleven weeks.

It is interesting to note that many industrialized nations have experienced economic problems and higher unemployment during the first part of the twenty-first century. Is the future already here, or are these economic problems just temporary?

The undesirability of a higher rate of unemployment is obvious. However, to enact any of the more appealing ideas for distributing the limited available work, there will need to be a decline in materialistic attitudes. Implicit in accepting less work is accepting less pay and being able to buy less. What would you choose: a more expensive vacation or a cheaper, but longer one? People's attitudes toward that issue might very well determine the distribution of work and leisure hours in future society.

According to Proxmire (1993), Americans would be willing to sacrifice salary for more vacation time. He cites a Gallup poll indicating that most women and a large minority of men would be willing to give up a day's pay each week for a day off. Proxmire proposes a reduction of one hour of work per week every third year in order to share the limited work available. He feels that implementation of this plan would result in greater productivity, higher profits, higher wages, and increased leisure.

In summary, changes in most of the major factors that affect future leisure cannot be predicted with certainty. A review of literature on the topic of predictions for the future (e.g., from books and periodicals such as *The Futurist*) shows just how difficult it is to predict future trends. Before September 2001, many articles on the future were predicting a continued economic boom and growth in the tourism industry. After the terrorist attacks of September 11, 2001, the main concerns of most articles on the future seem to be terrorism and economic problems. However, two trends likely to continue are the aging of society and improved educational levels. The aging of society will likely create a higher demand for leisure services because of the increased number of retired (unemployed) persons in society. Improved educational levels will probably also create a greater demand for leisure services, because more highly educated people tend to have more varied leisure pursuits. As discussed in the next section, imminent technological advances might also expand leisure activity opportunities.

LEISURE INNOVATIONS

Most of the leisure innovations discussed in this section have not yet become commonplace in the United States in the twenty-first century, even though most of them were discussed in the 1980s. Interestingly, articles from 2001 to 2003 on the future are still discussing innovations such as robots becoming more of a factor influencing leisure and life. In the 1980s, experts made predictions that robots would be commonplace by the year 2000. Perhaps in the next twenty or thirty years some of these innovations will really affect leisure as predicted.

Superconductors are one example of technology that might revolutionize leisure in the future. According to Lemonick (1987), superconductors can conduct currents at super high temperatures without loss of any energy. The Japanese Railway Group has already utilized superconductor electromagnets to design a train that can travel 321 miles per hour. The leisure-related implications of superconductors are mind-boggling. Obviously, pleasure travel could become faster and more convenient. Aside from enabling faster transportation, superconductors could create entirely new leisure possibilities. For example, Lemonick (1987) writes of superconductor-powered skating rinks and dance floors that would enable skaters and dancers to float! Similarly, can you imagine basketball players or ice hockey players flying over their defensive opponents? The superconductor innovation could create a whole new array of leisure opportunities.

An already existing leisure innovation that has the potential to become even more popular in the future is submarines. According to Eichenwald (1987), leisure submarines were being sold for $2 million to $5 million, and business is booming. The submarines are operating in resort areas throughout the world, taking tourists on short trips to view undersea life in tropical areas.

A leisure innovation that might literally "take off" in the future is the paraplane, a small flying machine powered by two fifteen-horsepower engines. The pilot sits in a small cart, as an attached 400-square-foot parachute rises overhead and lifts the cart into the air. The paraplane's inventor claims it is the simplest and safest aircraft ever built.

Another technological advance that could have far-reaching leisure implications is robots. Cornish (1986) discussed the possibility of fights between robots becoming a form of entertainment, a prediction that came true in 1999 when the television show Battle Bots aired on the Comedy Central network and ran for three seasons (see <www.battlebots. com>). Conceivably, robots could replace humans in many spectator sports! In addition, robots in the home could perform many essential chores done by humans, thereby creating more free time.

Wallechinsky, Wallace, and Wallace (1981) also offer some predictions that would create an increase in free time. One is that humans will be living to the age of 120 by the year 2020. Coupled with their prediction of the average retirement age decreasing to fifty, the average person will enjoy seventy years of retirement living. Wallechinsky, Wallace, and Wallace also speculate that the workweek will decline to below thirty hours and that eventually work time might be totally a matter of choice (by the year 2029).

Wallechinsky, Wallace, and Wallace offer several other tantalizing leisure-related predictions, one being that solar satellites (by the year 2030) will be able to provide twenty-four-hour daylight. Another appealing possibility is the construction of enormous all-weather protective bubbles over city parks, enabling residents of cold-weather cities to enjoy "outdoor" sports all year round.

Smith (1993) speculates that technology will have a great impact on future entertainment. According to Smith, people will be able to enjoy spectacular, high-technology concerts, museums, and amusement parks. At home, Smith foresees opportunities for personal video interactive and virtual reality experiences.

However, technology might not have an entirely positive effect on leisure. Rybczynksi (1991, p. B5) expresses the concern that "too much technology will obscure the spontaneous, childish, and impulsive characteristics that are such an important element in play." He goes on to say that to avoid this problem, people will have to counteract the incessant drive for self-improvement and rediscover the pleasure of pure and simple leisure. In a related vein, because portable technology allows people to work anywhere, anytime, and the physical and temporal boundaries of the workplace no longer exist, people will need to find out for themselves how to maintain a balance between work and leisure (Anonymous, 1992).

Other concerns for leisure in the future stem from trends in social norms and overpopulation. Wallechinsky, Wallace, and Wallace (1981) predicted increased drug use, widespread use of cemetery land for recreational purposes, and gender distinctions becoming increasingly irrelevant. Which of these predictions will come true?

SCENARIOS FOR LEISURE IN THE FUTURE

The preceding section discussed possible leisure-related innovations for the future. In this section, a more comprehensive approach to future forecasting is examined. A scenario is a series of events forecasted for the future, based on a variety of factors. An example of an imaginative future scenario is Lang and Taylor's (1986) fictitious description of the life of Michael Smith, the typical baby born in 1986:

> Michael will grow up in a house laden with computer technology. He will learn to read and write by age 2 or 3 with the assistance of his home computer. As he grows up, he will not be too distracted from his education by household chores, because

household robots will take care of chores like vacuuming and raking leaves. (p. 116)

Lang and Taylor write that Michael's first job will most likely be in a service field such as leisure, tourism, health, or information sharing. He will need to take sabbaticals for reeducation several times in his career. Because of the fast rate of technological advances, reeducation will be necessary to keep pace with change.

His workweek might be only thirty hours and eventually shrink to twenty hours because of increased productivity made possible by advanced technology. Because of the shortened workweek and a life expectancy of 100, Michael will have ample free time to pursue activities such as travel. Flights in hypersonic jetliners will take passengers halfway around the world in only an hour.

Despite all these advances, Michael Smith will not necessarily be happier than people are today. He will likely be married and divorced three or four times in his lifetime. Despite medical advances that will prevent infectious diseases and cancer, he will still suffer from problems such as headaches and indigestion. Other problems, such as crime, will also continue to plague society.

Although Lang and Taylor's (1986) future scenario is more of an overview of life in general, not just about leisure, most of their predictions have strong implications for leisure. An interesting statement is that Michael Smith will not necessarily be any happier than people are today. It seems that people today should be working to shape the future so that people can lead happier lives. Are technological changes really "advances" if people's quality of life (as measured by perceived happiness) is not improved?

Young (1980) offers some other scenarios for leisure in the future. Rather than describing one specific scenario, Young discusses four possible scenarios for leisure in the future: traditional, humanistic, pessimistic, and optimistic.

The traditional scenario basically assumes that current trends will continue, such as the aging of society, a decline in the workweek, and growth in wealth. The work ethic will prevail, and people will continue to use recreation as a means to escape the tensions of work and living in an urban environment. More specialized and expensive activities will gain more appeal. In essence, the traditional view foresees little change in leisure in the future, aside from technological advances and a somewhat greater amount of free time.

Meanwhile, the humanistic scenario foresees an almost radical change in work and leisure. In this view, a leisure ethic will prevail to such an extent that education will focus more on leisure enhancement than on career preparation. In addition, the nature of work will change, as it will become more people oriented than object oriented. Humanism will replace materialism. Open space will be preserved for future use rather than exploited for profit. The humanistic scenario presents an interesting forecast of attitude change, focusing less on the technological advances on which many futurists tend to concentrate.

In contrast, the pessimistic scenario describes a much less desirable future. In this view, open space for recreation will be an almost impossible luxury, and in general, there will be a scarcity of natural resources. People will suffer "future shock" because of the intensely fast pace of change in society. A "throwaway" attitude will prevail. Not only will people discard material items rather than clean them or repair them, but relationships will also be temporary. People will increasingly seek identity through leisure-based subcults, to an even greater extent than the "punk rockers," "tennis bums," and "beach bums" of the 1980s or the "rappers" of the early twenty-first century.

The optimistic scenario presents a much happier view of the future. Open space will be preserved through planning, enabling outdoor recreation activities to continue to be enjoyed. There will be more time for leisure as a result of a three-day workweek, flextime, job sharing, and extended vacations. Despite the increased travel opportunities, a great deal of recreation will continue to be home based or close to home, and people will rediscover the joys of simple activities. It sounds like a much brighter future than that offered by the pessimistic scenario!

The four scenarios raise some interesting questions.

1. Which scenario is most likely to come true?
2. What can people do today to help make the more positive scenarios come true?
3. Is it possible that leisure will not be substantially different in the future than it is today?
4. What changes can you foresee in future leisure that are not forecasted in any of Young's (1980) four scenarios?

EXERCISE IN SCENARIO WRITING

The purpose of Exercise 17.1 is to write a comprehensive forecast for leisure in the future. The scenario should carefully consider all of the factors that can influence the direction of future leisure. First, identify changes you feel are likely in each of the factors listed. Then discuss the leisure-related implications of each of these changes. After completing the exercise, write a narrative on your scenario and incorporate the information from the exercise. Try to be as specific as possible. For example, for technology and innovations, comment on which of the leisure innovations discussed in this chapter you feel will actually be influential in your lifetime and what you think the leisure-related implications of these innovations will be.

After writing your scenario, critique the likelihood of its validity, as well as its desirability. Which of Young's four scenarios does it most closely resemble? How does your scenario compare with those written by your peers?

SUMMARY

A major purpose of this chapter was to foster a more proactive, positive approach to the future. Present-day actions determine the events of tomorrow. People should determine what changes are desirable and which are not and try to steer the future course of events in the positive direction. You can be the creator of change, not the victim of change. This concept, more than any other presented in this chapter, should encourage a positive attitude toward the future. It is the positive energy of people today that can make the future a great place in which to live!

EXERCISE 17.1. Leisure in the Year 2050

Factor	Predicted change(s)	Leisure-related implication(s) of the change(s)
Leisure attitudes	_____	_____
	_____	_____
Religious influence	_____	_____
	_____	_____
Population trends	_____	_____
	_____	_____
Education	_____	_____
	_____	_____
Natural resources	_____	_____
	_____	_____
Energy resources	_____	_____
	_____	_____
Technology and innovations	_____	_____
	_____	_____
Influential people	_____	_____
	_____	_____
Social norms	_____	_____
	_____	_____
The economy	_____	_____
	_____	_____
Consumption	_____	_____
	_____	_____
Work patterns	_____	_____
	_____	_____

REFERENCES

Anonymous (1992). Talking about portables. *The Wall Street Journal,* November 16, pp. R18, R19.

Briscoe, D. (1992). Consumerism: Materialism replaces money as the root of the world's evil. *Chico Enterprise-Record,* July 26, p. 5B.

Cornish, E. (1986). Future free time: How will people use it? *Parks and Recreation,* May, pp. 57-60.

Durning, A.T. (1993). Long on things, short on time. *Sierra,* 78(1), 60-68.

Eichenwald, K. (1987). Latest in leisure gear: Submarines. *International Herald Tribune,* September 10, p. 24.

Lang, J.S. and Taylor, R.A. (1986). For a baby born in 1986 . . . *U.S. News and World Report,* January 6, pp. 116-117.

Leitner, M.J. and Leitner, S.F. (2004). *Leisure in later life* (Third edition). Binghamton, NY: The Haworth Press.

Lemonick, M.D. (1987). Superconductors! The startling breakthrough that could change our world. *Time,* May 11, pp. 64-75.

Proxmire, W. (1993). Letter to Senator Edward M. Kennedy. *Society for the Reduction of Human Labor Newsletter,* 3(3), 2.

Rybczynski, W. (1991). The death of leisure. *The New York Times,* October 8, p. B5.

Smith, A. (1993). The electric circus. *The Economist,* September 11, pp. F78-F81.

Veal, A.J. (1987). *Leisure and the future.* London: Allen and Union Publishers Ltd.

Wallechinsky, D., Wallace, A., and Wallace, I. (1981). *The book of predictions.* New York: Morrow.

Young, J. (1980). Ever wonder what recreation will be like 50 years from now? *National Recreation and Parks Association Bulletin,* January, pp. 6, 9.

Appendix

Categorization of Recreational Activities

Simple Entertainment

auctions
concerts
dance presentations
exhibitions (e.g., flower shows, auto shows)
films
lectures

poetry reading
radio
spectator sports (e.g., baseball, football)
storytelling
television
theater

Mental Activity/Contemplation and Self-Awareness

academic classes (e.g., psychology, philosophy)
human growth groups
lectures
meditation
museums
poetry

seminars
skill improvement classes (e.g., cooking, design)
tai chi
travel
writing/reading
yoga

Sports and Exercise

aerobics
archery
auto racing
badminton
ballooning
baseball
basketball
bicycling
billiards
bobsledding
bowling

boxing
canoeing
cricket
croquet
curling
diving
dog racing
fencing
football
field hockey
Frisbee

Frisbee football
golf
gymnastics
handball
hang gliding
horseback riding
horseshoes
ice hockey
ice-skating
jai alai
jet skiing
jogging
judo
karate
kayaking
kite flying/kite surfing
lacrosse
mountain biking
paddle tennis
paddleball
parasailing
platform tennis
polo/bicycle polo
racquetball
rafting
roller-skating

rowing
rugby
sailing
shooting
shuffleboard
skateboarding
skin diving
snorkeling
snow skiing
snowmobiling
snowshoeing
soccer
softball
squash
surfboarding
swimming
table tennis
tennis
track and field
volleyball
water polo
waterskiing
weight lifting
windsurfing
wrestling
yachting

Music

attending concerts
attending music appreciation
    classes
attending nightclubs
attending symphonies
composing music
conducting musical groups
formal singing (chorus)
humming

informal group singing
listening to records
playing musical instruments in a
    band
playing musical instruments
    nonprofessionally (with friends)
solo singing
whistling

Art

art appreciation
calligraphy
ceramics
design
drawing

glass sculpture
ice sculpture
metal sculpture
mosaics
oil painting

papermaking
photography
sketching
stained glass

stone sculpture
watercolor painting
wood carving

Dance

aerobic dance
ballet
ballroom dance
belly dance
ceili dance (Irish dancing)
clogging
contra dance

disco dance
folk dance
jazz dance
modern dance
square dance
sufi dance (mystical group dancing)
tap dance

Hobbies

antique collections (e.g., dishes, cars)
baking
basket weaving
cake decorating
candle making
card making
carpentry
clothes design
clothes making
collections (e.g., stamps, coins, dolls)
cooking
crocheting
decoupage
dyeing textiles
electronics
embroidery

felt crafts
finger painting
floral arranging
holiday decorating
jewelry making
kite making
knitting
leather crafts
macramé
metal crafts
model building
paper crafts
papier-mâché
pets
quilting
soap carving
tapestry making
woodcrafts

Play/Games

active games (e.g., tag)
adult board games
art games (e.g., Pictionary)
card games
children's board games
computer games

drama games (e.g., charades)
dual board games (e.g., checkers and chess)
games of chance (e.g., bingo)
guessing games
human interaction games

imagination games
indoor games
juggling
knowledge games
memory games (e.g., Concentration)
money board games (e.g., Monop-
oly)
new games (e.g., noncompetitive
sport)

paper-and-pencil games (e.g.,
tictactoe)
puzzles (e.g., crossword puzzles)
spelling games (e.g., Scrabble)
table sports (e.g., table hockey)
target games (e.g., darts)
throwing games (e.g., Frisbee)

Relaxation

hot mineral springs immersion
hot tubbing
listening to music
massage
meditation

mud baths
reading
sunbathing
watching a sunrise/sunset

Social Activity

art clubs
athletic clubs (e.g., tennis)
attending conventions
book clubs
collecting clubs (e.g., stamps)
combative sports clubs (e.g., karate)
country clubs
craft clubs (e.g., sewing)
cultural groups (e.g., music)
dance clubs
drama groups
educational groups (e.g., historical)
family gatherings
fraternities
game clubs (e.g., chess)
groups for the elderly
gun clubs
hobby clubs (e.g., animals)

international clubs
investment clubs
language preservation groups
large social functions
outing groups (e.g., hiking)
parties
political groups
professional organizations
religious groups
singing groups
sororities
toastmaster groups
track-and-field clubs (e.g., jogging)
veterans groups
visiting friends
water sports clubs (e.g., swimming)
winter sports clubs (e.g., skating)
youth groups

Humanitarian Services

aid to disabled (e.g., mental health
facilities)

aid to elderly (e.g., nursing homes)

aid to homeless (e.g., meal preparation)
aid to sick (e.g., hospitals)
community endeavors
conservation/ecology
educational groups (e.g., libraries)
fundraiser events (e.g., PTAs)

humane societies (e.g., ASPCA)
international groups
national groups
person-to-person aid groups (e.g., homebound)
protection groups (e.g., firefighters)

Nature Activities/Outdoor Recreation

animal observation walks
backpacking
beachcombing
bird-watching
campfire activities
camping
fishing
gardening
gathering of wild fruits, vegetables, nuts
hiking
hunting
mountain climbing
nature walks

night walks
picnics
plant-identification walks
river walks
rock climbing
scuba diving
snowboarding
spelunking (cave exploration)
trapping animals
tree climbing
whale watching
wilderness exploration
wildflower walks

Travel and Tourism

beach resorts
day trips
domestic travel
ecotourism
educational trips
foreign travel

health spas
island resorts
mountain resorts
organized tours
sports resorts

Index

Adapted sports equipment, 346, 349, 353, 354

Adolescence
and binge drinking, 294
consumption of soda, 202
and drug use, 289, 291, 402, 416
global comparisons, 409, 426, 438
leisure activities of, 321, 329-332, 352
and leisure hours per week, 60
physical activity participation rates, 73-74, 167, 170-171
and popular music, 266
television's effect on socialization, 261
and video games, 265
violence prevention, 265, 352

Adulthood, 64, 67, 331, 333

Aerobics
components of, 181-182
enjoyment of, 5, 7, 164, 190-196
intensity of, 164, 184-187
physiological benefits of, 168-169, 180, 229, 379
recreational activities, 17, 163, 183, 188-196, 379, 459

African Americans, 70-71, 74

Aggression
binge drinking's effects on, 285-286, 288, 290-292
effects on socialization, 269
and females, 74
outdoor recreation as an outlet for, 381
popular music's effect on, 266
sports participation effects on, 89-90
television's effect on, 262
video games' effects on, 265

Aging
and free time, 27, 60, 336
in the future, 33, 55, 449, 451, 454
and leisure activities, 333-335, 350-351
and leisure in various countries, 405, 411, 431-434, 436, 439, 441

Alcohol
and accidental deaths and injuries related to use of, 284-289, 299, 329
binge drinking, 284-294
ethics of recreational use, 53-54, 298-299
health implications of use of, 203-205, 299
leisure-related alternatives to, 202, 265, 290-294, 416
money spent on, 38, 284, 287
prevalence of the use of, 37-38, 49, 50, 65-66, 284-287, 349-350, 416
recreational use of, 124, 127, 196, 203-205, 284-287, 402
societal costs of abuse of, 38, 287, 299
theoretical causes of use and abuse of, 11, 105, 290-293

Americans with Disabilities Act, 359

Amusement parks, 52, 308

Anaerobic activity, 163, 196

Ancient civilizations, 49-50

Animals, 385, 389, 463

Antisocial behavior
historical perspectives, 49, 50
in other countries, 402, 404, 409
among youth, 50-51

Aquatics. *See* Swimming